Principles of Transport Economics

Principles of Transport Economics

Emile Quinet

Professor, CERAS,
Ecole Nationale des Ponts et Chaussées, Paris, France

and

Roger Vickerman

Jean Monnet Professor of European Economics,
University of Kent, Canterbury, UK

Edward Elgar
Cheltenham, UK • Northampton, MA, USA

Published by
Edward Elgar Publishing Limited
Glensanda House
Montpellier Parade
Cheltenham
Glos GL50 1UA
UK

Edward Elgar Publishing, Inc.
William Pratt House
9 Dewey Court
Northampton
Massachusetts 01060
USA

Paperback edition 2005
Reprinted 2008

A catalogue record for this book
is available from the British Library

ISBN 978 1 84064 865 2 (cased)
     978 1 84542 256 1 (paperback)

Printed in Great Britain by the MPG Books Group, Bodmin and King's Lynn

Contents

Figures

Tables

Preface

Transport continues to present considerable challenges to both policy makers and to conventional economics. It is the firm belief of both authors that only policies based on a thorough understanding of the economics of transport can any progress be made in solving some of the current issues facing governments across Europe. Although there are many books on transport, and not a few dealing with the economics of transport, we identified a real need for a book which provides a consistent and detailed treatment of all the various aspects of transport. This relates not just to the issues of the demand for and supply of transport services, problems of transport market regulation and the key issues of public policy, but also to the role which transport plays in the economy at large.

Transport issues dominate in discussions of location, of urban and regional development and of economic growth and we reflect this by placing these issues prominently in Part I. Here we show the links between those matters traditionally the province of transport economists and those which have been more the preserve of urban and regional economists, and increasingly of those interested in economic growth.

The traditional core of transport economics, factors affecting the demand for transport and the structure of costs, are placed in the centre of the book in Part II. Here we deal not just with the underlying economics, but also show how practical models can be related to the theory and empirical results derived from these.

Part III deals with the way transport is supplied. Here we deal both with the market structures of competition, monopoly and oligopoly, and the development of policy and institutional structures designed to regulate the market. As part of this we discuss the different ways in which policy has developed in different European countries and the emerging issues in the EU. This part concludes with a chapter which aims to draw together some of the problems we face in moving from the rationale for policy in the theories and models we develop to the implementation of specific policy measures.

The present book has its origins in a book written in French by one of the authors, *Principes d'Economie des Transports* (Paris: Economica). It is our

xi

intention here to make this available, in a substantially revised and updated form, to a wider audience. The principal geographical focus of the book is Europe because we wanted to draw on our own experiences of applying the analysis contained in this book to policy problems both within individual countries and more widely at the European Union level, not least with regard to the transport questions posed by EU enlargement. The examples and evidence are drawn from across Europe, but we have relied heavily on examples from France and the United Kingdom, not just because of our personal familiarity with these, but because in many policy areas they represent two contrasting positions over the concept of public service and the role of the private sector. However, the examples are meant to be illustrative; it was not our intention to write a book on transport policy in Europe, but to provide a set of universal tools to analyse and inform policy at all levels.

The book assumes that the reader is familiar with some basic economics. To get the most from the book a knowledge of Intermediate Microeconomics is desirable, but in order to make it as accessible as possible to as wide a set of readers we have placed some of the more technical material in boxes throughout the text. These can be skipped without any loss of the main argument, but provide both supporting evidence and the basis for those wishing to pursue a more advanced study of certain aspects. Some of the analysis is, however, essential for any real understanding of the issues; we have therefore left considerable technical material in the main text and encourage the reader to work through this carefully.

Any work such as this depends on the sharing of knowledge and research. We consider ourselves fortunate to be members of a worldwide community of scholars devoted to understanding the economics of transport and transport policy. We have benefited enormously from the opportunities, not just to discuss with, but also to work alongside many of these people. Within Europe we have been particularly fortunate to benefit from the European Commission's research programmes which encourage, not just the exchange of ideas, but provide the opportunity to consider their practical application.

Emile Quinet
Roger Vickerman

PART I

Transport in the economy

1. Transport and Economic Activity

Transport has a key role in economic activity. It is first of all a sector of economic activity which contributes to a share of national output. It is, however, also an essential means of realising that output. This has two dimensions. In the aggregate, transport is a derived demand and growth in the transport sector follows the growth of the economy as a whole; it is necessary to understand the nature and the intensity of this link. The opposing causality is also often argued, that transport improvements themselves can determine the rate of growth of the economy. This second dimension is that, as an input to the process of production, transport is like any factor of production which can be substituted for others, dependent on technology and on relative factor prices. In addition to these direct links, transport is also argued to have the potential to engender positive externalities in the economy. We need to consider these elements in turn.

1. THE ROLE OF TRANSPORT IN ECONOMIC ACTIVITY

1.1 Transport in the National Accounts

The national accounts of European Union countries show that transport accounts for around 8 per cent of the GDP. For most countries the contribution of transport in current prices has remained fairly stable, but in terms of constant prices these ratios have tended to fall over the long period demonstrating the extent to which the real price of transport has fallen, reflecting an effective increase in the productivity of the sector. However in recent years there has been a tendency for the measured output of the sector to grow faster than GDP overall.

There is a problem in determining the exact size of the transport sector, since the national accounts only record transport which is marketed and hence ignore such important sub-sectors as private transport undertaken within households and freight transport undertaken by firms on their own account. Thus the figures given above do not give an accurate picture of the true place of transport in overall economic activity. An alternative concept, which would provide a better picture, is current expenditure on transport

Table 1.1 *Household expenditure on transport, EU15 2000*

	Final consumption in transport as % of total consumption	Total consumption in transport, bn €	of which: personal transport equipment	operation of personal transport equipment	purchased transport	Consumption per Capita, €
B	15.7	20.2	7.9	11.1	1.1	1975
DK	12.4	10.1	3.2	5.5	1.3	1884
D	14.5	161.8	60.6	80.1	21.0	1969
EL	8.6	7.9	1.6	3.7	2.6	746
E	13.0	50.1	22.6	20.1	7.4	1296
F	15.5	118.5	31.0	69.7	17.9	1957
IRL	12.6	6.0	2.2	2.6	1.2	1587
I	12.5	88.8	27.7	48.1	13.0	1540
L	*15.4*	*1.5*	*0.8*	*0.6*	*0.1*	*3345*
NL	*12.4*	*24.8*	*10.0*	*12.1*	*2.7*	*1559*
A	12.9	15.1	5.1	7.6	2.4	1864
P	17.4	12.7	*5.4*	6.5	0.8	1269
FIN	13.8	8.6	3.1	3.9	1.5	1659
S	*13.2*	*16.6*	*3.5*	*9.4*	*3.6*	*1869*
UK	14.7	141.9	49.8	55.2	36.9	2377
EU15	*14.2*	*684.4*	*234.6*	*336.2*	*113.6*	*1811*

Source: Eurostat, national statistics (figures in italics are estimates)

which represents the sum of intermediate and final consumption and net transfers. Expenditure on transport in EU countries amounted to between 9 per cent and 17 per cent of total household expenditure in 2000 (Table 1.1), rather more than the estimates of transport output in GDP. This, however, excludes capital expenditure on transport, which typically accounts for 9–10 per cent of gross fixed capital formation and much expenditure on transport as an intermediate good in the production process. These figures are larger than the simple share of the sector in GDP.

However, these estimates do not include the share of transport in non-transport goods, which means that conventional national income accounting estimates will always tend to under-estimate the real share of transport. Estimates for France for 1998 as part of the satellite accounts for transport suggest a much larger contribution (Table 1.2).

Table 1.2 Components and origin of total expenditure on transport, France, 1998 (€ billion)

	Households	Firms	Public admin-istration	Total
Current expenditure	109.27	68.15	18.98	192.21
Capital expenditure	29.30	19.60	9.20	58.09
Depreciation	24.77	12.06	1.19	38.55
Total	113.80	75.69	26.99	211.76

Source: Le compte satellite des transports (CCTN), December 2001

Of this total €176 billion (83 per cent) is spent on road transport, 60 per cent of this by households. Households spend over 90 per cent of their transport expenditure (net of depreciation) on road transport and over 20 per cent of their gross expenditure on transport is spent on vehicle purchase.

1.2 Employment and External Trade

The role of transport in overall economic activity can also be measured through the share of total employment in transport. In the EU as a whole this amounted to some 6.2 million people in 1999 in the sector as strictly defined, around 4 per cent of total employment (Table 1.3). If we add those

Table 1.3 Employment by mode of transport, 1999 (1000 persons)

	Railways	Pipelines	Road Passenger	Road freight	Sea	Inland water-way	Air	Travel agencies & tour operators	Other* auxiliary activities	Total
B	41.4	0.02	26.8	57.4	0.5	0.8	13.0	7.4	44.0	193.2
DK	10.3	0.20	30.6	40.3	10.6	0.1	11.7	6.2	25.2	135.2
D	272.0	1.00	162.0	381.0	12.0	8.0	49.0	89.5	489.3	1463.8
EL	n.a.	n.a.	n.a.	n.a.	n.a.	n.a	n.a.	n.a.	n.a.	n.a.
E	39.8	-	152.2	292.2	7.3	0.1	36.3	37.8	126.7	692.5
F	174.8	1.02	168.6	305.1	12.4	2.9	62.7	38.2	213.6	979.3
IRL	5.2	-	7.1	11.9	1.6	0.0	7.0	3.3	6.8	42.9
I	137.7	0.52	136.6	298.7	15.4	4.6	25.2	35.6	195.0	849.3
L	3.1	-	2.0	4.8	n.a	0.5	2.6	0.6	1.3	n.a.
NL	24.0	0.15	n.a.	108.5	6.8	8.8	33.0	23.2	57.3	n.a.
A	52.0	n.a.	37.3	45.7	0.0	0.3	8.0	10.3	23.6	n.a.
P	6.3	-	38.6	50.0	1.3	0.6	10.9	7.8	24.4	139.9
FIN	12.7	-	23.7	36.8	8.2	0.3	9.7	5.2	18.0	114.6
S	12.1	0.03	55.1	62.1	13.2	1.3	13.9	12.4	37.9	208.0
UK	48.0	1.00	136.0	297.0	16.9	0.1	77.0	102.0	230.0	908.0

Note: * cargo handling and storage, other supporting activities, activities of other transport agencies

Source: Eurostat (employment according to NACE classification), national statistics

Table 1.4 Imports by Mode of Transport, 2000

	Value				Weight			
	Extra-EU15		Intra-EU15		Extra-EU15		Intra-EU15	
	bn €	(%)	bn €	(%)	mn tonnes	(%)	mn tonnes	(%)
Sea	420.9	40.7	316.1	21.3	1008.0	70.1	311.4	27.6
Road	175.9	17.0	886.4	59.6	75.0	5.2	492.1	43.7
Rail	18.4	1.8	51.2	3.4	55.4	3.9	53.6	4.8
Inland Waterway	5.7	0.6	16.0	1.1	28.0	1.9	130.4	11.6
Pipeline	39.3	3.8	19.3	1.3	209.3	14.6	97.6	8.7
Air	249.3	24.1	61.1	4.1	2.5	0.2	1.0	
Other/unknown	123.9	12.0	136.9	9.2	59.3	4.1	40.7	3.6
Total	1033.3	100.0	1487.0	100.0	1437.7	100.0	1126.8	100.0

Source: Eurostat

Table 1.5 *Number of enterprises by mode of transport, 1999*

	Railways	Pipelines	Road Passenger	Road freight	Sea	Inland waterway	Air	Travel agencies & tour operators	Other* auxiliary activities	Total
B	4	12	2187	7 461	74	259	101	1 064	2 069	13 231
DK	22	4	4140	7 996	461	37	148	578	1 574	14 960
D	132	138	32 023	52 708	1 013	1 573	505	11 345	21 564	121 001
EL	n.a.	n.a.	n.a.	n.a.	n.a.	n.a.	n.a.	n.a.	n.a.	n.a.
E	6	0	67 518	131 225	214	7	47	5 454	12 211	216 682
F	27	35	33 691	45 703	733	1 191	537	4 166	6 359	92 442
IRL	2	0	260¹	2939¹	41²	0	34²	303¹	541¹	4 120
I	131	20	23 366	113 882	507	850	196	8 164	14 590	161 706
L	1	0	170	460	13	76	13	119	96	948
NL	5	10	3 325	9 825	595¹	3915¹	140¹	2 200	3 495	23 510
A	17	2	4 092	4 846	19	59	78	1 223	983	11 319
P	1	0	11 008	6 246	74	25	27	934	1 402	19 717
FIN	3	1	9 058	12 002	198	101	65	685	1 126	23 239
S	30	11	9 552	15 703	438	338	194	2 023	2 342	30 631
UK	116	21	9 402	37 610	1 027	228	971	6 507	10 522	66 404

Note: * cargo handling and storage, other supporting activities, activities of other transport agencies
¹ 1998 ² 1997

Source: Eurostat (according to NACE classification)

8

employees in the private sector (truck drivers for example) plus all those employed in activities directly related to transport (e.g., construction and maintenance of infrastructure and vehicles, the oil industry directly related to its use in transport) we come to a total of some 11 million or 7 per cent.

Transport also facilitates international trade. As Table 1.4 shows, both the external and internal trade of the EU depend on transport. External trade relies most heavily on sea and air transport, but internal trade is most dependent on road transport, although there are differences if we measure by the value or the weight of goods transported.

1.3 Firms

Transport activities in the EU are realised by some 800000 firms which differ considerably in both number and size between the different modes and between the different member states (Table 1.5). Some 450000 of these firms are in the road freight transport sector. The largest relative number of individual firms is in Spain which has some 27 per cent of all transport firms in the EU15. Even in the rail sector, which is still dominated by large state–owned companies in most member states there are over 100 separate firms in Germany, Italy and the United Kingdom. However, the most deregulated market, the UK, has only around 8 per cent of firms, but around 14 per cent of employment. This suggests that there are substantial variations in the nature of the organisation of the transport markets in the different EU states.

1.4 Traffic

The output of the transport sector in terms of the services it provides can be measured in a number of different ways, but the most common is in terms of physical quantities which combine the volume (number of passengers or tonnes of goods) with the distance these are carried (kilometres) to give passenger-km. or tonne-km.) as shown in Tables 1.6 and 1.7.

These suggest a number of issues: the large and growing share of road transport, the rapid growth of air transport, the decline of rail despite the increasing investment in the renewal of the rail network in several countries with the advent of high-speed rail, and the overall decline in the share of public transport. Although there are differences in degree between European countries, the overall trends are similar everywhere.

One further aspect can be noted, the development of international traffic. This can be seen in various ways, but the available figures show that international road freight transport has grown at about twice the rate for national traffic and international rail freight has roughly maintained the same level whilst that for domestic traffic has fallen substantially.

Transport in the Economy

Table 1.6 *Passenger transport – performance by mode of transport, EU15 (1000 mn pkm)*

	Car	Bus & coach	Tram + metro	Rail	Air	Total
1970	1 582	269	39	219	33	2 142
1980	2 295	348	41	248	74	3 006
1990	3 199	369	48	268	157	4 041
1991	3 257	378	48	276	166	4 126
1995	3 506	382	47	274	202	4 410
1996	3 558	391	48	282	209	4 488
1997	3 622	393	49	285	222	4 571
1998	3 702	402	50	287	241	4 682
1999	3 788	406	51	295	260	4 801
2000	3 789	413	53	303	281	4 839
1991–00	+16%	+9%	+10%	+10%	+70%	+17%

Source: EUROSTAT

Table 1.7 *Goods transport – performance by mode of transport, EU15 (1000 mn tkm)*

	Road	Rail	Inland water-ways	Pipe-lines	Sea (intra-EU)	Total
1970	487	282	102	64	472	1 407
1980	717	290	106	85	780	1 978
1990	974	256	107	70	922	2 329
1991	1 006	235	106	79	956	2 382
1995	1 139	220	114	82	1 071	2 627
1997	1 206	237	118	82	1 124	2 768
1998	1 265	240	121	85	1 142	2 852
1999	1 322	236	121	85	1 197	2 960
2000	1 348	249	125	85	1 270	3 078
1991–00	+ 34%	+ 6 %	+ 18%	+ 8 %	+ 33 %	+ 29%

Source: EUROSTAT

The figures for traffic expressed in passenger- or tonne-km only represent one aspect of the economic importance of different modes; a given passenger-km does not represent the same economic impact if undertaken by, for example, high speed train or bus. Similarly a given figure for tonne-km does not reflect the value of the goods moved. To take account of this we could weight passenger-km or tonne-km by their costs or, better still, by the value added from the corresponding transport service. However, this does not lead to any significant differences from the traditional approach: data for France for the period 1990–1995 (taking 1990=100) showed that rail traffic fell to 87 per cent in tonne-km but 91 per cent in value added whilst the corresponding figures for road showed a rise to 118 per cent in terms of the physical measure or 119 per cent in terms of value added.

If, however, we weight freight traffic by the value of the goods transported we do obtain some important differences from the more conventional analysis. Data for France (Table 1.8) shows considerable differences from the more usual analysis by tonne-km (Gerondeau, 1996). These results show the specific nature of freight transport and the difficulty of measuring it effectively without reference to the context of the goods carried.

This is a reflection of considerable differences in both the modal distribution of traffic between different types of goods and the substantial differences in the average length of haul. The average length of haul by road in the EU is 110 km, that by rail is 245 km and by inland waterway 280 km. Average load values, however, are €1674/tonne by road, €924/tonne by rail and just €87/tonne by inland waterway. In international traffic, road carries only 4 per cent of the tonnage, but 20 per cent of the tonne-km, whereas rail carries 20 per cent of the tonnage and 45 per cent of the tonne-km.

Such differences also exist between different countries within the EU as a reflection of differences in the structure of production, the structure of trade and geographical structures (such as the density of population, distances between major settlements and the overall area of the country).

Table 1.8 Share of modes of transport according to the value added of goods transported (%)

	By tonne-km	by value added
Rail	22.4	4.5
Road	74.5	95.3
Inland waterway	3.1	0.2

Source: Gerondeau (1996)

1.5 Prices

Transport prices are very badly understood and the statistics cover different modes unevenly. Price indicators show important differences in the development of prices between modes. Thus maritime and air transport, and to a lesser extent, road haulage, have shown particularly strong falls in prices since 1980, whilst urban and interurban passenger transport have moved in the opposite direction. Whilst cars generally cost less to buy in real terms, the cost of using them has been rising in recent years. Prices of public passenger transport have tended to rise strongly in real terms, although the price of air travel has fallen quite markedly.

Table 1.9 presents some detailed data on the evolution of prices for land transport in the United Kingdom. This shows clearly how private motoring costs have risen less rapidly than rail or bus fares, despite stronger rises in fuel prices and tax and insurance. Generally however, transport prices have shown a stronger rise than the index of all prices during the decade and this has been a useful development compared with the generally slower rise in the cost of transport over preceding decades which had helped to increase the relative consumption of transport.

Table 1.9 Evolution of transport prices, UK, 1991–2001 (1991=100)

	All items	Motor vehicles					Rail fares	Bus fares	Fares & other travel costs
		Pur-chase	Mainten-ance	Petrol and oil	Tax and Insur-ance	All motor			
1991	100.0	100.0	100.0	100.0	100.0	100.0	100.0	100.0	100.0
1992	103.7	105.1	107.9	102.9	117.2	106.8	107.3	107.0	106.2
1993	105.4	104.0	114.2	111.0	132.4	111.4	114.8	111.7	111.7
1994	108.0	106.8	117.1	116.1	138.5	115.2	119.9	114.7	114.7
1995	111.6	108.6	119.3	122.1	135.0	117.3	125.2	118.9	117.5
1996	114.4	112.1	124.7	128.3	130.6	120.8	129.9	123.3	121.1
1997	118.0	114.8	131.4	141.0	135.9	127.3	132.9	127.7	125.1
1998	122.0	113.5	136.8	148.0	148.2	131.3	138.4	131.9	127.9
1999	123.9	108.7	142.2	160.5	159.9	134.4	143.5	136.7	131.9
2000	127.5	102.8	148.1	181.6	176.9	139.6	145.9	142.3	136.2
2001	129.8	101.4	155.3	172.4	186.2	138.8	151.5	148.2	140.6

Source: Transport Statistics GB 2002

1.6 Transport and the Public Budget

Transport is both a major contributor to, and a major recipient from, national public budgets. Transport pays a number of specific contributions to such budgets, in particular through fuel taxes, mostly paid by road haulage, but also through licence fees and other specific charges, as well as the normal contributions through direct and indirect taxes. Some countries charge higher (luxury) rates of VAT on the purchase of cars, although there are some concessions over the payment of VAT on public transport fares. In the other direction transport receives substantial sums from the public budget composed largely of local and national contributions to infrastructure investment and public subsidies to local passenger transport and to national railways.

For France, Orfeuil (1997) estimated the balance of contributions by road users and public expenditure on roads in 1991 to be a net payment by users of some FRF52 billion (€8.5 billion) about half of the actual public expenditure. Such figures have to be treated with care, however, since the budgetary balance of receipts and expenditures ignores the contribution which road users might be expected to pay towards the external resource costs associated with pollution, global warming, etc. Furthermore most national governments resist strongly the idea of hypothecating revenues obtained from particular sectors to expenditure on that sector; decisions on taxes and decisions on public expenditure are entirely separable.

2. THE RELATION BETWEEN TRANSPORT AND ECONOMIC GROWTH

In the preceding section we have shown the importance of transport in overall economic activity in terms of a range of different measures. We have also seen that, despite many differences, there are considerable similarities between different European countries. Given that EU countries at least have experienced similar patterns of economic growth and development this suggests that there are some strong links between the economy and transport which we now turn to examine in more detail.

This link works in both directions. First of all economic activity requires a certain amount of transport. According to this causality, the volume and nature of transport are explained by the level and structure of economic activity and it is this which we shall explore further in this section. The following section will be devoted to the analysis of the reverse causation according to which transport improvements induce economic development.

First, we consider some results from an analysis of the long period; we then look at alternative ways of modelling the demand for freight and passenger transport.

2.1 Analysis of the Long Period

An historical analysis over the long-term provides a perspective which enables the observation of certain relationships, and in particular the distinguishing of situations where transport has accompanied economic growth and development from those where transport developments appear to have been critical in allowing development to take place.

It would be interesting and instructive to study the development of transport from ancient times through to the Industrial Revolution, but the data are only available from more recent times. Prior to the Industrial Revolution inland transport depended on roads, except where there were good navigable rivers. Although the art of road building had been developed as far back as Roman times, and Roman roads were an important instrument of the development of the Empire, roads were slow. The early period of the Industrial Revolution in the late eighteenth century led to a demand for more reliable transport. This was met initially by the development of canals, overcoming the lack of natural navigable waterways by artificial ones. However, this could only provide a temporary solution. The Industrial Revolution led to profound and rapid changes in the structure of the economy. This led first to a major increase in the demand for transport, notably for the increasingly heavy loads associated with the development of coal mining and the iron and steel industry, but it also provided the means of providing this transport – rail.

Railways began in Europe in the 1820s. The first railway was in Britain. The Stockton and Darlington Railway, opened in 1825, was built primarily to carry coal and the small number of passengers were carried in coal trucks. Similarly, in France the first line was opened in 1828 between St Etienne and Andrezieux. Again it was a private line built mainly to cater for the transport of coal from mines to factories. Railways spread rapidly, catering increasingly for passengers as well as freight, and rail transport replaced the previous domination of slow and unreliable road transport. Rail dominated land transport until 1930, the date when the truck powered by the internal combustion engine began to return the highway to dominance.

During this period from the early nineteenth century to the late twentieth century there was a remarkable parallel between the growth of freight transport and that of total output. The relationship between the two was not completely stable and shows some deviations, but it held remarkably well.

Towards the end of this long period however the close relationship appears to have broken down rather more fundamentally. The general interpretation of this phenomenon is that, notably in periods of crisis or the growth of competition, users of transport revise their logistics policy, adjusting stocks, modifying sources of supplies, searching for new customers, all actions which decouple the link between the volume of transport and the volume of production.

2.2 Economic Activity and Freight Transport

Modelling freight transport has traditionally used a simple multiplicative relationship of a Cobb-Douglas form in which the coefficients represent the elasticities:

$$y = kx_1^{\alpha} x_2^{\beta} x_3^{\gamma} ...$$

Thus α is the elasticity of y with respect to the variable x_1 and represents the proportional rate of change of y for a given proportional change in x_1.

The usual specification of this model is expressed in terms either of total traffic, or the traffic by each mode, in tonne-kilometres. The explanatory variables represent economic activity, GDP or industrial production for example; rather more rarely the prices of different modes are introduced.

The French Report *Transport 2010* (1992) includes the elasticities used by the Ministry of Transport. These vary between modes and for different categories of traffic, but generally are in the range 1.2 to 1.8 for the impact of industrial production or GDP on tonne-km of freight traffic. In addition studies for OEST (Girault *et al.*, 1995; Giraud and Blain, 1997; Meyer, 1997) have distinguished short and long-term elasticities of freight traffic with respect to economic growth using a cointegration method. The short term elasticity is quite high (of the order of 2), but the long-term elasticity is rather smaller, around the average of those estimated previously. However, it is noted that there has been tendency for these elasticities to increase in recent years. Van de Voorde and Meersmann (1997), also using a cointegration model on data for Belgium, found short-term elasticities of the effect of industrial production on traffic in the range 0.89 for road to 1.45 for rail, but long-term elasticities as high as 2.38 for road, but only 0.45 for rail and −0.34 for inland waterway. A cross-section study for developing countries by the World Bank (Bennathan *et al.*, 1992) obtained elasticities with respect to GDP of 0.67 for total traffic (road + rail), 1.25 for road and 1.00 for rail.

Elasticities with respect to prices have been more difficult to derive. In the development of the French Infrastructure Plan (Schémas Directeurs d'infrastructures) the elasticity of road traffic with respect to road haulage (own) prices was assumed to be −0.4 and the cross-elasticity of rail traffic with respect to road haulage prices, +0.6. Quinet (1994a) provides estimates of both own and cross-price elasticities for long distance rail and road traffic on sections of networks where competition is the strongest. This gives own price elasticities of −1.0 for rail and −0.7 to −0.9 for road and cross-price elasticities of 0.5 to 0.7 for road with respect to rail prices, but 1.3 for rail with respect to road prices.

Econometric relationships, even adjusted by the considerations above, do not take into account the factors which are likely to lead to changes with respect to historical trends or behavioural relationships. Such changes need alternative approaches to identify future trends, for example *Delphi* methods in which a panel of experts is asked independently for opinions on a given subject and then invited to respond to the results of the first round of the inquiry. Such an inquiry was used by OEST in 1996 during the development of the Schémas Directeurs d'infrastructures in France. The factors cited included policy measures in transport, a possible growing indifference to the costs of transport, a growing need for flexibility, the development of internationalisation, uncertainty in the development of European integration, increasing sensitivity to the environment and possible problems with the public financing of transport.

2.3 Economic Activity and Passenger Transport

Rather more work has been carried out on forecasting aggregate passenger transport, which has tended to display a rather greater elasticity with respect to the growth in economic activity and a rather smaller own-price elasticity than freight transport.

It is also clear for passenger traffic that there are substantial differences between short-term and long-term price elasticities, with the latter typically being larger than the former. For example, in a study of the impact of tolls on French motorway traffic, the short-term elasticity with respect to the toll charged is −0.96 whereas the long term elasticity is −1.28. Using a series of studies from different countries, Goodwin (1992) estimated short-term elasticities of traffic with respect to fuel prices of −0.2, and long-term elasticities of −0.3, but more pronounced were the effects on fuel use with a long-term elasticity of −0.8. This shows the greater effect of fuel prices on the efficacy of fuel use rather than on travel.

Johansson and Schipper (1997) estimated elasticities in 12 OECD countries based on data for the previous 20 years. They distinguished elasticities for car ownership, average annual fuel consumption, annual kilometres driven, the demand for fuel and the volume of automobile traffic. The elasticities were calculated with respect to income and to fuel prices. With respect to income, elasticities varied from zero to +1.2; with respect to fuel prices the impact was around −0.1 on car ownership, but as much as −0.7 on aggregate fuel consumption.

Selvanathan and Selvanathan (1994) estimated the own and cross-elasticities of personal transport, public transport and communications (post, telephone, etc). They used a complete model of demand functions, utilising the properties derived from a utility function in which consumers choose between four goods, public transport, private transport, communications and all other goods. Using data for the United Kingdom and Australia produced overall income elasticities of between +0.5 and +2.3 (with both countries having values of 2 or above with respect to private transport) and own price elasticities of −0.1 to −0.6. The cross-elasticities were positive and of the order of +0.1, except for the cross-elasticities of public transport and communications with private transport which are of the order of +0.5.

The elasticities presented so far have been derived from correlations between aggregate time series data or cross sections of aggregate series across countries or regions. Elasticities can also be calculated from traffic models which estimate traffic on each link of a geographical network (such models are considered in more detail in Chapter 5), but varying one of the parameters, for example the price of one mode (for example changed proportionately on each of the links of the network) or the price of fuel. The elasticities which are derived are obviously highly dependent on the local conditions of competition between the modes and the values which can be derived for a given network differ from one network to another and depend on the average of different conditions within any one network.

The direct own-price elasticities of urban public transport have been surveyed in a variety of studies for different countries (e.g. Kechi, 1996; Goodwin, 1992; Oum *et al.*, 1992). These suggest an average elasticity of around −0.3 and in general range from −0.1 to −0.6 in the short term, and up to about double these values in the long term.

Oum *et al.* (1992) also survey the own price elasticities of other modes. For air transport they identify a wide range of values from −0.5 to −2; the range for interurban rail transport is a little narrower, from −0.5 to −1.5. These values are derived from aggregate models; those from disaggregate models tend to be a rather lower.

These values all reflect relationships observed in the past. The possibility of changes to these through time has been studied qualitatively through interviews with experts as with the values for freight. The uncertainty factors judged the most important appear to include decisions on transport policy, changing demographic factors, the concentration of locations, the reorganisation of working time, internationalisation, the development of tourism, possible changes in the process of European integration with a return to a more national focus, a growing sensitivity to the environment and increasing pressure on public finances. These factors could all move in very different directions.

2.4 Forecasting

Forecasting future transport demand has become a more difficult task due to the general breakdown of some of the regular patterns and trends in traffic of the past (see ECMT, 2003, for a detailed discussion of some of the main futures of these changes). Figure 1.1 illustrates the pattern of these expected trends from a study for the European Commission concerned with both transport demand and energy usage. In the past such forecasts were used mainly to plan the capacity of the network – a so-called 'predict and provide' regime. Increasingly such forecasts are needed as the basis for planning how to constrain future demand.

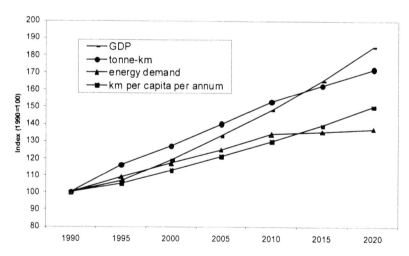

Figure 1.1 Traffic growth and forecasts (1990=100)

3. TRANSPORT AS A DETERMINANT OF ECONOMIC GROWTH

In the preceding section we looked at the effect of economic growth on transport, in this section we reverse this in order to examine the role which improvements to transport can have on economic growth. This effect can take many forms. The most obvious is that which results from the development of infrastructure and the activity which accompanies this development. The second is associated with the reduction in the cost of transport which leads to the development of markets and economic activity. The third, which has become a major area of research in recent years, considers the effects of externalities which derive from a better transport network. We take each of these points in turn.

3.1 The Direct Impact of Infrastructure Investment

The impact of investment in transport infrastructure has become a topic of some considerable controversy in recent years. From a position where such investment was often seen as an example of unproductive public sector investment likely to hinder growth by crowding investment out of the more productive private sector, the 1990s introduced a number of studies which, by various methods, claimed substantial growth impacts.

The most immediate macroeconomic consequences of the development of infrastructure obviously arise directly from the construction itself. This makes such investment attractive during periods of slack economic growth or depression. A pioneering study in this area was that of Charmeil (1968) which developed a basic methodology for this type of analysis and estimated, for the period 1965–70 for France, that the impact on GDP of road construction was of the order of 0.25 per cent.

3.2 The Effect of a Reduction in the Cost of Transport

However, the key role of infrastructure is not just in its construction, but also the impact of its use on the wider economy. The overall impact on the economy of a reduction in the cost of transport is easy to understand. Just like with any good, if the cost of production is reduced, price can fall and the quantity bought will increase. For the movement of people, a reduction in cost can change the pattern of consumption and movement as well as the distribution of income. Nevertheless, estimating the actual total impacts of infrastructure has become a topic of some considerable debate.

In the first of the recent studies to address this issue Aschauer (1989) used an augmented aggregate production function including public infrastructure as an additional input. This produced elasticities of public capital of the order of 0.4 to 0.5, well in excess of the usual elasticity of private capital and suggesting very high rates of return to any investment in infrastructure. Criticism of the approach, especially the econometric detail led to a large number of subsequent studies for a wide range of geographical situations. These tend to suggest that there is a positive elasticity of public infrastructure, but that the value is nearer to 0.1 (Lau and Sin, 1997). We look at this approach in more detail in section 3.3 below.

A second type of study, exemplified by the work of Baum and Behnke (1997) used a growth accounting approach which allocates total growth in the economy to the growth of labour and capital and then the unexplained residual to other relevant factors, such as transport infrastructure investment. Applying this method to Germany for the previous 45 years, Baum and Behnke suggest some 50 per cent of total growth can be attributed to the transport sector, most to the growth of roads and road transport. The problem with this approach is that it simply assumes that the unexplained residual in the accounting matrix is attributable to the one factor and ignores all the other changes in the structure of the economy over this long period of time.

A third approach has been used by the European Commission (1997). This treats transport improvements which arise through infrastructure investments like autonomous increases in productivity. This is justified through, in particular, the impact on time savings which can be reallocated to more productive use. The impact can then be worked out through the application of a macroeconomic model of the economy. This approach also produces substantial estimated impacts with the priority Trans-European Networks estimated to add 0.25 per cent to GDP and 0.11 per cent to employment over 25 years. The main problem with this approach is in the fundamental assumption of the link between time savings and productivity; how are such time savings paid for and will they really be devoted to productive use? At such an aggregate level it is difficult to determine the detail of the relationships in the economy. This may be easier to examine at the level of the individual project or at least in terms of an investment programme in one mode.

Bureau and Cipriani (1986) investigated the macroeconomic impact of the TGV Sud Est high-speed train line in France using a mini dynamic macroeconomic model (a simplification of the D.M.S. model) to which a transport sector has been added. The model is essentially Keynesian: the principal mechanisms are those of the multiplier and accelerator, the indexation of prices and wages, external competitiveness, and a Philips relationship in the labour market. The production functions are Leontief. Concerning transport, each sub-sector depended on a fixed-coefficients function and demand determined by price. Public policy (investment, taxation, etc.) is exogenous, the infrastructure is financed by borrowing, taking account of the external constraint of maintaining a current balance of payments equilibrium. The authors established that the overall change in the GDP was closely related to the profitability of the project.

More ambitiously, Morisugi and Hayashiyama (1997) attempted an ex-post evaluation of the impact of Japanese railways on the growth of GDP over the period 1875–1940. They used a computable general equilibrium model assuming an economy of identical individuals, private enterprises, a transport sector and a government which balanced budgets. The utility function of consumers included the value of goods and the value of travel which depended on the level of equipment. Likewise production depended on the transport of freight, labour and capital using a constant elasticity of substitution production function. The model depended on parameters derived from historical data and suggested that the contribution of the rail network to the growth of GDP, which depended essentially on the reduction of transport costs, was 0.5 per cent in 1875, the date when construction of the network started, and had grown to 12.3 per cent in 1940.

This work was essentially the Japanese equivalent of the work of Fogel (1964) on the contribution of the rail network to American growth. Although Fogel did not use a formal model, but reconstructed by inference what would have happened, in the absence of the railways, the alternative means of transport, their costs and the consequences on economic activity. He suggested that, at the global level, in the absence of the railways, United States GDP would have been reduced by between 10 and 20 per cent.

3.3 Positive Externalities and Implications for Growth

Thus far we have considered transport as a typical factor of production, entering into the classical production function but at constant returns to scale. We now turn to consider an alternative possible role of transport services in which they appear as a public good and which is related to new theories of endogenous growth (see Box 1.1)

BOX 1.1

Theories of growth and endogenous growth

The classic Solow–Swan model of growth has been the basis of the analysis of economic growth for decades. In its most simple form it uses the following variables:

K capital
L labour force, assumed to follow a constant geometric rate of growth, n, given exogenously
Y output
δ rate of depreciation of capital
s rate of savings of households
C household consumption
I gross investment

It is assumed that output Y depends on the factors K and L as given by the production function:

$$Y = F(K, L)$$

which has the following properties:

$$\frac{\partial F}{\partial K} \geq 0 \; ; \; \frac{\partial F}{\partial L} \geq 0 \; ; \; \frac{\partial^2 F}{\partial K^2} \leq 0 \; ; \; \frac{\partial^2 F}{\partial L^2} \leq 0$$

$$F(\lambda L, \lambda K) = \lambda F(L, K)$$

The last equation expresses the constant returns to scale in the aggregate national production function. This is necessary to relate to the classical analysis of market equilibrium, based on constant returns in the productive sector.

From the above equations we can derive:

$$\frac{dK}{dt} = sY - \delta K = sf(K, L) - \delta K \qquad (1.1)$$

It is usual to express this in terms of capital per head and output per head, such that if:

$$y = \frac{Y}{L} \text{ and } k = \frac{K}{L}$$

equation (1.1) becomes

$$\frac{dk}{dt} = sf(k) - (n + \delta)k \qquad (1.2)$$

If we know the function f, we can solve this differential equation completely. But we can portray graphically a qualitative view of the evolution of k through time in terms of the curves presented in the graph. Intuitively we can see that k tends towards the value k^*. In effect if:

$$k \geq k^*$$

then:

$$\frac{dk}{dt} \leq 0$$

and vice versa.

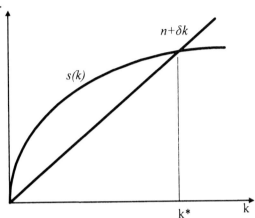

This model produces a result which tends towards a stationary state where capital per head and thus output per head tend to a unique value. This result is contradicted by the facts, which show a growth in income per head and the absence of convergence in countries or regions with low incomes. How do we escape from this contradiction?

A first response is to introduce an external factor, in the form of technical progress, but this cannot account for the divergence of incomes per head. Another response is to modify the model to introduce an exogenous growth factor. For this one approach is to assume:

$$y = Ak$$

This breaks the assumption of diminishing returns, but this is upheld more easily if we consider that K and k represent not just physical capital, bust also human capital, the stock of knowledge, or the stock of public capital, which is not just available to each enterprise but to the economy as a whole. Thus taking account of equation (1.2), it can be seen that the rate of growth of the economy is constant and positive, and of the value $sA - (n + \delta)$.

An analogous form is that used by Aschauer (1989) in which the production function is written:

$$Y = AL^{1-\alpha} K^{\alpha} G^{\beta}$$

where G represents public capital public, A, α, and β are parameters.

This effect is expressed through the production functions of enterprises which depend not just on private capital and the consumption of intermediate goods – these latter of course disappear when we aggregate the production function to the level of the economy as a whole – but also on public capital, and particularly here on transport infrastructure capital. For each of these, the production function can be written:

$$y_i = f(k_i, l_i, t_i, x_i) * A_i(G)$$

where:

k_i is the private capital.

l_i is the labour force.

t_i is a vector representing the cost and quality of transport.

x_i is a vector representing all other factors.

G is a parameter related to transport, represented by the capital in transport infrastructure or by an index of accessibility (for example the number of customers it is possible to reach within a given time or the size of the agglomeration, or another accessibility index).

In this expression transport enters in the form of an intermediate good t_i. This is the effect analysed in section 3.2 above. However it also enters as an intermediary in the expression $A_i(G)$. This can represent a number of different types of effect, for example:

- The improvement of communications allows enterprises better information about production technology, a more rapid diffusion of technical progress, and better information on the activities of competitors.
- The improvement of communications gives access to larger markets which allows enterprises to satisfy its needs more effectively, for example to match jobs and workers through access to larger labour markets.
- Other mechanisms which for example allow enterprises to develop scale economies through extension of their markets.

Relationships of this type have been the object of numerous statistical tests, using both geographic and sectoral aggregations (see Transportation Research Board, 1997; SACTRA, 1999 for detailed reviews and Vickerman, 2002 for further discussion).

3.3.1 Regional and national level evidence

Tests of this model at the national level have, for the most part, used aggregate public capital as an explanatory variable; rather few have specified the effect just of transport infrastructure capital. Table 1.10, taken from Hakfoot (1996), summarises the results in terms of the elasticity of output with respect to public capital from a range of he earlier studies. For the most part these studies assumed a Cobb–Douglas production function and were estimated for time series data. The results of these studies are, as can be seen, very varied.

Table 1.10 Evidence from studies of public capital elasticities

Author of study	Year of publication	Geographic coverage	Elasticity of GDP with respect to public capital
Ratner	1983	USA	0.06
Costa	1987	USA	0.20
Aschauer	1989	USA	0.39
Duffy-Deno and Eberts	1991	USA	0.08
Munnell	1990	USA	0.15
Berndt and Hansson	1991	Sweden	0.69-1.60
Toen-Gout and Jongeling	1993	Netherlands	0.48

Source: Hakfoot (1996)

Many criticisms have been levelled at these types of study (see for example Quinet, 1992; Vickerman, 2000a):

- There are problems of reliability with the data used. Series for capital are always difficult to determine, notably of public capital. By its nature the value of public capital is more difficult to determine than for private capital since it is less likely that prices reflect market valuations of the capital. Moreover the boundary between public and private capital is not clear and varies from one country to another.
- The use of the Cobb-Douglas production function is open to criticism, especially when the model is applied to less developed economies.
- The empirical results suggest an elasticity of public capital of the order of 0.3 to 0.4 which appears rather high. It is arguable that such values may be applicable to key elements of physical infrastructure such as

transport or energy, but these values may be more difficult to justify on the case of education or health care.

- All of this depends largely on the estimation of time series which cannot separate out the effects of supply and demand, and notably the effects of the short-run multiplier. Public investment is frequently the consequence rather than the cause of growth.

There have also been a number of cross-section studies which estimate the effects of different levels of provision of infrastructure across a set of geographical areas, often averaging growth and provision over long periods to reduce the effects of short-term fluctuations. Studies of this type have been carried out by, for example, Barro (1991), Looney and Frederiksen (1981), Ford and Poret (1991), Eberts (1986), Costa *et al.* (1987).

These studies, which eliminate the effects of an inverse causality (the more GDP grows, the more one has the need for, and the means of financing, public investment), nevertheless produce rather varied values of the elasticity (since the other sources of error have not been eliminated), but overall tend to be much lower.

Aschauer (1989) produced a set of widely discussed estimates, but ones regarded as not so rigorous, for the main industrial countries in the Group of 7 for the same time period. This showed a strong positive correlation between public investment and productivity growth in the 1980s in these countries. It is particularly noticeable that the 'natural' profitability of public investment appears so high, but this is rather difficult to justify in terms of conventional calculations of the rate of return on such projects.

Few studies have specified the individual effect of transport infrastructures. Looney and Frederiksen specified road investment and found a significant impact, similarly to that of Mera (1973). Prud'Homme (1996) and Fritsch and Prud'Homme (1997) who estimated the effect of road investment on productivity in France using a cross section across the 21 regions. They found an elasticity of regional GDP to road infrastructure of the order of 0.08 to 0.10.

3.3.2 Sectoral evidence

Sectoral tests have been carried out, notably by Nadiri and Mamuneas (1996), who estimated cost functions by sector and examined their evolution through time, relating the change in productivity by sector to changes in road capital. They found a contribution of road investment to productivity which varied according to sector, but with a mean value of 0.05 per cent, a figure rather smaller than those found in other studies.

3.3.3 Are there positive externalities?

What do these results suggest about the existence of positive external effects? It is not possible to draw any direct conclusions. In effect the estimated correlations identify the global effect of the improvement of infrastructure, public or transport, on the growth of production; but they do not identify the share within this global effect which can be attributed to the reduction in the costs of transport, and the distribution of this between those effects internal to the production function, and those which are external.

It is possible to infer this distribution through further reasoning. The elasticity of public capital translates into an ex post rate of return on the relevant investment. Comparing this ex post rate of return at the aggregate macroeconomic level with the rates of return estimated for each investment ex ante it is possible to obtain an estimate of the increase due to the external effect, because the effects are assumed to be present in most calculations.

From equation (1.3) the cost function for an enterprise can be derived:

$$C_i(y_i, r, w, c, \pi, G) = \underset{k_i, l_i, t_i, x_i}{Min} (rk_i + wl_i + ct_i + \pi x_i)$$

with:

$$y_i = A_i(G) f(k_i, l_i, t_i, x_i)$$

An investment translates into a marginal change of G, and a change in c, and leads to a change of costs C, such that according to the envelope theorem:

$$\frac{\partial C_i}{\partial c} = t_i \quad \text{and} \quad \frac{\partial C_i}{\partial G} = \frac{\partial C_i}{\partial y_i} y_i \frac{A_i'}{A_i}$$

The usual calculation of the rate of return does not take into account the second term, the ex post evaluation of rates of return integrates the two.

The elasticities of public capital in the various studies discussed above lie between 0.05 and 0.30. Quinet (1992) and Prud'Homme (1996) have calculated the ex post rates of return on corresponding investments in addition to the reduction of costs to producers and the consumers' surplus to the final consumers of transport. The results are approximately doubled, in the range 0.10 to 0.60. Nadiri and Mamuneas (1996) suggest a mean rate of return on road investments of 28 per cent. Morrison and Schwartz (1996) obtained similar results from an analysis which involved both geographical and sectoral comparisons. The ex ante rates of return lay in the range 0.05 to 0.20. At the very least these studies suggest the existence of substantial external impacts of such investments which are worth further investigation.

3.3.4 Historical evidence

Other consequences, difficult to quantify, are fundamental. These are the ones which emerge in the long term following transport developments. They result in changes in the way economic and social life is organised, both quantitatively and qualitatively.

Several examples could be quoted, but above all the creation of national markets in the course of the nineteenth and twentieth centuries in Europe, which enabled the elimination of famine due to the possibility of transporting foodstuffs throughout a country with both acceptable costs and times, is clear evidence of the wider role of transport. The improvement of transport is also a factor in the development of international trade: centuries ago it was just spices, expensive and rare, which were traded from the Far East; now all sorts of primary materials, even those of low value, can be imported without difficulty.

Relocation, which has now become one element in the essential strategy of firms, has become a major factor depending on changes in transport. Transport changes allow firms to change the sources of supply of materials and the locations of consumers such that production can benefit from scale economies. It can be argued that one of the fundamental enabling factors in globalisation lies in the improvement of transport and the reduction in its costs.

The same analysis can be applied to the transport of passengers with the development of tourism, the extension of business trips, or the changes in the way of life resulting from more frequent and extended contacts, urban development and the phenomenon of metropolitanisation. The progressive abolition of distance is one of the characteristics of modern life, though the 'death of distance' may not yet have occurred (Rietveld and Vickerman, 2003).

4. IMPLICATIONS

The belief in a link between transport and economic activity has for a long time supported policy intervention. Even before Keynes's support for a policy of intervening in the economic cycle and reducing unemployment through major public works there had been examples of using transport in this way. In France, for example, there were examples from as early as 1848 and the Freycinet Plan of 1870, named after the Minister of Public Works who adopted it, had also had the objective of boosting the iron and steel industry through the construction of a rail network and canals.

The economic analysis presented above allows us to determine more precisely the impacts and the limits of this type of action to affect the rate of economic growth and employment. Above all, the effects of the decision to proceed with an investment take time to have an impact: from the moment when a project is launched and the land is made available it takes one or two years before construction begins, and construction itself may take many years. These lags in the realisation of a project have to be allowed for as exogenous elements of the models, since the impacts may well be felt rather later than the needs of the economic cycle. They also may show that these effects are ephemeral, once an investment is completed there may be a slow return to the initial situation.

Besides, macroeconomic models rarely integrate all the consequences of a particular action which we are seeking to measure. Thus the models we have discussed above assume that prices are fixed, an assumption which might be thought reasonable in the short term, but not in the long term. Other models allow for this modification, but do not go as far as endogenising the rate of interest, or when they do it is at the cost of a simplification in the sectoral structure of the economy which may make the results less useful. It is necessary to treat with great reserve any claims of the type 'this project will create several thousand jobs'.

Such models only deal with one part of the impacts of the actions which they analyse, the most direct consequences on the productive system. In addition to any macroeconomic constraints, large investment projects may often need to be accompanied by other measures. For example, the finance of a new infrastructure from a government budget may have a favourable impact on employment, but if this puts the budget, or the public debt, out of equilibrium it may require compensating actions which would have a deflationary effect and the final impact may be indeterminate. If the project is financed by additional taxes then a theorem of Haavelmo says that the increase of the GDP which results is just equal to the size of the investment, assuming fixed prices.

It could be asked if the practice of decision making gives a sufficient weight to the positive external effects which can be created by the transport system. That transport has an effect on growth more profound than implied by a naive view of it as simple factor of production can clearly be seen. The provision and improvement of transport enables the development of contacts, better information and communication, the growth of market size, a better matching of needs with means of satisfying them. But the precise way of measuring all this remains elusive.

The practical consequences of implementing such programmes can be important. In terms of infrastructure it is convenient to develop networks above the level which would be implied by conventional cost-benefit evaluations. Perhaps it has been the intuition of this type of consequence which has inspired certain types of programme. We could note here the

Freycient Plan launched in France at the end of the nineteenth century, the debates in the United States over the increasing lack of public infrastructure and the interest in developing a large infrastructure programme in the original platform of Bill Clinton. Above all we can note the adoption of the Trans- European Networks Programme by the European Union as a means of accelerating European integration and promoting the development of the European economy.

Another consequence of allowing for the existence of positive externalities concerns pricing policy in transport. If the empirical results of the effects of infrastructure capital relate to the externalities of the network or to the growth in profitability of those using it, then a reduction in prices may be justified. Can we believe that the underpricing of transport, which is often observed, is part of an overall public policy, which is inspired by this intuition?

It should be possible to bring together these various factors, which affect every geographical area, be it a region, a city or a commune, to define a level of infrastructure which it requires according to the need for access or the needs of its economy. Certainly there is evidence that better infrastructure develops productivity, but it is also certain that good access is a factor of attraction to firms. Thus although good transport can be argued to be the basis for a favourable location, it is an argument which needs to be seen to be well founded rather than just assumed.

2. Transport and Location

The interaction between transport and location can be studied at different levels. At the microeconomic level, it involves the way in which economic agents take decisions about the location of their activities as a function of the availability and provision of transport. At the macroeconomic level, we are concerned with the way the structure and level of economic activity in a particular geographical area, city, region, or country, relates to the availability and quality of the transport system which serves it. We look at each of these aspects in turn in the first two sections of this chapter. The third section considers some of the practical consequences of the analysis.

1. TRANSPORT AND THE LOCATION OF ECONOMIC AGENTS

We concentrate here on the location of firms, the detailed discussion of household location decisions is deferred to Chapter 3 which deals in more detail with transport in urban areas.

The classic theory (Weber, 1909; Isard, 1956) gives transport an essential role in the choice of location for firms: firms locate in the place which enables them to minimize the total cost of transport, taking into account both the supply of inputs, including labour, and the delivery of outputs. The application of this principle leads to a unique location, independent of the volume of production or the technology used, which will maximise profits, but subject to a number of restrictive assumptions: constant returns to scale and production coefficients, the absence of externalities, the level and spatial distribution of demand given. We consider the significance of each of these conditions in turn.

1.1 A Given Level and Location of Demand

This hypothesis is essentially the transition to a spatial economy of the classic model of perfect competition in which the price is given for the individual firm. However, the introduction of space results in a situation

where firms do have some market power over those customers who are closer
to them because of the protection which the cost of transport provides. In
order to examine this in more detail it is useful to use a simple model of
spatial duopoly. We assume there are two identical firms, which can fix the
prices they charge to their customers, competing along a linear market space
within which customers are distributed at a uniform density, each having a
given and equal demand for the good (one unit) at prices below the limit of a
maximum price P.

It is assumed that each firm faces the same marginal cost of production c
and the cost of transport per unit is t. Thus for each location on the axis x,
the total cost (production+delivery) for the firm at location $(-L)$ is:
$c+t|x+L|$ and is represented by the cone shaped function based on location
$(-L)$. The equivalent applies to the firm at $(+L)$. If the firms follow, for each
customer defined by a given location x, a competitive strategy of the
Bertrand type, we can determine (see Figure 2.1):

- the actual prices (the segments defined by thick lines) which correspond
  to the costs of the least well performing firm;
- the market areas (0–A for firm 1 and 0+A for firm 2), each firm operating
  within the market where is has a cost advantage;
- and the profits of each enterprise, defined by the shaded areas.

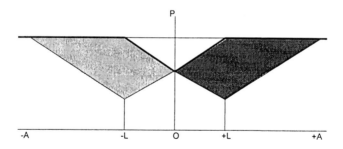

Figure 2.1 Spatial duopoly pricing

This shows that the introduction of space results in a major difference in
comparison with the aspatial situation since each firm can exercise some
market power over a neighbouring firm. The reduction of transport costs will
increase competition between enterprises and allow for an increase in the size
of market areas. Better transport should, in this simple model, therefore be
pro-competitive in the sense of reducing prices, but at the cost of allowing
firms the potential to grow in size.

This leads to strategic interactions between firms in terms of their choice
of location. We can see this by modelling the strategies of the two firms

considered above in the form of a two-stage game. The first stage involves the choice of location for each, the second the choice of a price. Assume that the relevant space is limited to the area between the locations −M and +M (Figure 2.2). It can be shown that the solution to this game (the Nash equilibrium) corresponds to the locations −M/2 and +M/2 for each firm respectively; this is the location which for each firm minimises the costs of transport for the given market area (0 to −M for firm 1 and 0 to +M for firm 2), but the market area is not given exogenously, it results from the conditions of transport and the strategic decisions of the firms.

The case of the spatial duopoly with delivered prices to the consumer can be compared with the case of spatial duopoly, but with factory gate prices. In the latter case there is only one price per firm whereas in the former prices differ for each customer according to their location. It is possible to show that, with transport costs proportional to distance, it is possible that at a given location there is no price equilibrium. The equilibrium location is thus at points −M/2 and +M/2 and the common factory gate price is $C+2tM$ (Thisse, 1988).

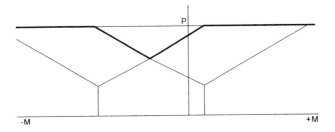

Figure 2.2 Location of firms

It is easy to determine the factors which enter into the choice of these locations: for each firm to move towards the other leads to enlargement of its market, but because of the increased competition which will ensue, to reduce its price. The optimal locations are those where these opposing factors balance out. Of course this result depends on the form of the function which links transport costs to distance. We assumed above that transport costs are a linear function of distance. Under a frequently used alternative hypothesis, that transport costs vary with the square of distance, the firms will seek the maximum differentiation and locate at the extremities of the available space.

We can also examine the case in which two firms are assumed to be in imperfect competition (Cournot duopoly) and to serve markets situated at nodes in transport network. In this case the optimal location of each firm will be at the nodes of the network (Thisse, 1993). This result is confirmed by empirical evidence and gives a certain robustness to the idea that the structure of transport costs and the conditions of competition lead to locations at the nodes of transport networks and thus towards a polarisation of economic activity in space.

1.2 Constant Returns and Externalities

It could be thought that the continuing reduction in the costs of transport and thus of their share in the cost of production would have led to a diminution of the role of transport in location and hence to a more uniform distribution of economic activity in space. This intuition is contradicted by the facts. In most countries and in the world as a whole, there has been a gradual process of urbanisation which has accelerated into a tendency towards metropolitanisation (see Rietveld and Vickerman, 2003, for a fuller discussion and Savy and Veltz, 1993, for evidence from France).

Such an empirical observation, implying that the traditional theory of self-balance in the relative growth of different regions is flawed, has led to a considerable increase in the exploration of the theory of the way a spatial economy is organised (see Fujita *et al.*, 1999; Fujita and Thisse, 2002, for more complete explorations of these effects). The essential features of such models are that consumers can express preferences for variety, which increases with increasing wealth, that firms face increasing returns to scale and that agglomeration economies arising both within and outside the industry reinforce the cumulative process.

A key debate in this literature is the extent to which it is factors internal to the process of production: specialisation, scale economies and the division of labour, or the external economies of urbanisation which dominate. Thus Henderson, (1988; 2003) is clear that it is essentially within industry effects which dominate whereas other writers (e.g. Ciccone and Hall, 1996; Ciccone, 2002) have identified rather more general measures of employment density as determinants of increased productivity in urban areas.

The general argument is, however, essentially the same. Firms prefer locations which have larger markets to supply, larger labour markets and a wider range of specialised services. In turn, these specialised services, which themselves can benefit from increasing returns, need larger markets to spread their fixed costs. These agglomeration effects were first recognised by Marshall (1920) who identified, in what he termed 'industrial districts', that, through the market for specialised services and both backward and forward linkages in the labour markets, there would be tendencies for industrial clustering. These tendencies, though clear, were, however, less easy to explain in terms of conventional economic logic, but relied on what we now term externalities, in Marshall's words 'the mysteries of the trade become no mysteries because they are as it were in the air'.

This agglomeration of activities allows each firm to benefit from greater diversity and to contribute themselves to this diversity, which is a means of mitigating the penalty of being nearer to competitors. These benefits also accrue to employed consumers who benefit from a wider range of goods and services available at lower prices and at the same time from higher nominal wages. The resulting higher real wages induce individuals to move into the larger urban areas and the growing benefits of agglomeration outweigh, up to a point, any tendency for productivity loss or competition which would hold wages down and force prices up. Thus there is a reinforcing tendency for an upward spiral of growth in the agglomeration.

Thus geographic polarisation appears to have become one of the characteristics of growth, resulting from factors very different from transport as embodied in Marshall's industrial districts or Perroux's (1955) 'development or growth poles', but transport changes are clearly implicated in these developments, they accompany them and accentuate them.

It could be considered that the representation of transport in these developing models of the spatial economy is very schematic. Peeters *et al.* (1997) have attempted to model it more fully using a simple representation of a network. Two hypotheses are considered: one with a rectangular network, the other with a radial network. Within these, a solution for the optimal location of factories is sought which minimises total costs for serving a demand which is uniformly distributed across all the nodes of the network. The existence of fixed costs determines that there cannot be a factory at each node, and that the higher the fixed costs the less numerous are the optimal factory locations. It emerges that the tendency towards central locations is stronger in the concentric network than in the rectangular, which shows that the shape of the infrastructure network does influence location and the degree of centralisation. This theoretical result can be compared with different observed structures. For example, at a national level there is an obvious comparison between the observed French structure, highly centralised around Paris and based on the development of a star shaped infrastructure centred on the capital, with the less centralised structure observed in Germany where the national infrastructure network is more rectangular based on a large number of more equal nodes. The tendency towards centralisation in a radial network is attenuated when, for example, a ring road is added not too far from the centre. The study also considers the case of two neighbouring networks, one radial, the other rectangular, with a frontier between them which is reduced or removed, for example through the development of a common market. It emerges that locations are not greatly modified by this case except that there is some tendency towards locations closer to the old frontier.

This analysis is close to the classical theories of urban hierarchies in the tradition of Christaller (1933) and Lösch (1940) (Figure 2.3) according to which cities are organised in nested networks which grow as one moves up the hierarchy to larger cities; this rise up the hierarchy being accompanied by an increasing diversity in the services offered, these services becoming increasingly specialised as their markets extend to a growing area.

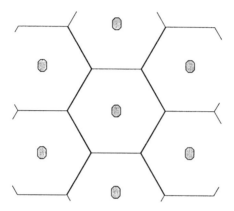

Figure 2.3 Spatial structure on two levels

2. TRANSPORT AND REGIONAL DEVELOPMENT

The considerations discussed above lead us naturally to an interest in the effects of transport on regional development which are developed in two stages, modelling and empirical evidence.

2.1 Transport in Regional Models

In regional modelling, transport plays a central role through the two following mechanisms:

- First, within each region, the reduction in the cost of transport leads to a reduction in the costs of production and hence to effects on the level of demand within the region, and on the structure of economic activity as evidenced by input-output tables. However, since most models assume constant returns and there is no recognition of product diversity, contrary to the considerations raised in the previous section, the effects of polarisation are usually badly treated.

- Second, between regions, a reduction in the costs of transport leads to a change in the trade, imports and exports, between the regions. We develop this below in a case where, for simplicity, there is no trade initially (infinite transport costs) and after a reduction in the costs of transport prices in the two regions converge to a point where the difference is equal to the cost of transport.
- Third, there is the more complex case, allowing for increasing returns, factor mobility and changing transport costs in which the final outcome is less determinate.

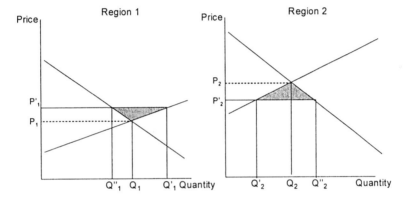

Figure 2.4 Gainers and losers in the development of trade

		Region 1	Region 2
Before	Quantity produced	Q_1	Q_2
	Quantity consumed	Q_1	Q_2
	Price	P_1	P_2
After	Quantity produced	Q'_1	Q'_2
	Quantity consumed	Q''_1	Q''_2
	Price	P'_1	P'_2

Figure 2.4 shows the gainers and losers from the development of trade which arises when one of the two regions puts in place an improvement of infrastructure allowing trade to take place more easily. The table below Figure 2.4 shows the quantities produced and consumed in each region before and after the change and the prices in the two markets. In the situation

after the change the difference in prices $(P'_2 - P'_1)$ is equal to the price of transport between the two regions. The gainers are the consumers in region 2 and the producers in region 1. Others lose (it can be shown, using the tools developed later in Chapter 7, that the aggregate balance over gainers and losers is exactly equal to the surplus realised by the new infrastructure). This result supports the general idea that when the trading arrangements between two regions are improved, there is specialisation by sector and that globally the producers in the region with the greatest initial advantages will benefit. This leads to polarisation and this polarisation is typically undervalued because the fundamental drivers of increasing returns and product diversification are omitted.

In most models, interregional trade is modelled according to this principle, but typically rather less crudely, taking account of the multiplicity of regions. For each product, the amount of trade between two regions depends on the difference in price and the cost of transport between the two, according to a relation of the form (Rietveld and Nijkamp, 2000):

$$t_{irs} = k_{is} \exp(-\beta_i (p_{is} + u_{irs})) / \sum_q k_{iq} \exp(-\beta_i (p_{iq} + u_{riq}))$$

in which :

t_{irs} is the share of traffic in good i between r and s
k_{iq} is the capacity of region q in the production of good i
p_{iv} is the price of good i in region v
u_{irs} is the cost of transport of good i from r to s

These models can also be used to explain the role of transport in the location of factors of production. For example, the migration of population between regions is determined, at least in part, by the relative incomes per head, the level of employment (or unemployment) and distance or the cost of movement. Whether people move both their jobs and their residence on any given change in transport costs and the impact of families with more than one employed person on the choice of locations further complicates this issue (see Vickerman, 1984, for evidence from an urban situation and Papapanagos and Vickerman, 2000 for a discussion of inter-regional migration).

2.1.1 An example of a multi-region transport-economy model: MEPLAN
To explore the characteristics of such a model we use here the MEPLAN model as applied to examine the impact of the Channel Tunnel between France and the United Kingdom on the regions of the European Union (COST 317, 1995).

The model produces a joint evaluation of regional economic activity and transport flows based on a regional input-output structure. The demand for transport and regional development depend on the characteristics of transport supply. In the application Europe is divided into 33 regions and the model comprises three modules:

- A regional economic module which evaluates the transformations in the structures of production and consumption in each region, on the basis of the growth of population and incomes, and differences in regional accessibility. In each region, the links between the sectors are represented by the coefficients of an input-output matrix. The demand for each good is satisfied through domestic production and imports, the volume of which depends on a comparison of prices with other regions and the costs of transport.
- A module which translates trade flows into transport flows.
- A transport module which relates these flows to the costs of transport which, when reinserted into the economic model, must, in equilibrium be coherent with the costs of transport chosen in the preceding step of the iterative process.

This model generates large numbers of results. We only consider here those which relate to the changes in regional GDP resulting from the completion of the Channel Tunnel.

The result of the theoretical model presented in Figure 2.4 can clearly be seen in Figure 2.5: there are gainers and losers from the development of a new infrastructure; positive effects on some regions, negative on others. The polarisation of activity resulting from this new infrastructure can also be seen: activity tends to grow in those regions most directly affected at the expense of those both far away or in the 'shadow' created by the infrastructure.

Developments of this model have been widely used over the past decade in evaluations of the wider impacts of Trans-European Networks (Wegener and Bökemann, 1998; Bröcker *et al*, 2002).

2.1.2 Other transport-land use models

There are many other regional models developed to a large extent from the pioneering study of Amano and Fujita (1970), which are represented by the structure in Figure 2.6.

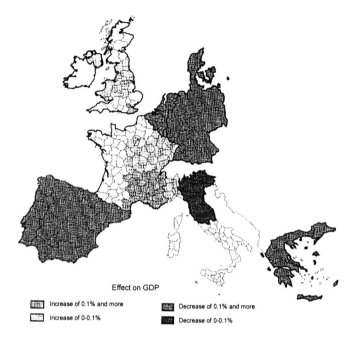

Figure 2.5 The effects of the Channel Tunnel estimated by the MEPLAN model

Transport features in this structure in many different ways:

- For the choice of mode and route which depend on the characteristics of transport supply, that is to say, on the quality of infrastructure and the volume of traffic;
- The amount of traffic induced determines the cost of transport between regions;
- Interregional trade depends on the allocation of the trade of one region with each other region, this depending on the nature of the good transported, the price of the good in each region, and as an element in this, the cost of transport for that good;
- The evolution of transport costs affects the change in the coefficients of the input-output matrix and the share of transport in the value-added of each good;
- The migration of population between regions is determined by incomes per head, (un)employment levels and distance (cost of transport);
- Investment by region and by sector depends on changes in (expectations of) production levels in each region, which can be altered by proposed changes in transport and accessibility.

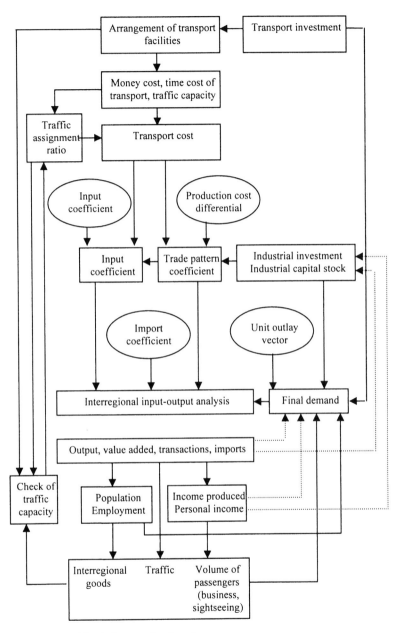

Note: A dotted line indicates a time lag of one year

Figure 2.6 Structure of the Amano and Fujita model

This model has been used in Japan to estimate the effects of construction of a bridge between the islands of Hokkaido and Shikoku, in particular the consequences for different locations resulting from changes made feasible by the completion of the bridge.

The UrbanSim model is a more recent model, designed at the end of the 1990s, which became operational in 2002. Its aim is to develop a tool to understand metropolitan land-use, urban planning, transport and environmental planning, representing interactions of policies and markets, including dynamic disequilibrium, through tools to analyse city and county planning policies. The behaviour of land markets and government policies is represented through multinomial logit functions applied at a highly level of spatial disaggregation, through household mobility and location choice, business mobility, land developers and real estate markets. The dynamics is time dependent, through annual steps. Data requirements are exacting. They concern households, business, land use and environmental constraints, and development costs. The outputs are: population by type (size, age, income, number of children and workers), employment by industrial activities, land use and density, housing units, commercial square footage, housing units. The travel components use accessibility indices which enter the housing and business location models and influence land prices and development decisions, which are calculated as the *logsum* (see Chapter 5) of multinomial logit models. Equilibrium between travel and other models is reached through fixed point equilibrium: at each run, location models provide travel demand patterns, which are inputs to the travel models to give transport costs and times, then accessibility indices which are used for the next run as input for location models.

As well as these formal models which can be quantified, other methods have been used to evaluate the effects of an improvement in transport.

A first set of methods uses accessibility indicators of the form:

$$A_i = \sum_j E_j \exp(-\mu c_{ij})$$

where

A_i is the accessibility of region i
E_j is the weight (GDP, population) of region j
C_{ij} is the cost or the time of transport between i and j

The relative importance of the effects of a change can be measured by:

$$\Delta q_i = \Delta \left(\frac{A_i E_i}{\sum_j A_j E_j} \right)$$

and the change relating to region i will be of the form:

$$\Delta E_i = \sigma E_i \Delta q_i$$

where σ is a response parameter calculated on the basis of earlier studies.

This method has been used by Simmonds and Jenkinson (1996) to assess the impact of the Channel Tunnel, by Botham (1983) to evaluate the impact of the British roads programme and by Vickerman *et al.* (1999) to assess the overall impact of the high speed rail programme in the Trans-European Networks.

Other methods are more qualitative. They seek to describe in a reasoned way the consequences of investments by using a mixture of statistical information and interviews with economic agents on their opinions. Spiekermann and Wegener (1997) discuss forecasts of the effects resulting from the Channel Tunnel in this manner.

In sum the regional macroeconomic analyses suggest evidence in favour of the polarising impact of infrastructure, benefiting regions which are close at the expense of those further away. But this result is typically implied by the assumptions underlying the models and which are not always fully justified. The modelling approach gives a degree of authority to the outcomes, but does not enable the validation of these assumptions. Thus it may be preferable to undertake more limited analyses, but which are nevertheless more solidly based on the observation of facts.

2.2 Empirical Studies

These are numerous and we can only present a sample of them. We discuss first some French evidence, and then some studies from other countries, before drawing some overall conclusions.

2.2.1 French studies

A large number of studies have been undertaken in France dealing with both autoroutes and the TGV, reflecting the importance attached to increasing accessibility to the regions. A substantial review of these has been made by Denan-Boemont and Gabella (1991)

The most complete studies of the TGV are those of Plassard (1990b) concerning the TGV Paris-Sud Est. These have suggested that the effects of the TGV on the structure of the economy have been relatively weak and slow to emerge. The existence of the TGV has only been a factor in location for a relatively small number of firms. This could be explained by the situation of economic crisis which followed the introduction of the first TGV in 1981 during the course of which the rate of formation of new firms was much weaker than previously. The decision to relocate seems not to have resulted from the existence of the TGV, but once this decision had been taken, the presence of the TGV could influence the precise location chosen. This is a familiar result from many studies of both firm and household location.

The presence of a high speed line does not by itself lead to development, as for example shown by the example of Le Creusot, an old industrial town, which was relying on the arrival of the TGV to support restructuring, but where it is difficult to discern any real impact.

In Lyon, following the arrival of the TGV more obvious effects could be identified, but in a fairly subtle way. The district of La Part Dieu, immediately surrounding the new TGV station experienced the strongest impacts. Land prices rose substantially and there has been considerable relocation of tertiary activities. Thus a new inter-regional link has had the most profound impacts on the intra-regional and indeed intra-urban distribution of activity.

The overall impact of the TGV has been in the increasing size of markets. Traffic surveys have shown the sensitivity of service sector activities and above all business services, which is explained by a dynamic response of the most dynamic Lyon based firms with respect to markets in the Paris region. The TGV had the effect of extending the market area of firms in Lyon to include the Paris markets. The reverse, however, does not seem to have been as pronounced and Paris-based enterprises have benefited less significantly from accessibility to markets in the Lyon region. A further effect has been the development of tourism associated with the TGV with coach firms reorganising their activities to serve the TGV stations and provide links to tourist destinations in the Burgundy region.

Table 2.1 Net employment change as a function of the time to access road infrastructure

	1975–1982				1982–1990			
	<20 mn	20–40 mn	>40 mn	Total	<20 mn	20–40 mn	>40 mn	Total
Urban areas	18663	3463	2933	25059	12207	−976	1212	12443
Rural areas	−101	1115	90	1104	−4540	−3252	−162	−7954
Total	18562	4578	3023	26163	7667	-4228	1050	4489

Source: Orus (1997)

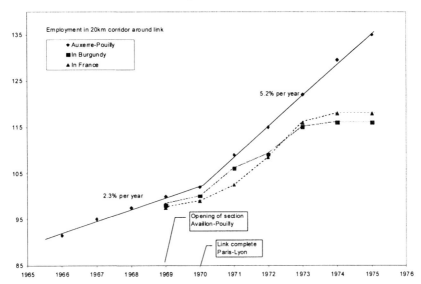

Figure 2.7 Evolution of socio-economic indicators along the Autoroute A6 in France

Turning to the impact of autoroutes in France, the responsible agency SETRA has created a series of statistical observatories in connection with the major new infrastructures. The economic changes which have followed their completion has thus been traced and evaluated. Certain changes are particularly significant, for example the impact on employment in a corridor of up to 20 km around the Autoroute A6 from Paris to Lyon and southern France (Figure 2.7).

In the most general sense, the quality of the road network is a factor in the maintenance or development of employment, as suggested in Table 2.1 which summarises evidence relating to the more favoured urban areas and the less favoured rural areas from highway development in France.

It is clear from these studies that road infrastructure has been a factor in economic development; but typically requires additional factors to be present if it is to be successful. Thus the impact has only been favourable if the potential to benefit from the autoroute existed initially.

This potential depends particularly on the following factors:

• the existence of tourist potential. The infrastructure does not of itself create tourism, but it allows its development;
• a developed tertiary sector, and an urban environment which is welcoming to enterprises, in general a tertiary sector which is well developed and interested in the possibilities provided by road transport;

- accompanying public policies, comprising particularly a policy which is welcoming to enterprises, policies towards land development and the development of general urban infrastructure and spatial planning;
- the availability of a well qualified workforce, and industrial structure which is sensitive to transport and a favourable demographic structure.

More recently Burmeister and Colletis-Wahl (1996) have analysed the consequences of the TGV Paris–Nord on tertiary activity in Lille and Valenciennes. The authors hypothesised that a high speed train will have a particular impact on the high quality service sector and on firms depending on network relationships (the reciprocal dependence of firms on access to resources controlled by others). The results of surveys undertaken on firms in the Nord region of France demonstrate limited impacts: a certain enlargement of market areas, from which Lille-based firms had benefited, but had also suffered; positive impacts for Lille locations, but also negative impacts for locations in Valenciennes where competitiveness and the possibilities to develop networks were reduced. The authors conclude by underlining the importance of accompanying programmes to accentuate the possible favourable impacts from the new infrastructure.

Brua (1993) studied the effects of improved accessibility in areas of low population density (mountain areas and scarcely populated rural areas). The conclusion was that economic development could not be produced solely by the development of high level infrastructure such as the TGV or autoroutes, but required a more complete and diversified network, not just over long distances but also, and above all, at regional and local levels, as well as actions external to transport.

Plassard (1990a) surveyed the experiences of the impacts of autoroutes on regional development. Recalling the points we have already identified (the absence of automatic effects, the need for local authorities to have an accompanying development strategy based on clear objectives) he underlined that the economic impact that infrastructure will produce depends on the strategies of economic agents. This will differ in cases where firms simply seek to profit from a transport policy for which they have not been responsible, without having to modify their production, and those where firms seek to establish a synergy between their production structure and the development of the infrastructure, eventually leading to an influence on that development. Battiau (1991) has stressed the effect of the concentration of large infrastructures which are associated with the concentration and internationalisation of flows, developing the idea of the reshaping of space through the accumulation of many infrastructures on the same axis, with the development of particular nodes (rail stations, autoroute interchanges) to the detriment of impacts on the regions which are crossed, in contrast to the impacts of ordinary road networks. Quinet (1988) suggested this was equivalent to a dualising of space between modern zones, geographically separate but linked by high speed means of transport, which reflected the same dynamism and where progress and change are diffused rapidly, and the remaining zones, separated and isolated, where growth is much less rapid.

2.2.2 British studies

Dodgson (1974) studied the impact of the M62 Motorway, which links the main old industrial areas either side of the Pennines in Northern England. Using a model with 66 zones, he related the rate of growth of employment to the costs of transport and other variables such as industrial structure and the natural rate of growth of the active population in each zone. From the regression analysis it was concluded that the coefficients were significant and had the expected sign (growth was stronger where transport costs were lower), but this factor alone did not explain a large share of the variance between zones.

Simon (1987) analysed the effects of the Humber Bridge using a survey of firms in the region. This suggested a wide range of possible adaptations and developments which could emanate from the new opportunities provided by this bridge across a wide estuary. However, these aspirations were not to be realised in practice, the overall impact was weak, albeit this was at a time of poor general economic conditions. This is another example which shows that although infrastructure may be a necessary condition for economic development, it is rarely sufficient.

Botham (1983) also used regression analysis to assess the variation in employment in the period 1960-65 across 30 regions of the UK as a function of both accessibility, transport quality and costs, and non transport variables such as regional policy, wage rates, etc. Accessibility was specified in different ways: accessibility to markets, accessibility to non-competing markets, accessibility to sources of supply. It appeared that accessibility to markets was the most significant variable and had played an important role in the development of employment.

2.2.3 Other studies

The effects of the Shinkansen high speed train in Japan have been examined in a before and after study by Nakamura and Ueda (1989). The results, shown in Table 2.2 are broadly comparable with those of the French studies and show the rate of growth of income per capita according to zone and whether it is served by the Shinkansen and/or the parallel motorway.

Table 2.2 Effect of Shinkansen: rate of growth of income per head (1981–
           85)

	Shinkansen and motorway	Motorway alone	Neither	All communes
Communes where population has grown	23.7	18.2	19.3	19.7
Communes where population decreased	10.9	11.6	4.4	5.5
All communes	15.7	14.7	5.7	8.2

Source: Nakamura and Ueda (1989)

A discriminant analysis of the data identifies the main conditions under which the Shinkansen led to population growth:

• tertiary sector activities based on the exchange of information hold an important place in the zone;
• the availability of higher education facilities;
• good accessibility of the Shinkansen station.

In contrast the following factors led to a negative impact on local development:

• a large share of manufacturing industry;
• a large share of older persons in the population;
• poor accessibility to the motorway.

Briggs (1982) studied the impact of the Interstate Highway system in the United States on the development of non-metropolitan zones. He concluded that counties with a highway, taken as a whole, had a rate of growth (of population and employment) between 1950 and 1975 which was above the mean. But access to the highway is far from sufficient to assure growth, in the same way that the absence of access does not guarantee decline. If tourism was the activity which seemed to be that most closely associated with the Interstate system, manufacturing industry and trade as a whole did not seem to be so clearly associated. Moreover, the system improved the overall accessibility for all regions and does not seem to have only benefited countries situated close to the network.

Mills and Carlino (1989) examined the growth of population and employment of US counties through the 1970s. Their general analysis identified a large number of factors, such as the initial level of population and employment, taxes, household incomes, crime rate, etc., and included the density of the Interstate Highway network in each county. The latter variable emerged as a very significant determinant of the rate of growth and the authors concluded: 'the Interstate Highway system has had a significant effect on the location of both population and employment'.

Miller *et al.* (1985) examined the effect of public transport on the development of urban areas in the US, drawing from experience with the Bart (the rapid transit system in the San Francisco area), the Dade County Metrorail and the Metromover. These infrastructures had had marked impacts on the polarised development of office construction, and, to a lesser degree, on residential construction. Metrorail and Metromover had been linked with a coordinated policy of urban development in their respective regions which the authors cited as being necessary in order to obtain the maximum impact from the new infrastructure.

Jensen-Butler and Madsen (1996) have developed a modern version of the Amano-Fujita type of model to study the impact of the Great Belt Bridge in Denmark. This showed the extent to which Copenhagen, as the major metropolitan area tends to benefit in relative terms at the expense of the more peripheral regions, even though some of these show substantial rates of growth. Further studies have been carried out on the Oresund link between Denmark and Sweden to examine the relative impacts on Copenhagen and Malmo at each end of the link.

In summary, the effects on location are difficult to quantify precisely, but are nevertheless important. The major impacts tend to be felt within a geographically limited area, probably of the order of 10 to 20 km from a major highway, more limited around a rail station. Regional macroeconomic models allow a tentative valuation of these effects, but the results must be treated with extreme caution since, like all models, they are highly dependent on the initial assumptions.

2.2.4 New approaches

A number of recent attempts have been made to introduce some of the ideas of the 'new economic geography' discussed in section 1.2 of this chapter. These use spatial computable equilibrium models to get round the difficulty of estimating the complex interactions between firms' and households' behaviour in a world of differentiated products (see Bröcker, 2003) for a valuable introduction to these models. The advantage of such approaches is that they provide a direct estimate of the change in welfare resulting from the investment, as measured by the assumed utility function, rather than the usual narrower measure of GDP or employment change. The precise impacts on the overall welfare change and its distribution is parameter dependent and therefore differs from case to case (Venables and Gasiorek, 1999).

Bröcker (1998, 2000) has used this model to estimate the impacts of the development of the EU's Trans-European Networks and their extension to include the new member states joining the EU in 2004. This shows modest net gains in welfare (up to 3 per cent) resulting from the improvements to the network, with these gains concentrated around the new corridors and major nodes. Thus a more sophisticated model provides similar qualitative results to those from the simpler tracking of changes from the French autoroute example.

In a more geographically focused application, Oosterhaven and Knaap (2003) have applied a similar model to a regional structure of the Netherlands to investigate the impacts of possible high-speed 'maglev' lines (using magnetic levitation propulsion methods) around the Randstad and between Amsterdam and the North Netherlands. This suggests substantial relocation and employment growth could occur, especially in those regions which benefit from a major change in both accessibility and level of service.

3. CONCLUSIONS

The empirical studies shed further light on theoretical analyses in suggesting that transport constitutes an important factor, but one which is far from the sole determinant, in the location of activities. It would appear to be the case that the existence of transport is a necessary, but not sufficient, factor in location decisions. But this has to be made more precise. If transport does lead to an increase in the level of economic activity in certain zones, there may also be zones where this level is reduced. There is therefore a redistribution element involved in improving accessibility. However, it can also be seen that due to an increase in the overall level of provision (reduction in aggregate transport costs) in the economy as a whole the positive effects will be expected to outweigh the negative. This should of course be expected where any evaluation of the project produces a positive rate of return since the value of the project to users should reflect the value of the activities which will use it (see Dodgson, 1973; Jara-Diaz, 1986; SACTRA, 1999).

This discrimination imposed by transport, creating advantaged and disadvantaged zones, implies polarisation, the reinforcement of stronger zones. But this polarisation is selective. It works through moderating the effects of distance over certain ranges, and to differentiate zones which are already very unequal; high speed rail for example has not reduced the influence of major regional centres, mainly because they are sufficiently far apart from each other. On the other hand both high speed rail and motorway developments have developed regional metropoles at the expense of their surrounding regions. It seems that horizontal polarisation over short distances has been much stronger than vertical polarisation over longer distances. It also operates differentially according to individual sectors of economic activity. Tertiary activities appear to have been much more sensitive than traditional secondary industrial sectors.

The effects of location are also different between different modes of transport. Railways, and more specifically high speed railways, appear to have had more limited spatial effects; concentrated around stations and limited largely to tertiary sector activities which generate a lot of business trips. The effects of major highways are more extensive, not only because such highways have a larger number of access points, but also because road transport is the dominant mode of transport. These effects thus impact on a much wider range of activities, although they appear to have a less profound direct effect on the organisation of firms, the degree of decentralisation between establishments and the structure of contacts with both customers and suppliers.

Taken together these results constitute a substantial body of evidence. They provide a certain justification for the frequent claims made by local politicians in favour of the beneficial effects of transport improvements. However, they also suggest that these effects are not guaranteed, and typically involve some redistribution between different zones – it is this which leads to the view that the structural effects of transport can be considered as a political myth (Offner 1993).

Because of these complications it is clear that trying to take the effects on location into account as part of the process of decision making in transport is a difficult task in terms both of knowing what these effects are and of incorporating them effectively into a decision making procedure.

3. Transport and the Urban Economy

Urban transport is of direct concern to most individuals. In most European countries more than three-quarters of the population lives in towns and cities and that is where they undertake most of their journeys. This gives rise to a number of different problems: environmental issues; the management of public transport, its costs and the quality of service; and the relationship between transport and the development of the urban space and its economy. We shall deal with the first two of these issues in more detail in subsequent chapters. It is the final aspect which forms the subject of this chapter: how transport affects the process of urban development and its relationship with urban structure. Interestingly this is not so much the issue which preoccupies politicians and public opinion, but it is from this which the other problems have their origin.

In order to understand this relationship it is necessary to start with the economic characteristics of the city, noting that these do not always conform to the usual assumptions of the neoclassical competitive equilibrium; this forms the subject of the first section. The second section is devoted to the place of transport in this development, particularly the duality between transport and land use. The third section considers several issues relating to problem of urban transport policy, in particular the role of transport in the processes of urban change and urban planning.

1. TRANSPORT AND URBANISATION

If the economy behaved strictly according to the assumptions of the neoclassical competitive equilibrium model, there would be no reason for individuals and activities to agglomerate. In the presence of constant returns to scale, and in the absence of public goods and externalities, the best organisation would be a uniform spatial distribution of all activities; this would minimise the costs of transport and hence total costs. The existence of cities proves that this assumption cannot hold. Following Fujita (1989), Fujita and Thisse (1996, 2002), Duranton (1998), Duranton and Puga (2000) and Fujita *et al.* (1999) it can be seen that the forces which lead to the agglomeration of individuals and firms, and thus to the creation of cities, depend to a great extent on the quality of transport.

1.1 Location of Natural Resources, Indivisibilities

Why cities develop where they do can be determined by many different factors: the existence of concentrations of natural resources (around which industries which use the resource have congregated); or particular geographical features, such as crossing points of rivers or mountain ranges, which are, in economic terms, examples of indivisibilities and scale economies in transport: a port, a bridge, a relay post. Once begun, however, for one or other of these reasons, a city develops because of cumulative forces of agglomeration which give an advantage to those activities located within the city. These cumulative forces relate both to factors affecting market size, but particularly to various forms of externality.

1.2 Externalities

In a very fundamental way the city is a concentration of externalities. In order to analyse this fully we need first to understand the distinction between technological and pecuniary externalities (Box 3.1)

BOX 3.1

Technological externalities and pecuniary externalities

Technological externalities lie outside the price mechanism; they arise when one agent or firm directly affects the utility of another agent or the profits of another firm by its actions; for example, by depositing waste material in a river a firm reduces the quality of fish in the river and reduces the utility of fishermen, or raises the costs of production of another firm by making it purify the water which it needs to use.

Pecuniary externalities correspond to the idea that one agent benefits (or suffers) from the action of another without paying the cost (or being compensated), but where that cost or benefit is reflected in the price. For example, the hairdresser in a large urban area may see his or her wages increase, not because productivity has increased, but because other wages have increased; or the rent for a given property may rise and benefit its owner, not because of any improvement to the property, but due to the provision of public services in the area.

Both types of externality are present in agglomerations. Technological externalities include the effects on the environment and congestion of which transport is a major source. Pecuniary externalities include the impact on rents, particularly land rents though the mechanisms we shall discuss in section 2.

Externalities of communication or agglomeration are technological; they arise because the productivity of firms is augmented by the existence of other enterprises in the neighbourhood, allowing communication and the exchange of information, analogous to the mechanism discussed in chapter 1 (section 3.3). The totality of firms in the same location gives rise to the possibility of exchange between these firms and the productivity of each rises. The theoretical models presented by Fujita and Thisse (1996, 2002) assume that the productivity of each firm depends on its accessibility to all other firms. This accessibility can be measured for example by the expression:

$$A(x) = \int a(x, y) f(y) dy$$

where:

    $A(x)$ is the accessibility at point x
    $f(y)$ is the density of firms at point y
    $a(x,y)$ is the distance (or the time, or the transport cost) between the points
        x and y.

From this it can be shown that several equilibria are possible giving rise to one or more urban centres according to the values of the key parameters, most particularly the cost of transport.

The development of communication between the departments of a given firm, a development allowed by modern telecommunications, can therefore have a centrifugal effect; firms maintain in a given agglomeration the activities which benefit from the effects of that agglomeration and locate those services which cannot benefit from the proximity to other firms in locations where the cost of land is lower.

Externalities of communication apply equally to consumers and impact on their evaluation of social contacts.

1.3 Economies of Scale

The development of cities can also be explained through the existence of economies of scale which lead to the concentration of the production of a given good in one location. A particular case of scale economies is the existence of indivisibilities associated for example with public infrastructure: schools, universities, specialised hospitals, etc. In their presence the means of organisation of these activities can allow the reduction of the negative effects of geographical dispersion. One form of scale economy generic to the agglomeration of activities is the source of the endogenous growth identified in chapter 1, and can equally mask the agglomeration externalities described in section 1.2 above. Thus the production function for each firm j (supposing that all firms have identical technologies to simplify the expression), related to its labour force N_j, is of the form:

$$f(N_j) = N_j \, g(N)$$

where:

N is the active population of the city,

$g(N)$ is an increasing function of N

Assume that, at the level of each firm, there are constant returns to scale; but the productivity of each firm depends on a factor outside its control, an agglomeration externality depending on the size of the agglomeration. Thus the production function at the level of the city, F, is of the form:

$$F(N) = N \, g(N)$$

This formulation reconciles the possibility of constant returns to scale at the level of the firm and increasing returns at the level of the agglomeration, and explains how, in a perfectly competitive market for each firm, the tendency towards the concentration of activities results in the positive externalities which each new firm contributes to those firms already in the market.

There is considerable evidence for the existence of these productivity effects within cities. Ciccone (2002) has shown how productivity across a set of EU countries is related to employment density. The elasticity of around 4.5 per cent is very close to that found for the US by Ciccone and Hall (1996). Henderson (2003) has concentrated on the within–industry linkages and shows that these differ considerably between sectors with much stronger effects on the high technology sectors than in traditional manufacturing suggesting that, despite the apparent footloose nature of such modern industries which would be suggested by traditional location models on the basis of their lower levels of transport costs, clustering effects are even stronger.

1.4 Preference for Diversity

Cities allow the satisfaction of preferences for diversity by both firms and consumers (Box 3.2).

BOX 3.2

The taste for diversity

Consumers preference for diversity can be expressed and illustrated imply in the following way, where the consumer devotes a given budget to one type of expenditure, drinks for example. If there are two types of drink the consumer can attain the utility u_1; if there is only one the level achieved will be u_0.

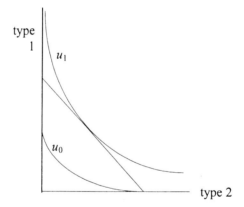

The preference for diversity results in the concave nature of the utility function. If the function was convex the consumer would consume only one good. Thus the preference for diversity can be expressed in terms of a utility function of the form:

$$U = (\sum_{i=1}^{i=n} x^\rho)^{\frac{1}{\rho}}$$

The individual is subject to a budget constraint:

$$\sum_i p_i x_i = r$$

If the concavity of U is positive, which happens when $\rho < 1$ (as in the diagram), the maximum utility that the individual can attain increases with the number of goods. If $\rho > 1$ the positive effect of diversity will provide that, contrary to the assumption of the model, chosen quantities will dramatically differ between individuals. The addition of a new good to those already offered would give nothing to person 1 but would be appreciated by individual 2 who would switch consumption towards the new good and benefit from an increase in utility.

If $\rho=1$ preference is zero; it becomes stronger as $\rho \to 0$.

At the level of the firm, the preference for diversity of new entrants can be expressed in terms of the following production function:

$$F = N^* \left(\sum_{i=1}^{n} y_i^\rho \right)^{\frac{1-\alpha}{\rho}}$$

In this expression, α and ρ are parameters, N is the labour force of the firms, and y_i are the different services which the firms uses in production. The preference for diversity is measured by the inverse of the parameter ρ. If $\rho<1$, then it is better for a given total of entrants that this quantity would be divided among a number of differentiated goods rather than concentrated in one.

The advantages of diversity are simple to understand in terms of the consumer and the range of goods available. For firms the diversity of factors of production allows a better adaptation to the needs of the firm's activities; one can think of the diversity in the types of service required by the firm, for example the range of legal services required which may not be found in a single person or specialist firm. Given that each of these activities may benefit from scale economies their profitability depends on there being a sufficiently large range of clients.

An improvement in transport, allowing the enlargement of supply areas for consumers and firms, increases access to greater diversity and thus utility or profit.

1. 5 A Cumulative Process of Agglomeration

The combination of external economies of agglomeration, economies of scale in certain sectors of the economy, and a preference for diversity, lead to a cumulative process of agglomeration described and modelled in particular by Fujita and Thisse (1996, 2002) (see also Fujita *et al.*, 1999). This model considers an economy which comprises:

- Industrial firms facing constant returns to scale in which productivity grows with the diversity of services to which they can gain access; thus the firm production function is of the form:

$$F = N^a \left(\sum_{i=1}^{n} y_i^\rho \right)^{\frac{1-a}{\rho}}$$

N is the labour force of the firm

y_i represents the services on which they can call

- Services facing increasing returns due to the existence of fixed costs. These services fix their price on the basis of a mark-up over marginal costs which is inversely proportional to the elasticity of demand (following the Cournot assumption of oligopoly).
- Consumers who have a utility function which is increasing with the diversity of goods consumed:

$$U = \sum_{i=1}^{n} x_i^\rho$$

The model shows that an increase in the size of the agglomeration leads to an increase in the productivity and the number of services and hence to the productivity and number of industrial firms. This leads to increased diversification which results in a reduction of the prices of goods and an increase in the utility of consumers. This leads in turn to an increased attractiveness of the location to population and hence an increase in the demand for labour and better conditions in the labour market. A larger labour market allows an increase in the diversity of jobs available as well as a wider range of people and skills to fill those jobs. Wages and productivity will increase, maintaining the increase in real wages and these two factors will generate the continuing growth in the size of the agglomeration.

These effects can be obtained as a result of a reduction in the cost of transport which would allow firms access to a wider range of services, which would increase their numbers of customers as well as inducing an increasing number of suppliers. Thus market areas would increase in size and firms would find suppliers and labour in greater numbers, of a greater diversity and better adapted to specific needs as well as a more diversified market of consumers for final goods.

The eventual increase in the cost of transport and congestion among those services provided at fixed costs are the constraints on the cumulative process of growth. The limits to this process can occur at a number of different equilibrium points depending on the precise values of the relevant parameters of the model: concentration into a single large city or the emergence of several centres. This is equivalent to the result noted above (section 1.3) for the case of the individual city with increasing returns.

Whilst it is clear that a model of the individual growing city can be developed which depends on the existence of scale economies and externalities, two key questions remain: are there limits to the growth of the individual city and how does the growth and optimal size of one city relate to the urban structure of the wider economy or a region or country? The answers to both of these questions implicate transport.

The simplest answer to the question as to what sets the limit on city growth is that similar factors to those which cause cities to grow can cause them to stop growing: principally that external economies can become diseconomies. Hence, whilst efficient transport is a major feature in city growth, congestion caused by that growth increases the costs to both firms and households of being in the city. As real wages begin to fall, the attraction of moving to the city is reduced for mobile labour and the profitability of alternative locations is increased. It is not just congestion which is the key feature of the overdeveloped city. A whole set of other external diseconomies can be identified such as increasing crime, increasing pollution, problems of urban physical decay and the increasing inability of city administrations to manage the city when faced with increasing costs and falling tax bases (Glaeser, 1998).

Why does this process not produce a self balancing outcome as would be implied by traditional equilibrium theories? And why, if similar conditions are available to most cities in an economy, does it not produce a set of optimal cities all the same size? Models of the optimal size of a city show quite simply that there are processes at work which prevent self-balance (Dixit, 1973). We have already seen the way in which the growing city may increase the productivity of firms faster than the expected diminishing returns would reduce it, hence real incomes continue to rise faster than nominal wage rates. But there is a further factor which causes cities to continue to grow, the asymmetry of information between those already located in the city and those outside. As diseconomies set in the marginal social cost of living in the city is rising faster than the average cost and it is the latter which is relevant to the marginal migrant. The city will continue to grow beyond the point which is optimal for the current population.

Turning this into a model of urban structure, or an optimal system of cities, is much more difficult. Mirrlees (1972) attempted to do this within the structure of optimal tax theory models, but the difficulty of obtaining analytical solutions to such complex structures led to something of a hiatus in the development of optimum geography until the development of the computable models of the 'new economic geography'. Krugman (1993a, 1993b) showed the way in which quite small differences in parameters could produce a substantially different pattern of cities and relative sizes. The development of such approaches has, however, had to depend on the use of rather simple stylistic geographies, such as where the number, and relative sizes, of a set of cities strung out around a circular 'racetrack' is shown to be fundamentally unstable (Fujita *et al.*, 1999). Hence accident matters, and history matters, in determining how and where cities start to grow, and their future growth depends on what has happened in the past. One of the critical parameters in the solution is the level (and rate of change) of transport costs, but lower transport costs can lead to either concentration or deconcentration according to the initial level and the importance of market size and scale economies in the cities' activities.

1.6 The Effects of Segregation

If there are many forces leading towards agglomeration, there are also many which push towards the segregation of populations within urban zones

First, the positive externalities of agglomeration, which result in the clustering of firms, often operate preferentially towards firms of the same type which need the same type of labour, the same suppliers, etc. This results in high concentrations of similar firms in particular locations. Some of these are of international significance in the high technology sectors such as Silicon Valley in California, but all countries have similar clusters and there has been a particular interest recently in the clustering of the so-called knowledge economy of universities, research establishments and embryonic firms of which perhaps the best known is the Cambridge region in the UK, but similar examples can be found in the southern suburbs of the Paris region or near Schiphol Airport, Amsterdam.

This latter form of segregation is similar to that which is also found in social groups where some groups cluster together and others have a strong repulsion to proximity. Factors which give rise to these responses include education, age, income, occupation, but above all in many urban areas differences of race or religion. These segregation effects emerge in critical economic variables such as differential land prices, housing rents, etc. Periods of change in the characteristics of a given area, where for example households with different characteristics start to move in, can lead to external effects which are greater than the initial change in values would suggest – hence a process either of increasing values (gentrification) or of falling values (ghettoisation) relative to surrounding areas. This has a further impact on incentives for households to move into or out of the area and thus a continuing impact on land rents, the quality of the housing stock due to maintenance and new investment and the quality of public services, given the rising or falling tax base of an area.

In the following section we look in more detail at models of the relationship between land rents and the cost of transport in urban areas.

2. TRANSPORT, LAND RENTS AND LOCATION

2.1 Land Rents and Transport Costs

Any analysis of the role of transport in the urban economy needs to include an analysis of land rents. Here we present an overview of the basic model, then draw from this several rules concerning the effect of transport on urban structure and finally examine the way in which the empirical evidence corresponds to these expectations. The theoretical development is based on a schematic case in which, following the effects of the process of agglomeration, activities exist within a unique constrained area which is assumed to be represented by a point (the Central Business District), and the remainder of the city is occupied by residential housing.

The city is assumed to have been established on land for which the alternative use is agricultural, the price of which (over unit time and area) is R_A. Residents located at a distance x from the centre pay a cost of transport $T(x)$ per unit of time, occupy a residential space of area $S(x)$ for which they pay $R(x)$ per unit of time and area to a landowner who rents properties in a competitive market. Thus,

$$R(x) \geq R_A$$

because otherwise landowners would prefer to rent the land to an agricultural user. It is assumed that the city has a given number of inhabitants N. Each inhabitant consumes a quantity Z of a composite good (an aggregate of all the other goods available) and has a convex utility function $U(Z, S)$ which is assumed to be the same for all inhabitants. The problem is then to determine the relationships between $T(x)$, $R(x)$, and $S(x)$.

It is assumed first that the area of the residence of each inhabitant is fixed:

$$S = S_0$$

Hence the density is constant and equal to S_0 and the city extends to a distance x_M from the centre such that:

$$\int_0^{x_M} \frac{2\pi}{S_0} x\,dx = N$$

and the utility of each individual depends just on Z, the choice between different locations, reduced by an interaction between the cost of transport

$T(x)$ and the cost of housing $SR(x)$. Each individual seeks to minimise the sum of these two, thus for each location chosen we must have:

$$T'(x) + S_0 R'(x) = 0$$

Alternatively, it can be assumed that, for each location, rent is fixed through a bidding process; the result is a Nash equilibrium such that $T(x)+SR(x)$ is the same at each location (i.e. for each value of x).

From this we can derive:

$$R'(x) = -\frac{T'(x)}{S_0} \qquad (3\text{-}1)$$

and hence:

$$R(x) = -\frac{1}{S_0} T(x) + \text{Constant}$$

The constant determines that at the boundary x_M, the rent is R_A:

$$\text{Constant} = R_A + \frac{T(x_M)}{S_0}$$

From which the value of the land rent at any location x:

$$R(x) = -\frac{T(x)}{S_0} + R_A + \frac{T(x_M)}{S_0}$$

Note that in this situation individuals will be indifferent with respect to their location; all possible locations face the same total costs, only the division between transport costs and rent costs will differ between individuals.

At each point the land rent actually paid results from the maximum bid-rent which any user is prepared to pay; the bid-rent is the highest amount the owner can receive and which potential users are prepared to pay taking account of the alternatives offered at all other locations in the urban space. Because of the existence of positive transport costs these bid-rents and hence the equilibrium land rent will fall as locations move outwards from the centre. At the edge of the city this is equal to the agricultural land rent R_A.

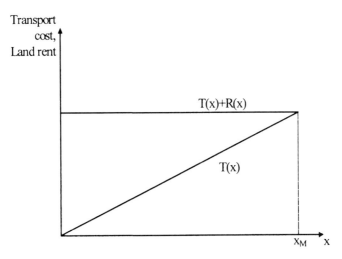

Figure 3.1 Land rents and the cost of transport

It can easily be seen that, if

$$T(x) = ax^a \frac{1}{2}$$

then

$$RDT = \frac{\alpha}{\alpha + 1} CTT \qquad (3-2)$$

where:
RDT represents the total rent differential:

$$RDT = 2\pi \int_0^{x_M} (R(t) - R_A)t \frac{dt}{S_0}$$

CTT represents the total cost of transport:

$$CTT = 2\pi \int_0^{x_M} \frac{t}{S_0} T(t)dt$$

In particular, if the cost of transport $T(x)$ is proportional to distance ($\alpha = 1$), then:

$$RDT = \frac{1}{2}CTT$$

This shows very clearly in a simple model the links between the cost of transport and land rents. We can also use this simple model to deduce the consequences of a reduction in the cost of transport. Land rents will fall similarly at each location since the transport cost line in Figure 3.1 becomes less steep, but the disposable income available to residents for non locational (housing plus transport) use will rise as will residents' utility. There are further consequences from this; the increasing real wages in the city will encourage in-migration and the city grows. The increase in income will lead to an increase in demand for goods produced in the city, thus the profitability of enterprises rises and they need more space to produce, this leads to a rise in land rents at the centre, and if the CBD needs to increase in size this will spill over into the residential market. Richer households may also seek to increase the space they wish to use. Hence there may be a self-correcting mechanism in the city where some of the consequences of reduced transport costs are an increase in the overall level of rents appropriate to the city. This in part also explains why we might expect land rents to be higher in larger cities than in smaller cities.

The model can be developed to allow the space of residential units to vary and become part of the decision making of each resident, and for there to be different groups of resident determined by income levels and differences in their utility functions. However, the basic results remain unchanged, in particular the key relationship, equation 3-1, except that there will be an increase in the size of plot with distance from the centre;

$$R'(x) = -\left(\frac{T'(x)}{S(x)}\right)$$

The results concerning the links between the cost of transport and land use are also confirmed. If the cost of transport falls:

- The city grows in size.
- Rents will fall in the centre and rise in the periphery.
- Utility increases.
- The size of housing unit increases.

Similar results also emerge from an increase in wage rates in the city. This is a little more complicated since wages are measured in money terms and transport costs in terms of time. An increase in wages leads to an increase in incomes and an increase in the cost of transport. The size of residential unit changes under the influence of these two contradictory factors; they will increase under the influence of rising incomes but they may be reduced as opportunity cost of leisure time rises. The result depends on the relative importance of the two parameters.

2.2 Public Amenities and Local Transport

In the models developed so far transport infrastructure only has one use, the role of allowing individuals to travel from their residence to their workplace which is assumed to be in the Central Business District (CBD). In reality the situation is much more complex; alongside the key radial routes used for commuting, there is a considerable local infrastructure which has the character of a public good and enables the social interaction between households which forms the basis of much leisure activity. If, following Fujita (1989), we define the general level of this local transport infrastructure as K and $E(K)$ the utility of each individual (assumed identical) with respect to this infrastructure which, alongside Z and S, forms one of the arguments of the individual's overall utility, we can write:

$$U = U(Z, S, E(K))$$

We can then study the behaviour of an agent who aims to maximise the expected profit from economic activity in the city and compare this with the social optimum. This analysis is developed in the context of an open city in which the agent is the owner of land. We can envisage this agent as a financier who buys agricultural land at price R_A, pays for the public infrastructure K, provides work for the N inhabitants for which he receives their product YN generating a level of utility U. The problem is thus:

- to minimise cost:

$$C(U, N, K) = \underset{X_u, s(r)}{Min} \int_0^{X_u} (T(x) + Z(S, U, E(K)) + R_A s(x)) dx$$

$$\text{with} \quad \int_0^{r_u} \frac{2\pi x}{s(x)} dx = N$$

- and to maximise profit:

$$Max_{N,K} \Pi = Max_{N,K} YN - C(U, N, K) - K$$

It can be shown that this problem of financial planning gives the same solution as a decentralised market situation in which the planner would buy the optimal amount of land, establish the public infrastructure at the optimal level K^* and allocate the land according to competitive tender. The population is given at the optimal level N^*, and the developer receives the rent $RDT(N^*)$. Competition between cities would lead to this profit being eliminated and thus in equilibrium:

$$Y(N^*) - C(U, N^*, K^*) = RDT(N^*) = K^*$$

Thus the developers finance the cost of the public good through the land rents obtained through competition between inhabitants in the land market, or by a tax on the price of land fixed at the right level by the developer. This result, which can be found in a number of models, is known as the Henry George Theorem after the late nineteenth century economist who first enunciated it (Arnott and Stiglitz, 1979). What it shows is that the level of public goods which attracts people to a city increases the level of land rents or the price of land in that city by enough to pay for the provision of the level of public goods.

The equilibrium thus obtained corresponds to a situation of competition between cities to attract economic activity; all the cities will offer the same level of utility in equilibrium and will have the same population. It is also an optimum in the sense that the cost of obtaining the given level of utility is minimised. Through subsidising – or taxing – in the manner used by the developers, it is possible to obtain a pre-determined level of utility.

It has been assumed up to now that the advantages conferred by the public good, such as local infrastructure are independent of the level of use. If that were not the case, for example in the presence of congestion, it would be necessary to adjust the tax as a function of the cost of congestion which the inhabitants cause. This would determine the general principle of congestion charging which will be examined in detail in Chapter 7.

The model above can be applied in the case where the parameter K represents not just transport services but any kind of public infrastructure, or even where the infrastructure does not extend over the whole city, but just in one zone. In the latter case the equality found between the cost of K and the rent differential will be restricted just to that zone.

3. EVIDENCE ON THE ADEQUACY OF THE MODELS IN PRACTICE

How do these models accord with the real world? It is not necessary to undertake detailed statistical analyses to verify whether the form of cities accords with the theory, or whether land values decrease regularly when moving from the centre to the edge of a city.

The inadequacy of the theoretical model can be explained by a number of reasons. First, land is not typically the flat featureless uniform plain of the theory. Natural obstacles occur, areas where construction is not possible because of relief, rivers, etc. It is also unrealistic to suppose that the centre can be reduced to a single point where all economic activity is concentrated. There are many activities, local services, convenience shops, etc. which it is obvious will need to be distributed throughout the city. Generally therefore the monocentric urban model is not a theory of the location of activities.

The model in the form presented above also excludes consideration of many of the local public goods (parks, school, libraries, etc.) which are an important part of the typical urban fabric and which modify the relative attractiveness of specific locations and hence the structure of land prices and rents. The model is also an equilibrium model, it assumes that any shocks caused by exogenous factors have had the time to work through and adjustments have taken place. This is unlikely to take place in reality. Moreover, it is possible that there are several equilibria, some of which may not be stable. In such a situation we have different possible courses of action. First we could construct much more complex models which take into account some or all of these considerations such as the non-uniformity of space, dynamic adjustments through time, mechanisms determining the location of local productive activities. We shall look further at such models in the context of demand in Chapter 4, although it has to be recognised that such models are very demanding in terms of data to calibrate in practice.

The second approach is to retain the fundamental qualitative conclusion of the monocentric model, the link between transport costs and land rents, and to examine if this can be verified in principle. Thus we can observe the way in which land values and land use within a city change in response to changes in the transport system and the positive relation between land values at particular locations and the accessibility of that location. Thus the statistical results from limited applications can be used to verify the general conclusions of the overall model.

A number of studies have used this approach. Mills (1993) and Gravel *et al.* (1996) used hedonic price methods (of which more in Chapter 5) to analyse factors determining land prices. Mills studied the price of offices in Chicago as a function of the existence of a range of services in the neighbourhood and the accessibility of the location. Accessibility was clearly a factor, but was only one of the factors which determined prices. Gravel *et al.* studied the factors influencing the determination of average rents in different urban areas in one French département, Val d'Oise. Again it emerged that accessibility and the level of transport service was only one element in determining rents, together with factors such as the level of crime or the relative level of educational achievement.

Huang (1997) examined the link between density and accessibility in a sample of zones in Washington DC. A very significant relation was identified both for the density of housing and the density of employment, but with relatively weak correlation suggesting again that this was only one of many factors. Similar results were found in a study in Nevada by Song (1996).

Other studies have looked at the effect of changes in the transport system on land prices and land use, either through before and after studies on a set of zones or through a comparison between different zones in the same agglomeration. The results of these have tended to be rather mixed with strong effects close to new infrastructure or access points to a network but no consistent pattern throughout the network.

Generally the more subjective studies suggest that certain simple rules can be used to determine the pattern of land prices and uses; the development of new highway, location close to a highway interchange and the general character of a neighbourhood are the principal influences and dominate complex accessibility indicators.

In sum, experimental verification of the major lessons from the core model of the link between land values and costs of transport, suggests results which are much less strong than the model claims. This is, first, because the observed value of land depends on a number of factors of which transport is only one; these are typically assumed constant in the theoretical model.

The second reason is due to the absence of the competitive market which the theoretical model assumes. Public powers intervene, both to regulate and also as an economic actor to develop and provide certain urban activities directly. These all lead to distortions in the expectations of the theoretical model and hence we need to examine various relevant issues arising from urban transport policy.

4. TRANSPORT POLICY AND URBAN POLICY

Transport is an important factor in urban development apart from its influence on land values. This fact has numerous consequences in terms of urban policy, some of which we examine in more detail below.

4.1 Urban Planning

The first of these concerns the approach to urban planning. This is often conceived as a sequential process which depends on the ultimate urban form desired, as represented for example in an urban plan. From the plan the relevant flows of transport and locations of activities can be deduced and the appropriate infrastructures to accommodate the flows determined and prioritised according to the implicit rate of return. The preceding analysis shows that this procedure is not sufficient; each new infrastructure has an impact on land prices and on locations which leads to repercussion on the urban structure which may take it away from the planned structure.

It is of course possible to impose the land use plan through policy rules. But it is also clear that if this policy is too constraining in the sense that it attempts to impose an urban structure very different from the structure towards which the underlying market forces are leading it will lead to problems. The progress of urban planning must therefore be iterative and take account of the bi-directional causality between transport and urban structure, and not just the single direction from urban structure to transport.

4.2 Urbanisation and Suburbanisation

The sizes and structures of cities have gone through many transformations in different countries and different periods of time (Gannon, 1996; Wiel, 1997; Duranton, 1998). The phenomenon which has been observed in many cities in developed economies in recent decades has been a relatively stable metropolitan population combined with continuing depopulation of rural area, but a growth of communities on the fringe of the metropolitan region. At the same time residential densities have become more uniform and employment has decentralised from the urban core to the periphery.

This movement has been dominated by the dynamics of housing markets, with an increasing desire for independent housing by larger numbers of independent households within a stable population and the availability of new housing land on the urban fringe. This process has been associated with an increase in traffic and an increase in typical journey lengths (Gannon, 1996, Vickerman, 2002b). The associated increase in infrastructure provision itself provides an incentive for these trends to continue. This process of change has numerous consequences for society way beyond the strict economic consequences. For our purposes the key factor is the impact which the relatively low cost of urban transport relative to other prices in the economy has contributed to this decentralisation of the urban structure, a factor to which we return in Chapter 7.

4.3 Problems of Distribution

Efficiency is a primary concern of economic analysis, but in transport, both urban and interurban, there are important distributional issues which must not be ignored. These can be substantial: a new highway causes large and persistent nuisances and the choice of route has to consider the neighbouring areas affected. Furthermore, because the choice and priorities concerning urban policy (the development of employment, remedial policies to zones needing regeneration) affect the economy, it is important that policy makers define the complete set of values and social objectives which define the overall objective of policy. The economic analysis can then help the decision makers to evaluate the consequences of their choice including the consequences for distribution. This is seen in the way in which changing urban structure leads to the decline of certain areas through the concentration of the old or the poor in areas such as those towards the centre of a city with poor urban infrastructure whilst other zones face increasing pressures of growth.

Another example of the effects of redistribution can be seen in the consequences of the creation of new urban infrastructure. First, new commercial centres grow up around interchanges leading to further decline in traditional commercial centres in the urban core. The extension of these commercial pressures along the corridors around these interchanges imposes environmental pressures which degrade these zones as residential zones.

4.4 Fiscal Federalism

Taxes are raised at different spatial levels, local, regional and national. The exact division of powers differs considerably between different tax systems in different countries but many of the same principles arise of the relative power of each level to impose taxes and to compensate different levels for any fiscal inability to cove the cost of providing local services. These differences can affect the ability of the responsible authorities to provide the necessary level of transport services to support the urban structure (Henderson, 1988, Wiel, 1997).

The rivalry between communities to attract firms leads them to switch designated land uses from residential to commercial, or to reduce tax rates on firms moving into designated development areas with an overall impact on the authority's budget for the provision of general urban infrastructure.

PART II

Demand and Costs

4. The Demand for Transport

Transport demand and its causes can be analysed at an aggregate level, for instance at the level of a country; this aspect has been presented in Chapter 1. It can also be analysed at a spatial level, the level of a geographical network; in that case its goal is to estimate the traffic level mode by mode on each of the links of the network, according to the characteristics of transport supply, i.e. quality of service and prices on these links. The present chapter is devoted to this latter aspect.

The analysis of demand is based on the theory of consumer behaviour, which will be reviewed in the first section. The adaptation of this theory to transport problems is then presented, first for the case of passenger traffic, using alternative approaches; the following section is devoted to the forecasting of freight flows, which has been given less attention in the past. A final section draws conclusions on the limits of the methods, and on the implications for transport policy.

1. THE THEORETICAL BASIS

1.1   Consumer Behaviour

The basis of traffic modelling is the theory of consumer behaviour, in which the main hypothesis is that each consumer is assumed to have a utility function, which is an increasing function of the quantity of each good consumed. This function is concave. The behaviour of the consumer can be symbolised by the following constrained maximisation:

$$Max\ U(x_1, x_2,\ x_n)$$

with:

$$\Sigma p_i x_i \leq r$$

so that the consumer is assumed to try to maximise his or her utility under the constraint that expenditure cannot exceed income. The solution of this problem leads to the demand functions of the goods, which are especially simple when U is a quasi-linear function, for instance in the case of three goods:

$$U = x_0 + u(x_1, x_2)$$

Usually x_0 is a composite of all the existing goods, except the ones on which the attention is concentrated, and its price is normalized to one. It can then be shown that the demand functions for x_1 and x_2 do not depend on income. The maximal value of U, which is a function of parameters p_i and r, and which is named the indirect utility function, has a simple expression:

$$V(p_1, p_2, r) = r + v(p_1, p_2)$$

The classical theory of the consumer's choice has to be extended in two directions for the application to transport.

1.2   Extension to Discrete Choices

If for instance, a consumer cannot consume both of two goods 1 and 2 (for instance 1 and 2 are two different transport modes between which the traveller has to choose), this is equivalent to the consumer having two utility functions:

$$U_1 = U(x_0, x_1, 0)$$
$$U_2 = U(x_0, 0, x_2)$$

and the corresponding indirect utility functions: $V_1(p_1, r)$ and $V_2(p_2, r)$.

If the utility functions depend also on the quality parameters q_1 and q_2 which correspond to modes 1 and 2 respectively, these parameters will also appear in the indirect utility functions. A special case often used in transport corresponds to stochastic utility functions where the probabilistic element can represent changes of the tastes of the consumer, i.e. that the choices depend on a variable which has not been identified; then the indirect utility functions are:

$$V_1 = r + v_1(p_1, q_1) + \varepsilon_1$$

(4.1)

$$V_2 = r + v_2(p_2, q_2) + \varepsilon_2$$

It is not possible to predict exactly the choice of the user between 1 and 2, but only the probability of this choice, or (in the aggregate) the proportion of the population which will choose 1; for instance:

$$Pr(1) = Pr(V_1 \geq V_2) = Pr(\varepsilon_1 - \varepsilon_2 \geq v_2(p_2, q_2) - v_1(p_1, q_1))$$

Knowledge of the distributions of the stochastic elements ε_1 and ε_2 (or of the distribution of their difference) allows the calculation of $Pr(1)$ if v_1 and v_2 are known. Two of the distributions frequently used (Ben Akiva and Lerman, 1991) are:

- a normal distribution, leading to the probit model:

$$Pr(\varepsilon \leq x) = \frac{1}{\sigma\sqrt{2\pi}} \int_{-\infty}^{x} \exp(-\frac{t^2}{2\sigma^2}) dt$$

If ε_1 and ε_2 follow a normal distribution with the mean zero and variances are σ_1^2 and σ_2^2 and covariance is σ_{12} then $(\varepsilon_1-\varepsilon_2)$ is distributed normally with the mean zero, and the variance:

$$\sigma'^2 = \sigma_1^2 + \sigma_2^2 - 2\sigma_{12}$$

so that:

$$Pr(1) = Pr(\varepsilon \geq v_2 - v_1) = \frac{1}{\sigma'\sqrt{2\pi}} \int_{-\infty}^{v_1 - v_2} \exp(-t^2 / 2\sigma'^2) dt$$

- a Gumbel distribution, a particular case of the law of Generalised Extreme Values (GEV).

Generalized Extreme Values distributions have the following shape:

$$F(\varepsilon_1 ... \varepsilon_n) = \exp(-G(\exp(-\varepsilon_1)....., \exp(-\varepsilon_n)))$$

where G is defined by the following properties:
- G is positive
- G is homogeneous of degree μ

- The Nth partial derivative of G is non negative if N is odd, non positive if N is even and if the probabilities are independent and follow a distribution of the form:

$$Pr(1) = \frac{\exp(v_1 G_1'(\exp(v_1)....\exp(v_n)))}{\mu G(\exp(v_1)...,\exp(v_n))}$$

The Gumbel distribution is:

$$Pr(\varepsilon \leq x) = \exp(-\exp(-\mu(x-m)))$$

The mean value of this distribution is: $(m + \dfrac{\gamma}{\mu})$, γ being the Euler constant

$(\gamma = 0,577....)$ with the variance $\dfrac{\pi^2}{6\mu^2}$

If ε_1 and ε_2 are independent and distributed as the Gumbel distribution, the parameters of which are $(\mu, 0)$, then $\varepsilon = (\varepsilon_1 - \varepsilon_2)$ is distributed as a logistic distribution, according to the logit model such that:

$$Pr(\varepsilon \leq x) = \frac{1}{1 + \exp(-\mu x)}$$

In the specific case of a discrete choice between two alternatives as defined by (4.1):

$$Pr(1) = Pr(\varepsilon \geq v_2 - v_1) = \frac{1}{1 + \exp(\mu(v_2 - v_1))} = \frac{\exp(\mu v_1)}{\exp(\mu v_1) + \exp(\mu v_2)}$$

Staying with the case where ε_1 and ε_2 are independent and distributed as a Gumbel distribution, the parameters of which are $(\mu, 0)$, then : $Max(V_1, V_2)$ is also a Gumbel distribution with the parameters:

$$\mu \text{ and } \frac{1}{\mu} \log(\exp(\mu v_1) + \exp(\mu v_2))$$

There is a possible extension to the case where there are more than two alternatives. Let n be the number of alternatives, the utilities of which are, omitting the term r:

$$V_i = v_i(p_i, q_i) + \varepsilon_i$$

If the distribution of ε_i is known, the probability of alternative 1 is:

$$Pr(1) = Pr(U_1 \geq U_2 \, and....U_1 \geq U_n)$$

$$= \int_{\varepsilon_1 = -\infty}^{+\infty} \int_{\varepsilon_2 = -\infty}^{v_1 - v_2 + \varepsilon_1} .... \int_{\varepsilon_n = -\infty}^{v_1 - v_n + \varepsilon_1} f(\varepsilon_1, \varepsilon_2 ... \varepsilon_n) d\varepsilon_1 d\varepsilon_2 ... d\varepsilon_n$$

If the ε_i follow a normal distribution with zero mean and a known covariance matrix, the previous formula does not lead to an algebraic expression, even if the probabilities are independent.

- If they follow a Gumbel distribution, $Pr(1)$ has a simple expression provided that the probabilities are independent, and have the same parameters $(\mu, 0)$:

$$Pr(1) = Pr(v_1 + \varepsilon_1 \geq \underset{j \in [2, n^\circ]}{Max} (v_j + \varepsilon_j)) = \frac{\exp(\mu v_1)}{\displaystyle\sum_{j=1}^{j=n} \exp(\mu v_j)}$$

Furthermore, $Max(V_1 .... V_n)$ follows a Gumbel distribution with the parameters μ and $\dfrac{1}{\mu} \log(\displaystyle\sum_{j=1}^{j=n} \exp(\mu v_j))$, this last expression is named the 'logsum'. It expresses, to a constant γ/μ, the average utility derived from the choice.

A specific property of this law, named IIA (Independence from Irrelevant Alternatives) is that $\dfrac{Pr(1)}{Pr(2)}$ does not depend on the characteristics of the other possibilities.

This result is in contradiction with some intuitions, illustrated in the transport field by the classical 'blue bus–red bus' paradox. Assume that a user, whose preferences are described by a logit model, has to choose between two transport means, car and bus, the utilities of which are equal:

$$v_A = v_B$$

Then the probabilities of choosing car or bus are both equal to 0.5. Let us now assume that one of the modes of transport is divided into two modes with identical characteristics, e.g. through painting half of the buses blue and the other half red, or in a more realistic way that another mode is introduced, which is very close to bus (for instance trolley-bus) which presents the same utility for the user. Then the IIA property shows that each of the three modes would have a one-third probability of being chosen, which is clearly not a sensible result. To overcome this inconvenience, it is necessary to give up the hypothesis of independence of the probabilities. This can be done through a probit model in which the probabilities are correlated; this cannot be written easily or solved analytically, but can be solved numerically through the use of computer algorithms.

Another way is to develop a nested model. Let us for instance consider the simultaneous choice of the destination d among D alternatives, and of the transport mode m among M alternatives, and let us assume that the utility is:

$$U_{dm} = v_d + v_m + v_{dm} + \varepsilon_d + \varepsilon_m + \varepsilon_{dm}$$

with a correlation between the U_{dm}

$$\mathrm{cov}(U_{dm}, U_{dm'}) = \begin{vmatrix} \mathrm{var}(\varepsilon_d) & d = d' \\ \mathrm{var}(\varepsilon_m) & \text{if } m = m' \\ 0 & \text{otherwise} \end{vmatrix}$$

assuming that : $Var(\varepsilon_m) = 0$

Then:

$$U_{dm} = V_d + V_m + V_{dm} + \varepsilon_d + \varepsilon_{dm}$$

If we furthermore assume that εdm follows a Gumbel distribution $G(\mu m, 0)$, the parameters of which are $\mu = \mu m$ and $\eta = 0$, and that εd is such that $\underset{m}{Max}\, U_{dm}$ follows a Gumbel distribution $G(\mu d, 0)$, this ad-hoc assumption allows us to make calculations more easily (it is made more sensible by the fact that the maximum of several stochastic variables is a stochastic variable the law of which tends to a Gumbel distribution when the number of the variables increases to infinity). Then:

$$\Pr(d) = \Pr(\underset{m \in Ddm}{Max\ U}_{dm} \geq \underset{m \in Dd'm}{Max\ U}_{d'm})$$

$$= \Pr[(V_d + \varepsilon_d + \underset{m \in Ddm}{Max}\,(V_m + V_{dm} + \varepsilon_{dm}) \geq (V_{d'} + \varepsilon_{d'} + \underset{m \in Ddm}{Max}\,(V_m + V_{d'm} + \varepsilon_{d'm}),$$

$$\forall d' \in Ddm, d' \neq d$$

As $\underset{m \in Ddm}{Max}\,(V_m + V_{dm} + \varepsilon_{dm})$ follows the distribution

$$G(\mu_m, \frac{1}{\mu_m} \log(\sum_{m \in Ddm} \exp[\mu_m (V_m + V_{dm})]$$

or

$$G(\mu_m, V_d') \text{ with } V_d' = \frac{1}{\mu_m} \log[\sum_{m \in Ddm} \exp \mu_m (V_m + V_{dm})]$$

Then:

$$\Pr(d) = \Pr[V_d + V_d' + \varepsilon_d + \varepsilon_d' \geq V_{d'} + V_{d'}' + \varepsilon_{d'} + \varepsilon_{d'}'], \forall d' \neq d$$

Due to the distributions followed by ε_d' and $(\varepsilon_d + \varepsilon_d')$ it follows that :

$$\Pr(d_i) = \frac{\exp(v_{d_i} + v_{d_i}')\mu_d}{\sum_{d_i} \exp(v_{d_i} + v_{d_i}')\mu_d}$$

with:

$$v_{d_i}' = \frac{1}{\mu_m} \log(\sum_{m_j} \exp(v_m + v_{md\,j})\mu_{md_i})$$

and:

$$\Pr(m_i \text{ if } d_i) = \frac{\exp(v_{d_i} + v_{m_i d_i})\mu_{md_i}}{\sum_j \exp(v_{d_i} + v_{m_j d_i})\mu_{md_i}} = \frac{\exp(v_{m_i d_i}\mu_{md})}{\sum_j \exp(v_{m_j d_i}\mu_{md})}$$

In this model everything happens as if in the first stage the user chooses, for each possible destination, the mode to be used through a specific logit model; then chooses the destination through another logit model where the utilities are the sums of the utilities of the destinations, plus the utilities drawn from the chosen modes through the first stage. So the expression of the nested logit model will also be of the 'logsum' form already met in the simple models above.

1.3   Extension to Time. The Generalised Cost of Transport

The second extension of the classical theory of consumer behaviour takes into consideration the fact that any travel involves the expenditure of time as well as money. Time is often the more binding constraint, which leads to the concept of a value of time, more specifically a value of time savings. Several models can be used to introduce this idea; three are presented here, a simple model, the activity model and the opportunity model.

1.3.1 A simple model

The simplest model assumes that the consumer, in optimising behaviour, is subject to both an income constraint and a time constraint. In order to consume one unit of good i, time t_i, has to be spent and the total time available is constrained. Thus the consumer has to maximise:

$$U(x_1...x_i...x_n...)$$

With not only:

$$\sum_i p_i x_i \leq r$$

but also:

$$\sum_i t_i x_i \leq T$$

Assuming that λ and μ are the dual variables relating to the two constraints, we obtain:

$$\frac{\dfrac{\partial U}{\partial x_i}}{\lambda p_i + \mu t_i} = \tau$$

where τ is a constant. U^*, the optimal value of utility, depends on p_i, t_i, r and T. In the same way as λ represents the marginal utility of income, r, through the envelop theorem, μ represents the marginal utility of time T, and μ/λ can be called the value of time: to increase the available time T by one unit is equivalent to increasing income by μ/λ.

1.3.2 Activity model

It is clear that the simple model is naive. The time spent on each activity is not proportional to the quantity consumed, and it does not have the same value for each activity the consumer undertakes. Moreover, for many activities it is not appropriate to assume that the consumer wishes to minimise the amount of time spent on that activity, positive utility can be obtained from the time involved. However, since time spent on consumption cannot be spent on working there is assumed to be a trade-off between consumption and work, determined by the wage rate, which is the opportunity cost of income forgone. A more elaborate modelling framework to incorporate these ideas assumes that the utility of a consumer depends on two kinds of arguments, the quantity of goods consumed x_i and the time spent on the activities t_j :

$$U = U(x_1...x_n, t_1...t_m)$$

with the constraints:

$$\sum_{i=1}^{i=n} p_i x_i - (wt_w + r) \le 0$$

$$t_w + \sum_{j=1}^{j=m} t_j \le T$$

$$\overline{t}_j - t_j \le 0$$

In this expression w is the hourly wage, t_w the time spent working, $\overline{t}_j$ the minimal time which can be devoted to activity j and T is the total available time. Calling the dual variables λ, μ, v_j respectively, the Lagrange technique yields:

$$\frac{\partial U}{\partial t_j} - \mu - v_j = 0$$

$$-\frac{\partial U}{\partial t_w} + \lambda w - \mu = 0$$

$$(t_j - \overline{t}_j)v_j = 0$$

Thus we can derive the indirect utility function:

$$V(p_i, \overline{t}_j, w, T, r)$$

and the value of time spent in j activity is:

$$h_{\bar{t}_j} = \frac{\partial V}{\partial \bar{t}_j} \Big/ \frac{\partial V}{\partial r} = \frac{v_j}{\lambda} = \frac{\dfrac{\partial U}{\partial t_j} - \mu}{\lambda}$$

or:

$$h_{\bar{t}_j} = w + \frac{1}{\lambda}\left(\frac{\partial U}{\partial t_j} - \frac{\partial U}{\partial t_w} \right) \qquad\qquad (4.2)$$

Two cases can be considered:

- If $t_j > \bar{t}_j$, then $v_j = 0 = \dfrac{\partial U}{\partial t_j} - \mu$

and the marginal value of time spent in activity j is zero. This is the case of pure leisure activities.

- If $t = \bar{t}_j$, then $v_j \neq 0$

This is the case of intermediate activities, which include transport. Equation (4.2) tells us that the marginal value of time spent in this activity is equal to the hourly wage, plus the difference between marginal disutility of work and marginal disutility of the jth activity.

It is clear that here the value of time $\dfrac{\partial V}{\partial \bar{t}_j} \Big/ \dfrac{\partial V}{\partial r}$ depends not just on the income forgone, but also on the activity for which that time is used. It will additionally depend on the characteristics of the individual which determine preferences. For instance many models use values of time which depend on income and the purpose of travel, as well as on, for example, the level of comfort.

1.3.3 Opportunity models
This kind of reasoning only holds for consumption activities, which in the case of transport concerns only non-work travel, including commuting. Hensher (1997) analysed the opportunity costs for work travel, leading to the following expression for the value of work travel time:

$$h = (1 - r - pq)PM + \frac{1-r}{1-t}VW + \frac{r}{1-t}VL + \Delta PM$$

where:

r is the proportion of time used for leisure activities.

p is the proportion of time devoted to work.

q is the ratio between productivity of work whilst travelling and average productivity

PM is the marginal productivity of work

VW is the difference between the disutility of transport and the disutility of work

VL is the disutility of transport for the worker

ΔPM is the extra production allowed by the decrease of tiredness which an improvement in transport would permit.

t is the income tax rate

1.3.4 The generalised cost of transport

With this understanding of the value of time, it is now possible to introduce the notion of generalised cost of transport. In the case of the simple model, if x_i represents the quantity of transport, a unit variation of this quantity leads to a variation of utility as given by the expression:

$$\frac{\partial U}{\partial x_j} = \frac{\partial V}{\partial r} p_. + \frac{\partial V}{\partial T} t_.$$

and $\left(p_. + \frac{\partial V}{\partial T} / \frac{\partial V}{\partial r} t_. \right)$ plays the same role as the price in the classical case,

$\left(\frac{\partial V}{\partial T} / \frac{\partial V}{\partial r} \right)$ being the value of time.

In the activity model, if transport represents the *j*th activity, the money cost of which is p_j, it can be seen that:

$$\frac{\partial u}{\partial x_j} = \frac{\partial V}{\partial r} p_j + \frac{\partial V}{\partial t_j} t_j = \frac{\partial V}{\partial r} \left(p_. + \frac{\partial V}{\partial t_j} / \frac{\partial V}{\partial r} t_. \right)$$

It is thus possible to define a generalised cost, which is the sum of the factors which influence the utility derived from transport *j* for the given consumer, and which will thus help determine the travel decisions made. This generalised cost takes the form:

$$p_i + \frac{\partial V}{\partial \overline{t_j}} / \frac{\partial V}{\partial r} t_i$$

2. APPLICATION TO TRANSPORT: TRAFFIC FORECASTING MODELS

The first traffic models were developed by geographers and engineers. They sought to find similar regularities to human behaviour as found in the physical world, and indeed were based largely on the ideas of 'social physics' which had emerged in the 1940s. Thus we find the dominance of these models by the concept of the 'gravity model' or by the idea of distance and the associated transport costs being referred to as impedance. These models are typically aggregate in that they seek to model flows of trip making, not individual trip decisions, although to do this they need to make assumptions about human behaviour and models have become more behavioural through time. The most common modelling framework is known as the four–stage model, which comprises:

- a generation sub-model which determines the number of trips from a given zone, i.e. total trip making;
- a distribution sub-model which determines how these trips are distributed according to the various destinations, i.e. allocation to specific origin-destination (O-D) pairs;
- a mode choice sub-model which determines how these O-D flows are distributed between the different modes;
- a route choice sub-model which determines the allocation of mode-specific O-D flows to the network, mainly for road traffic.

It has become more common to add a fifth stage, dealing with departure time choice to allow for cases where travellers change the time of their journeys rather than change route to cope, for example, with congestion.

Before analysing each of these four stages, it should be noted that they are not independent of each other. If, for instance, there are more, and more interesting, destinations, we should expect generation to be larger; if there is a better rail service between two points, we might expect both the generation and distribution of trips to reflect this better supply as well as the division of these trips between available modes. There needs therefore to be recursive links between the stages and some indication of how to deal with this is given below. Furthermore, since the model is typically concerned with estimating the number of trips on the links of a network between zones, the definition of these zones is a critical stage of the modelling process.

2.1 Generation Models

There are basically two kinds of generation model. In the first, the aggregate model, the number of trips is estimated in total for a given zone. This variable is related to several other ones representing the level of activity and the characteristics of the population in the zone. For instance:

$$T_i = kr_i^a p_i^b$$

where:

T_i is the number of trips per unit of time, averaged over the population of the city or zone i.

r_i is the average income per inhabitant of the relevant population

p_i is the car-ownership rate

k, a and b are parameters.

In the second, the disaggregated approach, the population is subdivided into homogeneous categories, within which it might be expected that trip-making behaviour is relatively stable, for instance according to journey purposes:

- home to work (commuting) travel
- business travel
- personal business and shopping travel
- leisure travel
- holiday travel

and travellers are classified according to criteria such as:

- income
- size and structure of the household
- age
- car ownership
- occupation
- location

The assumption is that within each category behaviour is similar, a fact which makes transpositions easier both through time and space. Let Π_{ijk}^t be the proportion of users the characteristics of whom are: income (i), household size (j), age (k), and g_{kij} the rate of mobility of this category of users at time t (or in city t).

Then the average trip generation is given by:

$$G^t = \sum_{ijk} \Pi_{ijk..}^t g_{ijk..}$$

and in another city (or at another time) t' it is given by:

$$G' = \sum_{ijk} \Pi'_{ijk..} g_{ijk..}$$

What does experience tell us about the validity of these generation models? A considerable amount of evidence has been produced from around the world. The most important results are about daily trip making in urban areas, mainly commuting trips, which present a picture of considerable uniformity in trip making behaviour.

The most remarkable feature is the constancy in the daily number of trips made within a specific area over long periods of time. Although there are significant differences between levels of trip making in different types of area, these are not large. For example, Coindet (1996) and Guider (1996) report on trip making in France. In the Ile de France region this amounts to some 3.5 trips per person and per day (including walking), a number which has been constant over the twenty past years. Outside Paris the figure is a little lower, but also fairly constant, varying between 3.2 and 3.4 trips per day.

The UK National Travel Surveys also provide a long period of data on rates of trip making (DTLR, 2001). For the past 30 years the average number of trips made by Great Britain residents has been close to 1000 a year, or about 20 per person per week (Table 4.1). In 1998/2000 the average trip rate was only 8 per cent higher than in 1972/1973.

Table 4.1   Personal travel in the UK

	No. of journeys	Distance travelled (miles)	Time travelling (hours)	Average trip length (miles)
1972/73	956	4476	353	4.7
1975/76	935	4740	330	5.1
1978/79	1097	4946	376	4.5
1985/86	1024	5317	337	5.2
1989/91	1091	6475	370	5.9
1992/94	1053	6439	359	6.1
1995/97	1052	6666	355	6.3
1998/00	1030	6843	360	6.6
% change	+7.7	+52.9	+1.9	+40.4

Source: DTLR (2001)

However, over this period, the average trip length increased by over 40 per cent, from 4.7 miles to 6.6 miles (7.5 km to 10.6 km) and hence there was a more than 50 per cent increase in the annual distance travelled per person a year. There has been rather less change in the proportion of trips made for different purposes, but most have been affected by the trend towards longer trips (Table 4.2).

Table 4.2 Personal travel by journey purpose, UK, 1998/2000

	Trips %	Distance %	Average trip length (miles)
Commuting	15.6	19.7	8.4
Business	3.5	10.2	19.5
Education	11.3	4.3	2.5
Shopping & personal business	31.0	20.0	4.3
Visiting	17.5	20.7	7.9
Other	21.1	25.1	7.9
Total (=100%)	1030	6843	6.6

Source: DTLR (2001)

But this stability covers large discrepancies between individuals. For instance, Lefevre and Offner (1990) have shown for France that the modal split varies strongly with the trip purpose and the distance to the central business district. Walking and public transport dominate in the centre and car use in the outskirts; the number of motorised trips is more stable, but nevertheless varies between 1.7 and 2.1 per person and per day according to distance from the centre.

There have, however, been substantial changes in the destinations of these trips, and therefore in the trip distribution, which is characterised by an increase in the length of trips. This has amounted to an increase of 0.85 per cent per year in Ile de France, and nearly 3 per cent for other French agglomerations. In the UK, work trips have increased in length by around 16 per cent on average between 1989/1991 and 1998/2000 (Table 4.2) and the average length of shopping trips increased by over a quarter. The biggest changes were in business and other leisure travel.

Interestingly, as people have shifted to the use of private motorized transport and transport speeds have typically also increased for most modes, the average time spent in travelling has remained roughly constant. This statistical result is called 'Zahavi's law'. In France the daily figure is around 29 minutes in Ile de France, 17 minutes elsewhere. In the UK the average time spent travelling (including walking time) remained almost constant over the period from 1972 (Table 4.1) at around 360 hours per year or 59 minutes per day.

This increase in journey length has two important consequences. First, it is linked to the growth of urban sprawl; if people can live further from the centre without expending more time on their journeys, but where they can find cheaper living costs from lower land prices etc. there is pressure for decentralization leading to sprawl (see for example Prud'Homme and Lee, 1999; and the discussion in ECMT, 2001). Second, increasing journey lengths for the same amount of activity implies increased transport intensity in the economy as discussed in Chapter 1.

In these models, mobility does not depend on supply, but solely on the characteristics of the individual and the zone of residence. Logically a reduction of transport cost would be expected to induce an increase of mobility, but this has rarely been explored in the modelling framework. The effect is believed to be small compared to the effect of income or car ownership, and since mobility changes are slow and correlated with other factors, they are far from easy to detect statistically.

2.2 Distribution Models

The core relation for distribution models, which allocate trips generated between alternative destinations, is the gravity formula, the standard formulation of which is:

$$T_{ij} = k \frac{(P_i P_j)^a}{d_{ij}^b}$$

where:

T_{ij} is the traffic from zone i to zone j
P_i and P_j are the populations of zones i and j
d_{ij} is the distance between i and j
a and b are parameters

A more general formulation, which uses the information available from the generation stage is:

$$T_{ij} = k O_i D_j f(c_{ij})$$

where:

    O_j is a generation factor related to the origin zone i
    D_j is an attraction factor of the destination zone j
    f is a decreasing function sometimes called the impedance function
    C_{ij} is the generalised cost of travel between i and j

According to the nature of the constraints imposed on the previous equation we can determine three alternative formulations:

- the non constrained model
- the singly constrained model (the sum of the traffic out of each zone is exogenously fixed, i.e. $\sum_{j} T_{ij} = O_i$)

- the doubly constrained model (the sums of both the traffic out of and into each zone are exogenously fixed)

This formulation can be deduced from several principles; the most established is through an analogy with the physical concept of entropy (Ortuzar and Willumsen, 1994). Assuming the number of trips from each origin is fixed, likewise the number of trips to each destination, the distribution maximises the probability of possible arrangements of users respecting the margin constraints:

$$W(\|T_{ij}\|) = \frac{T!}{\prod_{ij}(T_{ij}!)}$$

Using Stirling's equation this can be re-written as:

$$\log(W) = \log T! - \sum_{ij}(T_{ij} \log T_{ij} - T_{ij})$$

The entropy of this expression is then maximized subject to the constraints:

$$\sum_{i} T_{ij} = D_j$$

$$\sum_{j} T_{ij} = O_i$$

and an additional constraint which fixes the total cost of transport at a given level:

$$\sum_{ij} T_{ij} c_{ij} = C$$

The maximisation of the Lagrangian, of which the dual variables are λ_i, μ_j, ν, leads to

$$T_{ij} = \exp(-\lambda_i)\exp(-\mu_j)\exp(-\beta c_{ij})$$

which can be written as:

$$T_{ij} = O_i a_i D_j b_j \exp(-\beta c_{ij})$$

Without the total costs of transport constraint, this would give:

$$T_{ij} = O_i a_i D_j b_j$$

The singly constrained model can be written:

$$T_{ij} = O_i \frac{D_j \exp(-\beta c_{ij})}{\sum_k D_k \exp(-\beta c_{ik})}$$

It is possible to use the model without the total costs of transport constraint by using a known existing O-D trip matrix $\left\| t_{ij} \right\|$ which has been updated by information on the new marginal values. Thus it is quite common to seek to maximise (Ortuzar and Williumsen, 1994)

$$W = -\sum_{ij} \left(T_{ij} \log \frac{T_{ij}}{t_{ij}} - T_{ij} + t_{ij} \right)$$

from which it can be shown that:

$$W' = -0,5 \sum_{ij} \frac{(T_{ij} - t_{ij})^2}{t_{ij}}$$

from which a result of the form:

$$T_{ij} = a_i O_i b_j D_j t_{ij}$$

is obtained.

The T_{ij} are calculated through iterations on the matrix t_{ij} where the rows and columns are multiplied alternately by the coefficients allowing a successive adjustment of the marginal values towards a converged solution.

These developments of the gravity model lack conviction because they proceed by analogy and not from a rigorous reasoning based on assumption and hypothesis. Some economic fundamentals can be identified within the model based on the theory of discrete choice discussed in section 1 of this chapter. In the case of the home to work commuting journey, assume that an individual resident in zone i seeks to maximise the utility derived from work, equal to $s_k + c_{ij}$, where s_k is the wage obtained from employment k, j is the location of employment k. Assume that wages are distributed independently of location according to $s_k = \overline{s} + \varepsilon_k$ where the ε are distributed according to a Gumbel distribution of mean μ and variance $\eta = \overline{s} - \dfrac{\gamma}{\mu}$. Suppose also that there are D_j jobs in zone j. Then the maximum utility, net of transport costs, which can be achieved in location j will be a stochastic variable u_j equal to the maximum of $(s_k - c_{ij})$ which is distributed as a Gumbel distribution with parameters μ and

$$\frac{1}{\mu}\log(\sum_i^{D_j} \exp \mu \eta) = \frac{1}{\mu}\log D_j \exp\left(\overline{s} - c_{ij} - \frac{\gamma}{\mu}\right)\mu$$

Its mean will be:
$$m_j = \frac{1}{\mu}(\mu(\overline{s} - c_{ij}) + \log D_j)$$

and the probability that destination j will be chosen will be:

$$\Pr(j) = \frac{\exp(\mu m_j)}{\sum_k \exp(\mu m_k)} = \frac{D_j \exp \mu(\overline{s} - c_{ij})}{\sum_k D_k \exp \mu(\overline{s} - c_{ik})} = \frac{D_j \exp(-\mu c_{ij})}{\sum_k D_k \exp(-\mu c_{ik})}$$

and total traffic will be:

$$T_{ij} = O_i \frac{D_j \exp(-\mu c_{ij})}{\sum_k D_k \exp(-\mu c_{ik})}$$

This is the singly constrained gravity model where the destinations are not mutually exclusive. From this model it is possible to derive an equation for the doubly constrained model (Cochrane, 1975; Koenig, 1974), on the assumption that individuals who stay in location j are those who receive the highest utility from this decision. This gives:

$$\Pr(j) = O_i \frac{D_j \exp(-\mu c_{ij})\exp(-\beta_j)}{\sum_k D_k \exp(-\mu c_{ik})\exp(-\beta_k)}$$

Koenig (1974) shows that this expression remains valid if the probabilities are distributed according to any distribution, not necessarily double exponential, as long as the number of jobs (the attraction) at each destination D_j are large.

Finally, the model can be extended to the unconstrained case: the individual travels as long as the utility derived from that travel is positive. Thus it is possible to show (Cochrane 1975) that:

$$T_{ij} = kO_iD_j \exp(-\mu c_{ij})$$

This is the gravity model in its original form.

The appropriate model to use in each situation depends essentially on the particular circumstances. Though deriving from the same mathematical relationship, the various models have different uses; the unconstrained model assumes an elasticity with respect to the cost of transport and thus deals with both generation and distribution and hence is mainly used for intercity problems; the singly and doubly-constrained models are more adapted to urban problems for instance home to work trips or recreational trips.

2.3   Modal Split

Modelling modal split is based on the idea that the allocation of travel between different modes depends on the difference (or sometimes the ratio) between the transport costs of the various modes. A general formulation is the logistic function:

$$Pr(1) = \frac{1}{1 + \exp\mu(C_1 - C_2)}$$

in which:

$Pr(1)$ is the proportion using mode i
C_1 and C_2 are the generalised costs of the two modes,
μ is a positive parameter.

According to the value of μ, the choice is more or less sensitive to the difference of transport costs (Figure 4.1).

The all–or–nothing choice corresponds to a value of μ of infinity, a situation in which the distribution is insensitive to costs corresponding to the value 0. This general principle can be applied at either an aggregated or a disaggregated level.

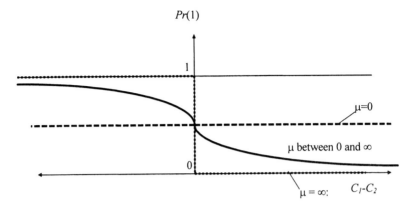

Figure 4.1 Form of logistic curve

2.3.1 Aggregated level

At an aggregate level, the unit of observation is the data on flows between one origin-destination pair. *Pr(1)* represents the share of passengers using mode 1, for instance the proportion of passengers using rail to go from one city or zone to another. The logistic formula can be justified in the following way: Each user faces generalised costs of each mode given by:

$$C_1^i = C_1 + \varepsilon_i$$

$$C_2^i = C_2 + \varepsilon_i'$$

The stochastic elements ε have zero mean and are independent; they represent the effects coming from either non-identified variables in the generalised costs, or from the idiosyncratic behaviour of the users

2.3.2 Disaggregated models

At a disaggregated level, the observed unit is the user, and the utilities of each mode are arguments of the logit function; they are indirect utility functions in the sense of the theory of consumer behaviour and depend on the price of the mode, the travel time, and other characteristics of the user or of the mode:

$$U_{ij} = \sum_k \beta_{ij}^k X_{ij}^k + \varepsilon_{ij}$$

where:

- i is the user
- j is the mode
- k represents each of the attributes which characterize the pair (i, j)
- β_{ij}^k are parameters
- ε_{ij} are the random elements affecting utility

According to the assumption made concerning the distribution of the random terms, several models can be derived. The most frequently used are logit models, which are simple to implement and estimate, but which can produce some paradoxical consequences. As well as the problem of the IIA property, already encountered, which can be addressed through the use of nested models, there are other anomalies. For instance the equation:

$$\frac{P_i(j)}{P_i(l)} = \frac{\exp(\mu V_{ij})}{\exp(\mu V_{il})}$$

yields:

$$\Delta\frac{P_i(j)}{P_i(l)} = \frac{P_i(j)}{P_i(l)}\exp(\mu \Delta V_{ij})$$

From this, it would appear that a change of quarter of an hour in the travel time of one mode has the same effect on modal split regardless of whether the total travel time is half an hour or 10 hours. Similarly, it can be seen that the direct and cross elasticities are:

$$E(P_i(j)/X_{il}^k) = -P_i(l)\beta_{il}^k X_{il}^k$$

From these equations, any changes affecting one mode affects the share of the other modes in a similar way, which is a very restrictive result. Finally the linear specification does not allow us to take into account threshold effects on variables X_{ji}. These drawbacks can be overcome through a Box-Cox transformation, which uses the transformed variables:

$$Y_{ij}^k = \left| \begin{array}{ll} \dfrac{(X_{ij}^{\lambda_k}) - 1}{\lambda_k} & \text{if } \lambda_k \neq 0 \\[3mm] \log X_{ij}^k & \text{if } \lambda_k = 0 \end{array} \right.$$

Gaudry (see for example Gaudry and Wills, 1978) has studied the properties of this transformation and Mandel *et al.* (1996) applied the method to traffic forecasting in Germany, illustrating the improvements it can produce.

Disaggregate models are based on a unit of observation which corresponds to the choice of the individual user whereas aggregate models reflect the average choice of a group of users in a given O–D pair. This creates a number of problems both for the calibration of the model and for the forecasting process. Even if the explanatory variables are the same, it will suffice in the aggregate model just to know the mean values which can often be observed without specific data collection. In the disaggregate model it is necessary to know the values of these variables for each user and each choice by that user and not only their average value over the users. This implies costly data collection.

Calibration is usually carried out in both cases through maximum likelihood methods. The larger number of observations in disaggregate models (it is typical to use data for about 200 users in disaggregate models whereas aggregate models can be calibrated on perhaps 30 O–D pairs) allows the introduction of a larger number of explanatory variables than in aggregate models, which tend to be restricted to the basic components of generalised cost such as money cost and time.

Once it has been calibrated the disaggregate model determines the probabilities of each choice for an individual of given characteristics, but it does not provide forecasts of the usage of each mode. These forecasts have to be implemented through various aggregation methods (Ben Akiva and Lerman, 1991):

- Classification of users in homogeneous categories defined by the values of the variables explaining the utilities. Each class is assumed to be represented by a mean observation.
- Integration, a limit form of the classification when the number of categories tends to infinity.
- Sample enumeration, consisting of drawing a sample of the population, determining the choices of each of the individuals of the sample, and finally aggregating them.

It is clear that to estimate the behaviour implied in a disaggregate model by using an aggregate model can lead to significant errors (Small, 1992). This is shown in more detail in Box 4.1

BOX 4.1

Aggregation bias (after Small 1992)

Consider le choice between car and bus, modelled by a logit model of the form:

$$P_b^i = \frac{1}{1 + \exp(\beta_1 (c_a^i - c_b^i) + \beta_0)}$$

where:

P_b^i is the probability of choosing bus

c_a^i, c_b^i are the money costs of car and bus for all

i represents the individual

β are parameters

The values of the parameters and variables are such that half of the users have a probability of taking the bus of 0.9 and the other half a probability of 0.1. The mean modal split is thus half and half between bus and car.

If the cost of using bus increases by dc, the probability of taking the bus changes according to the equation:

$$\frac{dP_b^i}{dc} = P_b^i (1 - P_b^i)\beta_1$$

The aggregate model gives a mean rate of change of this share of:

$$0.25\beta_1$$

The application of the disaggregate model to each of the two population groups gives a mean rate of change of the share of bus:

$$0.9 \times 0.1\beta_1 = 0.09\beta_1$$

This produces a result which is confirmed by other model applications.

Although it would be useful to be able to transfer disaggregated models between different applications, for example a model calibrated in one city to another, the need for these to be based on detailed knowledge of the specific circumstances and an understanding of behaviour in these circumstances, largely prevents this from happening. Transferability remains a distant goal.

2.3.3 Price-time model

As an alternative to disaggregated choice models the price-time model has been developed. This approach has been used particularly in France by SNCF and by the Civil Aviation Administration to model the competition between rail and air. The model is analogous to the models of product discrimination used in industrial economics, and is intermediate between aggregated and disaggregated models. It is based on the following principles, explained in the case of air-rail competition:

Assume that each user makes decisions according to the generalised costs of each mode:

$$C_f^i = p_f + h_i t_f$$

$$C_a^i = p_a + h_i t_a$$

Where:

C_f^i, C_a^i are the generalised costs of rail and air

p_a and p_f are the prices of the two modes

t_a and t_f are the travel times

h_i is the value of time of the user i

User i chooses rail if:

$$C_f^i \leq C_a^i$$

or:

$$h_i \leq \frac{p_a - p_f}{t_f - t_a}$$

Knowledge of the supply allows us to calculate:

$$h_b = \frac{p_a - p_f}{t_f - t_a}$$

which can be called the 'switch value'.

It is generally assumed that values of time are distributed in a similar way to incomes, which follow a log-normal distribution (Arduin, 1993); this allows us to calculate the share of users choosing rail:

$$\Pr(f) = \Pr(h \leq h_b)$$

This model is disaggregated in the sense that it analyses behaviour at the individual level, but it needs only aggregated data. It can equally be used to model the route choice which we shall consider in a subsequent section, but first we review some empirical evidence on estimates of the values of travel time, which have been provided from modal split models.

2.3.4 Values of time

Values of time are deduced from models of travel behaviour, and most commonly from modal split models; they are calculated as the marginal rate of substitution between time and price:

$$-\frac{\partial V}{\partial t} \Big/ \frac{\partial V}{\partial c}$$

The derived values of time vary considerably (see Table 4.3).

Table 4.3 Synthesis of values of time

Car: personal trips	
Value of time (personal) 1997€/hour	Country
1.5 – 2.5	Finland
2.5 – 4.5	Germany, Denmark, Netherlands, Portugal, United Kingdom
4.5 – 8.5	Ireland, Sweden
Train: business trips	
Value of time (business) 1990€/hour	Country
5.2	Spain
10.1 – 13	Denmark, Italy, United Kingdom, Germany, Ireland, Netherlands, Belgium
17.2	Sweden
24	Finland
Train: personal trips	
Value of time (business) 1990€/hour	Country
1.6 – 2.3	Denmark, Sweden, Belgium, Germany, Finland.
2.7 – 2.9	Spain, Netherlands
3.4 – 4.2	United Kingdom, Ireland, Italy

Source : EURET (1996)

In France, the Boiteux Report (Boiteux, 2000), established the unitary values to be used in cost-benefit analysis shown in Tables 4.4 and 4.5.

Table 4.4 Value of time in an urban context, France (1998)

Journey purpose	% of wage costs	% of gross salary	France €	Ile-de-France €
Business travel	61	85	10.5	13.0
Home-work travel	55	77	9.5	11.6
Other travel (shopping, leisure, tourism, etc.)	30	42	5.2	6.4
Mean value for all travel when journey purpose not known	42	59	7.2	8.8

Source : Boiteux (2000)

Table 4.5 Values of time in interurban travel, France (1998 € per hour)

Mode	For distances less than 50 km	For distances less than 150 km	For distances between 50 km and 400 km (road) or 150 km and 400 km (rail)	For distances greater than 400 km
Road	8.4	–	$(d/10+50).1/6.56$	13.7
Rail 2nd Cl.	–	10.7	$1/7(3d/10+445).1/6.56$	12.3
Rail 1st Cl.	–	27.4	$1/7(9d/10+1125).1/6.56$	32.3
Air	–	–	45.7	45.7

Source : Boiteux (2000)

The calculations in Table 4.4 assume that the mean value of time for all travel is based on a distribution of trips by journey purpose of 10 per cent for business, 35 per cent for home–work commuting trips and 55 per cent for other purposes. The values are based on the average monthly gross salary in 1998 assuming a 39–hour working week. Wage costs are on average 1.4 times the gross salary. Salaries in the Ile-de-France region are about 23 per cent higher than the national average. The value for business travel assumes that the travelling time is completely lost for any business activity and leads to no fatigue, no loss of productivity such that any saving of time is, for the employer, equal to the wage cost saved. However, the gain to society is reduced to the net salary since social security payments are unchanged. It is only when the time saved is reused for an activity which generates extra payments that we can begin to consider that the social benefit is equal to that to the employer. This is assumed not to be that frequent and the net salary (equal to about 85 per cent of the gross salary is used by default in Table 4.4).

Segonne (1998) analysed surveys of car users which provide useful additional information on travel times estimated by the users in comparison with the real travel time. Users overestimated the potential gain in travel time from using a new infrastructure at 16.5 minutes against a real saving of 0, and those actually using the new infrastructure estimated a time saving of 23 minutes against a modelled saving of just 8 minutes. The same study compared the results of revealed preference studies of the type discussed above which observe what users have actually done, with those of a stated preference survey in which potential users play a game in which they make hypothetical choices. This also revealed a significant difference with the median value of time being FFR35 (€5.34) per hour in the stated preference study against FFR47.1 (€7.18) per hour in the revealed preference study.

Hensher (1997) also demonstrates the differences between values of time drawn from a behavioural model and the opportunity cost of time, based on evidence for Australia (Table 4.6).

Table 4.6 Values of time for different journey purposes and modes, Australia

	Value of time in US dollars per hour	
	Drawn from a behavioural model	Opportunity cost
Home to work		
Private car	4.65	4.08
Firm car	7.87	6.90
Train	2.43	2.13
Bus	4.00	3.51
Long distance trip		
Personal purpose	6.52	5.72
Professional purpose	12.50-25.00	21-25
Urban travel for professional purpose	10.10	20.20

Source: Hensher (1997)

Small (1992) surveyed values of time and drew the conclusions that:

- Value of home to work (commuting) travel time is roughly half the gross wage
- Value of business travel time is higher, around the gross wage
- Value of personal and leisure travel time is close to the hourly wage.

In price–time models the value of time is roughly equal to the hourly income. Merlin (1991) and Small (1992) also show that value of time is different according to the nature of the transport activity. Waiting time is valued roughly 2 or 3 times more than in-vehicle transport time. There is some evidence that value of time varies with the length of the trip (Massiani, 1997).

Many models, particularly those dealing with situations of congestion, use the value of time implied by delays in departure or having to arrive late or early as summarised by de Palma and Rochat (1996) (Table 4.7). This shows the very high cost associated with a late arrival.

Wardman (1998, 2001) has reviewed a wide variety of values of time for Britain, including walking, waiting, delays and interchange penalties. Wardman's use of meta-analysis on some 143 studies suggests that walking and waiting time is on average valued at 1.58 times in-vehicle time, rather less than the values in the studies quoted above and the conventional wisdom that it is around 2 to 3 times in-vehicle time. However, the value of lateness was considerably higher (on average 7.4 times in-vehicle time) and interchange penalties were valued much higher (equivalent to an average 28 minutes time loss). Reliability thus becomes a key issue in both the perception and evaluation of transport choices (see Bates *et al.*, 2001; Lam and Small, 2001, for some further discussion).

Table 4.7 Evidence on the value of waiting time and congestion

		Ratio to the cost of travel time	
Author	Country or city	Of the cost of arrival in advance	Of the cost of delayed arrival
Small (1992)	USA	0.64	2.39
Khattak *et al* (1995)	Brussels	0.38	1.03
De Palma and Rochat (1996)	Geneva	0.327	2.69

Source: de Palma and Rochat (1996)

Finally, the EU research programme UNITE (Nellthorp *et al.*, 2001) has drawn together a number of state-of-the art studies of the value of time, which are based essentially on the approach developed by Wardman (Table 4.8). These were based on a number of value of time studies including the 1994 *UK Value of Time Study and the 1985-1996 Dutch Value of Time Studies*, both undertaken by the Hague Consulting Group; the Swedish national value of time study and the *Freight and Coach Value of Time Studies.*

Table 4.8 Values of time based on state-of-the-art studies, UNITE (1998€)

Passenger (VOT/person hour)		Freight (VOT)	
Car/motorcycle		Road transport	
Business	21.00	LGV	40.00
Commuting/private	6.00	HGV	43.00
Leisure/holiday	4.00		
Coach (inter-urban)		Rail transport	
Business	21.00	Full trainload	725.00
Commuting/private	6.00	Wagon load	30.00
Leisure/holiday	4.00	Average per tonne	0.76
Urban bus/tramway		Inland navigation	
Business	21.00	Full shipload	200.00
Commuting/private	6.00	Average per tonne	0.18
Leisure/holiday	3.20		
Inter-urban rail		Maritime shipping	
Business	21.00	Full shipload	200.00
Commuting/private	6.40	Average per tonne	0.18
Leisure/holiday	4.70		
Air traffic		Air transport	
Business	28.50	Average per tonne	4.00
Commuting/private	10.00		
Leisure/holiday	10.00		

Source: Nellthorp et al (2001)

2.4 Route Choice

This modelling stage is mainly used for road transport where it is necessary to assign a given volume of trips between a given origin and destination to the actual road network. Route choice has many similarities with mode choice. In both cases, the problem can be expressed as a discrete choice situation determined by the cost and quality characteristics of the (links of the) network. The main difference arises when the characteristics of the supply, mainly the travel time and the generalised cost of the routes, depend on traffic levels.

The key relationship in route choice studies is the speed–flow function (Figure 4.2) which relates speed to the level of flow on a particular link, measured in passenger car units (pcu). From this can be derived the congestion function (Figure 4.3) which relates the time taken to travel a given distance to the aggregate level of travel demand (see De Borger and Proost, 2001, for a further discussion and evidence for some European cities.

2.4.1 Wardrop's first principle

In an urban situation many links are close to saturation and traffic speed varies considerably with traffic flows. Furthermore the structure of the network is generally much more complicated than for intercity traffic. The problem is solved by application of the first principle of Wardrop (1952): 'in the equilibrium situation, the generalized cost of each used route between a given origin and a given destination are equal and lower than the generalized costs of any unused route'.

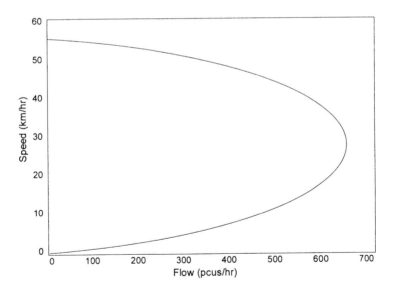

Figure 4.2 Speed–flow function.

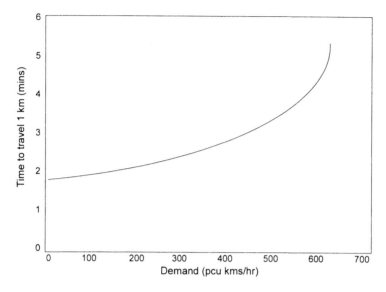

Figure 4.3. Congestion function

In order to explain the use of this principle, we use the following notation (Leurent 1991, Florian 1991):

$a \in A$ link

v_a flow on link a

$i \in I$ origin-destination pair

$k \in K_i$ route , the set of routes relating the O-D pair *i* being K_i

h_k the flow on each route *i*

δ_{ak} index denoting whether link a belongs to route k

g_i the flow on the O-D pair *i*.

The conditions are:

$$v_a = \sum_{i \in I} \sum_{k \in K_i} \delta_{ak} h_k$$

$$g_i = \sum_{k \in K_i} h_k$$

$$h_k \geq 0$$

The transport cost on link a is given by:

$$s_a = s_a(v_a)$$

and the cost of route k is:

$$s_k = \sum_a \delta_{ak} s_a(v_a)$$

Define u_i by:

$$u_i = \underset{k \in K_i}{Min} \, s_k$$

Assume that g is a function of u only

$$g_i = g_i(u_i)$$

and that functions $s_a(v_a)$ are increasing and functions $g_i(u_i)$ are decreasing.

Wardrop's first principle says that for equilibrium values, noted by $*$:

$$s_k^* - u_i^* \begin{vmatrix} = 0 \text{ if } h_k^* > 0 \\ \geq 0 \text{ if } h_k^* = 0 \end{vmatrix}$$

This relation may also be written:

$$(s_k^* - u_i^*)(h_k - h_k^*) \geq 0$$

h_k is a distribution which ensures compliance with the constraints. Summing these relations for all routes and O–D pairs leads to:

$$\sum_i \sum_k s_k^*(h_k - h_k^*) \geq \sum_i u_i^*(h_k - h_k^*)$$

or

$$\sum_a s_a^*(v)(v_a - v_a^*) \geq \sum_i u_i^*(g_i - g_i^*)$$

This inequality means that any variation around the equilibrium costs (left-hand side) is greater than the amount users are willing to pay (right-hand side). It can be shown that, assuming continuity and monotonicity of functions s_a and g_i, the previous inequality has a unique solution; and that it is equivalent to the optimisation problem (Beckmann 1956):

$$MinZ = \sum_a \int_0^{v_a} s_a(x)dx - \sum_i \int_0^{g_i} u_i(x)dx$$

with the same constraints as previously. Most optimisation algorithms to find an equilibrium use this equivalence.

It is possible to gain a more intuitive view of these results in the simple case where there is just one O-D pair and two routes 1 and 2, and where total traffic is constant.

$$G(u) = T$$

It is then possible to use a graphical representation (Figure 4.4) where traffic is measured from left to right for route 1 (v_1) and from right to left for route 2 (v_2), since $v_1+v_2=T$. The vertical axis represents costs. The Wardrop equilibrium is defined by v_1*, v_2* and $s_1* = s_2*$. This point is in fact the only one which satisfies:

$$Min(\int_0^{v_1} s_1(x)dx + \int_0^{v_2} s_2(y)dy)$$

in an optimum situation or:

$$s_1^{\cdot}(v_1^{\cdot})(v_1 - v_1^{\cdot}) + s_2^{\cdot}(v_2^{\cdot})(v_2 - v_2^{\cdot}) \geq u(T - T) = 0$$

in a situation of inequality with:

$$v_1+v_2=T$$

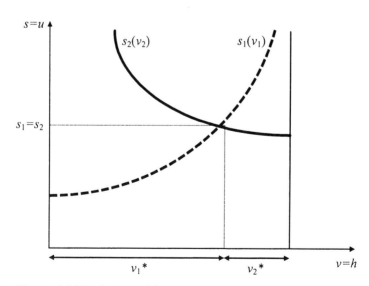

Figure 4.4 Wardrop equilibrium

2.4.2 Wardrop's second principle

It is clear that the equilibrium of the first Wardrop principle, which defines an optimum for the users, is in general different from the social optimum; this second optimum corresponds to the second Wardrop principle. It is defined by the programming problem:

$$\underset{v_1, v_2}{Min}(v_1 s_1 (v_1) + v_2 s_2 (v_2))$$

Which leads to the value $v_1^{\cdot}$ such that:

$$s_1 (v_1^{\cdot}) = s_2 (T - v_1^{\cdot}) - v_1^{\cdot} \frac{ds_1}{dv_1^{\cdot}} + (T - v_1^{\cdot}) \frac{ds_2}{dv_1^{\cdot}}$$

In general, the social optimum is defined as:

$$MinZ' = \sum_a v_a s_a (v_a) - \sum_i \int_0^{g_i} u_i (y) dy$$

But, this does not lead to the same result as the previous one. The discrepancy between them is the source of some paradoxes, the most famous one being the Braess (1968) paradox, which shows that it may be uneconomic to build a new link in a network. Assume a network as depicted in Figure 4.5, which has a single O–D pair, with 6 users going from 1 to 4, and 2 available routes.

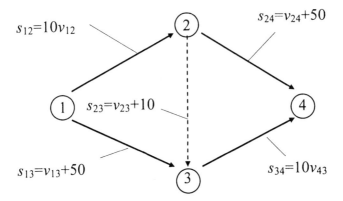

Figure 4.5 The Braess paradox

It is easy to check that both the first and second principles lead to a split of 3 users on route ① ② ④ and 3 on route ① ③ ④. Let us now add a new link from ② to ③ and for which:

$$s_{23} = v_{23} + 10$$

The individual equilibrium now has 2 users on each of the three routes ①②④, ①③④ and ①②③④, while the social optimum has not changed and still has 3 users on each of the two previous routes.

Another less well known paradox has been identified by several analysts in France (Ville (1970). Two routes provide the same O-D traffic. The first is a long ring road with low congestion and the travel cost is independent of the traffic. The second is a short urban road with considerable congestion. The route split is such that the generalised costs are the same on both routes. A myopic analysis of the congestion on the second route may induce a decision to widen it. After the widening, the route split changes, and the number of users of route two increases, but their travel costs do not change as they must, for equilibrium, be equal to the cost of using route one, which is constant. The widening has just transferred some users from route 1 to route 2, without any gain in time or cost. The net social impact is however an increase in total costs.

Up to now we have assumed the equilibrium is deterministic, and the cost of travelling on each route is assumed to be without uncertainty. This case is similar to the situation of an all-or-nothing split in the problem of modal choice. There are also stochastic models, in which the costs on each route are associated with a probability, which may represent either differences in perception of reality, or differences in preferences of users. The generalised cost is then of the form:

$$s_h^j = s_h + \varepsilon_h^j$$

where j are the passengers. Depending on the assumptions made about the ε_h^j it is possible to obtain either a logit or a probit model, according to whether or not the probabilities are correlated. With the assumption of probabilities, which are independent and identically distributed according to a Gumbel distribution, the equation giving the route split is:

$$\Pr(h) = \frac{\exp(-\mu s_h)}{\displaystyle\sum_k \exp(-\mu s_k)}$$

This assumption of independent and identically distributed probabilities is not fully satisfactory; it is more sensible to assume that their dispersion is linked to the generalised cost:

$$Var(\varepsilon_h^j) = k\sigma_h^2$$

Experience suggests intuitively that stochastic models are better than non-stochastic models especially when networks are simple and without congestion, and when costs are relatively independent of traffic flow; all cases where the all-or-nothing allocation of deterministic models does not work well (Florian 1991; Kawakami *et al.*, 1989).

3. MODELLING IN PRACTICE

The theoretical refinements of the previous section are at odds with the generally poor quality of data used for their implementation.

3.1   Statistical Information

Data collection is generally time consuming and expensive, while the studies which use the data generally have short time scales and limited budgets. In studies related to new infrastructure it is interesting to note the disproportion between the sums devoted to forecasting the costs of construction and those to the forecasting of traffic and revenue (for some evidence see Flyvbjerg *et al.*, 2003). Hence the choice of models is often more dictated by the availability of data and by the cost of implementation, than by the theoretical adequacy to the problem.

Information about traffic and transport flows may come either from traffic counts or from surveys. Traffic counts can be automatic or involve the manual counting of vehicles, tickets sold by railways or air companies, or the number of passengers boarding or alighting from a bus at each stop. The cost of such surveys is lower, but they do not provide any information about the origin or destination. Nevertheless, origin and destination can be inferred through specific surveys or by using a gravity model and combining it with the results of the traffic counts.

Surveys of travellers are more expensive, whether carried out during the journey or at home. For urban traffic and for road traffic, surveys of travellers are not easy to carry out. Simple ones can simply involve the distribution of a questionnaire, to be returned by mail, handed out to those passing through a cordon around a city or a region.

The most comprehensive O–D surveys are carried out in respondents' homes, using face-to-face interviews. These make it possible to ask a much larger number of questions about the characteristics of the interviewee and household, about his or her job and the trips undertaken during the previous day or week. This often involves respondents being asked to complete a travel diary for the period in question, recording full details of all trips made, which is collected at the end of the period.

BOX 4.2

Trade-off between model quality and data quality

The problem of the trade-off between the quality of the model and the quality of the explanatory variables can be illustrated by the following example derived from Ortuzar and Willumsen (1994). Suppose there are two specifications for explaining variable y. The first, the perfect model without error, uses two explanatory variables x_1 and x_2, each known to have errors (which are independent). Thus:

$$y = a_1 x_1 + a_2 x$$

The second specification is an approximation, it uses just one variable x_1 which is known perfectly, but the model includes an error term:

$$y = cx + \varepsilon$$

With the first model, the expected variance is:

$$(\sigma_y^1)^2 = a_1 \sigma_1^2 + a_2 \sigma_2^2$$

and with the second:

$$(\sigma_y^2)^2 = \sigma_\varepsilon^2$$

If the variables x_1 and x_2 are known with a very large error it is better to use the imperfect model. Moreover, the efforts to improve the information must, for a given level of cost, be preferable to using the less well known variable (or more precisely that for which $a\sigma$ is the greater).

Another kind of survey is the stated-preference study. Here the interviewee is presented with several possible trade-offs between well-defined alternatives. The answers are then introduced directly as input data in a traffic model. This method requires considerable caution to ensure that the answers are sufficiently reliable: the alternatives must be described very precisely, and should not be very different from the situations of which the interviewee has direct experience. This makes it difficult to use when no validating data is available or when the situation to be studied has no actual equivalence (for example in the case of a new transport mode).

A final form of enquiry is to use panels composed of a carefully selected sample of people which is surveyed at regular intervals. Panel surveys give good insights into temporal changes in travel patterns and are widely used by transport operators who need up to date knowledge of changes in the market.

Traffic studies also require information on network characteristics. It is not uncommon to have one to two hundred nodes and a few thousand links which produces an O–D matrix with tens of thousands of cells. Since it is not usually possible to fill all the cells with collected data, values have to be estimated from other data. Such data include socio-economic characteristics (numbers of households, household size, incomes, occupation, age, etc.) of the population at each node, which leads to huge data files and the scope for many errors, uncertainties, and side-problems.

3.2 Computer Programmes

Traffic studies of the type discussed above require computer programmes to manipulate the large quantities of data and the complex calculations. Many different versions of these are available which, although based on similar principles, differ in the ways they manage databases, carry out estimations, and present results. Choosing between these competing models depends on a number of criteria: their ease of use, the range of alternative assumptions which can be built in, the speed of execution of calculations based on alternative assumptions and the degree of fit between forecasts and outturns.

One problem with such models is that they are often developed for a specific set of circumstances and are not easily transferable between different geographical locations, even within countries. The commercial nature of the organisations developing such models has not always led to convergence on the use of the best elements of different approaches, although there have been some attempts to verify the predictions of different models against each other.

3.3 Comparisons of Forecasts and Reality

The availability of many different models would suggest that the best practice would have been identified leading to high levels of forecasting accuracy. Unfortunately the accuracy of traffic forecasts is low as shown by

Demand and Costs

Table 4.9 for French motorways. Although on average actual traffic was overestimated by a small margin of 2 per cent, there were enormous variations with over–estimations of 25 per cent and under–estimations of 70 per cent. The UK National Audit Office (1988) came to the similar conclusion, that traffic forecasts for British motorways, were largely inaccurate, but unpredictably so.

Table 4.9 Actual against forecast traffic, French autoroutes

Autoroute section	Actual/forecast traffic (% error)
A8 – Aix-Fréjus	-3.2
A61 – Toulouse-Narbonne	+5.3
A10 – Poitiers-Bordeaux	+6.3
A81 – Le Mans-Rennes	-21.6
A40 – Macon-Genève	+54.4
A42 – Lyon-Pont d'Ain	+48.4
A62 – Bordeaux-Toulouse	-5.8
A11 – Angers-Nantes	-25.3
A31 – Toul-Langres	+0.9
A11 – Le Mans-Angers	+69.2
A72 – Clermont Ferrand-Saint-Étienne	-21.2
A71 – Bourges-Clermont-Ferrand	-12.5
A51 – Aix-Manosque	-11.1
A26 – Reims-Arras	-15.3
Mean	-2.0

Source: SETRA (1993)

A detailed survey of the discrepancies between forecasts and reality for most of the large transport infrastructure projects all over the world leads to the same conclusions (Skamris and Flyvbjerg, 1996). Important errors appear (Table 4.10), and they are biased towards over-estimation, suggesting strategic biases by the analysts, usually reporting to the promoters of the project. These biases seem to appear irrespective of whether the promoter is in the public or private sector.

Flyvbjerg *et al.* (2003) surveyed 210 projects (27 rail and 183 road) worldwide. For rail projects they identified that in 85 per cent of cases there was an error of more than 20 per cent in forecasts and on average traffic was 39 per cent lower than that forecast (i.e a 65 per cent overestimate on average). For road projects forecasts were more accurate, on average traffic was 9 per cent higher than forecast, but there were still 50 per cent of cases where the error was more than 20 per cent. They identify seven reasons for inaccuracy:

- methodological problems
- poor data
- behavioural change
- unexpected exogenous factors, e.g. unpredicted changes in fuel prices
- unexpected political factors
- appraisal bias of consultant
- appraisal bias of project promoter

Table 4.10 Discrepancies between forecasts and reality for several studies

Projects	Under–estimation 0 to 20 %	Over–estimation 0 to 20 %	Over–estimation 20 to 50 %	Over–estimation > 50%
Metros in developing countries (source TRRL)	1	1	2	5
Roads in United Kingdom (source TRRL)	5 %	10 %	25 %	60 %
Bridges and tunnels in Denmark	1		2	
10 suburban railway projects in USA	Over–estimation by an average of 61%			

Source: Skamris and Flyvbjerg (1996)

However, these results are not as unsatisfactory as might appear. First, projects are rarely implemented in the same way as the traffic forecast has assumed due to modifications made during construction or a change in circumstances during a long construction period. Second, forecasts assume the prediction of an equilibrium value which is assumed takes place instantaneously, whereas in reality traffic takes time to attain its final value. SNCF French Railways has shown that that for new TGV services this delay is roughly of about 3 to 5 years.

Furthermore, when forecasts have to be made for a long period into the future many of the assumed exogenous variables, such as the price of fuel, the growth rate of GDP and the political situation may all change.

3.4 Directions of Improvement

There are deep-seated reasons for the inaccuracy of models, the temporal horizon is often badly defined, and long; transport demand is derived from that for other activities, the means of production of which may be changed to use relatively more or less transport.

3.4.1 Short timescales: dynamic models

At one point on the timescale, where adjustment can take place over a short period, less than one hour, the previous models fit badly because they are based on stationary situations, when in reality traffic conditions are constantly changing between departure and arrival time, especially in congested situations. In practice, users adapt their behaviour, mainly through changing departure times, but also through changing route, or even in some circumstances destination. These characteristics require the development of dynamic models which allow for real-time adjustments of traffic to changing circumstances. These models permit the achievement of other goals such as the evaluation of new policies (modular pricing, modular access control, implementation of flexible and staggered hours, parking management, information to road users), and the design of new technologies such as users' information and road guidance technologies.

Dynamic models are presently used mainly for route choice decisions by explicitly taking into account time variations of demand. Time is split into blocks of about one minute and in many models users can choose their departure times according to their desired arrival time and the traffic conditions. The model uses a generalisation of the first Wardrop principle (Wie *et al*, 1995) in which for each O-D pair, the total cost for each possible O-D pair at each departure time is equal and minimised for all pairs where traffic is non-zero.

De Palma and Marchal (1996) and de Palma *et al*. (1997) have developed the Metropolis model, which has been adapted to large networks, such as important parts of the Ile–de–France region. This model is based on a learning process of the users, which takes into account some imperfect knowledge of congestion in order to choose at the same time the hour of departure and the route. Metropolis can simulate traffic for large-scale urban networks up to several thousands of links. It combines a graphical interface with a core simulator that models traffic congestion in large urban areas, describing minute by minute the congestion on each link of the car network. The users' decisions that are modelled are the mode choice, the departure time choice and the route choice.

The exogenous parameters are not numerous, many of them are calibrated through the model itself. Metropolis is mesoscopic on the supply side (it uses speed/occupancy functions) and microscopic on the demand side (vehicles are simulated individually). It is a fully dynamic model in the sense that departure time is modelled endogenously and that it does not require the acquisition of dynamic O–D matrices. Indeed, the input data requirements of the model are very small: a coded network (oriented links, nodes and zones), a set of congestion laws on each link (speed/occupancy functions), a static O–D matrix and behavioural parameters about users' schedule constraints. The output data consist of the dynamic patterns of the traffic variables (speed, flow and density) on each link and at any time of the simulated period. The simulator also outputs indicators about the users' schedules, delays, schedule delay costs, collected tolls, etc. Metropolis offers several other useful modelling features. Figure 4.6 illustrates, as an example of the output, the distribution of departure times.

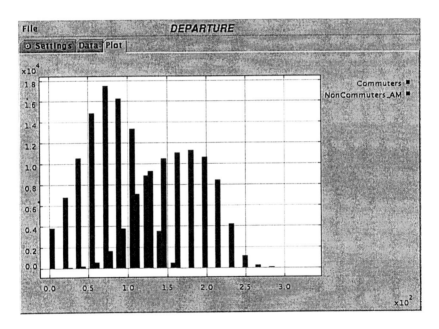

Figure 4.6 Metropolis output on distribution of departure times

3.4.2 Long timescales: location models
At the opposite end of the timescale, where adjustment may take several years, changes in transport supply lead to changes in the number of trips, changes in vehicle ownership and, more fundamentally, in the location of home or work. In the previous models it was not clear which of these effects

were actually taken into account; a priori all long term decisions are embedded in induced traffic, but this induced traffic is the most difficult part to model.

This suggests the need for location models which integrate both transport and land use, the principles of which have been presented in Chapter 2, in the framework of the explanation of locations between regions. Here we present an urban model, building on Webster *et al.* (1988), Anas (1987) and Clement (1996).

These models comprise three parts:

- A 'transport' model which defines, for a given transport system, and given locations, the transport flows and costs. This part describes the equilibrium of the transport market, through sub-models analogous to those which have been described previously.
- An 'economic' model, generally based on input-output matrices. The activities of a zone are classified into base activities, which are exogenously given, and other activities, the level of which is determined by the level of domestic demand, itself depending on the location of households.
- A 'land use' model, which aims at determining the locations of households and firms, based on the Von Thünen model (see McCann, 2001, for a more detailed discussion of such models).

In these models time is split into several periods, each one of around five years. They are very exacting in data provision, as they require knowledge of household characteristics and the production structure for each of the zones into which the area studied is divided. Nevertheless, despite the difficulties of implementation, these will be more and more widely used as they allow a better integration of transport and land-use policies, and they provide insights on the distributional effects of transport policies on the geographical level (Wilson, 1998). This has particularly been possible with the development of both GIS (Geographical Information Systems) as a means of obtaining and using large quantities of spatial data, and of micro-simulation studies which enable better representation of household behaviour.

3.4.3 Transport as a derived demand and activity models

Activity models aim at taking into account the fact that transport demand is a derived one. Trips are the means of achieving a programme of activities mixing imposed needs and individual preferences. Furthermore, these activity patterns are conditioned by more or less rigid constraints in terms of their duration and their location in time and space (Fischer, 2000).

There is a large diversity in travel behaviour; behaviour does not result from individuals undertaking a formal optimisation, but from a progressive learning process, which displays both inertia or a routine elements and a random character. Modelling such behaviour poses several problems, and especially the difficulty of defining precise categories of behaviour. Furthermore, behaviour is increasingly determined not just by the individual acting independently, but by factors affecting the household in which the individual lives.

Activity models have two kinds of outcome:

- First, the construction of computer programs to model the decisions resulting from new transport conditions (Ben Akiva *et al.*, 1996).
- Secondly, to induce an improvement of the traditional models, for instance through the incorporation of new socio-economic variables in them, as for instance in the Matisse model (Morellet 1997).

4. FREIGHT TRAFFIC MODELS

Freight transport modelling has not been developed to the same extent as passenger travel modelling (Vickerman, 2003a). Most models start from a potential volume of freight to be forwarded, which is then distributed between the various modes, according to the performances of the modes in terms of cost, time and reliability. Route choice is preceded by the translation of tonnages into the number of vehicles, generally through a simple ratio. This type of model is used in particular in multi-regional studies; trade between regions is modelled through distribution models linking the share of one region in the imports or exports of another to the accessibility of the regions.

More sophisticated models integrate several of these steps, for instance through a nested model, which takes into account the fact that freight transport is just one part of the total logistics policy of a firm, including the management of inventories and the size and frequency of shipments (McKinnon, 2003). This requires disaggregated models. But even if they are more satisfactory in terms of explanatory power, they are more difficult to use for forecasting, because they need a lot of input data at the level of the firm, data which are often not available.

Regional models of the type seen in Chapter 2, analyse generation and distribution together using regional input–output matrices. Here the demand of one region for a particular product is satisfied by 'domestic' production and 'imports' coming from other regions. The transport flows implied by the satisfaction of these demands can be modelled by logit models which use information on the prices of production in each region and the costs of transport between the two regions.

Modal split models use the value of time for freight as an input parameter. This parameter can be estimated in a similar way to that for the determination of passenger values of time. For example, Calzada and Jiang (1996) and Jiang and Calzada (1997) have explored both opportunity cost methods and revealed or stated preference methods. De Jong and Gommers (1992), using stated preference data, have also shown the importance of reliability, which seems to be as important as time and the risk of damage to the goods.

5. CONCLUSION

A tremendous amount of knowledge has been gained through the analysis of demand, both in terms of the data collected and the theoretical refinements of modelling. However, the accuracy of forecasting is much lower than would be expected in the physical science or engineering sciences and much lower than is desirable given the costs of the investments often being modelled.

The best developed elements are those for modal split and route choice. When correctly applied, these can lead to useful and accurate forecasts. This is less true for generation and distribution models. These are more crude; for instance neither phase routinely takes into account the importance of the quality of transport, for both passenger and freight traffic. This is understandable since the effects of transport improvements on generation and distribution take a long time to be realised and are therefore difficult to determine, often being mixed with many other changes.

These changes are particularly relevant in the long run where such features as urban sprawl and increasing freight transport intensity have been observed and taken as evidence of poor forecasting. However, other factors such as the growth of information technology and telecommunications have also had a major impact on both the total demand for transport and its distribution. This has not typically resulted, as might have been expected, in a reduction in the need for transport (Crowley, 1997; Madre, 1997). Thus firms can use better information technology to improve the quality of transport and lower its overall cost; use of the telephone or the Internet by consumers purchasing goods may substitute several delivery trips for a single shopping trip; tele-commuting by workers may lead to their moving residence further from the workplace thus reducing the number of commuting journeys, but increasing the total distance travelled within a working week and possibly substituting non-commuting journeys for the journey to work saved.

The development of intelligent transport systems (ITS) will also change traffic management through development of more efficient use of vehicle fleets, an increase in road capacity, and a consequent decrease in travel time, congestion and accidents. This may work against the tendency for the price of transport to be increased through higher fuel prices and attempts to make all modes of transport cover their full costs including all the environmental impacts. Due to these probable dramatic changes, demand analysis will need to be reconsidered in the near future; new models and consideration of new explanatory factors and new parameters will be needed, and it is probably one of the most exciting challenges of transport analysis to try to prepare for this new era.

5. The Costs of Transport

The previous chapter has introduced the cost of transport for the user as an element in the determination of demand. But the concept of transport cost, in a wider sense, goes far beyond this definition, which has so far included only the direct expenses of road users, or the price of the ticket for public transport users, and the non-monetary costs directly borne by the user such as time taken. In addition we need to include the non-monetary costs borne by the rest of the community; these include infrastructure costs, conventionally borne by public authorities, environmental costs and accident costs. Also for public transport, there are the costs borne by operators, which are not necessarily equal to the price of the ticket.

Table 5.1, based on Greene *et al.* (1997), provides a schematic outline of the different types of cost involved in transport, according to who bears them, who causes them, and also according to whether they are tradable or not, internally or externally.

Knowledge of costs is necessary for the decision-maker. At a micro-economic level, detailed information on costs, on the factors which govern variations in costs and the distributions of these variations, are the basis for decisions such as pricing, investment choice, and the management of transport enterprises. At a more general level, that of a country or a city for instance, knowledge of costs is necessary to inform public debates about modal shares, charging for infrastructure, or equity issues. For those purposes, it is necessary to know, not only the level of costs, but also the cost function which shows how costs vary with respect to various parameters.

There are various ways of gaining this information. First, it is possible to use the accounting framework of firms; but accounts provide information only the present level of costs, they do not give information on the cost function.

Another way is to simulate the expenses which a firm would incur to provide a given service. This method is based on engineering knowledge and has been used quite frequently in the past on transport questions due to the dominance of engineers in the development of transport planning. The method most frequently used by economists is based on statistical analysis of data on traffic, pertinent parameters, and costs. We discuss this approach in subsequent sections. Assumptions on the shape of cost functions and their properties, are discussed in the first section. A section is devoted to each of the categories of costs we have identified above: monetary costs, expenditure of time, infrastructure cost, environmental costs, costs of safety provision and operator costs. Some empirical evidence is presented in a final section.

Table 5.1 Structure of transport costs

Total costs	External costs	Environmental costs	Fauna and flora Energy Noise Pollution of air, water and soil Landscape Vibration
		Congestion Accidents Use of space	
		Infrastructure costs	
	Internal costs	Private costs	Fuel Maintenance Repairs Insurance Taxes Depreciation

Source: Based on Greene et al. (1997)

1. COST FUNCTIONS: THEORETICAL BASIS

We start by summarising the general properties of cost functions. The cost function of a transport operator is the minimal cost which must be incurred to produce a given quantity q (which can be either a scalar, or a vector in the more general case of a multiple product operator). If the operator can use production factors x, y, z, the prices of which are p_x, p_y, p_z, the cost function can be written:

$$C = C(q, p_x, p_y, p_z)$$

From this function, we can define some key economic concepts:

- marginal cost: $\dfrac{\partial C}{\partial q}$

- economies of scale, which can be defined at two levels:

  the one global: $C(\lambda q) \le \lambda C(q)$ $\lambda \ge 1$

  and the other local: $\dfrac{C(q)}{q} / \dfrac{\partial C}{\partial q} \ge 1$

- the existence of a natural monopoly: $C(q) < C(q_1) + C(q_2)$

- given q_1 and q_2 such that $q=q_1+q_2$. Sufficient conditions for existence imply:

  economies of scale: $C(\lambda q) \le \lambda C(q)$ $\lambda \ge 1$

  and, if the firm is multiproduct, economies of scope: $C(q_1,q_2)<C(q_1, 0)+C(0, q_2)$

To conclude this synthesis, it should be noticed that production functions and cost functions are not simply determined by the techniques of production and the prices of inputs. They also depend on market structures; for example a market with poor competition induces low productivity efforts and results in increased costs. The same occurs when a firm is linked to a customer by a contract with a low incentive, for example where there is asymmetric information.

2. THE MONETARY COST TO THE USER

For public transport the cost for the user is the price paid to the operator, which is in effect just a transfer from user to operator, the amount of which depends on the commercial strategy of the operator. For private transport, which forms the main focus here, a deeper analysis is necessary, and we concentrate on the example of costs for the car user. These comprise:

- A fixed part, paid yearly through insurance premia, annual licence fees, vignettes or permits, etc.
- A semi-fixed part, which is mainly composed of vehicle depreciation, and depends on the age and on the mileage of the vehicle.
- A part which is variable with the mileage, corresponding to maintenance, petrol, oil, tolls, etc.

BOX 5.1

Amortisation: an economic analysis

Given a durable good whose value decreases over time due to usage, obsolescence etc., for which the value at the start of year t is V_t , then the economic cost for the use of good during the year is given by:

$$A_t = V_t - V_{t+1} + iV_t$$

This can be demonstrated by considering that the user has financed the use of the good during year t through borrowing for one year the sum V_t corresponding to the purchase price, which costs:

- interest on the sum: (iV_t)
- repayment of V_t at the end of the year, reimbursement of V_{t+1} through resale of the good leaving the remainder as expenses to the user of $(V_t - V_{t+1})$

The relative shares of each of these parts and their total amounts depend on the type of vehicle, on its yearly mileage, and on the traffic conditions under which it is used. Fuel costs, maintenance costs and depreciation can be estimated by surveys of the costs incurred. In most countries the payment for infrastructure use is made by means of an annual licence fee which does not vary with usage; in some countries there are tolls for the use of specific types of highway which can either be a fixed annual fee (such as the 'vignette' system for the use of major highways in Austria and Switzerland) or a direct user charge (as in France or Italy). These may be levied on all traffic or just on certain classes of vehicle (such as the 'Euro-vignette' system for heavy goods vehicles in some EU countries). There are other resource costs, such as parking, which are often inadequately accounted for (see Peirson and Vickerman, 2001, for a more detailed discussion of the conceptual issues involved).

Some evidence, taken from Roy (2000) on the mean total costs is shown in Table 5.2 for the users of small cars in the UK and France. The figures for large cars are about 1.5 times higher. The figures differ between countries because of differences in the annual kilometres driven (British vehicles are used more intensively) and due to differences in taxation.

These figures are the result of accurate economic calculations, but are they really used by the users in their decisions? Surveys show that there is a gap between calculated costs and cost as perceived users (Small 1992), the latter being lower than the real cost. In fact users tend just to take into account fuel expenses and underestimate other expenses, especially amortisation.

Demand and Costs

Table 5.2 User costs for small cars, UK and France(€/vehicle-km)

	Money price (including tax)	Tax
United Kingdom – London		
Small gasoline car, peak	0.562	0.117
Small gasoline car, off-peak	0.547	0.105
United Kingdom – Other Urban Areas	0.462	0.108
Small gasoline car, peak	0.449	0.098
Small gasoline car, off-peak		
United Kingdom – Non Urban Areas		
Small gasoline car, peak	0.308	0.099
Small gasoline car, off-peak	0.301	0.093
France – Urban Areas		
Small Gasoline car	0.497	0.127
Small diesel car	0.310	0.074
France – Non Urban Areas		
Small Gasoline car, toll motorways	0.576	0.202
Small Gasoline car, other roads	0.497	0.127
Small diesel car, toll motorways	0.382	0.145
Small diesel car, other roads	0.310	0.074

Source: Updated from Roy (2000)

3. TIME COSTS

Transport users spend time on making journeys, which can be expressed in money terms, using the concept of the value of time which was introduced in the previous chapter. The focus here is on the physical aspects of the time spent travelling. This is complex because travel time for a given journey is not fixed, but will depend on traffic levels, which implies that transport is a good of variable quality (Levy-Lambert, 1968) or subject to delay (Kolm, 1968). This variability varies according to the mode.

3.1   Road Congestion

Road congestion depends on the laws of traffic flow. Limiting ourselves to an aggregate analysis (as opposed to trying to model the behaviour of each vehicle in the flow), and taking into account just the situation of the flow of a given number of vehicles along an infinite road, the following relation holds:

$$D = \frac{V}{Q}$$

where:

V is the speed (distance covered by the vehicles in one unit of time)
Q is the flow (number of vehicles passing through a given section of the road within one unit of time)
D is the traffic density (number of vehicles on a unit length of road at a point in time)

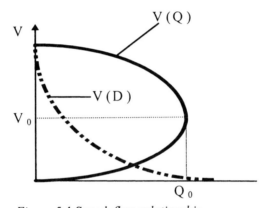

Figure 5.1 Speed–flow relationship.

Experience shows that speed V decreases with density D. It follows that the flow Q is related to speed according to the curve V(Q) which has the shape indicated in Figure 5.1. The upper part of this curve corresponds to a stable flow, the lower part to an unstable flow, where there is a low average speed, and a lot of stop and go, which happens in a situation of high density. Q_0 is the capacity of the road.

A typical algebraic expression for the relation V–Q, takes the form:

$$T = t_0\,(1.1 - A.S)/(1.1 - S)$$

where A is a parameter which characterises the type of road and, for example in France, takes the following values:

0   for urban roads in the centre of towns
0.3 – 0.5 for primary urban roads
0.666   for highways
0.92   for motorways

S is the ratio Q/Q_0

Q is the flow counted in pcu (passenger car units) a standardised measure
    of traffic volume

Q_0 is the flow at capacity or the saturation point.

This type of relation is valid only when $S < 1$, i.e. when the flow is lower
than the capacity of the road (the capacity of a road is generally estimated at
1800 pcu per lane).

Beyond this threshold, the following formula is generally used:

$$T=10t_0(1.1-A)/S^2$$

But this procedure is just an approximation. When traffic faces a bottleneck,
the capacity of which is lower than the traffic flow, in order to be more
accurate it is necessary to take into account the queuing process, in the way
indicated in Figure 5.2, drawn from Arnott *et al.* (1994), and originally from
Vickrey (1963).

Cumulative Flow

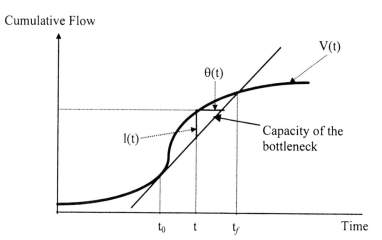

Notes: $V(t)$ cumulative upstream flow at time t
       t_0 time at which the queuing process begins
       t_f time at which the queuing process ends
       $l(t)$ length of the queue at time t
       $\theta(t)$ duration of the queue for the vehicle entering the queue at time t

Figure 5.2 Traffic flow through a bottleneck

3.2 Air Congestion

Congestion in air transport is quite different from road congestion in that it is
not simply expressed through an increase in the travel time. Its main effect is
a gap between the desired and the effective arrival time. When total traffic

exceeds the capacity of the runways or of the air traffic control system, flights have to be postponed or brought forward. The scarce resource of take-off or landing times, the 'slots', can be distributed arbitrarily by the airport or air traffic control authorities, or allocated through procedures such as auctions, or through 'grandfather rights' procedures which give priority to the existing users. Congestion in such a system is planned, it is not directly visible to the user, except in terms of an inconvenient timetable, flight times are not increased as long as there is no unexpected incident. When there is an incident which delays a flight, the immediately following flights have to be delayed too.

3.3   Rail Congestion

Rail congestion has the same features as air congestion; it is revealed in the gap between desired and effective arrival time in the published timetable. But it is much more complex in that there is a fixed infrastructure on which the speeds of all trains are not the same and their stopping patterns can differ. Unlike planes, faster trains can only overtake slower trains according to a pre-determined pattern according to the configuration of the tracks. This point clearly appears on a graph of time paths, as shown in Figure 5.3 which presents the example of trains between station A and station B. Each train is represented by a broken line, the slope of which is proportional to the speed of the train on each section, stops are represented by a step in the line. This diagram shows several features of the rail congestion problem.

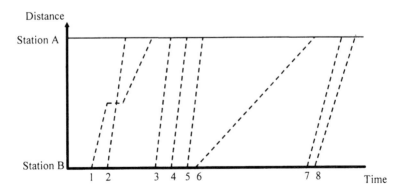

Figure 5.3 Rail paths

When the trains have the same speed (as in the case of trains 3, 4 and 5) the capacity is high. A slow train (train 6) takes much more capacity. In order to allow fast trains not to be penalised, it is necessary to stop a slower train

(train 1) in order to allow the faster train (train 2) to overtake. The characteristics of rail congestion are then clear. It does not occur where there are dedicated tracks used by trains with identical speed profiles, as in the case of the TGV, or where passenger intercity trains are run during daytime and freight trains are run during night. But congestion can be serious around large cities, especially at peak hours when the traffic is composed of a mix of trains with different speeds, slow commuting trains, fast intercity trains, and slower freight trains (especially for combined transport), all having strict arrival times, or on intercity routes where different trains have different stopping patterns to meet different traffic objectives.

3.4   Congestion in Urban Public Transport

Congestion in urban public transport is quite different from other situations. The core of the difference lies in the fact that on, for example, a metro line, the operator reacts to the volume of traffic. When demand increases, the operator increases the frequency of the service, decreasing the waiting time for all the users. There is an externality, but it is a positive one, as shown in Box 5.2, which develops a model drawn from Small (1992).

BOX 5.2

External cost of urban public transport
(based on Small, 1992)

Assume an urban public transport line, the flow on which is q, the operating cost of the buses is CV, each having a capacity of N, and the time interval between them is e. The travel time is θ, and the value of time is unity.

The operator has to solve the following programme:

$$\underset{e}{Min}\, C = q\theta + q\frac{e}{2} + \frac{c_v}{e} = C^* \text{ with } qe \leq N$$

There are two cases to consider:

1. $qe < N$

The optimal interval between two buses is $e = \sqrt{\dfrac{2c_v}{q}}$

The cost for the operator is $\dfrac{C_v}{e} = \sqrt{\dfrac{qC_v}{2}}$

which is an increasing returns to scale cost function, and the total social cost is $C^* = q\theta + \sqrt{2qC_v}$.

2) $qe = N$

the total social cost is $C^* = q\theta + \dfrac{N}{2} + q\dfrac{C_v}{N}$

The cost for the operator is $q\dfrac{C_v}{N}$, which is a decreasing returns to scale cost function

The move from the first process to the second one occurs for a flow such that $\dfrac{N}{q} = \sqrt{\dfrac{2C_v}{q}}$ or $q = \dfrac{N^2}{2C_v}$

In this limit situation, the waiting cost is equal to the cost of the operator.

4. INFRASTRUCTURE COSTS

Infrastructure costs have traditionally been borne either by public authorities (in the case of roads or inland waterways), or by operators more or less linked to the public authorities. This is still largely true for the public road network and in many countries rail infrastructure is provided by publicly owned companies, as is air traffic control, ports and airports. There has, however, been a strong trend towards privatisation of infrastructure, and even to the direct provision of new infrastructure by the private sector, although frequently the private sector enterprises operate subject to a franchise or concession granted for a limited period by the public sector and in almost all cases are subject to some form of regulation.

These organisations, whether public or private, exhibit some common features. First, the quality of the service they provide depends on the level of demand, through the mechanism of congestion as discussed above. Second, they provide, not a single service, but several services which may be differentiated by the nature of the transport (passenger or freight), or by time (which implies different qualities of service), or by the size of vehicle. Third, the production function, and thus the cost function, displays lumpiness and discontinuities. It is not possible to provide a fraction of an airport runway, motorways have an even number of complete lanes. For roads the possibility of roundabouts or grade separated intersections does provide some element of continuity in the service provided (Small 1992).

It follows that the cost function presented in section 1 of this chapter needs to be adapted to take into account these features, especially in the case of roads. The analysis concentrates first on this mode of transport, then on air infrastructures; railways are dealt with in detail in section 7 where we discuss operators' costs.

4.1   Road Infrastructures

Road infrastructures produce both a quantity of traffic and a quality of service, this quality varies according to the quantity. The cost function needs to include both elements, and can be expressed as (Small *et al.*, 1989):

$$C(q,Q) = qht(q,Q) + \rho K(Q)$$

where:

h is the value of time, assumed to be the same for each user
q is the traffic flow per unit of time, assuming that there is just one category of traffic and that the flow is the same over the time. It would be possible to relax this assumption in which case q would be a vector.
Q is the maximum capacity of the road
$t(q,Q)$ is the travel time for a user, which depends on the level of the traffic and on the capacity of the road
$k(Q)$ is the construction cost of the road whose capacity is K
$\rho K(Q)$ is the annual capital charge, including depreciation and maintenance costs, assumed here to be independent of the traffic level and proportional to the construction cost.

The short run marginal cost is thus:

$$\frac{\partial C}{\partial q} = ht(q,Q) + qh\frac{\partial t}{\partial q}$$

If Q can only be varied discretely, it is possible to draw a curve $C(q,Q)$ for each value of Q, and the long run cost function is the envelope of the lower parts of these curves for each value of q, shown as the bold line in Figure 5.4.

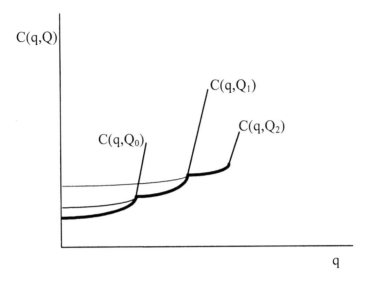

Figure 5.4 Long-run cost function with discrete capacity variations

If Q can be varied continuously, the long-run cost function is determined by:

$$\frac{\partial C}{\partial Q} = 0$$

or:

$$qh\frac{\partial t}{\partial Q} + \rho\frac{\partial K}{\partial Q} = 0$$

In order to clarify the central question of economies of scale, it is interesting to ask under what condition they are constant. It is easy to see that this will be realised if:

$$K = aQ$$

and if the function $t(q,Q)$ has the shape:

$$t = t(\frac{q}{Q})$$

Then the long-run cost function is determined by:

$$q^2 h \frac{t'}{Q^2} = \frac{\rho K(Q)}{Q}$$

and the long run marginal cost and the average cost are equal; the former is:

$$\frac{dC}{dq} = ht\left(\frac{q}{Q}\right) + \frac{q}{Q} ht'\left(\frac{q}{Q}\right)$$

and the latter is:

$$\frac{C}{q} = \frac{1}{q}\left(qht\left(\frac{q}{Q}\right) + \rho K(Q)\right) = ht\left(\frac{q}{Q}\right) + \frac{q}{Q} ht'\left(\frac{q}{Q}\right)$$

Turning to the evidence on the costs of roads, the evidence for interurban highways in France (Table 5.3) shows that construction costs increase with capacity, but at a decreasing rate.

Table 5.3 Costs and capacities of intercity highways

	Number of lanes	Capacity (PCU/hour)	Average cost (€mn/km)	Average cost per lane km (€mn)
Main road	2	2000	2.44	1.22
Main road	3	2700	3.43	1.14
Main road	2×2	4000 to 5000	4.43	1.11
Motorway	2×2	6000	6.11	1.53
Motorway	2×3	9000	7.63	1.27

Sources: Memento de la Route (1996) and Guide des Etudes de Trafic Interurbain (1992)

On the other hand, if the function $t(q,Q)$ does not have the form $t = t\left(\frac{q}{Q}\right)$ but exhibits increasing returns to scale then, for a given value of q/Q, t is a decreasing function of Q. This point is clear in the equation of the time-flow relation from section 3 above.

These two factors, acting in the same direction as each other, induce increasing returns to scale in intercity road infrastructures. The same is not true of urban roads where time-flow functions are similar, but construction costs are likely to be increasing with Q, due to land prices and environmental constraints.

It has been assumed thus far that the maintenance cost, included in the term ρK, is independent of the traffic flow. This is a simplification. Maintenance costs vary with traffic flow and depend on the weight of the vehicles. The relationship differs between the categories of costs. It is approximately proportional to the fourth power of axle-load for the pavement and proportional to traffic for other types of expenditure (Small, *et al.*, 1989; Brossier, 1991; Newbery, 1988b).

4.2 Air Transport Infrastructure

There is relatively little evidence on the cost functions for air transport infrastructure, as opposed to that for air transport operators. Here we look in turn at the cases of airports and air traffic control.

4.2.1 Airports

Keeler (1973) found constant returns to scale and Doganis and Thompson (1975) found the same result, with a Cobb-Douglas cost function. Tolofari, *et al.* (1990) studied the cost functions of British airports, using a translog cost function, providing evidence on variable costs, short-run marginal costs (excluding capital cost) and total costs, with optimised capital infrastructures, corresponding to long-run marginal costs. It was identified that:

- The short-run marginal cost is much lower than the average cost (the ratio is about 1 to 2)
- This result is due to the fact that airport infrastructures have tended to be of excessive size, actual capacity is larger than optimal capacity, partly due the indivisibility of infrastructures.
- In the case of optimal infrastructures, the returns to scale would be about 1.4

Current airport practice tends to lead to increasing returns to scale due to:

- The 40th peak hour, which is used to scale the infrastructure, is linked to annual traffic by the linear equation:

  40th peak hour = 400 + 3.5(annual traffic in million passengers)

- There are productivity effects in terminals: up to 20 million passengers, total costs increase less than traffic; and the same holds for variable costs.
- There are also returns to scale for runways.

These qualitative results are confirmed by Quinet (1992b) who used a Cobb-Douglas cost function to exhibit slight economies of scale (about 1.1) in French airports.

4.2.2 Air-traffic control infrastructures

This difficult field has been explored through productivity analysis which shows that the cost of air control depends on a number of various factors such as traffic flows, direction, hourly distribution, and displays far reaching geographical consequences (congestion in the Balearic Islands may cause delays in Amsterdam). However, there are almost no econometric studies; so only general assessments can be presented:

- For a given level of equipment, marginal cost is initially small, than increases (each air controller cannot deal with more than a maximum number of airplanes; the size of the sectors cannot be reduced without increasing the transaction costs between sectors).
- When the level of equipment varies, marginal costs decrease and the saturation level increases.

These considerations induce us to believe that there are increasing returns to scale, but how large are these? Best estimates suggest they lie between 1 and 2: the marginal cost is between half the average cost and the average cost.

5. ENVIRONMENTAL COSTS

Transport has substantial and manifold impacts on the environment:

- Noise
- Air pollution, both regional and global
- Barrier or segregation effects
- Ground and water pollution
- Landscape and aesthetic effects

Only the three first items have been subject to any rigorous monetisation, this being made difficult by the fact that environmental effects are external ones, and are not marketable goods. It is thus necessary to estimate the price through various surrogate methods.

5.1 Methods of Estimation

The most important methods are (following Pearce and Markandya, 1989, and Quinet, 1994b, on which this section is based):

Surrogate markets: which can be dealt with in a number of different ways:

- The cost of trips necessary to benefit from an amenity can be used to value that amenity; this method is used, for example, for the evaluation of leisure parks;
- The use of hedonic prices: the price of some marketed goods depends on their exposure to characteristics such as air pollution or noise. Variations in the price of the marketed good with respect to variations in the environmental factor can thus be used to estimate the implicit value which individuals attach to the environmental quality.
- Estimates of the cost of environmental protection. Observing the amount which individuals are prepared to pay to reduce or eliminate negative environmental effects provides an estimate of their implicit valuation.

These methods pose several difficulties. For instance, hedonic relations are not true demand functions. The residents of the most exposed houses may have chosen them partly because they are less sensitive to the environmental factor, e.g. noise, in which case the value of dwellings would decrease less than if the sensitivity were the same for everybody. Furthermore, there is the problem of distinguishing the individual impacts of each of the environmental variables, which are often closely linked to each other. Moreover, we have to assume for accurate hedonic valuations that people are well informed and aware of the damage caused by the nuisance at stake.

Contingent valuations: consist in asking people what they are willing to pay to avoid the nuisance, or what they are willing to receive in order to continue suffering from it. Difficulties of implementation are, however, numerous:

- In order to get reliable answers, it is necessary to devote a lot of care to devising the questionnaire, and to administer it through very sophisticated controlled procedures;
- Psychological biases lead to the result that willingness to pay to avoid a nuisance is consistently lower than the willingness to accept compensation to continue to suffer it;
- As is the case for other methods, the results can be biased by poor knowledge of the actual damage.

Indirect methods: avoidance cost, damage cost: are implemented in two stages. The first is technical and aims at estimating the consequences of the nuisance in physical units, for instance, in the case of air pollution, the frequency and significance of any impacts on health, or the damage to buildings. The second stage is the monetisation of the damage, either through the market prices for the damaged goods, or through the cost of repairing the damage, such as the health care costs of injured or sick people, or through more subjective valuations (e.g. the value of human life). This method gets round the problem of the lack of information, but monetary valuation of environmental damage is hazardous. For example, the cost of repair overestimates the willingness to pay when the repair is not actually carried out and the repair implies the definition of a zero level for the nuisance, and this definition is often arbitrary (in the case of noise for instance).

As can easily be seen, the methods of surrogate markets and contingent valuations estimate the willingness to pay of those who bear the nuisance; they deal with demand. Avoidance or repair costs deal with supply. If the decisions were optimal, these methods would produce the same result and the following double equality would hold (Figure 5.5):

Price = marginal cost = marginal willingness to pay

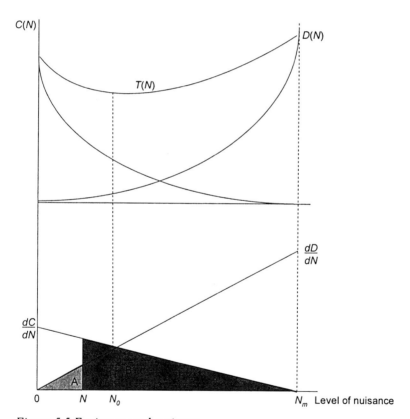

Figure 5.5 Environmental optimum

Figure 5.5 displays the total costs in the top part of the diagram and the corresponding marginal curves in the lower part. $C(N)$ represents the cost to the polluting producer, showing how marginal costs fall as the level of the polluting activity rises whilst $D(N)$ is the external cost of the polluting activity (willingness to pay for pollution reduction). Without any intervention the producer would seek to produce at N_m. The social optimum, where total costs, $T(N)$, are minimised is at N_0. If the polluting activity were reduced too far, say to N, then the gains from the loss of pollution would be outweighed by the loss of benefit to the consumers of the polluting activity.

However, in practice these methods do not provide equal values. Thus we have to take the decision as to which one to choose. The answer will typically depend on the nature of the problem which has to be solved (Quinet 1994b; Mauch and Rothengatter 1996).

Moreover, both cost and willingness to pay methods imply several different actors. In the case of noise, the willingness to pay is based on the willingness to pay of agents who actually suffer from the noise. Similarly, the protection cost function includes both the cost of a noise barrier, paid for by the public authorities, and the costs of double glazed windows paid for by the residents.

When the effect is permanent (in the case of global warming for instance), its valuation needs to include the effects on future generations. This raises two problems, how to estimate the value for these future generations and what discount rate to choose. It is often argued that three categories of values need to be taken into account, the sum of which is the total value of the good:

- the value in use, which corresponds to the actual revealed consumption of the good;
- the option value, which corresponds to the possibility of a future consumption of the good;
- the existence value, which corresponds to the value obtained by an individual who never consumes the good, but appreciates its existence so that other people can use it, or simply just as a resource.

These three values also exist for marketed goods, but it is often thought that option value and existence value are pre-eminent in the case of environmental goods, especially for the case of depletable resources. Cost of travel or hedonic prices only provide values in use; for contingent valuations the outcome will depend on how the questions are asked.

5.2 Valuation of External Effects – Evidence

It is clear from these considerations that the empirical results from valuation studies are likely to be extremely varied. We consider this evidence for each type of environmental damage in turn.

5.2.1 Noise

The effects of noise are not easy to measure. The most frequently used unit is the *Leq*, an integral, for a given duration, of the logarithm of the power of the sound, in which frequencies are weighted according to the sensitivity of the human ear. It is scaled in Decibel A (dBA). According to many authors, there is a difference of 5 dBA between the noise of railways and the noise of road traffic. The usual methods to value noise are hedonic: they are based on the loss of value of buildings associated with exposure to noise. The studies are remarkably consistent and suggest that an increase of 1 dBA induces about a 1 per cent reduction in the value of housing, the results of the different studies fall in the interval 0.5 per cent to 1.2 per cent (Kail *et al.* 2000). Studies using the contingent valuation methodology produce similar results.

Noise also has effects on health including impacts on the cardiovascular system and effects on sleep which impact on the general state of health. The most important studies of this effect have been in Germany (Infras-IWW, 2000), including that by Ising *et al.* (1995), which identify and measure the effects, but do not proceed to give them monetary values. One of the rare studies which does include monetisation concludes that these effects represent a rather small part of the total problem, perhaps 20 to 30 per cent (Weinberger, 1992).

5.2.2 Local air pollution

Local air pollution attributable to transport is caused by a number of chemical emissions from vehicles: nitrous oxides, which generate ozone, sulphuric oxides, non-burnt hydrocarbons, volatile organic particulates. These emissions cause damage to human beings, to animals and plants, and to buildings. There is considerable uncertainty about the size of these effects, especially about the long-term effects of particulates upon cancer. Valuation methods include the direct cost of any damage, the costs of protection against the emissions, and the willingness to pay to avoid damage (through contingent valuation procedures). There have been numerous studies to evaluate these effects (see Friedrich and Biekel, 2002).

This evaluation of environmental impacts involves a series of stages, from source to target, and from physical to economic impacts, known as the impact pathway (Figure 5.6). Several types of data and analytical techniques may be required, and each of these can affect the accuracy of the final results.

To take the example of air pollution, we must successively:

- Estimate, in kind and in quantity, the gaseous emissions produced by a transport activity.
- Determine how these gases move in the atmosphere, both in time and space, taking into account any chemical transformations they may undergo.

- Calculate the effect they will have on targets such as humans, wildlife, and buildings. If we take effects on health as an example, the result for this stage would be a number of deaths and sick persons, or in the case of wildlife, the number and kinds of animal species killed or made ill.
- Finally, the monetisation stage applies monetary cost values to these damages, including estimates of the value of human morbidity and mortality, plus losses of commodities such as reduced agricultural production.

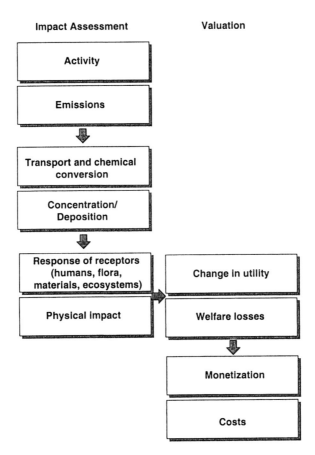

Source: Friedrich and Biekel (2002)

Figure 5.6 The Impact Pathway Approach

5.2.3 Global warming

The most important greenhouse gas is CO_2, emitted by the burning of hydrocarbons and transport (especially road transport) is the major producer of greenhouse gases. The increase of CO_2 in the atmosphere has been recorded since the beginning of the Industrial Revolution, and has induced warming of the atmosphere. Models aiming at forecasting this phenomenon provide a large range of estimates, between about 0.1 to 0.5 degrees per decade in the future. The consequences of global warming are various. Some species will disappear and sea levels will rise, so that some entire countries, like Bangladesh, may disappear. Studies which estimate the cost of this damage are scarce, and the bulk of them have concentrated on the consequences for North America, suggesting a decrease of US GDP of about 1 to 2 per cent. Other studies suggest that the consequences could be much more dramatic in other parts of the world such as Southern Asia or Southern Africa where the figure could reach 10 per cent. Table 5.4 provides a summary of some results (ECMT, 1998).

Table 5.4 Some estimates of the effects of global warming

Study	Basic hypothesis	Range of estimates (%GDP)
Nordhaus (1991)	2*CO_2 - 3°C	0.25%+... for omissions 1% most plausible estimate 2% maximum
Cline (1992)	2*CO_2 – 2.5°C	1%+...for omissions 2% possible/probable
	2*CO_2 – 4.5°C	2.1% – 4.3%
	Long-term – 10°C	6% – 12%
	Long-term – 18°C	13% – 26%
Tol (1994)	2.5°C – OECD	1.6%
	2.5°C – non OECD	2.7%
	2.5°C – whole world	1.9%
Fankhauser (1994)	2.5°C – OECD	1.3%
	2.5°C – non OECD	1.6%
	2.5°C – whole world	1.4%

Source: ECMT (1998)

On this basis, it is possible to estimate the cost of one tonne of carbon, through the calculation of the marginal cost of damage. The values depend critically on the assumptions and on the part of the world concerned. The effects for the US are quite weak, but those on Central Africa much greater. For Europe, estimates are in the range of €4 to €20 per ton of carbon (Friedrich and Bickel, 2002). Other studies have calculated the charges which would need to be imposed in order to reduce CO_2 emissions to an acceptable level. This level is in general taken as corresponding to the Kyoto agreement, but even using this assumption leads to results which are very sensitive to decisions over the market in emission rights and the time horizon. The expected values are between €20 per ton of carbon, the value used in the UNITE study (Nellthorp *et al.*, 2001) which corresponds to satisfying the Kyoto accords for Germany, and €135 per ton of carbon, which is the value used by Infras-IWW (2000) and which corresponds to the strongest reduction objectives for the year 2030.

5.2.4 Other environmental impacts

Current research is focussing on a varied range of impacts such as:

- upstream-downstream effects, which result in impacts on the environment arising from the construction of infrastructure or vehicles, the production of fuels, or the disposal of waste from scrapped vehicles. The evaluation methods are similar to those described above, but applied, not to transport itself, but its upstream and downstream effects.
- the effects of severance resulting in the segregation of habitats for fauna and flora and posing difficulties for humans in crossing the barrier created by the route of the infrastructure. These impacts can be evaluated in terms of the cost of re-establishing previous levels of communications.

The consequences for landscape and nature can be assessed either by the cost of restoring it to its original state or the cost of compensating local residents.

6. ACCIDENT COSTS

Problems of safety and the incidence of accidents is a characteristic of transport, particularly of road transport. In the EU, in 2000 there were 41 018 recorded fatalities for all modes, of which 40 812 were on roads, 22 517 in passenger cars. In comparison, only 92 railway passengers and 114 airline passengers were killed. There were nearly 1.3 million road accidents involving personal injury. Road fatalities have fallen by about a half since 1970 and by over a quarter since 1990 despite road traffic having increased by 2.4 times over that period. Accidents involving personal injury have fallen by only about 7 per cent since 1970 and have been static since 1990.

Accident rates differ substantially between modes and between countries (Table 5.5).

These accidents have an enormous cost, a cost which depends on the numbers of fatalities and injuries and the monetary value which can be placed on human life or on an injury. Determining this value is a controversial and sensitive issue.

Table 5.5 Accident rates, EU15, 2000

	Road fatalities/ billon pkm	Personal injury road accidents/ billion pkm	Rail fatalities/ billion pkm	Air fatalities/ billion pkm
Belgium	13.88	463.6	0.38	
Denmark	7.82	109.6	0.57	
Germany	10.37	529.3	0.51	
Greece	27.08	310.0	10.5	
Spain	17.40	306.7	—	
France	11.54	173.2	0.21	
Ireland	12.46	234.2	1.43	
Italy	9.64	318.6	0.18	
Luxembourg	14.90	176.5	—	
Netherlands	7.14	250.2	n.a	
Austria	14.10	608.4	0.48	
Portugal	21.38	511.0	0.56	
Finland	7.11	118.5	0.59	
Sweden	6.36	170.0	n.a	
United Kingdom	5.73	387.4	0.33	
EU15	10.77	342.0	0.36	0.40

Source: European Union Energy and Transport in Figures, 2002

6.1 The Value of Human Life

Let us first emphasise that the value of human life is a statistical concept, it represents the marginal value of an unidentified life, corresponding to the valuation of a small risk.

Two methods are currently used. The human capital method is the oldest one, based on the calculation of the discounted loss of production caused by the death. Several alternative approaches are possible. The loss of production can be calculated on either a net basis, excluding the discounted consumption which will not take place, or a gross basis, not excluding this consumption. The implementation of the calculation poses a number of difficulties: the choice of discount rate, to which the result is very sensitive; uncertainty over future levels of production, over a long period; and ethical considerations, the values associated with several groups of people, pensioners or the unemployed, are zero. In addition, this method takes no account of the value of pain and suffering.

The second method is based on willingness to pay, which can be implemented in two different ways. The first is based on revealed preference, such as the extra wage for risky jobs; the second is based on contingent valuation, through interview techniques. Contingent valuation is open to the difficulties already identified, plus the problem that people are often not aware of the actual risks from transport, and are not able to identify and evaluate the consequences arising from the very small risk levels implied by safety in transport. This is clear from the differences in the two possible values: what individuals are prepared to pay to reduce an already very small personal risk of death compared with what they are prepared to pay to reduce the risk of a fatal accident in the community at large.

Results are again widespread, the values given by human capital methodology being generally lower. The UNITE research programme of the EU (Nellthorp *et al.*, 2001) has assembled a large amount of evidence on the values of human life currently in use in different countries for the appraisal of investment projects (Table 5.6).

A further question is whether altruism influences the value derived from willingness to pay methodologies. Jones-Lee (1990) suggests that the value of human life procured by this method should not be modified in order to take altruism into account, provided that altruism is not influenced by the kind of good at stake (i.e. there is no paternalism).

A particular problem is to determine whether the value of human life should be the same in all transport modes. Taking as a basis the value of human life in road transport, let us consider the reasons why there should be any difference from other modes. The first, and simplest, reason is the difference in the socio-economic characteristics of the users of each mode. Of these, income is probably the most important factor; for this reason, the value of human life would normally be lower in urban public transport than for car users, and higher in interurban public transport, less so for standard or coach class passengers on trains or planes, more so for first or business class users. This effect is amplified by the fact that the choice of the mode is partially influenced by the value of life: people whose value of life is higher than the average (mostly people with higher incomes) are more likely to choose the safer mode, in much the same way as those with a higher value of time will choose the faster mode. Though this point is logically sound, it has

Demand and Costs

Table 5.6 Values of statistical life: proposed UNITE values by country compared to official values, 1998

Country	Official values in use (mn €)	UNITE VOSL (mn €)	(Official-UNITE)/Official %
Austria	1.52	1.68	10
Belgium	0.40	1.67	312
Denmark	0.52	1.79	244
Finland	0.89	1.54	73
France	0.62	1.49	141
Germany	0.87	1.62	87
Greece	0.14	1.00	588
Ireland	1.04	1.63	57
Italy	n.a.	1.51	–
Luxembourg	n.a.	2.64	–
Netherlands	0.12	1.70	1269
Norway	1.49	1.93	29
Portugal	0.04	1.12	2896
Spain	0.07	1.21	1625
Sweden	1.48	1.53	4
Switzerland	n.a.	1.91	–
United Kingdom	1.53	1.52	1
Hungary	n.a.	0.74	–
Estonia	n.a.	0.65	–

Source: Nellthorp et al. (2001)

never been introduced in transport modelling, which means at least that its size has not been important in estimates. Another reason why this effect does not appear is that people are not aware of the real conditions of safety in transport. Viscuse (1993) has shown that people underestimate risks in private transport, and overestimate them in public transport.

Another reason for a discrepancy between road and other modes as far as value of life is concerned is the correlation between the effort to reduce the risk and the willingness to pay for safety. According to Kolm (1970a), an improvement of a road implies a reduction of risk (for example through more prudent driving behaviour) which is greater for those who have a high value of life than for the others who trade off the possibility of increased safety which is offered to them against the possibility of higher speed on the improved road. The consequence is that public decisions should be taken with an average value of life lower than the average willingness to pay for safety of the users.

Jones-Lee and Loomes (1994) have suggested two more reasons for the difference between road and other modes: first the context effect, which means, for example, that people place a higher value on avoiding dying in a tunnel than dying in the open air. The difference between modes could be up to 50 per cent. A second cause is the mass effect: when a large number of people die together, the value of life of each of the fatalities is higher. This point is made clear by the impact on the media, but contingent analysis surveys of this issue do not show any clear statistical result. A theoretical justification for this kind of effect can be found in the behavioural theories of altruism and risk aversion (Galland and Quinet 1995).

These reasons support the idea of a value of life which is higher in public transport than in road transport. Jones-Lee and Loomes (1994), as well as Galland and Quinet (1995), suggest a ratio of 1.5 to 2. The last two authors give the following theoretical reasons. First, as public transport users have no direct responsibility for safety, they need to be more protected (this position can be justified through a model of imperfect information of the operator about the value of life of the users, coupled with decreasing returns in the technical function of safety procurement). Second, the mechanism of legal responsibility induces the managers of a public transport operator to spend more money than would an agent working with his own money. Moves to make operators and their managers corporately liable in the case of accidents have followed a recent spate of rail accidents in the UK. Individual behaviour in this respect appears perverse in that following rail accidents (despite all the evidence on the statistical greater safety), travellers switch to using their cars on much more risky roads.

6.2 Other Accident Costs

In order to calculate the costs of accidents, it is necessary to take into account, not only the value of human life, but also the cost of injuries and damage to property and the net loss of production due to the accident. The valuation of damage to property is of course based on the monetary cost of the damage. The value of injuries adds direct costs (medical care, transport of the injured people, etc.), indirect costs (loss of production) and an estimation, very subjective, of the pain and grief. Table 5.7 provides some evidence from the values used by the Swedish Road Administration in its evaluation of road investments.

There are some further issues in the evaluation of accident costs, especially for road traffic. First, there is disagreement on how far these costs are internalised through insurance and through drivers' willingness to pay to avoid accidents. Second, there are some interesting issues surrounding the extent to which accidents rates are related to, on the one hand, traffic flow, and on the other hand, speed.

Table 5.7 Components of costs of safety, Sweden, 1997

Components	Death		Serious injury		Minor injury	
	€000	%	€000	%	€000	%
Willingness to pay for safety	1484	91.1	234	79.9	10	60.7
Net loss of production	111	6.8	29	10.0	1.6	9.3
Hospital costs	4.0	0.2	22	7.5	1.2	7.1
Administrative costs	6.6	0.4	1.3	0.5	0.6	3.6
Material damage	24	1.5	6.4	2.2	3.3	19.3
Value of statistical life and injuries	1630	100	293	100	17	100

Source: Swedish National Road Administration (SNRA)

This gives rise to an interaction between congestion and accident rates: the more vehicles there are on a road, the more likely it is that they collide, but the greater is congestion, the lower are speeds and hence the less serious is the accident likely to be. Furthermore, as traffic volumes rise, drivers cannot be assumed always to behave in the same manner and simply accept an increased risk of collision. They are likely to modify their behaviour and this will reduce the likelihood of accidents (Peirson *et al.,* 1998; Dickerson *et al.,* 2000).

7. OPERATOR COSTS

7.1 Concepts and Methods of Analysis

Transport operators include airlines, road haulage firms, urban public transport operators, railway companies. A common characteristic of these firms are that they are multiproduct firms: they may carry both freight and passengers and within each category provide a range of different services to different groups of customers, but using a number of common inputs. The costs of freight and passenger transport are different, costs vary according to the destination or to the time of day. The cost function should ideally depend on a wide range of variables, which would be impossible to determine through statistical methods. This multiplicity of arguments can be replaced by a small number of statistical indicators which include for instance:

Total traffic expressed in passenger-km: Qv
and in tonne-km: Q_M
average weight: T
average length of haul: L
total length of the network: N

to give cost functions, called 'hedonic cost functions', written as:

$$C = C(Qv, Q_M, T, N, L)$$

Starting from this type of function, it is possible to define several indicators the value of which allows us to judge whether or not the activity is a natural monopoly:

- Economies of scale, estimated by an homothetic variation of all the arguments. Jara-Diaz and Cortes (1996) argue that all the characteristics of the network should not be included in this expression:

$$EE = \cfrac{C}{Q_v \dfrac{\partial C}{\partial Q_v} + Q_M \dfrac{\partial C}{\partial Q_M} + N \dfrac{\partial C}{\partial N} + T \dfrac{\partial C}{\partial T} + L \dfrac{\partial C}{\partial L}}$$

$$= \cfrac{1}{\varepsilon^c_{Q_v} + \varepsilon^c_{Q_M} + \varepsilon^c_T + \varepsilon^c_N + \varepsilon^c_T + \varepsilon^c_L}$$

  It is true that a proportional increase of the number of nodes and of the number of links is not consistent, and that it has no real economic or managerial meaning to increase both the traffic and the size of the network.
- Economies of density, calculated holding the network (number of nodes, length of the arcs) constant:

$$ED = \cfrac{C}{Q_v \dfrac{\partial C}{\partial Q_v} + Q_M \dfrac{\partial C}{\partial Q_M}} = \cfrac{1}{\varepsilon^c_{Q_M} + \varepsilon^c_{Q_v}}$$

In these equations, ε are the elasticities of the cost with respect to the indexed variables.
- Economies of scope can be approximated through the index:

$$\frac{C(Q_v,Q_M)-C(0,Q_M)-C(Q_v,0)}{C(Q_v,Q_M)}$$

Or through the concavity of the isocost function, such as:

$$C(Qu, QM) = Constant.$$

The most used frequently used forms of cost function are translog functions, second order expansions of the logarithm of the cost function. A particular case of translog function is the Cobb–Douglas function, expansion to the first order:

$$C = Q_v^a Q_M^b N^c L^d$$

The superiority of the translog function compared to the Cobb–Douglas is that the elasticity of substitution between factors can take any value whereas in the Cobb-Douglas it is restricted to unity or in CES functions of the type:

$$y = (\sum_j a_j x_j^\rho)^{\frac{1}{\rho}}.$$

it is restricted to a constant value.

7. 2   Results

Winston (1985) surveyed the cost functions of transport operators using an analysis based almost exclusively on economies of scale through Cobb-Douglas functions. These results showed important economies of scale in railways, but almost no economies of scale in other modes (Table 5.8).

Recent studies have made more extensive use of the translog function which more systematically takes into account the multi-product character of transport firms. The results of these studies slightly modify the conclusions which were drawn in 1985.

The most studied mode has been road freight transport, probably due to the wide availability of data. Harmatuck (1991) used a hedonic translog cost function distinguishing between truck load and less than truck load consignments, taking into account network characteristics. This estimated that scale economies were of the order of unity or rather larger, but that some important variations occurred in this value. Economies of scope depended on the firm in question, but it appeared that in general these were more important for larger firms, a result also identified by Harmatuck (1981) and by Chiang *et al.* (1984). Beuthe and Savez (1994) analysed cost functions for long distance road haulage in France, distinguishing three types of transport, tankers, refrigerated vehicles and others, finding a variety of results, but with a tendency for small scale and scope economies, similar to Harmatuck (1991).

Table 5.8 Cost elasticities in the production of transport

Study	Functional form	Type of production	Mean cost elasticity
Rail			
Keeler (1974)	Non linear	Multiple	0.57
Harris (1977)	Linear	Simple	0.64
Friedlander and Spady (1981)	Translog	Mulrtiple	0.895
Caves *et al.* (1981)	Translog	Multiple	0.605–0.716
Jara-Diaz and Winston (1981)	Quadratic	Multiple	0.352–0.787
Road haulage			
Koenker (1977)	Log-linear	Simple	>1
Spady and Friedlander (1978)	Translog	Simple	>1
Spady and Friedlander (1978)	Translog	Simple	<1
Harmatuck (1981)	Translog	Multiple	=1
Wang and Friedlander (1981)	Translog	Multiple	=1
Airlines			
Eads *et al.* (1969)	Non linear	Simple	≥1
Keeler (1972)	Linear	Simple	=1
Douglas and Miller (1974)	Semi-log linear	Simple	=1
Caves *et al.* (1984)	Translog	Simple	=1

Source: Winston (1985)

Other studies have concentrated on the effects of networks. Walker (1992) used a simulation study to investigate the effects of size and number of firms to serve a market of given geographical structure coming to the conclusion that scale economies existed in such a situation. Callan and Thomas (1992) used a translog function to examine the effects of the composition of loads and the size of networks, identifying economies of density, but not economies of scale.

By use of linear regression these studies assume implicitly that the explanatory variables are exogenous, and not determined by the firms. In the regulated markets which existed prior to the 1980s this was not an

Demand and Costs

unreasonable assumption, but in a deregulated market in which firms can determine their own optimum network size, average length of haul, mean load size etc., this requires a simultaneous equation approach. These tend to suggest a greater significance of scale economies. Xu *et al.* (1994) analysed the cost functions for less than truck load traffic in the deregulated market in the US (1988-90). Using a translog function with the equations:

$$C = f(TM, D, T) \qquad (5.1)$$
$$D = g(TM)$$
$$T = h(TM)$$

where   .

C is total cost
TM is output in tonne-miles
D is average length of haul
T is average load

The results (Table 5.9) show first that there is a significant positive correlation between D and TM and between T and TM, suggesting that large firms specialise in long distances and large loads. They also suggest that the estimated elasticities of the cost function will be biased if these simultaneous relationships are not taken into account as shown below.

Table 5.9 Scale economies in truck traffic

Variables	Coefficients	
	Single equation model	Simultaneous equation model
TM	1.08 (0.038)	1.13 (0.035
D	-0.07 (0.074)	-0.55 (0.074
T	-1.40 (0.089)	-0.93 (0.087)

Source: Xu et al.(1994)

Simple regression suggests a weak influence of distance D, but the more complete model suggests a much larger and significant effect, and distance and average load are strongly correlated with total traffic, TM. Large firms operate in long-distance markets where they can compensate for the lack of large scale economies by increases in distance, load size and thus gain a cost advantage which can be used to reinforce market dominance through the use of information technology, more diversified services, wider geographical coverage or a greater financial capacity.

These considerations can also be applied to other modes of transport. Studies of air transport have identified substantial network economies and scale economies close to unity (Kirby, 1986, for internal Australian carriers; Oum and Zhang, 1991; Gillen *et al.* 1990, for Canadian companies; Caves *et al.*, 1984, for American companies). These studies have demonstrated the importance of the multiproduct character of air transport, the number of locations served, the length of links and the density of traffic. Oum and Zhang (1997) used the methodology of Xu *et al.* (1994) and the data of Caves *et al.* (1984) to show that, taking into account the correlation between length of haul and the size of firm, scale economies were rather larger than initially believed.

Evidence on cost functions for bus transport is more scarce. Berechman (1983) suggested substantial scale economies in the Israeli bus industry in contrast to earlier studies. Tauchen *et al.* (1983) also found scale economies for small companies, but close to constant returns to scale for large companies, but with substantial economies of scope between scheduled services, school transport and charters.

Rail cost functions have two main characteristics: first, they cover both infrastructure and services; second, for rail there is a less close link between the level of capital and the level of production. Taking these factors into account there is evidence of significant network economies as shown by McGeehan (1993) for Ireland and Preston (1994) for 14 European railways. Scale economies depend on the size of the network according to Preston (1994), greater than unity for the smaller networks (Switzerland, Portugal, Belgium, Netherlands), but less than unity for the larger networks (UK, France, Germany). Cantos (2000) for Europe and Ivaldi and McCullough (2001) for the USA applied translog functions to railway data allowing for complementarities between infrastructure and operations and passenger and freight services. The results showed that infrastructure and freight services are complements, but infrastructure and passenger services are substitutes. Friedlander *et al.* (1993) used a translog variable cost function dependent on the characteristics of the product carried, length of the network, length of haul and level of equipment, to study the costs of 27 US rail companies over 12 years. This suggested that almost all companies had an oversupply of capital, but that there were significant network economies and rather weak scale economies.

As a whole, it appears that economies of scale in railways are less than thought ten years ago and much less important than economies of density. Economies of scale and density are generally constant in road haulage, although it is also possible to find situations of increasing returns to scale. Air transport is in an intermediate situation. These results depend on the geographical structure of the networks, and on the degree of optimality of the capital goods. It is also clear that firms can use their size to choose niches in the market which allow them to compensate for the negative effects of any diseconomies they incur; large firms compensate for any decrease in the economies of scale due to their size by economies of density and longer average hauls.

8. EMPIRICAL EVIDENCE

It is much more difficult than might be thought to provide a simple guide to estimates of total transport costs. Despite attempts to synthesise the results of various studies, a survey of some recent studies suggests that these are heterogeneous both in the way they are presented and in the definition of the types of costs. Some general remarks are possible:

- The types of cost included are almost exclusively social costs: external costs and costs incurred by public authorities. Monetary costs for users are rarely calculated and time costs are treated in a very heterogeneous manner: these can be marginal cost, average cost, or the additional cost incurred relative to some situation of 'normal' traffic speed.
- The distribution of costs is also arbitrary: in several types of costs, such as infrastructure costs or operator costs, there are important fixed costs, the distribution of which can be achieved through various methods between which it is difficult to choose (see Box 5.3), but which lead to very different results. Furthermore, some authors calculate a short-run cost including congestion costs, but not infrastructure capital costs, others calculate a long-run cost, including infrastructure capital costs.
- The calculations are often made in order to compare what users pay (through taxes, charges, etc) and what they cost to the nation, rather than as an estimate of resource costs.
- There are large differences between American and European results, due mainly to fuel taxes, which are much lower in the former. American studies, however, usually take into account parking costs, while European ones generally do not (see Calthrop *et al.*, 2000)

BOX 5.3

Some aspects of the distribution of fixed costs

The distribution of the fixed costs of a multi–product activity has no uncontestable solution. This problem can be seen both from an efficiency point of view, where the outcome is a formula of the Ramsey-Boiteux type and from an equity point of view, which we develop further here.

Let us take the situation where various kinds of traffic – we assume that there are three of them – bear only fixed costs. The total cost is

$$C(q_1, q_2, q_3)$$

and the incremental costs are:

$$C(q_1, 0, 0); C(q_1, q_2, 0)$$

It may seem sensible to allocate to each traffic the extra costs it gives rise to, but this extra cost depends on the order in which we introduce the types of traffic, such that;

$$C(q_1, q_2, q_3) - C(0, q_2, q_3)$$

is generally different from:

$$C(q_1, q_2, 0) - C(0, q_2, 0)$$

It may also be tempting to use an allocation such that no subset gains by merging with another to build and use another infrastructure. This idea leads to the core of the cooperative game, the characteristic function of which is C. But the core may be empty (this situation happens if the monopoly is not sustainable). Let us take the case of three types of traffic which require two lanes, while two types of traffic require only one lane. In algebraic terms:

$$C(q_1, q_2, q_3) = 2$$

and for any other combination:

$$C = 1$$

It is easy to see that there is no allocation P_i which satisfies:

$$P_1 + P_2 + P_3 = 2 = C(q_1, q_2, q_3)$$

and:

$$P_1 + P_2 \leq 1$$

and similar relations obtained through permutations of this.

Another possible procedure is to take a weighted average of the possible incremental costs, for instance for traffic q_i

$$P_1 = \tfrac{1}{3}((C(q_1, q_2, q_3) - C(0, q_2, q_3)) + \tfrac{1}{2}(C(q_1, q_2, 0) - C(0, q_2, 0))$$
$$+ \tfrac{1}{2}(C(q_1, 0, q_3) - C(0, 0, q_3)) + \tfrac{1}{2}(C(q_1, 0, q_3) - C(0, 0, 0)) + \tfrac{1}{3}C(0, 0, 0)$$

More generally:

$$P_i = \frac{1}{n!}\left(\sum_{s=0}^{s=n-1} s!(n-s-1)! \sum_{\bar{s}} (C(q_{\bar{s}}, q_i) - C(q_., 0)) \right) + \frac{C(0)}{n}$$

In this equation $\sum_{\bar{s}} C(q_{\bar{s}}, q_i)$ represents all the possible combinations of choosing s products among the $(n-1)$ other than i, plus i. This allocation presents interesting properties: it is independent of the order of the products, it depends only on the incremental costs, and it provides a zero price for a product which costs nothing to produce. But it can lie outside the core of the corresponding cooperative game (Curien and Gensollen 1992).

Other allocation procedures, also based on cooperative games, have been developed, especially in the USA (see Quinet, 1997b).

8.1   American Studies

There have been many American studies which have been surveyed by Gomez-Ibanez (1995, 1997). They have focused mainly on road transport and typically exclude congestion costs and private costs for the user. Direction (1992) provides estimates of the costs per passenger-kilometre for the various transport modes in Canada. Levinson *et al.* (1996) provide the following figures (Table 5.10), in dollars per passenger–km, from an intermodal study on the Los Angeles – San Francisco corridor.

Table 5.10   Long-term costs on the Los Angeles–San Francisco corridor (US cents per passenger-km.)

Cost category	Air	High speed train	Freeway
Infrastructure (construction, maintenance)	1.82	12.90	1.20
Operator: capital	6.06	1.00	0.00
Operator: operational costs	3.40	5.00	0.00
Accidents	0.04	0.00	2.00
Congestion	0.17	0.00	0.46
Noise	0.43	0.20	0.45
Pollution	0.09	0.00	0.31
User: monetary cost	0.00	0.00	8.60
User: time	1.14	4.40	10.00
Total	13.15	23.50	23.02

Source: Levinson et al. (1996)

Littmann (1999) has provided a very full analysis of automobile costs in an urban context (Figure 5.7) including the value of time and the running expenses of the car.

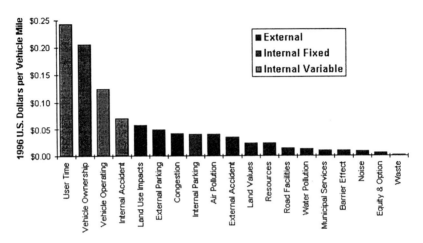

Source: Littman (1999)

Figure 5.7 Automobile costs ranked by size

8.2 European Studies

Examining costs according to their type Quinet (1994b) provides the following estimates, expressed as a percentage of GDP:

Monetary expenses:	14
Time:	8
Safety:	2
Pollution:	0.5
Noise:	0.3

A number of much more detailed studies have recently been carried out in different countries and at the European level. Sansom *et al.* (2001) have carried out one of the most comprehensive studies on data for Great Britain, aimed at calculating both full and marginal social costs of transport for several modes and comparing them to the revenues obtained from transport operation (Tables 5.11 to 5.14). These, based on data for 1998, show clearly that there are substantial differences between calculations based on full cost

Demand and Costs

and marginal cost bases such that although on average the users of the road network come close to covering the full costs on the basis of high cost estimates and cover more than double the costs on a low cost estimate, they only meet between one-third and one half of the marginal costs (Table 5.11).

Table 5.11 Road sector costs and revenues, Great Britain (pence/vehicle–km)

Cost or revenue category	Full costs		Marginal cost	
	low	High	low	high
Costs				
Cost of capital for infrastructure	0.78	1.34	n/a	n/a
Infrastructure operating cost and depreciation	0.75	0.97	0.42	0.54
Vehicle operating cost (PSV)	0.87	0.87	0.87	0.87
Congestion	n/a	n/a	9.71	11.16
Mohring effect (PSV)	n/a	n/a	-0.16	-0.16
External accident costs	0.06	0.78	0.82	1.40
Air pollution	0.34	1.70	0.34	1.70
Noise	0.24	0.78	0.02	0.78
Climate change	0.15	0.63	0.15	0.62
VAT not paid	0.15	0.15	0.15	0.15
Sub-total	**3.34**	**7.20**	**12.32**	**17.05**
Revenues				
Fares (PSV)	0.84	0.84	0.84	0.84
Vehicle excise duty	1.10	1.10	0.14	0.14
Fuel duty	4.42	4.42	4.42	4.42
VAT on fuel duty	0.77	0.77	0.77	0.77
Sub-total	**7.14**	**7.14**	**6.17**	**6.17**
Difference (cost-revenue)	**-3.79**	**0.07**	**6.15**	**10.88**
Ratio (revenue/costs)	**2.13**	**0.99**	**0.50**	**0.36**

Source: Sansom et al. (2001) Table B

However, there are substantial differences between types of vehicle (Tables 5.12 and 5.13). Most vehicle classes, except buses and coaches, more than cover their full costs on the basis of low cost estimates; only cars cover their full costs on the basis of the high estimates. No road vehicles cover their marginal costs, although this is of course averaged over the whole road network and hides the substantial variations which occur between different road types and different types of area. However, even on the basis of low cost estimates it is only on non-main roads in smaller towns and rural areas that cars cover their marginal costs (by about 2.5 pence/vehicle-km). In large conurbations the excess of marginal costs over revenue is of the order of 50 pence/vehicle-km and in Inner London it reaches more than 100 pence/vehicle-km. This shows how important it is to consider marginal costs rather than just make a comparison of total costs and revenues.

Table 5.12 Fully allocated costs and revenues by vehicle class, Great Britain (pence/vkm)

Category of vehicle	Revenues	Low cost estimates		High cost estimates	
		Costs	Costs– revenues	Costs	Costs– revenues
Car	5.6	1.6	-4.0	4.3	-1.2
LDV	5.6	2.4	-3.1	7.5	1.9
HGV-rigid	17.6	9.1	-8.6	22.0	4.3
HGV-artic	19.5	14.1	-5.4	29.9	10.4
PSV	83.6	106.1	22.6	128.1	44.6

Source: Sansom et al. (2001) Tables 7.2, 7.3

Table 5.13 Marginal costs and revenues by vehicle class, Great Britain (pence/vkm)

Category of vehicle	Revenues	Low cost estimates		High cost estimates	
		Costs	Costs– revenues	Costs	Costs– revenues
Car	4.5	10.1	5.6	13.8	9.2
LDV	4.5	10.8	6.2	16.6	12.1
HGV-rigid	17.6	24.1	6.5	38.2	20.6
HGV-artic	19.5	34.9	15.4	51.0	31.5
PSV	83.6	106.3	22.8	131.6	48.0

Source: Sansom et al. (2001) Tables 7.4, 7.5

The evidence for rail (Table 5.14), based on a mid-point between low and high cost estimates, shows a closer relationship between full costs and marginal costs. Passengers appear to pay something fairly close to the marginal costs of operation relative to train-km, although this will be less closely related to the costs per passenger-km, but passengers are being heavily subsidised on the basis of the full cost analysis. On the other hand freight seems to be paying a rather larger share than might be justified. If the argument for rail subsidy is to counter the under-charging of road, this might be rather odd given that it is freight vehicles which are more seriously undercharged than cars for their use of roads.

Table 5.14 Rail sector costs and revenues, Great Britain (pence/train km)

Cost or revenue category	Fully allocated cost		Marginal cost	
	Passenger	Freight	Passenger	Freight
Costs				
Infrastructure	5.33	3.41	0.42	1.19
Vehicle operating costs	7.07	9.28	7.07	9.28
Electricity	-	-	0.23	-
Congestion	n/a	n/a	0.18	0.00
Mohring effect	n/a	n/a	-1.05	n/a
Air pollution	0.46	0.68	0.46	0.68
Noise	0.16	0.37	0.16	0.37
Climate change	0.10	0.33	0.10	0.33
VAT not paid	1.32	n/a	1.32	n/a
Sub-total	**14.44**	**14.07**	**8.89**	**11.85**
Revenues	**7.52**	**13.41**	**7.52**	**13.41**
Difference (cost-revenue)	**6.92**	**0.66**	**1.37**	**-1.56**
Ratio (revenue/costs)	**0.52**	**0.95**	**0.85**	**1.13**

Source: Sansom et al. (2001) Table C

Although this study is one of the most comprehensive analyses carried out, it is only based on evidence for one country, Britain. For comparison Table 5.15 presents some evidence for Italy drawn from a study by Amici della terra and Ferrovie dello Stato (2002). Note that these are based on passenger-km and by converting the low cost estimate figures for car from Samson *et al.* to euro and assuming an average car occupancy of around two or less, gives very similar figures for total marginal external costs. The components of these costs do differ however with the Italian figures showing much greater pollution and accident costs but very much lower congestion costs. The latter dominate the British estimates.

Table 5.15 External costs by mode, Italy (€ cents/pkm or tkm 1999)

	Green-house gases	Air pollu-tion	Noise	Acci-dents	Con-gestion	Total
Road						
Passenger	0.74	2.37	0.75	3.27	0.99	8.11
Private use	0.81	2.45	0.80	3.67	1.08	8.80
Automobiles	0.83	2.52	0.52	3.19	1.18	8.23
Motorcycle	0.57	1.23	3.79	6.26	-	11.85
Moped	0.49	2.16	3.79	10.87	-	17.30
Bus, coach	0.24	1.72	0.37	0.27	0.33	2.93
Freight	1.04	7.26	2.09	0.77	1.35	12.51
Light vehicles	5.23	45.22	12.28	6,75	10.65	80.14
Heavy vehicles	0.78	4.94	1.47	0,40	0.78	8.38
Rail						
Passenger	0.31	0.88	2.46	0,16	0.07	3.62
Freight	0.33	0.65	4.16	0,05	-	5.19
Air						
Passenger	1.17	1.04	1.65	0.14	0.01	4.02
Freight	4.69	4.18	6.61	-	-	15.48

Source: Amici della terra and Ferrovie dello Stato (2002)

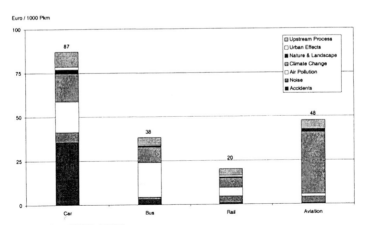

Source: Infras, IWW, (2000)

Figure 5.8 External costs, passenger traffic, 1995 (EU15, Norway, Switzerland)

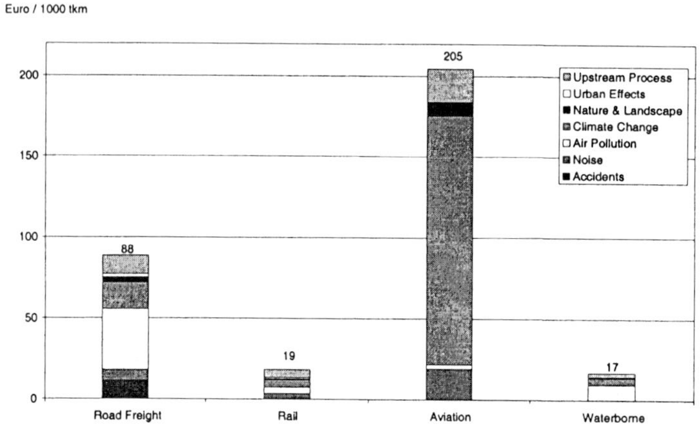

Euro / 1000 tkm

Source: Infras, IWW, (2000)

Figure 5.9 External costs, freight traffic, 1995 (EU15, Norway, Switzerland)

In a major study, Infras-IWW (2000) estimated the costs of accidents, noise, air pollution, climate change, nature and landscape, urban effects and up- and downstream effects for all modes, at the European level and for each European country (Figures 5.8 and 5.9). In addition, the costs of congestion have been estimated for several modes of passenger and freight transport (road, rail, aviation and waterborne transport). These are used to estimate total, marginal and average costs (per passenger or tonne-km). For car this gives very similar figures, €0.09/passenger-km., to the Italian and British studies; for other modes the comparison is not so close.

8.3   Monetary Costs

The costs faced by road users have already been discussed in section 2 of this chapter. Here we present some results concerning operators' costs from the same study (Roy, 2000). These are mean values (in € per passenger or tonne–km for 1995) around which we must expect considerable variation.

The figures include allowance for the cost of vehicles and load factors. Estimates are given for metropolitan regions, other urban areas and intercity transport (Tables 5.16 to 5.18). For urban public transport data is given for both marginal costs and the price to the user. Fixed costs are estimated to account for between 25 and 50 per cent of total costs, depending on networks and their form of organisation, frequencies and mode.

Table 5.16 Operator costs and revenues, metropolitan areas

	London		Ile–de–France		Dusseldorf	
Mode	Price for the user	Marginal cost ex VAT	Price for the user	Marginal cost ex VAT	Price for the user	Marginal cost ex VAT
Metro, peak	0.153	0.053	0.086	0.081	0.131	0.123
Metro, off-peak	0.124	0.030	0.086	0.130	0.131	0.050
Bus, peak	0.127	0.150	0.152	0.036	0.131	0.187
Bus, off-peak	0.113	0.140	0.152	0.407	0.131	0.070
Large truck, peak		0.037		0.092		0.153
Large truck, off-peak		0.037		0.093		0.149

Source: Roy (2000)

Table 5.17 Operator costs and revenues, other urban areas

	France		United Kingdom		Münster (Germany)	
Mode	Price for the user	Marginal cost ex VAT	Price for the user	Marginal cost ex VAT	Price for the user	Marginal cost ex VAT
Metro, peak	0.170	0.214	0.100	0.060		
Metro, off-peak	0.171	0.090	0.071	0.010		
Bus, peak	0.198	0.334	0.177	0.150	0.087	0.060
Bus, off-peak	0.198	0.254	0.153	0.130	0.087	0.020
Large truck, peak		0.090		0.044		0.152
Large truck, off-peak		0.090		0.044		0.152

Source: Roy (2000)

Demand and Costs

Table 5.18 Operator costs, inter-urban transport

Mode	United Kingdom	France	Germany (Westphalia)
Rail, peak	0.140	0.075	0.065
Rail, off-peak	0.055	0.057	0.037
Bus, peak	0.097	0.146	0.067
Bus, off-peak	0.078	0.136	0.025
Large truck, peak	0.039	0.092	0.153
Large truck, off-peak	0.054	0.090	0.150
Rail freight, peak	0.030	0.041	0.054
Rail freight, off-peak	0.030	0.041	0.054
Inland waterways		0.023	0.019

Source: Roy (2000)

9. CONCLUSION

The cost of transport is composed of elements which become less well known as we move from direct monetary costs of operation through infrastructure costs to environmental costs. Monetary costs for the car user should include an estimate of the depreciation of the capital value, but for most users amortisation is at least partly subjective. There is also some uncertainty about infrastructure costs; insofar as these costs bear an important part of fixed costs, the break-down of which is often arbitrary. Finally, environmental costs and safety costs and also, to a lesser extent, time costs, are subject to even more uncertainty, which is both physical (how much pollutant is emitted and suffered by the inhabitants?) and economic (what is the cost of the damage caused by these pollutants?).

Transport costs also vary according to a large number of factors: the type of the vehicle, the traffic mix, the location, the time, the nature of the infrastructure. If we just consider average values, this can lead to errors, as illustrated in Box 5.4.

An application of this fact can be found in many comparisons made between what some category of user pays and the true cost incurred. For instance, it is seen that on the whole, road users pay a bit more than the total costs imposed. But this reasoning, on the basis of averages, masks what a more precise analysis would show, that some categories pay far too little and some others pay too much. For example, there are differences between rural road users and those using urban roads in the peak, or between heavy truck users and light goods vehicles.

BOX 5.4

Errors stemming from averages

Let there be two modes F and R, the unit costs of which depend on one parameter L, uniformly distributed between 0 and L_1 (L may be for instance the length of haul or the size of the load).

$$CF(L)=a_F+Lb_F$$

$$CR(L)=Lb_R$$

The market is such that the loads for which $L<L_0 =(a_F)/(b_R - b_F)$ use R and the others F. Official statistics show an average cost (per km or per tonne according to the meaning of L) which is:

$CMR=b_R$ for mode R

$CMF=b_F+a_F/2(L_0+L_1)$ for mode F

And of course: $CMF<CMR$

A quick observation of the averages leads to a recommendation to transfer traffic from R to F. The error comes from the consideration of averages around which variations are not proportional.

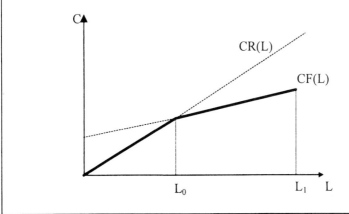

The same situation applies to returns to scale; the average result for a mode, for instance the fact that, on the whole, road haulage experiences constant returns to scale masks very different situations where some firms experience increasing returns while others experience decreasing returns.

Long–run changes are also important; monetary costs are decreasing in the long run, as we have seen in Chapter 1 in relation to changes in GDP, and particularly for certain modes such as the car. What the statistics do not show is that, at the same time, the quality of service has improved dramatically: compare, for example, the progress in speed, comfort and reliability of cars and airplanes during the last fifty years.

Meanwhile, as monetary costs decrease, other costs, those not borne directly by the user, are becoming more and more important. They still remain less important than the direct monetary costs, but their share is increasing. For infrastructure cost, this may be a transitory feature because of the need to match rapid increases in traffic by an appropriate increase in capacity, a situation which will not continue indefinitely. However, the situation will probably be more permanent for environmental costs. Their share in total cost has been growing, not least due to the increasing concern about them. Of course considerable action is being undertaken in order to reduce the emissions of pollutants, the effects on landscape, etc. and it is quite probable that in the near future some environmental effects will be mastered, such as local pollution due to NO_x. However, this abatement will take some time due to the cycle of vehicle renewal. Furthermore, it is probable that we will discover new effects either previously unknown or underestimated, such as, for instance, the long-term effects of particulates on cancer.

Thus we have seen that transport costs are marked by the divergence between the steadily decreasing evolution of direct monetary prices or costs and the tendency to increase of non-money prices or costs. Transport costs are becoming more and more external, and this implies a need for increasing public intervention in order to control these externalities and to correct the natural market forces.

PART III

The Organisation of Supply

6. The Nature of Markets and Public Intervention

Supply takes many different forms in transport. Some integrated operators provide a complete service, as was the traditional situation in the railways; others provide only one part of the service, for example in road haulage. This is not a fixed situation, however, as we have seen with the attempt to restructure railways in many European countries, most notably the UK. In certain sectors or sub-sectors we encounter monopoly or oligopolistic organisation; in others the number of firms is extremely large. There is, therefore, a varying role for government in transport from direct public sector provision, through various types of franchising or arm's length provision to varying degrees of regulation of private sector activity. We can characterise these differences in three dimensions: integration or fragmentation, monopoly or competition, liberalism or intervention. Any one type of provision may be located in a slightly different position on each of these dimensions, and indeed we can find very different patterns in different European countries, and in some cases even within countries. Box 6.1 illustrates these diversities for one EU country, France.

Similar types of structure can be found, with some variation, in all European countries. The strongest differences are found in the organization of the railways, which are often more fragmented and more remote from the State than in France, most particularly in the UK. The opposite situation is true for roads where France has developed most strongly the system of toll concessions. Airlines have been liberalised and privatised in the UK and, to a lesser degree, in Germany. Local public transport has been delegated to the private sector more in the UK than in other countries and the UK led the way in the deregulation and liberalisation of road freight transport. Nevertheless, some form of State interest is still found in almost all forms of marketed transport, either to regulate markets or to ensure that there is transport available to meet certain public service obligations.

BOX 6.1

Organisation of transport
The diversity of the situation in France

- Interurban rail services are provided by SNCF, a publicly-owned service, enjoying an almost total monopoly.
- Autonomous ports and airports are publicly established with exclusive concessions (franchises) to operate a public service on the territory for which they are awarded the rights.
- The same situation applies to RATP which provides public transport in the central part of the Ile-de-France region. Public transport in the outer part of the Ile-de-France region is provided by APTR and ADATRIF, which are groups of private operators under contract to the Region.
- Ordinary roads are constructed and maintained directly by public authorities (the State, départements, or communes).
- Companies which provide toll infrastructures (société autoroutières, bridges or tunnels) are concessionaires, awarded a concession for a period of several decades. They may have either public or private status.
- Urban public transport is provide in many agglomerations by municipal authorities, but in the majority of cases conceded or franchised to the private sector for periods of four to five years. In the majority of cases the capital equipment remains the property of the municipality.
- Interurban bus transport is provided in most cases by private sector enterprises, usually under contract to local authorities for regular services.
- Road freight transport is provided either by companies on their own account, or by private companies for hire and reward (although the largest of these are subsidiaries of SNCF) which are large in number and subject to a complex regulatory structure
- Inland waterway freight transport is also provided both on own account (for example by oil companies which operate through subsidiaries) or by professional transport companies (which include several large operators with a capacity of several thousand tonnes and many small operators, each of which has a capacity of only a few hundred tonnes).
- Air transport is provided through a structure which involves one very large national carrier, Air France, and a number of smaller private companies.

---

1. INTEGRATION OR FRAGMENTATION

1.1 The Three Levels of Organisation

We can distinguish three levels in the supply of transport:

- the infrastructure level, the most materially dense and physical in the system, which constitutes that part which can actually be seen on the ground, roads, rails, airports, ports;
- the infostructure level, which has the objective of ensuring the best utilisation of the infrastructure. This level, up to now rather less important than in other sectors, is developing rapidly. It is this level which is provided by air traffic control systems, or the signalling and information systems on the rail network, by traffic police and the information services used by road hauliers, the coordination of traffic signals in urban areas and information to road users on interurban roads and which lies behind the development of intelligent transport systems for vehicles which are in the course of development;
- the service level, that part of the supply which is purchased by the final consumers, characterised by price, frequency and quality of service. Within the internal organisation of operators at this level we can distinguish three similar levels of activity: thus a transport operator has infrastructure, such as depots, interchanges and vehicles; an infostructure which comprises a management system for managing both vehicles and demand (scheduling, reservation systems, etc.) and a service level which corresponds to the delivery of the complete service to the final consumer.

1.2 Coordination through Organisation or the Market

The links between these three levels can be articulated either through the operation of the market between different operators, or through an integrated operator providing two of three of the individual levels, or through a number of different enterprises working together. The advantages and disadvantages of each type of organisation have been evaluated differently in different countries and at different times. Thus, for example, the three levels are integrated in France, but have in recent years been largely separate in the UK.

Economic theory suggests the following main considerations on this topic:

- the market is not perfect: it only produces an optimum where there are many agents, each of which is small and possesses perfect information; it loses these advantages in a situation of monopoly or oligopoly;

- the market will tend towards an optimum, according to the Coase theorem (Henry 1997b), but with some important reservations;
  - all relevant agents must participate in the negotiation and have the power to effect transfers
  - negotiation is costless
  - information is perfect
- in many situations integration is preferable to this type of outcome due to the asymmetry of information (Box 6.2).

BOX 6.2

Market organisation and asymmetry of information

Suppose that a seller supplies a machine which is in the state θ: $\theta = 0$ if it does not work, and $\theta = 1$ if it does.

Taking account of this probability θ gives a value of the machine (the sum of the benefits achieved) of θV_1 for the seller and θV_2 for the buyer. If θ is known to the seller but unknown to the buyer, there is a risk that the exchange does not take place. In effect if the seller proposes a price p, the buyer infers that θ is less than p/V_1. In order to formalise this belief we hypothesise that he thinks that θ is uniformly distributed between 0 and p/V_1. Thus the most probable value of θ will be $p/2V_1$. If the buyer is risk neutral, the utility which he will gain will be:

$$pV_2/2V_1$$

and he will only make the purchase if:

$$pV_2/2V_1 > p$$

so that:

$$V_2 > 2V_1$$

which is a much more restrictive condition than the optimality condition which would apply in a perfect market, where exchange is advantageous if:

$$V_2 > V_1$$

This will also be the situation when the coordination of activities is essential. Thus the coordination of trains operated by different companies, but using the same track, cannot for obvious technical reasons be achieved by the same sort of simple procedures as those for cars on a road. It is thus necessary to have some form of contract between the train operators and the network owner, but the cost of such contracts, the transaction cost, may be considerable (see Box 6.3). Thus it is necessary to have a formal means of organising the allocation of slots for using the infrastructure. However, the separation of the management of the infrastructure risks introducing a number of inefficiencies: intervention in the case of accidents, maintenance of track, etc. It is not, of course, necessary to combine management of the infrastructure and the allocation of its use; where there is a dominant operator it can take charge of the allocation of slots.

BOX 6.3

Transaction costs

The concept of transaction costs was developed by Williamson (1975). Milgrom and Roberts (1992) provide a useful typology:

- costs of coordination: the transmission of information, based on decision making in a hierarchical organisation; organisation of the market.
- costs of motivation: the asymmetry of information; for example the buyer of a used car knows the condition of the vehicle much less well than the seller; the employer cannot measure exactly the amount of effort being put in by the employee; this relates also to the imperfect engagement of the parties, and the difficulty for each to identify the motivation of the other. Contracts are rarely complete, in the sense that it is impossible to envisage all possible circumstances which may arise.

The size of transaction costs is determined by (Dang N'Guyen 1995):

- the extent of information available to decision–makers
- the difficulty of putting in place complete contracts which foresee all possible eventualities,
- the specificity of transactions
- the bounded rationality of decision makers
- the opportunism of the parties
- the frequency of transactions
- the difficulty of measuring the results.

A similar situation arises in the case of specific investments, those which can only be used by the party for which they were originally intended and thus in case of default by that party are rendered unusable. For example, a road haulage operator which equips its vehicles for use in combined transport is subject to any decisions made by the rail operator for such a means of transport; a developer of a computerised reservation system depends on the airline company for which it is developed. Long-term contracts are thus necessary, but, given the complexity of such contracts, some form of integration may be advantageous.

BOX 6.4

Specific investments

Specificity of investment can be illustrated by the following simple model drawn from Tirole (1988). Assume two firms. Firm 1 produces a final good for the market for which the price is v. It purchases an input from Firm 2, at a price $p(I)$, I being the specific investment made by Firm 2, for which the cost of production is $c(I)$ (assuming $C'(I) < 0$ and $C''(I) > 0$). Thus the optimum I is that which satisfies:

$$Max_I(v - C(I) - I)$$

where $C'(I) = -1$.

Alternatively the negotiation of a price between the two firms would depend on achieving a level of investment based on a share of the profits from the investment compared with the situation without trade, leading to a price $p(I)$ such that:

$$V - p(I) = p(I) - C(I)$$

where:

$$p(I) = (v + C(I))/2$$

Thus Firm 2 fixes its investment such that:

$$Max_I(p(I) - C(I) - I) = Max_I\left(v - \frac{C(I)}{2} - I\right)$$

where

$$C'(I) = -2.$$

The value of I is sub-optimal, because of the opportunistic behaviour on the part of Firm 1.

2. BETWEEN MONOPOLY AND COMPETITION

2.1 Monopoly

Monopoly is normally encountered in the presence of economies of scale and scope. This is usually termed a situation of natural monopoly when monopoly is both the most efficient structure of production and the state towards which the organisation of production tends.

BOX 6.5

Structure of the market and the size of demand

The links between the structure of the market and the level of demand can be shown in the case of a single production activity. Assume that an activity is supplied by one or more producers, each of which faces the same U-shaped cost curve: $C(q)$, with a minimum at $q_0{}^*$. According to the level of demand, there will be, for efficient production, n firms in the market, defined by:

$$\underset{n}{Min}\, C(Q/n)$$

From the following diagram it can be seen that the cost function for the industry takes the form of a set of curves of equal size, but getting flatter and flatter as the quantity of production grows.

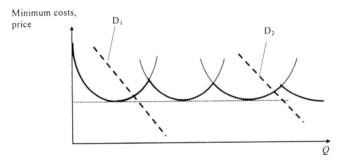

If demand is at level D_1, the most efficient situation from a social perspective would be a monopoly. This would be called a natural monopoly. At level D_2, we would be in a situation of oligopoly (in the case of the diagram, 3 firms). Eventually, in the event that demand increases, the situation approaches perfect competition, where costs are independent of the level of production where returns to scale are constant (a horizontal cost curve). If the cost curve $C(Q)$ show an asymmetry in the neighbourhood of the minimum cost point, the height of the 'festoons' will diminish and tend to disappear.

In effect, if at the start there are two firms, the dominant firm will have lower costs and can continue to take the advantage over the other. As has been seen in Chapter 5, the conditions of natural monopoly, economies of scale and of scope, will be found particularly in the provision of infrastructure which is characterised by high fixed costs and low running costs. Other reasons can justify, in the case of infrastructure, the attribution of special rights to the operator: the need for public authorities to have the right to acquire land for construction, the necessity for the police to have powers to maintain security and safety for the effective flow of traffic. In these two cases, leaving coordination to the market would imply costs, delays and risks of non–optimality in comparison with transferring these powers to a pubic authority.

Economies of scale and scope also arise in the provision of transport services, but they are much weaker than in the case of infrastructure.

2.2   The Extent and Form of Competition

The existence of monopoly power does not imply a particular form of competition. Ports on the same coast are in competition, whether or not they are close to one another. The major European hub airports of London, Paris, Amsterdam and Frankfurt are in competition for intercontinental traffic.

It is also important to distinguish between monopoly of a product and of a service. Thus a national rail company may have a monopoly of the provision of the rail product, but in terms of the service it provides it is in competition with other modes such as road and air.

It is not therefore possible to assess the degree of competition simply in terms of the number of operators in a given geographical area. It is necessary to analyse in more detail the conditions of supply and demand in order to identify the nature of the market and to judge its structure: in the case of transport it is necessary to apply the notion of the appropriate market used in competition law.

In a narrow sense a product of a transport activity and its market is defined by the transport of a person (or an object) from an origin to a destination in given conditions relating to costs, delays, safety and comfort. It can easily be seen that any change in any one of these characteristics changes the value of the good for the customer and thus changes both the product and its market. Among these characteristics, certain are fundamental. Origin and destination have limited possibilities of substitution. Quality of service is more substitutable. Substitution can be illustrated by the cross elasticities of substitution between modes which demonstrate, for example, how there is competition between air and high speed rail over long distances and between car and ordinary train over short distances.

BOX 6.6

The concept of the appropriate market

The concept of the appropriate market is used in the law of competition to evaluate the market power of a firm. This is the zone of competition within which the firm operates. The easiest way to define the extent of the market is in terms of the substitutability of products: two products are located in the same market if their cross elasticities exceed a certain critical value.

This criterion is well adapted to determine if two well identified products are in the same market. It is less so when applied to firms since in a perfectly competitive market the cross elasticities of a firm with respect to the price of another is zero. Each firm can be asked to define its competitors, but any response risks being biased for strategic reasons.

Another form of interaction between markets results from supply conditions. Thus the markets for transport between Milan–Amsterdam and Frankfurt–Madrid may not be linked with respect to demand, but can be provided for with respect to costs, due for example to economies of scope. The joint exploitation of these two links allows for a reduction in total expenditure resulting in a better servicing of generated traffic or a simpler management of incidents and breakdowns because the effects can be spread over a larger fleet. At the same time, for certain modes, rolling stock can be redeployed from a market where there is excess supply to one where there is a shortage, contributing to an equalisation of costs between the markets, thus producing a result similar to that of perfect competition even though the number of firms operating in the market is small. This phenomenon can be encountered in maritime transport, aviation and trucking. It is less likely in rail transport in cases where the displacement of rolling stock is costly or where rolling stock is specifically adapted to a particular infrastructure; redeployment from one country to another is not possible if technical standards are not compatible.

In the case of road freight transport many local markets are in a situation of oligopoly given the limited number of operators, often due to the structure of contracts where one customer uses one or two operators on a regular basis. But this situation does not result in the classic oligopoly outcome because, given the mobility of the capital employed in vehicles, any abuse of a dominant market position will lead to entry into the market by operators from neighbouring markets.

This phenomenon of flexibility in supply plays an important role in maritime transport where the possibility of entry into the market is very great.

For regular lines it is limited by Maritime Conferences, alliances of several companies which control prices, frequencies and profit shares in order to provide a regular service on a given line. These accords, which are not protected by any public authority, are limited in case of any excess by the potential for new entry.

The flexibility of supply and the integration of markets to which it leads play a varied role in aviation markets, depending on legal possibilities of market entry. In effect most international air transport is regulated by bilateral accords which, to a greater or lesser extent, extend the commercial activities of the airlines to the other country involved. According to the particular agreement the possibilities of market entry are more or less limited by the various 'freedoms' defined for different air travel markets (Box 6.7).

BOX 6.7

Air transport freedoms

The Chicago Convention of 1944 established the legal principles which govern air transport, based on the sovereignty of States and defining the 'freedoms' which can be determined bilaterally:

- 1st freedom: overflight without landing rights.
- 2nd freedom: landing rights for non-commercial reasons.
- 3rd freedom: right of disembarkation of passengers from a foreign aircraft.
- 4th freedom: right of embarkation of passengers to a foreign aircraft.
- 5th freedom: as 3rd and 4th freedoms, but from or to a third country.

The importance of intervention by the authorities can be seen from this example. Legislative and regulatory powers can modify the way natural forces work and, in particular create or limit monopolies, reduce or augment the number of operators and the degree of competition. These latter considerations lead to the tendency for the public sector to intervene in the market for transport; they provide both a *raison d'être* for, and set limits to, the extent of intervention.

3. BETWEEN INTERVENTION AND LIBERALISM

Transport policy in many countries has shown a perpetual oscillation between liberalism and interventionism. France took an essentially liberal stance from the middle of the nineteenth century until the period between the two World Wars. Railways were largely developed by private concessionaires, and the early development of private road transport was freely permitted. Only when the growth of road freight transport threatened the railways' traffic, and their profitability, did the public sector intervene, first through the grouping of the companies in 1937, then through nationalisation and the formation of SNCF, and finally through a series of controls and regulations designed to restrain the growth of road freight. This interventionist strategy developed in the post– Second World War period with the formation of other nationalised companies, for example, Air France in air transport, RATP in the provision of local transport in the Paris region.

Gradually, however, these nationalised companies faced increasing difficulties in balancing their budgets and the measures designed to control the competitive pressure from other, private, modes, especially road transport, failed to prevent their continued growth. During the 1980s, influenced by the experience of deregulation in the US and the new approaches being taken by the European Commission, there was a gradual move to a more liberal stance, first in road transport, then in air transport, although more slowly towards rail where SNCF has remained largely untouched.

The French experience is not unusual, although France has been more interventionist and slower to liberalise and deregulate than most northern European nations. The early history of transport organisation in the United Kingdom was very similar to France. Privately developed railways gradually merged into four companies (in 1920) and were finally nationalized into British Railways in 1947 at the same time as a large part of local public transport and of road haulage was taken into public ownership. Similarly the national flag carrier airlines were publicly owned. Deregulation started earlier in the UK, with road freight transport being deregulated from 1968, long-distance coach services in 1980, local bus services in 1986 (coupled with the privatisation of the National Bus Company and the encouragement of municipal authorities to divest themselves of their bus operations), the privatisation of British Airways in 1987 and finally the privatisation of British Rail in 1996.

Although the UK has gone further than most EU countries in the privatisation of transport, and the fragmentation of many sectors such as bus and rail in the desire to introduce competition, others have introduced elements of these approaches. In Sweden and Germany many local rail services are provided by private companies on a franchised basis. The Netherlands took the lead, along with the UK, in the deregulation of road freight transport. There has been a general move towards the deregulation of air transport. All these moves have been strongly promoted by the European

Commission, which, after a rather interventionist phase in the early years of the Common Transport Policy, followed by a long period of inaction, has taken a lead in moves to deregulation, in requiring the separation of infrastructure from the provision of transport services, and in promoting efficient pricing policies consistent across all modes.

BOX 6.8

Methods of public intervention

As well as the direct management by a government agency or by a publicly owned and controlled company, public control can be exercised through concessions granted for the construction and operation of infrastructure (e.g. Autoroutes in France, the Channel Tunnel, various major bridges and tunnels in the UK), or to provide services on a defined network (e.g. the provision of local public transport). Concessions can be granted to organisations which are publicly controlled, privately owned or some form of public-private partnership.

Public control is typically maintained over private enterprises by some form of regulation, which can take one of three main forms:

- technical regulation, which concerns the regulations under which construction should take place, traffic allowed to operate, etc.;
- social regulation, which concerns the conditions of employment of workers;
- economic regulation, which governs either prices charged (through fixing prices directly, or through the imposition of taxes) or quantities (authorisation to enter a market, control of capacity, etc.).

If there are historical or geographical reasons which explain the fluctuations in patterns of public intervention in transport markets, there are some fundamental reasons which can justify its continuation. These fall into two main categories: market failure and the concept of the public service obligation.

3.1 Market Failure

The state has a principal interest in ensuring a correct functioning of markets, ensuring for example the level of safety of each means of transport which the users would not be able to do individually. It also has an interest in minimising the impacts of specific types of market failure which are common in transport, essentially those concerning externalities and increasing returns. Certain activities in the transport sector can also be thought of as constituting public goods, the limiting case of which involves activities with only a fixed cost and zero marginal costs. A public good is one where consumption by a single user does not reduce the amount available for consumption by other users and pricing cannot be used to exclude a particular potential user from a given unit of consumption. Such goods need to be provided by the public sector and paid for out of taxation. Pure public goods (e.g. national defence, radio broadcasts) are rare in transport, but uncongested roads have many of the characteristics.

BOX 6.9

Externalities, monopoly and economic optimum

The links between the economic optimum and the market economy are determined by two fundamental theorems:

- a competitive equilibrium, where each agent determines their own behaviour and takes the price given by overall demand, is a Pareto optimum, and
- if total production is convex (no returns to scale) a Pareto optimum can be attained by a competitive market system.

These two theorems establish the optimality of the market system subject to the following two assumptions:

- the utility functions of consumers depend only on the goods they consume;
- the production function of each enterprise only depends on the inputs used by that enterprise and is subject to constant returns.

These assumptions exclude both externalities and monopoly. The effects of introducing these two distortions can be analysed in a simple partial equilibrium analysis.

External effects
The diagram below depicts:

- the demand curve D. the supply curve, which in the case of a good produced under competitive market conditions will be defined by the marginal (private) cost of production: C_{mp};
- the marginal social cost, C_{ms}, which in the case of a negative externality exceeds the marginal private cost.

The market equilibrium occurs at q_e, p_e, whereas the social optimum is at q_0, p_0. This social optimum can be achieved by imposing a tax t on production.

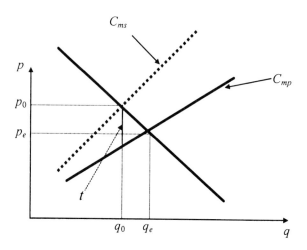

Monopoly

If the good is produced by a monopoly which aims to maximise its profit, as determined by the expression:

$$Max_q \, \Pi(q) = Max_q (p(q)q - C(q))$$

where:

Π is the monopoly's profit
$p(q)$ is the inverse demand curve
$C(q)$ is the cost function

The first order conditions for a maximum can be derived as:

$$p = dC/dq - q\,dp/dq$$

Whereas the social optimum, defined by the maximisation of consumer surplus, is given by:

$$Max_q \left(\int_0^q p(x)dx - C(q) \right)$$

and thus $p = dC/dq$.

The monopoly fixes price above marginal cost, and hence maximises profit at the expense of the consumers, who pay a higher price for a smaller quantity. Public intervention is one means of correcting this situation.

To control the negative impacts of externalities on social welfare and to internalise their consequences, the public sector has a number of means at its disposal: taxation (or subsidy in the case of a positive externality), regulation or the determination of clear property rights.

In the case of monopolies, there is a double inefficiency. The static inefficiency (as shown in Box 6.9) results in the monopolist charging a price above the optimum and reducing the quantity produced. The dynamic inefficiency results from the reduced market pressure exerted on the firm in a monopoly situation. There is considerable empirical evidence of these effects, principally that from deregulation, where a monopoly firm with exclusive rights has been replaced by competition concurrence.

3.2   The Rationale for Public Service

The second type of public intervention is the direct provision of services by the public sector. The concept of public service provision is well established in many countries and is recognised to have a number of important attributes: continuity, universality, adaptability and equality.

Despite this widespread recognition and use in different countries, albeit to a varying extent, the Treaties of the European Union (as amended by the Treaty of Nice) give scarcely any recognition to the concept of public service. The Treaties adopt the basic stance of promoting competition throughout the EU. For example, Article 82 refers to the problem of situations of a dominant market position; Article 87 deals with public intervention, noting that subsidy may undermine competition. Only Article 86 refers to 'public enterprises and enterprises to which (the State) accords special rights', and it is with the objective of restraining these rights, which must not interfere with free competition and the free movement of goods and services. The Treaties provide the European Commission with substantial powers to control public intervention by the governments of the member states of the EU, limited only by recourse to the European Court.

What sort of activities can be classified as being in the public interest? The Treaties are not very explicit, but the Court of Justice has recognised, for example in the Almelo and Corbeau decisions, a general economic interest of society in the Belgian postal service and in the regional distribution of electricity, based on the characteristics of their obligation to supply, continuity of service, uniformity of price, all under the general principle of universal public service.

Community law has a limiting view of the restrictions on competition permitted to provide a public service obligation (Stoffaes 1995). In the Almelo judgement the Court ruled that it was 'necessary to allow an enterprise invested with such an obligation of public service to accomplish that mission'. Thus the protection of profitable activities to compensate the losses resulting from the execution of a public service obligation is allowed, unless these profitable activities are seen to be 'specific activities which can be separated from the general public interest service and which represent the particular needs of operators and which involve certain supplementary activities which the postal service does not traditionally offer' (Corbeau judgement).

The gap between the restrictive interpretation of the EU and the traditional notion of public service applied in many member states, most notably France, has led to considerable reassessment. Stoffaes (1995) and Denoix de Saint-Marc (1996) have attempted to distinguish between the two principles which define the concept of public service: the essential nature of a service for the economic and social life of a country, and the correction of market failure. This suggests three fundamental categories of public services (Denoix de Saint-Marc 1996 and Henry 1997b):

- those which provide an accessible service to users who would otherwise be threatened with exclusion;
- those which contribute to social cohesion and the development of a community;
- those which contribute to a better utilisation of resources through both space and time.

There are many reasons for applying the public service concept in transport. It is necessary to ensure the existence and continuity of service for both the economic and the social good as, for example, demonstrated when strikes or accidents lead to the interruption of service. Some countries, for example the French law on inland transport (LOTI) of 31 December 1982, have written the principle into law, such that public authorities may intervene when this right to transport is not assured by natural market mechanisms.

This need might arise, for example, when the price is below the cost of providing the service or when universal or public service needs can only be met through the use of cross-subsidies by which the profits from one part of a network (such as the better used routes) are used to finance the deficits on unprofitable routes, thus allowing the operator to charge the same price to all users without resorting to external subsidies, despite the differences in the costs of provision of specific services. In this case a monopoly would be unsustainable (a so-called contestable market) because a competitor would be able to enter the market and cream off profits on the more profitable routes by offering a lower price, destroying the compensation mechanism ensuring the financing of a universal public service (see Box 6.10).

BOX 6.10

Sustainability, cross subsidy and creaming

Assume a firm producing multiple products given by the vector q, according to a cost function $C(q)$. There is cross subsidy between two groups of products q_1 and q_2, where $q=q_1+q_2$, which are sold with prices given by the vectors p_1 and p_2 if the following conditions are not satisfied:

$$C(q) - C(q_2) \leq p_1 q_1 \leq C(q_1)$$
$$C(q) - C(q_1) \leq p_2 q_2 \leq C(q_2)$$

and it can be seen that if $p_1 q_1 + p_2 q_2 = C(q)$ any one pair of inequalities results in the other two.

Thus if, for example, the first pair of inequalities are not satisfied, a competitor can produce q_1 alone and sell it at a price below p_1, and hence cream the market for goods q_1 eliminating the existing firm.

The use of cross subsidy has attracted considerable criticism. It distorts prices from costs and thus results in a loss of economic efficiency. It involves a lack of transparency over costs and can thus result in further distortions in resource allocation and the supply of goods and services. The main advantage is that it provides a means of financing public service obligations without recourse to tax revenues.

Cross subsidy is a source of unsustainability, a concept which can be defined thus if the existing firm produces q which it sells at price p, where $q = D(p)$ and $pq \geq C(q)$, there exists a price p_e $(p \geq p_e)$ and a quantity q $(D(p_e) \geq q_e)$ such that $p_e q_e \geq C(q_e)$.

A case of structural unsustainability is shown in the following figure which depicts the demand curve $D(q)$ and the average cost curve $C(q)$ and where the monopoly has achieved a financial equilibrium: the outcome (q_m, p_m) is optimal given the constraints imposed, but it is not sustainable since a competitor producing q_e at a price below p_m will destroy the monopolist's equilibrium.

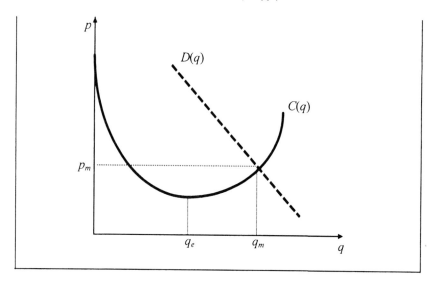

Thus, when the regulated monopolies for the provision of local bus services outside London were abolished in the UK in 1986 there was a considerable reduction in the provision of unprofitable routes which had formerly been sustained by cross-subsidies. Such routes had now to be supported directly from tax revenue rather than by the users of more profitable routes which became the subject of intense and often destructive competition. An alternative approach was used in London which allowed for the franchising of routes. In this case the benefits of competition are found in the process of competing for the franchise rather than directly in competing for the passenger; this helps to ensure efficiency and service quality without the destructive nature of direct competition.

3.3   Limits to Public Intervention

These limits are of two general types. First, they relate to the virtues of competition, described by Schumpeter (1942) as a process of creative destruction. Competition serves to reduce costs, to adapt products to the wishes and needs of consumers, and to progressive development: firms see their profits eroded by their competitors and seek to re-establish profitability through a dynamic process of innovation and adaptation. The public sector is immune from much of this and therefore tends to be less efficient and less innovative.

The other limit is that provided by a critical analysis of public action itself, recognising the inherent weakness of government. The public sector is not a unified entity which encompasses the public interest in the way supposed by the theory. In practice it is composed of a multiplicity of actors, each motivated by their own objectives: administrative organisations seeking to develop their power and the importance of their particular service in terms of, for example, the number of people under their control or the budget at their disposal. Politicians are constrained by the desire for re-election and thus are subject to both the political agenda and the electoral timetable. The control of elected bodies over the administration of public services is thus far from perfect. In all cases, public power is the victim of an asymmetry of information which works against it: the enterprises which it tries to control know the market conditions much better than those trying to exercise control. Careful selection of information ensures that administrators, politicians and regulators only receive that information, and in a form, which the enterprise wishes them to receive, thus satisfying neither economic efficiency nor the public interest. Even the replacement of state monopolies by regulated private sector firms can result in more resources going to 'deceiving' the regulator than to achieving the desired increase in efficiency, a process known as regulatory capture. This has been well documented in the case of the British process of privatisation of utilities, including that of Railtrack the regulated rail infrastructure monopoly. Even though Railtrack has now been replaced by a not-for-profit agency, Network Rail, the same issue of regulatory asymmetry remains.

4. CONCLUSION

The discussion of this chapter has outlined the reasons for the diversity of market structure which is found in the transport sector. These will be developed in more detail in the following chapters. Chapter 7 deals with the way in which the public sector makes optimal decisions when it is the direct operator of services, pursuing simply the goal of maximising the public interest, for example in the case of the management of infrastructure. Chapter 8 analyses different types of competition and the impact of regulation. Finally, Chapter 9 deals with the case of monopoly and the public interest.

7. Optimal Public Decisions

In this chapter we analyse the problem facing the public sector. In a situation where consumers and producers aim to maximise their utility or profit, the public sector seeks to satisfy the public interest through the various means at its disposal: information, regulation, direct imposition of taxes and prices, and the direct provision of goods and services themselves. In section 1 we recall the various ways in which the public interest can be expressed, and the criteria by which it can be measured, before applying these in the case where the public sector has been most directly involved: the provision of infrastructure. Section 2 deals with questions of price structure and regulation in infrastructure. Section 3 is concerned with the infrastructure construction decision and the choice of investments.

1. DEFINITION AND MEASUREMENT OF THE PUBLIC INTEREST

When the public sector makes a decision, this results in a modification to the equilibrium state of the economic system, leading to changes in prices and in the quantities of goods consumed. The mechanism of general equilibrium through the interdependence of all markets in the Walrasian system means that any initial change, even if it only affects one market directly, will result in changes to prices and quantities in all markets.

The theory of consumer behaviour demonstrates the effects of changes in prices and quantities on the utilities of each of the individuals in the society or community under consideration. This is based on the change in the utility of the individual from the initial state (referenced by the index 0) and the final state (referenced by the index 1):

$$\Delta U_i = U_i(q_{1i}^1, .., q_{ni}^1) - U_i(q_{1i}^0, ..., q_{ni}^0) = U_i^1 - U_i^0$$

Hence, for any decision considered, the resulting variations in utility for each individual can be determined. Suppose the society consists of two individuals, we can shown this graphically by reference to Figure 7.1 in which the axes represent the utilities of the two individuals 1 and 2. Given the constraint imposed by limited resources the range of possible outcomes is limited to those within the convex utility possibility frontier.

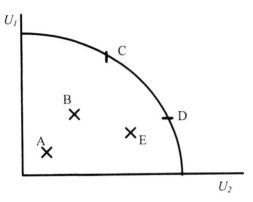

Figure 7.1 Pareto optimum

Here point B is clearly superior to point A because both individuals have a higher utility. In the same way C is superior to B and D is preferable to E. But we cannot compare E to B or E to C in the same unambiguous way, we can only say that E and B can be improved for all members of the society. But there is no situation which can be preferable to C for all members of society. In the same way we cannot choose between C and D, both represent Pareto optimal combinations like all other points defined by the frontier between what is possible and what is not given the limited resources.

Thus the Pareto criterion does not allow us to compare all situations; only those unambiguously preferable can be compared. But the situations where everyone will benefit from an action are rare in a society composed of a large number of individuals, comparisons between situations like B and E, where some gain and some lose, are often needed. It is certainly necessary that we can make choices between two alternative optimal situations such as C and D.

This analysis identifies a number of problems:

- how, for the same individual, can we calculate the change in utility between two different states?
- how can we define a global criterion which aggregates the changes in utility for all members of a given society?

1.1   Calculating Changes in Individual Utility

If the change is a marginal one, the variation in utility can be expressed in different ways according to the basic theories of consumer behaviour which can be summarised as follows:

If consumer *i* has a utility function:

$$U_i = (q_{i1}, q_{i2}, \ldots q_{in})$$

and a total budget of r_i, the consumer's behaviour is given by the following constrained maximisation problem:

$$\underset{q_{i1}, q_{i2}, \ldots q_{in}}{Max}\ U_i$$

subject to:

$$\sum_j p_j q_{ij} \leq r_i$$

from which the Lagrangian expression:

$$L = U_i - \lambda_i \left(\sum_j p_j q_{ij} - r_i \right)$$

gives:

$$\frac{\partial U_i}{\partial q_{ij}} = \lambda_i p_j$$

Hence:

$$dU_i = \sum_{j=1}^n \frac{\partial U}{\partial q_{ij}} dq_{ij} = \lambda_i \sum_{j=1}^n p_j dq_{ij}$$

or :

$$\sum_i (p_j dq_{ij} + q_{ij} dp_j) = dr_i$$

$$dU_i^* = \lambda_i \left(dr_i - \sum_j q_{ij} dp_j \right) \tag{7.1}$$

The calculation of *dUi* can be made through knowledge of the marginal utility of an increase budget (income) λ_i. This problem can be inverted such that the utilities are defined as a monotonic transformation and hence any marginal variation is simply a positive multiplicative factor. This can be given the value of one and hence we can rewrite equation 7.1 as:

$$dU_i = \sum_j p_j dq_{ij} \qquad (7.2)$$

If only one price is changed, with the other prices and income constant, this gives:

$$dU = -q_{ij} dp_j$$

Extension of these results to situations where the transformation is non marginal is not easy (see for instance Kanemoto and Mera, 1985, or Morisugi and Hayashiyama, 1997). By making simplifying assumptions (for example assuming a quasi-linear utility function) and assuming that only the price of one good changes, this results in the well-known relationship:

$$\Delta U_i = -\int_{p_j^o}^{p_j^1} q_{ij} dp_j \qquad (7.3)$$

which is the classic expression for consumer's surplus and which allows a comparison and a ranking of different transformations for a single individual based on the observed information of prices and quantities.

1.2 The Aggregation of Individual Utilities

Since utilities are based on the preferences of individuals, aggregating them to provide a measure for society as a whole is not straightforward. If the variations in utility between two situations are positive for all individuals the change is clearly beneficial. The difficulty arises when the change makes one individual better off and another worse off. One way forward is through a compensation criterion; if the gainers can compensate the losers for their loss and still remain better off there is an implicit gain.

The outcome is simplest in the case of marginal changes. Transfers will be equally marginal and their impact on the price system thus does not have to be taken into account. The compensation criterion thus reduces to:

$$\sum_j p_j dq_j \geq 0$$

dq_j being the algebraic sum of the variations in quantities of good j consumed by all the individuals.

These criteria are derived from a utility function which is composed solely of traded goods, but can be extended to include external effects and non-traded goods relevant to transport such as time (Morisugi, 1983).

An alternative way of presenting the surplus criterion for marginal changes involves assuming that the society itself has a utility function (its social welfare function) which depends on the utilities of each individual within that society:

$$W = F(U^1, ..., U^n)$$

Then the change in the social welfare resulting from a marginal change is given by:

$$dW = \sum_j F_j' dU^j$$

and normalising individual utilities by assuming the marginal utility of money of different individuals is constant and equal to unity we obtain:

$$dW = \sum_i \left[F_j' \sum_i (p_i dq_i^j) \right]$$

Assuming that the initial distribution of income is optimal society as a whole is indifferent to a marginal transfer between individuals; thus F_j' is independent of i, and:

$$dW = \sum_j p_j dq_j$$

dq_j being the total change in the quantity consumed of good j.

If society does not give the same weight to each individual, if for example it wants to favour certain groups, this can be translated into a distributional weight attached to each individual's utility.

1.3   Practical Problems in the Calculation of Welfare Gain

The calculation of surplus in the sense used by Dupuit and Marshall, or of the Hicksian equivalent variation, is very demanding in terms of information. At the end of the action which is proposed, the entire system of prices and incomes will have changed, as well as the quantities of all the goods consumed by all individuals. It would be necessary to calculate the gains for each individual in the society affected by the change.

This task can be simplified in two situations:

- If it is possible to aggregate the demand functions of individuals into one of a representative individual, this can result in two outcomes. The first arises when all individuals have identical utility functions and incomes. The second, already met in Chapter 5, arises when the individual demand functions are of the form (Varian, 1992):

$$q_i^j = \alpha_i^j(p_1,...p_n) + r^j \beta_i(p_1,...,p_n)$$

Thus the aggregate demand function can be written, where $R = \Sigma r^j$,

$$Q_i = \sum_j q_i^j = J\alpha_i(p_1,...p_n) + R\beta_i(p_1,...,p_n)$$

For a given good, it is only necessary to consider a single demand function instead of having to take account of all the individual demand functions.

- In the case of marginal changes, if the economic system is in a Pareto optimum situation in which firms maximise their profits at constant prices, then a measure based on one specific good can be obtained by analysing just the market in question; the total effect on the economic system can be measured through the consumer's surplus in that market. The proof, adapted by Lesourne (1969), and reproduced in Box 7.1 for a specific example, assumes marginal changes, full employment of resources and balance of trade equilibrium. If the change is not marginal the calculation would depend on modelling the entire system. Kanemoto and Mera (1985) have demonstrated the method necessary to achieve this. Morisugi and Hayashiyama (1997) carried out numerical solutions measuring the relationship between the Marshallian consumer surplus and the equivalent variation and showed that this is weak even in the case of major changes such as the programme of railway construction in Japan.

BOX 7.1

Equivalence between general and partial equilibrium analysis

Assume that transport simply uses quantity X_a per kilometre of a good a at price p_a. The change in social surplus is then:

$$dU = p_a X_a dT + \sum_i p_i dq_i \qquad (1)$$

where:
    dq_i is the change in consumption of good i

T is the distance in km.

To satisfy the equilibrium of supply and demand for each good i requires:

$$dq_i = \sum_h dq_{ih} + dq_{ia}$$

where:

  h represents the firms, and
  q_{ia} is the quantity of good i consumed by the firm making good a.

Hence given that variations in quantities with respect to price will be negative in the case of consumption and positive in the case of production we obtain:

$$\sum_i p_i dq_i = \sum_i \sum_h p_i dq_{ih} + \sum_i p_i dq_{ia} \qquad (2)$$

Assuming that firms seek to operate at an optimum, i.e. to maximise their profits with respect to given prices, we obtain:

$$dB_h = \sum_h p_i dq_{ih} = 0 \qquad (3)$$

and

$$\sum_i p_i dq_{ia} + p_a sq_a = 0 \qquad (4)$$

But the production of firm a, dq_a is equal to

$$dq_a = d(X_a T) = X_a dT + t dX_a \qquad (5)$$

and combining the above equations we obtain:

$$dU = -p_a T dX_a$$

which says that the social surplus is equal to the surplus of the user.
    In addition it can be seen, from equations (2) and (3), that if a firm h is not at an optimum it transfers to the user the change in profit at a constant price:

$$dB_h = \sum_i p_i dq_{ih}$$

We can now take this simplification into account. Suppose that the cost of transport on a particular route is reduced, ignoring for the moment any cost involved in achieving this reduction (assume for example a reorganisation of transport at a constant cost), what happens in terms of the use of transport? There will be changes in the prices of all goods in the economy and in the quantities consumed by each consumer. However, the result obtained in Box 7.1 allows us to calculate the social welfare change without having to calculate all these individual changes. It shows, in effect, that the social welfare is equal to the welfare change of those using the particular link, that is:

$$dU = -Tdp_t \qquad (7.3)$$

where:

T is the traffic on the link

dp_t is the change in the cost of transport on the link.

In effect, for each user j using the link:

$$dU_j = \sum p_i dq_{ij} = dr_j - \sum q_{ij} dp_i$$

as if neither their income changes nor the prices of goods other than that of transport, which changes by dp_t.

We can now lift the assumption that the change has been costless. If the change requires an additional cost of dC, the same reasoning shows that it is sufficient simply to include this cost which includes all the consequences of this additional cost in terms of changes in utility of individuals. Social welfare change thus becomes:

$$dU = -Tdp_t - dC$$

Of course this result does still depend on certain important initial assumptions: a marginal change, the economy at an optimum initially, the possibility of compensation or optimal distribution of income.

If the economy is not optimal, if for example certain firms enjoy monopoly power, the results presented in Box 7.1 show that it is possible to add to the users' surplus the changes in profits enjoyed by these firms at a constant price. If the distribution of income is not optimal, or if compensation is not possible, it becomes necessary to determine the gains and losses by each group and weight them according to their importance as determined by society. Finally we should note that this approach has ignored the presence of externalities.

Thus far we have looked at the basic theoretical tools necessary to take public decisions. Now we turn to study the way these tools can be used in the management of transport in terms of decisions about the management of infrastructure (in section 2) and investment decisions (in section 3).

2. INFRASTRUCTURE: PRICING, REGULATION AND PROPERTY RIGHTS

In this section we present first the rules for a first-best optimum in the management of infrastructure; then we analyse the way in which pricing can be used in the case of second-best solutions, for example where the operator of the infrastructure must break even or where the rest of the economy is not in a first-best situation; and finally we consider the practicalities of pricing.

2.1 Rules for the Optimal Management of Infrastructure

The initial problem is to set the optimal level of production. When there are no external effects, this level can be attained through the use of marginal cost pricing and when this price is fixed the optimal quantity can be derived from the demand curve.

The principle of marginal cost pricing can be derived in a number of ways. The most complete uses the basic theorems of welfare economics to show that, assuming convexity of the production set and the utility function, a·competitive equilibrium is an optimum (see Box 6.9). Thus in a competitive equilibrium, firms which maximise their profits at given prices will produce at the point where marginal cost is equal to the market price.

A simpler way of arriving at this result is to resort, in a partial equilibrium analysis, to the notion of consumers' surplus used by Dupuit and Marshall. The consumers' surplus is equal to the area under the demand curve less the cost of production:

$$S(q) = \int_{0}^{q} p(t)dt - c(q)$$

and is at a maximum where:

$$p(q) = \frac{dc}{dq}$$

This result will hold whether or not the producer faces decreasing returns. However, it assumes that there are no externalities and that the rest of the economy is at an optimum. The analysis has to be adapted to allow for these two assumptions not holding.

2.1.1 Taking account of externalities

External effects appear in an individual's utility function, but they do not depend on decisions taken by the individual, rather on decisions taken by others. The existence of externalities is an obstacle to the achievement of social welfare because those creating them do not take the effects into account as part of their own decision-making. Restoring the economic system to a Pareto optimum thus requires some correction to the existing price system.

These mechanisms can be illustrated by a simple example. Assume two firms, 1 and 2, each operating in a competitive market. The first produces product y at a cost $C_1(y)$ $(C'_1 > 0; C''_1 > 0)$. The second produces product x at a cost which depends both on the quantity of x it produces and on the quantity produced of y (for example because of effluent produced by producer 1):

$$C_2(x,y)=k(y)+c(x) \quad \text{with:} \quad dc/dx > 0, \quad dk/dy > 0 \quad d^2c/dx^2 < 0 \quad d^2k/dy^2 < 0$$

If the market price of good y is p_y and that of good x is p_x the output of x and y which maximise the profits of each firm can be derived from the normal rules for profit maximisation:

$$\frac{\partial C_1}{\partial y} = p_y$$

$$\frac{\partial C_2}{\partial x} = \frac{\partial c}{\partial x} = p_x$$

From which the solutions are x_n and y_n.

Firm 1 will produce until its marginal cost is equal to the market price, ignoring the costs which it imposes on firm 2. The firms' profits will be given by:

$$\Pi_1'' = p_y y_n - C_1(y_n)$$

$$\Pi_2'' = p_x x_n - C_2(x_n, y_n) = p_x - c(x_n) - k(y_n)$$

Since firm 1 does not take into account the effect of its activities on the profits of firm 2, the situation is not optimal for the two firms taken together. It is as if firm 2 has to meet a fixed cost *k(y)* over which it has no control and which depends on the decisions of firm 1. Their total profits could be increased if firm 1 fixed its output in order to maximise $\Pi_1 + \Pi_2$, which would require:

$$p_y = \frac{\partial C_1}{\partial y} + \frac{\partial k}{\partial y}$$

Thus firm 1 would need to fix its price taking account, not just of its own marginal cost, but also of the marginal cost which its production imposed on the output of firm 2. These results can be illustrated graphically (Figure 7.2), where the shaded area represents the loss of profit resulting from the externality.

We now need to explore ways in which this optimum can be attained, that is how to encourage firm 1 to produce at y_0 instead of at y_n. The first is through regulation. The public authorities fix a norm for the externality such as the emission of a pollutant which limits the production of firm 1 to y_0. The second is through the price mechanism. The authorities impose a tax on the polluting firm at a level given by dk/dy.

The third means is through a market mechanism using Coase's theorem (see Chapter 6). Firm 2 has an interest in making a contract with firm 1 through which firm 2 agrees to pay the sum of $(y_n - y_0)dk/dy$ if firm 1 limits its production to y_0. The optimum is achieved through a free market mechanism where each gains. In an extreme form firm 2 may purchase firm 1.

A fourth means involves the public authorities selling tradable permits, each of which permits a given level of pollution. The pollution permit becomes a factor of production; at a price q firm 1 will demand y permits:

$$y(p_1+q)=dC_1/dy$$

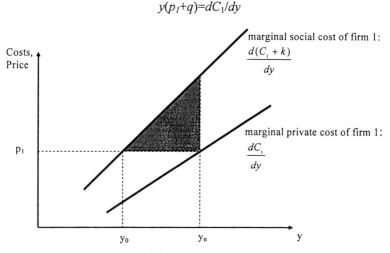

Figure 7.2 Externalities and the Pareto optimum

This equation defines a demand function for firm 1. If there are several firms of type 1, the sum of their demands defines a market demand curve which relates the quantity of permits to their price, thus allowing the authorities to determine the optimum level of pollution. In this case, given y_0 permits, the price of each permit is fixed at (dk/dy).

All of these methods are capable of re-establishing an optimum. This does not mean that there are no problems in their implementation. They all require there to be the necessary information, there are costs of implementation and implementation poses problems of delay and control. The difference between the different methods depends on the distribution of benefits between the three actors, firm 1, firm 2 and the public authority.

Given these tools, we can now analyse in turn three of the externalities we encounter in transport: the loss of time through congestion, impacts on the environment and safety.

The loss of time
Road congestion. We start with the case of road congestion, analysing first the simplest situation where there is a constant flow along a uniform continuous road. The conditions of traffic flow are shown in Figure 7.3. Assume that users make their decisions on the basis of generalised cost, and that this generalised cost is the same for all users, vehicles are homogeneous and the values of time are equal for all.

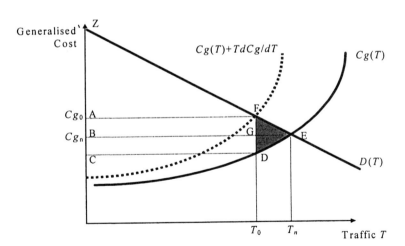

Figure 7.3 The marginal cost of congestion

Figure 7.3 shows:

- the demand curve $D(T)$, which defines the volume of traffic T wishing to use the road for a given generalised cost Cg;
- the average cost curve Cg (T), which defines the generalised cost for a given volume of traffic. The cost curve is increasing due to the mutual interference of vehicles with each other as traffic volumes increase occasioning a loss of time.

An equilibrium volume of traffic will be established at T_n leading to a generalised cost of Cg_n. For a larger volume of traffic, certain users will face a higher cost than that which they are prepared to pay, and vice versa. The single Nash equilibrium is at T_n, Cg_n. The corresponding level of social welfare can be written as:

$$S(T_n) = \int_0^{T_n} D(T)dT - T_n Cg(T_n)$$

However, social welfare is not maximised at T_n, but at traffic level T_0, since:

$$\underset{T}{Max}\ S(T) = \underset{T}{Max} \left[\int_0^T D(t)dt - TCg(T) \right]$$

where:

$$D(T_0) = Cg(T_0) + T_0 \frac{dCg}{dT_0}$$

It can be seen that at the optimum, the generalised cost differs from the average cost for that volume by:

$$T_0 \frac{dCg}{dT_0}$$

This amount represents the burden placed by one user on others. By the presence of others each of the T_0 users sees their own costs rise by dCg/dT_0. How can the traffic level be achieved at T_0 rather than at T_n? The most obvious way is by imposing a tax on the route, for example a toll of $T_0(dCg/dT_0)$, which changes the price to one of marginal social cost. It can be shown that this result can be generalised from the case of the single link to a complete network (see, for example, Yang and Huang, 1998). An optimum is reached where, on each link, the user pays an amount equal to the cost which the marginal user imposes on other users on that link.

Figure 7.3 can be used to show the effects of introducing such a charge. First of all social welfare increases from triangle BEZ to the area FDCZ. However, the distribution of that welfare changes; users lose surplus by the difference between BEZ and AFZ. The public sector gains through the revenue from the charge by the area AFDC, which revenue can be used to compensate users or non–users according to social preferences.

This model is rather basic, in particular it assumes that all users have the same value of time. If we change this assumption then some paradoxical results can emerge. Assume a very simple network comprising a single origin and destination, linked by two alternative routes with identical characteristics. It is worthwhile, in terms of social welfare, to install a toll on one of the links such that users with a higher value of time would tend to use the link with the toll whereas those with a lower value of time would choose the free link where they would face a longer journey. For an adequate level of tolls, the gains of one group would exceed the losses of the other group.

To provide a more complete analysis of congestion, we return to the model of congestion of Chapter 4 based on the model of Arnott *et al.* (1994). In this model, the N users have a preferred arrival time of t^*, and three values of different types of time loss:

α is the value of travel time
β is the cost of arriving ahead of the preferred time
γ is the cost of arriving late.

Assume that the travel time is dependent on the waiting time imposed by a bottleneck on the route of which the capacity is s. As seen in Chapter 5, the natural equilibrium could be represented by the situation in Figure 7.4, the queue begins to form at t_q, grows up to t_n, then reduces progressively and disappears at t_f. Travelling the route costs the same to all users. The first and last departures incur the costs of arriving at the wrong time. The user leaving at t_q arrives at the desired time t^* and only incurs the travel time. Hence we have:

$$t_q = t^* - \frac{\gamma}{1-\gamma} \frac{N}{s}$$

$$t_f = t^* + \frac{\beta}{\beta+\gamma} \frac{N}{s}$$

$$t_n = t^* - \frac{\beta\gamma}{\alpha(\beta+\gamma)} \frac{N}{s}$$

This situation is not optimal. The delay at the bottleneck could be reduced without the arrival time changing. Each traveller could have the departure time regulated so as to keep the flow constant and equal to the capacity of the bottleneck. Thus there would be no cost of waiting time and it can be shown that the total cost would be halved. However, the distribution between users would not be equal, some would face an increased cost, and others, those who are made to leave at t^*, a zero cost. Of course such a situation is impractical; it would not be possible to establish an order of priority between many users. However, one means of realising such a situation would be to impose a time-varying toll, equal at each moment to the waiting cost in equilibrium. The resulting Nash equilibrium would tend to eliminate queues.

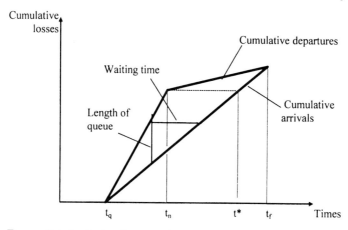

Figure 7.4 Analysis of congestion

The cost for users is the same as in the situation without the toll, but society benefits from the toll revenue equal to the average user cost. It can easily be seen that, at each moment, the toll paid by each user is equal to the total cost which that user is imposing on other users by their not being able to arrive at the desired time. Nevertheless the practical problems of putting such a variable charge remain, fixing such a charge requires precise information on the desired times of arrival, the value of time and traffic flow.

Models with different users are more complex. Arnott *et al.* (1994) explored the effect of introducing several types of user in terms of their values of time and desired arrival times. This results, in the case of a linear route with a single bottleneck, in a time-varying toll which eliminates queues and optimises the total cost of transport with varying impacts on distribution and a reduction in the total travel time which is less than in the case of a single type of user.

Another means of reaching an optimum depends on providing information to motorists, the subject of much research exploiting the possibilities offered by the development of information technology and telecommunications. The usefulness of such an approach depends on the ways in which users respond to such information (see for example Polydoropoulou *et al.*, 1997). Here behaviour is analysed in terms of how users actually respond to information (revealed preference) as well as their stated preferences from interviews. It appears that behaviour can be changed effectively through the provision of such information, including departure times and choice of routes.

The rate of change of behaviour is an essential component in the evaluation of information provision because, contrary to what may be thought, perfect information is not necessarily the optimum (de Palma, 1992) for a large number of situations.

Air transport. The same principles of the Arnott *et al.* (1994) model of bottlenecks can be applied to air transport, since the same problems of desired arrival or departure time lead to runway congestion at certain times of day. However, the economic loss is smaller than in the case of road congestion because there is not the same problem of queues. There is a pre-determined set of rules which fix the order of arrival or departure of planes. This is determined by an annual allocation of slots, although there is a tendency for slot allocations to remain fairly static year on year. The economic optimum would require that the best slots are allocated with respect to the time desired by the flights which produce the greatest social welfare, which would be in the main to the flights with the greatest number of passengers. One means of ensuring the optimal allocation would be by introducing a landing tax depending on the difference between the desired time and the actual time. Such a tax would translate the loss which each plane imposes on other planes. It would be related to the number of other planes and would increase towards the desired time, but this information is not sufficient to fix the tax.

One means of revealing the true value of slots is through bargaining between air companies. This has been used at many US airports (Starkie 1994). The resulting market is not completely free. There will typically be two separate markets, one for large planes and the other for small planes, without the possibility of transferring slots from one market to the other. This is necessary to protect the less used routes which serve markets with a lower density of traffic, but which are necessary for the maintenance of economic activity in these regions thus assuring a form of public service. This requires a break with the normal continuity of slot allocation (so-called 'grandfather rights') in order to open up the market. Unused slots can be reallocated and new entrants have priority rights over a share of the reallocated slots. Note that this type of market organisation is not an auction, though it may lead to a Pareto-optimal allocation if all stakeholders take part to the bargain and if all parties are fully informed. Note also that that the full efficiency of an auction is not achieved if auctions are coordinated between origin and destination airports.

Rail transport. Rail congestion, like air congestion, cannot be measured by waiting time since there are again rules which determine priorities, but nothing ensures that that these rules will result in an optimum. An optimum could be obtained through an appropriate pricing structure, but the calculation of such prices is complex. It would be necessary to evaluate the costs which a planned train movement imposes on other train movements, for example by assessing the loss of revenue from not running other services. This can be achieved by a single operator in possession of all the necessary information, but is much more difficult to put in place where a regulator or an independent track operator has to allocate slots between different train operators.

The main complication in establishing a pricing structure derives from the need to incorporate trains running at different speeds, for example freight trains, long-distance passenger trains and suburban trains. The movement of a given train is thus characterised by two parameters, its time of operation and its speed, whereas for air transport it is only the time. This complication is reduced by rules which attach a priority to a particular type of train at a particular time, for example commuter trains could be given priority at the morning and evening peak. Although it is also possible to consider the use of an auction, the problem arises where there are links owned or operated by different operators in different parts of the same train movement, for example trains between London and Paris need to use track in England between London and the Channel Tunnel, the Eurotunnel link and track in France between the Tunnel and Paris.

It also necessary to note that when congestion arises, a delay of one train with respect to the timetable causes delays to other trains on the same route and creates negative externalities. In order to correct this it may be necessary to impose penalties for poor timekeeping, as for example in the UK system of passenger train franchises, and equally bonuses for good timekeeping.

The environment.

In Chapter 5 we identified the possibility of translating environmental impacts into monetary terms. This implies that we can also correct for such externalities by use of appropriate taxes. In practice such taxes have not been widely used, except through relatively mild measures such as annual licences, and reliance has been placed on regulation as a means of correction. However, the use of direct monetary payments would offer some important advantages in terms of efficiency, as shown in Box 7.2).

BOX 7.2

Regulation, taxation and the decentralisation of decisions

Assume a situation of n firms ($i = 1,n$) of which each emits a quantity K_i of pollutant, which can be removed at a marginal cost which varies with the level of emission q_i according to a decreasing function which differs from one firm to another:

$$c_i(q_i)$$

the same level of total pollution Q can be obtained:

- either by fixing for each firm, through regulation, a level of emission G_i such that:

$$\sum_i G_i = Q$$

- or by fixing a tax t on each unit of pollution emitted. Each firm will minimize the sum of the cost of depolluting and the tax payable on the remaining pollution thus:

$$Min \int_{q_i}^{K_i} c_i(t)dt + tq_i$$

giving:

$$t = c_i(q_i)$$

The two approaches will give the same result if:

$$q_i = G_i$$

but determining G by the public authorities requires, especially if n is large, a lot more information than that of t, which can, in addition, be adjusted through arbitrage.

Moreover, the tax provides a strong incentive towards progress in the depolluting techniques since the firms will have a direct interest in these, as can be seen in situation following: a regulation which is set at N_1 has the same result as a tax t in the initial situation; but if a new technique becomes available, the tax would lead automatically to a greater reduction in pollution than a process of regulation: to the level N_2.

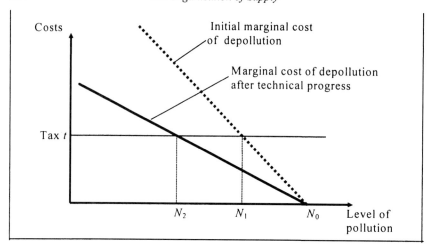

The choice between the two instruments depends also on the degree of precision with which the quantities and costs corresponding to the optimal level of pollution are known. If they are both known perfectly, the choice is purely theoretical, and we would be indifferent between the two approaches. If, however, there is some uncertainty, as shown in Box 7.3, which presents the result known as the Weitzmann theorem (Weitzmann, 1974), the choice between taxation or regulation will depend on the slopes of the cost and benefit functions. The ultimate decision will depend on the practical possibilities of establishing a tax or regulatory regime and of maintaining these effectively.

BOX 7.3

Information and the choice between taxation and regulation
The Weitzmann theorem

Assume that the true costs and benefits of pollution, only known inaccurately, are represented by the solid lines. The true optimum is defined by q_0, corresponding to a cost p_0. Suppose that the costs have been mis-estimated, the assumed cost curve is the dashed line. The economic loss resulting from the tax imposed is shown by the dark shaded area. If, in absolute values, b is the slope of the benefits curve, c that of the cost curve, ε is the uncertainty over costs (i.e. for a given value of q the distance between the dashed line and the true line is ε), then this loss is given by:

$$P_t = \varepsilon^2/(b+c)$$

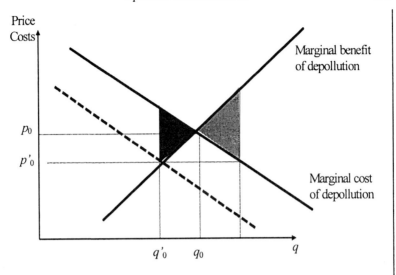

In the same way the economic loss resulting from regulation, given by the lightly shaded area, will be:

$$P_r = \varepsilon^2(b+c)(b/c)^2 = P_t(b/c)^2$$

Thus, if the benefits are independent of the level of pollution, regulation is preferable, because an error in the costs will have little influence on the optimum, and the inverse is true if the benefits vary a lot with the level of pollution (for example because of certain thresholds).

The results will be reversed in the case of uncertainty over benefits.

These principles can be illustrated in the case of air pollution. It is easy to apply either regulation or taxation on vehicle manufacturers to achieve a reduction in pollution because the technologies that each uses are similar. On the other hand detailed regulation of their users would require a multiplicity of restrictions and controls to be optimal. Taxation of use is difficult to envisage since the degree of pollution emitted depends on numerous parameters, all difficult to control. Given the choice between fixing norms or the use of taxation to control vehicle manufacturers, it will be dictated by the fact that uncertainty over the benefits to be attained by emission control is much greater than uncertainty over costs, but these costs vary much more than the associated benefits. This suggests that the control of emissions through taxation based on the level of emission (a tax on purchase or an annual licence) would be preferable.

A system of markets in property rights or tradable permits, suggested by economic theory, has been little used in transport. Two examples will suffice. In California, vehicle manufacturers are required to achieve an average emission level across all the vehicles produced, but are free to distribute this amongst the fleet as they wish. The system of traffic control in Singapore (Chin and Smith, 1997) also uses tradable permits. Control depended initially on the control of vehicle use, based on a system of permits relating to the destination zone. This was replaced by electronic tolling, and finally by the management of car ownership, initially through taxes on purchase, but now through a system of tradable permits issued in limited quantities. The authors analyse the efficiency of this system in terms of the minimising of the economic loss through errors in estimating the parameters.

Safety and accident costs.
Taking into account safety externalities poses particular problems as analysed by Jansson (1994). Consider, first of all, the situation where there is just one type of traffic:

where:

Q is the traffic volume
$r(Q)$ is the risk of accidents, which depends on traffic volume
a is the average willingness to pay to reduce the risk
c is the cost of an accident to society (loss of production, the cost of emergency services and medical care

Thus the total cost of accidents is given by:

$$TC = (a+c)rQ$$

We can thus ascribe to each user the difference between the social marginal costs and the private cost and thus derive an optimal price which consists of two terms:

- the costs of safety which are supported by society, c.

- the term $(a+c)Q\dfrac{\partial r}{\partial Q}$ which depends on the variation of the accident rate as a function of traffic Q. The analysis of accident statistics does not appear to reveal a net variation in the accident rate as a function of traffic volume, and the rate r is often considered to be a constant, even though some studies have suggested that it would be normal for the number of accidents to vary with the square of traffic volume (given the probability of two vehicles coming into contact) and thus that r should be proportional to traffic volume.

The analysis is more complex when traffic consists of different types of vehicle. Jansson (1994) suggests the following model in which accidents consist simply of encounters between cars and bicycles (accidents between cars follow the rules established above independently of what happens between cars and bicycles, and there are no accidents between bicycles); thus where:

Q	is car traffic
M	is bicycle traffic
$X(Q,M)$	is the number of accidents resulting from traffic volumes Q and M. These accidents only cause casualties to bicycles.

The total cost of accidents will be, on average:

$$TC=aX(Q,M)+cX(Q,M)$$

a represents the value of human life
c represents the social costs not covered by those involved in the accidents.

The tax to be applied is the difference between the marginal social cost and the marginal private cost (which is zero for car users). This differs for car and bicycle users as follows:

$$P(car) = dTC/dQ = (a + c)dX/dQ$$
$$P(cycle) = dTC/dM - aX/M = (a + c)dX/dM - aX/M$$

It can be shown finally that according to the values a and c and the function $X(Q,M)$, a variety of situations can be identified where car users pay nothing and only cyclists pay and where cyclists would be subsidised in order to reduce their number and hence accidents.

2.2   Pricing in a Non-Optimal Environment

In the models discussed so far, typically only a single mode has been considered. Other modes have implicitly been supposed to be operating optimally. The picture changes somewhat when imperfections exit in the rest of the economy, for example if competing modes do not have optimal prices or the operator is constrained by the need to break even.

2.2.1 Non-optimal pricing of competing modes
In these circumstances the optimal price is not simply marginal cost pricing, but must take account of the non-optimal price charged on the competing mode. A simple relationship can be derived, as shown in Box 7.4. If, for example, the competing mode is priced at below marginal cost, the mode

under analysis should also be priced at below marginal cost by an amount which depends on the size of the markets of the two modes and the elasticity of substitution between them.

BOX 7.4

Pricing in the case of non-optimal pricing of a competing mode

Assume q_1 and q_2 are the two substitute modes, c is the numeraire good in the economy with a price of unity, p_1 and p_2 are the prices of the two modes. Consumers are assumed to have identical utility functions $U(q_1, q_2, c)$ and the same income, which leads to the standard results of proportionality of the marginal utilities to prices and hence to demand functions.

Assume that the production of q_1 (q_2) requires a_1q_1 (a_2q_2) units of c, of which the total available resource is C, and that markets are competitive. The social optimum is achieved where:

$$U(q_1, q_2, c) \ Maximum$$

with:

$$q_1 = q_1(p_1, p_2, r)$$
$$q_2 = q_2(p_1, p_2, r)$$
$$c = c(p_1, p_2, r)$$
$$c = r - p_1q - p_2q_2$$

and the constraint:

$$a_1q_1 + a_2q + c = C$$

Let λ be the dual variable of this constraint, and by developing the Lagrangian, we can obtain finally:

$$q_1 = \lambda[q_1 + (p_1 - a_1)(\partial q_1/\partial p_1) + (p_2 - a_2)(\partial q_2/\partial p_2)]$$
$$q_2 = \lambda[q_2 + (p_1 - a_1)(\partial q_1/\partial p_1) + (p_2 - a_2)(\partial q_2/\partial p_2)]$$
$$1 = \lambda[1 - (p_1 - a_1)(\partial q_1/\partial r) - (p_2 - a_2)(\partial q_2/\partial r)]$$

It can be verified that:

$$\lambda = 1$$
$$p_1 = a_1$$
$$p_2 = a_2$$

is a first-best pricing solution.

If p_1 takes a value different from a_1, then the first equation of the preceding system does not hold, only the last two hold from which by eliminating λ we obtain:

$$(p_1 - a_1)[(\partial q_1/\partial p_2) + q_2(\partial q_1/\partial r)] + (p_2 - a_2)[(\partial q_2/\partial p_2) + q_2(\partial q_2/\partial r)] = 0$$

Introducing the direct and cross elasticities:

$$e_1 = (\partial q_1/\partial r)/(q_1/r)$$
$$e_{22} = (\partial q_2/\partial p_2)/(q_2/p_2)$$
$$e_{12} = (\partial q_1/\partial p_2)/(q_1/p_2)$$

and noting the divergence of prices from the first best prices:

$$\delta a_1 = p_1 - a_1$$
$$\delta a_2 = p_2 - a_2$$

we obtain:

$$q_1\delta a_1[e_{12}+(p_2q_2/r)e_1]+q_2\delta a_2[e_{22}+(p_2q_2/r)e_2]=0$$

If $(p_2q_2)/r$ is low (the position of mode 2 in the economy as a whole is small), then:

$$(q_2\delta a_2)/(q_1\delta a_1) = -(e_{12}/e_{22})$$

This equation can be generalized to the case of more than two modes and when transport is an intermediate good (Quinet, 1992a).

2.2.2 Balanced budget constraint of the operator

The model discussed in Box 7.5 is based on the work of Mohring (Mohring and Harwitz 1962). This does not take account of construction costs and generalises to the case of infrastructure the classic result in which, given constant returns to scale, pricing according to marginal cost covers all expenditures.

BOX 7.5

Optimal pricing under a budget constraint

The model is presented here in the form developed by Bernard (1983). Assume a society of *n* identical users with a utility function of the form:

$$U(q, T, l) = U[q, T, (\bar{t} - tT)]$$

where

    q is a consumption good
    T is the number of journeys made, each at unitary cost
    t is total time available
    l is time available for consumption activities

t is time spent in travel

the budget constraint is given by:

$$q + cT + \gamma T - r \leq 0$$

where γ is the tax on transport.

Assume in addition that travel time t is a function of traffic T and the characteristics of the infrastructure:

$$f(nT, K) - t \leq 0$$

Travel time varies with total traffic volume, but is given for each individual, to the extent that n is not large.

Moreover the annual running cost of equipment K is ρK, covering the fixed costs of interest and maintenance, the available stock of the consumption good, F is given by:

$$F = nq + ncT + \rho K$$

In these conditions, with γ and t given, each user maximises utility subject to the budget constraint and the tax on transport. The public authorities determine γ and K, subject to total resources for which utility is maximised.

The Lagrangian defining the consumer's behaviour can be written:

$$L = U(q, T, \overline{t} - tT) - \lambda(q + cT + \gamma T - r)$$

Maximising this with respect to q and T gives:

$$\frac{\partial U}{\partial q} = \lambda$$

$$\frac{\partial U}{\partial T} - t \frac{\partial U}{\partial l} = \lambda(\gamma + c) = \frac{\partial U}{\partial q}(\gamma + c)$$

The public sector's optimisation is given by:

$$\underset{q,T,t,K}{Max}\ U(q, T, \overline{t} - tT)$$

$$nq + ncT + \rho K - F \leq 0$$

$$f(nT, K) - t \leq 0$$

$$\frac{\partial U}{\partial T} - t \frac{\partial U}{\partial l} = \frac{\partial U}{\partial q}(\gamma + c)$$

Introducing the Lagrangian variables μ and ν with respect to the first two equations, we obtain:

$$\frac{\partial U}{\partial T} - t\frac{\partial U}{\partial l} - \mu n c - \nu\left(n\frac{\partial f}{\partial(nT)}\right) = 0$$

$$\mu\rho + \nu\frac{\partial f}{\partial K} = 0$$

$$-T\frac{\partial U}{\partial l} + \nu = 0$$

From which, taking account of the final constraint on the public sector:

$$\gamma\frac{\partial U}{\partial q} - (nT)\frac{\partial U}{\partial l}\frac{\partial f}{\partial(nT)} = 0$$

where $\left(\dfrac{\partial U}{\partial l} / \dfrac{\partial U}{\partial q}\right)$ represents the values of time h (in effect the marginal rate of substitution between time and money). From which:

$$\gamma = h(nT)\frac{\partial f}{\partial(nT)}$$

(which is the marginal cost of congestion, presented in a different way from that used previously) and:

$$\frac{\partial U}{\partial q}\frac{\rho}{n} + T\frac{\partial U}{\partial l}\frac{\partial f}{\partial K} = 0$$

or

$$\rho = -h(nT)\frac{\partial f}{\partial K}$$

If the function f is homogeneous of degree 0, which corresponds to a situation of constant returns (double the expenditure on infrastructure, traffic at a given speed doubles), then:

$$K\frac{\partial f}{\partial K} + (nT)\frac{\partial f}{\partial(nT)} = 0$$

The revenue from charges is:

$$\gamma(nT) = h(nT)^2 \frac{\partial f}{\partial(nT)} = -h(nT)K \frac{\partial f}{\partial K} = \rho K$$

This covers all the costs of the infrastructure.

This result can be extended to a situation where traffic varies seasonally, as can be seen through a simplified model:

Given:

Pt(T)	is the inverse demand function for year *t*
Tt	is traffic in year *t*
AC(Tt,K)	is the mean transport cost for infrastructure of cost *K* and traffic *Tt*
θ	is the (supposedly given) life of the infrastructure
j	is the rate of change/progress

Optimal management of the infrastructure corresponds to maximizing the social surplus.:

$$\underset{K,Tt}{Max}\left[\sum_{t=1}^{t=\theta}\left(\int_{0}^{Tt}Pt(u)du - TtAC(Tt,K)\right)\exp(-jt) - K\right]$$

The conditions for which are:

$$1. \quad Pt(Tt) = AC(Tt,K) + Tt\frac{\partial AC}{\partial Tt}$$

i.e. it is necessary to impose a tax equal to the difference between marginal private and marginal social costs.

$$2. \quad \sum_{t=1}^{t=\theta}Tt\frac{\partial AC}{\partial K}\exp(-jt) + 1 = 0$$

i.e. if the cost function of the infrastructure has constant returns, that is if:

$$AC(\lambda T, \lambda K) = AC(T,K)$$

then the revenue obtained at marginal cost is *K*. This result no longer holds when the investment is discontinuous (Oum and Zhang, 1990): then covering depends narrowly on the type of traffic.

As seen in Chapter 5 infrastructure cost functions which display constant or decreasing returns will generate sufficient revenue from marginal social cost pricing to cover costs, but in the case of increasing returns, marginal social cost pricing will entail a deficit.

Newbery (1988b) has shown that deficits are common in the case of road renewal. He assumes that damage to a road depends on two factors: climate which, even without any traffic, will lead to a deterioration of the road, and the number of axles passing over it (note it is the number of axles rather than the number of vehicles since large vehicles cause more damage than small vehicles). The passage of an axle brings forward the date when the road needs to be repaired and hence increases the present cost. If traffic does not increase and if the weather conditions do not change, in a stationary state where sections of road in the network are equally distributed in terms of their vintage, revenue from marginal cost pricing exactly covers the maintenance costs of the road. In the situation where traffic is growing and weather plays a role, revenues from marginal cost pricing will be smaller than the costs.

The situation where marginal cost pricing leads to a deficit are likely to be frequent with infrastructure. Such a deficit presents a number of problems. It will need to be covered by taxes, which will lead to a loss of efficiency elsewhere in the economy. Some of these efficiency problems are explored in more detail in Chapter 9. Finally there are equity considerations which arise if the full costs of the road network are not paid by those who directly benefit from its use.

For all these reasons it may be desirable to substitute for full marginal cost pricing an alternative which aims to maximise social welfare subject to a balanced budget constraint. Such a pricing principle is the so-called Ramsey–Boiteux pricing (Ramsey 1927, Boiteux 1956) which derives a price defined by (see Box 7.6):

$$\frac{p_i - c_i}{p_i} = \frac{\lambda}{\varepsilon_i}$$

where:

the subscript i refers to each good produced
c_i is the marginal cost of production of good i
p_i is the price of good i
ε_i is the own price elasticity of good i
λ is an adjustment parameter.

BOX 7.6

Ramsey-Boiteux pricing in partial equilibrium

Given a firm which produces i (i varies from 1 to n) goods, for which the demands are independent and the inverse demand functions are given by:

$$p_i(q_i)$$

and the cost of production is:

$$C(q_1,...,q_n)$$

Then the consumer surplus which results from a given production vector is:

$$CS = \sum_i \int_0^{q_i} p(u)du - C(q_1,...,q_n)$$

the budget constraint is:

$$\sum_i p_i(q_i)q_i - C(q_1,...,q_n) = 0$$

If μ is the corresponding dual variable and c_i the derivative of C with respect to q_i maximising CS gives:

$$p_i(q_i) - c_i - \mu p_i - \mu q_i \frac{dp_i}{dq_i} + \mu c_i = 0$$

Rearranging this equation and introducing the elasticity

$$\varepsilon_i = \frac{p_i}{q_i}\frac{dq_i}{dp_i}$$

we obtain:

$$\frac{p_i - c_i}{p_i} = \frac{\mu}{1-\mu}\frac{1}{\varepsilon_i}$$

The parameter μ is determined by the extent to which the budget constraint is respected.

If the production of i leads to externalities the equation can be extended. Calling $CE(q_1,...,q_n)$ the total external cost, then the problem becomes:

$$Max\ CS = \sum_i \int_{q_i}^{q_i} p_i(u)du - C(q_1,...q_n) - CE(q_1,...q_n)$$

with:

$$\sum_i p_i q_i - C(q_1,...q_n)$$

such that:

$$\frac{p_i - c_i - (\frac{1}{1-\mu})ce_i}{p_i} = \frac{\mu}{1-\mu}\frac{1}{\varepsilon_i}$$

Where ce_i is the marginal external cost, and μ is the dual variable ensuring meeting the budget constraint.

The analysis can be further extended to the case where there is a positive marginal cost to the use of public funds (for example the taxes used to finance the production do not meet an optimality criterion).

Then the problem becomes, in the case of two products:

$$MaxCS = \sum_{i=1}^{i=2} p_i(u)du - C(q_1,q_2) + \lambda\left(\sum_i p_i q_i - C\right)$$

from which we can derive:

$$\frac{p_i - \frac{\partial C}{\partial q_i}}{p_i(q_i)} = \frac{\lambda}{(1+\lambda)\varepsilon_i}$$

where ε is the inverse of the elasticity of demand for good *i*.

This is a little complicated if the goods are substitutes or complements:

$$\frac{p_i - \frac{\partial C}{\partial q_i}}{p_i} = \frac{\lambda}{\lambda+1}(\frac{q_1}{p_1}\frac{\partial p_i}{\partial q_1} + \frac{q_2}{p_1}\frac{\partial p_2}{\partial q_1})$$

which becomes:

$$\frac{p_1 - \dfrac{\partial C}{\partial q_1}}{p_1} = \frac{\lambda}{1+\lambda}\frac{1}{\varepsilon_1}\frac{\varepsilon_1\varepsilon_2 - \varepsilon_1\varepsilon_{12}}{\varepsilon_1\varepsilon_2 - \varepsilon_{12}\varepsilon_{21}} = \frac{\lambda}{1+\lambda}\frac{1}{\eta}$$

where η is called the super-elasticity.

Oum and Tretheway (1988) have extended this basic analysis to include the case where goods or services produce externalities, the general situation in transport (as shown in Box 7.6).

These solutions enable us to present a general conclusion: price will deviate from marginal cost the more inelastic is demand. Moreover the existence of externalities plays an important role when the deficit with respect to marginal cost is small, but when the deficit is more important their incidence is reduced with respect to marginal private cost.

Note that these various imperfections can be dealt with together in the framework of a general equilibrium model which is also able to take into account equity and distribution concerns (see for instance De Borger and Proost , 2001 for a theoretical presentation and some applications).

Up to now we have assumed no information problems. This is not the case in the real world, where imperfect information takes various shapes.

2.2.3 Problems of uncertainty, information and institutions

It appears that, on the grounds of efficiency and equity, marginal social cost provides valid answers and leads to better outcomes than other concepts such as average cost or long-run marginal cost. But up to now the argument has been developed in an ideal world where information is perfect and there is no uncertainty. We now turn to more realistic situations where agents are confronted by asymmetric information (for instance, the infrastructure manager has a better knowledge of costs and demand than the regulator); there are conflicting objectives between institutions (the regulator aims at welfare maximising and firms aim at profit maximising) and there is uncertainty (so that it is not possible afterwards to know whether good results on costs are due to the efforts of productivity of a firm or to chance).

It is clear that institutional structure is important for the analysis. Information asymmetry between infrastructure management and operations is much lower when both are in the same organisation than when they are run by two different organisations. We assume here that, in the line of the reforms of the European Union (and according to the real situation in most modes of transport), there is separation between infrastructure management and the operators, and that the third actor is the regulator. The objectives of the operators, which are generally private firms, is to make a profit. The objective of the infrastructure manager is a mix of profit, bureaucratic goals (such as maximising turn-over) and welfare maximising, according to its status (for example whether it is a public corporation or a public service agency of government). The objective of the regulator is to achieve some kind of collective welfare. In this framework, there are two types of relations and information situations to analyse from the point of view of infrastructure charges: downstream between the infrastructure manager and the operators, and upstream between the infrastructure manager and the regulator.

Relations between the infrastructure manager and the operators
In this case the important change vis–à–vis the previous analysis is that neither the infrastructure manager nor the regulator know accurately the private value or collective costs of the services to be run on the infrastructure. The challenge is to induce efficiency in the downstream market of the operators. This opens the case for quantity regulation instead of price regulation, and for the use of auctions instead of charges to select the efficient services.

Price or quantity regulation. In terms of costs, there is considerable uncertainty over environmental damage. Thus, charges are uncertain and the welfare gain is unpredictable so quantity regulation may have more predictable and reliable effects (Weitzman, 1974). Whether it is better to allocate through prices or quantities will depend on the relative slopes of the two functions, and the distribution of uncertainty on demand and costs. A correct charging system would require a lot of information and imply high transaction costs (mainly costs of information and enforcement).

The use of auctions. The efficiency of pricing is that it is a mechanism for selecting the most efficient services, a mechanism which works well when the values of the operators are simple and not related to each other. This is more likely to be the case in road transport than in other modes such as rail and air transport, or more generally when there are scarce resources to allocated. In rail for instance, the value of a service for an operator depends on whether competitors have another service close to the first one, or whether the first operator has another service on a complementary line. Here the values of services are not independent and it can easily be shown that in such cases direct charging cannot select the most efficient operator, and charging is best replaced by auctions.

How to induce efficiency in operations. Also related to charging is the problems of how to induce efficiency in operations. The solution depends on how the downstream market operates. If the downstream market is competitive, efficiency is implemented by competition itself, the infrastructure manager does not have to deal with it, and the regulator simply has to ensure that competition works well.

If the downstream market is not competitive, the goal of achieving productivity or providing effort incentives is to offer a menu of tariffs (Laffont and Tirole, 1994). The simplest version of this is the two-part tariff where a large quantity is associated with a low unit price, close to the marginal cost, and a small quantity is associated with a high unit price. Efficient users will choose the former and the latter will be chosen by relatively inefficient users. The problem is that this may hamper new entrants which are small users, compared with incumbent firms which are generally large users.

This can be applied to any regulated transport production where there is segmented demand: passengers and freight on railroads, goods vehicles and private cars on highways, or more simply large and small users of an infrastructure. Social surplus maximization leads to the following best incentive to the regulated operator: high consumption should not be distorted (i.e. price should equal marginal cost), but low consumption is lower than when the operator has perfect information about users' preferences. In fact, the shadow cost of public funds induces the regulated firm to behave somewhat like a monopolist and to distort the consumption vector.

Well devised tariffs can achieve this goal over time: when uncertainty is low, the charge is close to the 'price-cap' type, which has a strong incentive effect and does not leave too much information rent; when uncertainty is high, charging is close to the 'cost plus' type: incentives must be reduced in order not to imply too high an information rent.

Relations between the infrastructure manager and the regulator.
The task to which charging can contribute is for the regulator to induce efficiency in the infrastructure manager's behaviour. Efficiency here is taken to have a very wide meaning: first, to minimise the cost of infrastructure provision; then to ensure static efficiency (the infrastructure manager does not misuse monopoly power); and finally to achieve dynamic efficiency (mainly to induce a correct infrastructure investment).

The solutions, and their problems of implementation, are classical: regulation on prices to avoid monopolistic behaviour, price-caps for cost-minimisation. A specific issue in the case of transport infrastructure is that large fixed costs and returns to scale may lead to rent-seeking by infrastructure managers whose objectives are more bureaucratic than welfare maximising. Given the uncertainty over costs, they advocate low charges based on low marginal costs and receive subsidies to cover fixed costs and the investment needed to cope with the demand which is artificially increased by the low charge. This transfers the burden to the tax payer. This argument is advanced by those favouring charging based on average cost. The solution of economic theory is to propose a menu of charges to the infrastructure manager. It appears that charges will be higher, and closer to average cost, when uncertainty and information asymmetry are high.

A further argument in favour of charges related to average cost is that without a link between expenditure and revenues, and the possibility of penalty if expenditures exceed revenues, there is a risk of over-investment. This arises from the uncertainty of investment appraisal and from strategic behaviour by infrastructure managers, guided by the bureaucratic goals of extension in the size of their business. The criterion of average cost ensures that the investment is profitable, but it leads to the rejection of other investments which are also profitable but do not satisfy this criterion.

The main idea here is to find a way of putting a link between expenditure and revenue. However, this link need just be a simple equality. A well devised lump-sum subsidy linked to better estimated of fixed costs, coupled with a break-even or profit maximising (subject to price–regulation) goal, may achieve the target of enhanced managerial efficiency and still allow for market efficiency through charging based on marginal social cost. When there are specific investments, especially large ones, a partnership or a merger of infrastructure managers and operators is to be recommended.

The problem in implementing this kind of solution is the risk of regulatory capture. Through time, as there are renegotiations of the contract between regulator and infrastructure manager, the regulation becomes more and more discretionary, and the risk of regulatory capture increases. Specific attention has to be given to fine-tuning of the financial arrangements. For instance, a private infrastructure manager whose goal is profit should not be directly given the revenues from congestion costs as it induces him to under-invest in infrastructure capacity. Such revenues would be better channelled through lump-sum subsidies.

Problems of jurisdictions. Institutional arrangements should take into consideration problems of jurisdictions, which can have consequences on infrastructure charging. These problems arise particularly in the case of international traffic (Courcelle *et al.*, 1998; Bassanini and Pouyet, 2000). Separate pricing of the leg of the journey in each country has effects on the tax revenue and on the externalities in the other country. The pricing policy depends on the degree of cooperation or competition between the two countries, and on the technical and legal possibilities of discriminating between domestic and foreign traffic. This will also depend on the priorities of environmental goals and budget constraints.

The analysis also needs to address the question of the effect of the hierarchy of jurisdictions. The hierarchy will impact on the cost of information transmission and processing, the completeness of contracts between the centre and the periphery, the effort incentive (Caillaud *et al.*, 1996). On the other hand, taxes by lower level jurisdictions can lead to problems of tax exporting, competitive tax spillovers, and beggar–my–neighbour tax competition (Inman and Rubinfeld, 1996).

2.3 Infrastructure Pricing: From Theory to Reality

In practice the pricing of infrastructure is very different from that suggested by the theory. It tends to be based much more on considerations of finance than on consideration of optimising use. We take each mode in turn.

For roads the main pricing tools are taxes on fuel, tolls, licences and parking charges. None of these allow for variations in time or through space in order to produce, however imperfectly, an allowance for the costs of congestion or environmental damage. Newbery (1995) has estimated the marginal costs of road use in Britain in a variety of situations. His estimated costs vary between up to €1.5 per km in urban areas at peak times to a few cents per km on rural roads. Other studies have produced similar results for a variety of different situations (Peirson *et al.*, 1995; de Palma and Marchal, 1998; Newbery, 1998a; Nicolas, 1998). The most recent and detailed study has been discussed in Chapter 5 (Sansom *et al.*, 2001). In comparison, taxes on fuel amount to between €0.05 and €0.10 per km.

The environment has not directly been the object of road taxes. In all countries which use direct tolls, these have the objective of providing the resources necessary for financing construction and not to influence the choices of users in respect of the marginal costs of use. In most cases, tolls tend to be used on uncongested inter-urban routes and not on congested highways around urban areas. Parking charges do tend to be higher in more congested areas and at times when traffic is greatest, but they are a long way from representing true resource costs (Calthrop *et al.*, 2000). One problem is that by reducing the period when vehicles can be parked they may contribute to increased mobility, whilst transit traffic is not affected. The system which would allow the recovery of the exact marginal costs does exist, electronic road pricing, where electronic cards can be debited directly on passing signal posts. Attempts to introduce such systems have typically met with political problems (one experiment in Hong Kong was abandoned after two years), although such a system is in operation in Singapore in conjunction with a system of high ownership taxes and vignettes. Cordon charges have been implemented in some Scandinavian cities and a charge of £5 (about €7) for access to Central London was introduced in 2003. The need to consider packages of measures together in order to meet the need for consistent policy has been argued in detail by De Borger and Proost (2001).

Turning to truck traffic, cost calculations show that the heaviest loads should pay very high taxes due to the damage inflicted on roads used, and which increase as the fourth power of the axle weight (see the evidence in Table 5.9). Different European countries reflect this to a varying extent in the taxes charged on heavy trucks, but none charges an amount equal to the full estimated damage, and where taxes on axle weights have been imposed this has often been compensated by much lower taxes on diesel fuel.

The situation is not much better in the case of other modes. Price structures in rail transport pay little regard to the costs of congestion. Prices at airports typically reflect a situation where publicly owned airport authorities are concerned solely with balancing revenue and costs and not with allocating slots efficiently. Prices tend to be fixed with respect to aircraft size and not with respect to the true burden each flight imposes. This situation is compounded by the fear of competition between airports where there becomes a reluctance to charge full economic prices to airlines who may use their monopsony power to take flights elsewhere.

3. INVESTMENT CHOICE

Investment decisions and the choice between different investments depend heavily on the concepts involved in the notion of consumers' surplus. The models developed in section 2.2.2 of this chapter provide us with basic choice rules, but are rather too theoretical to be the immediate basis for practical evaluation.

Practical methods depend essentially on the ability to calculate net surplus in such a way as to capture all the effects of the investment. In this we follow the ideas set out by Boiteux (1994). We look in turn at the development of the criterion, then at the conditions under which it holds and finally consider some gaps and the possibilities of using it in some specific cases.

3.1 The Criterion of Net Benefit

The aim is to take into account all the effects on users, time savings and changes in the cost of provision, effects which have repercussions on the whole economy. If the rest of the economy is in equilibrium, a partial analysis will summarize the global effects and the consumers' surplus of users will be a complete measure of the social surplus (see Dodgson, 1973; Jara-Diaz, 1986).

In practice there are non-optimalities associated with transport infrastructure as shown earlier:

- environmental externalities
- increasing returns
- the existence of government, which requires taking into account changes to transfers occasioned by the investment.

We examine each of these elements in the case of a toll road, which allows us to encounter most of the issues involved in the calculation of a rate of return.

3.1.1 User surplus

In its simplest sense (Figure 7.5), user surplus is calculated as the change in the area under the demand curve (which defines traffic as a function of the generalised cost of travel) when, as a result of the investment, the generalised cost falls from Cg_0 to Cg_1. This is the direct application of equation 7.3. This area can be approximated by:

$$CS = T_0(Cg_0 - Cg_1) + (T_1 - T_0)(Cg_1 - Cg_0)/2$$

where T_0 and T_1 are derived from traffic studies and the generalised costs Cg incorporate the money costs of travel, time spent and a measure of comfort and convenience, delay penalties and the value of time.

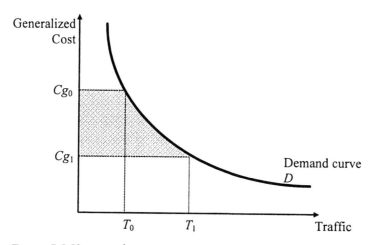

Figure 7.5 User surplus

The surplus comprises the reduction in costs to existing users T_0 and the surplus accruing to new users, induced by the reduction in costs to make journeys that were previously regarded as too expensive. Assuming a linear approximation of the demand curve these are valued (on average) at one half of the benefits to existing users (the so-called 'rule of a half').

An alternative way of calculating user surplus consists of basing it on the implicit law of demand contained in the traffic model itself. Thus, in the case of the discrete choice model, Small and Rosen (1981) have shown that he following expression defines user benefit:

$$CS = T \int_{U_0}^{U_1} \sum_{i=1}^{n} \pi_i(u) du$$

where:

i represents the available alternatives

U represents the indirect utility, indexed 0 in the initial situation and 1 in the final situation

$\pi_i(u)$ is the probability of choosing mode i when the utility associated with this mode is u.

If the choice model is of the logit type:

$$CS = (T/\lambda)\Delta[\log(\sum_i \exp(-\lambda u_i))]$$

which is equivalent to the accessibility equation used in Chapter 5. If the value of time used in the basic consumers' surplus approach is the same as that in the traffic model, and more generally if the generalized cost has the same formulation as that of utility in the traffic model, Jara-Diaz (1990) has shown that the two methods of calculating user benefit will give approximately the same result.

This supposes that the utilities defined in the traffic model represent the social value of transport. Considerations of equity or public service concepts suggest that there are differences between individual values and those of society as a whole. For this reason it is often decided to use, especially for the case of home-work journeys, the same value of time for all users rather than the ones suggested in individual behaviour.

We also need to question the degree of accuracy in the determination of values of time (and more generally other parameters relating to service quality) deduced from these models. It is easy to see that inaccuracies in their estimation could have little influence on the results of traffic studies, but have a considerable impact on the estimation of benefits (see Box 7.7). In these conditions it may be preferable to use a simpler model for calculating user benefits, using one value (or a range of values) of time (or service quality) based on various alternative methods, rather than just one implicit in a single model.

BOX 7.7

Sensitivity of benefits to values of time

The following simple illustrative example can easily be translated into real-world situations.

Assume that users consist of two groups of equal numbers. The first group has a value of time $h = 100$, for the second group the value is h', but h' is not known accurately and takes a value between 200 and 300.

In the initial situation, there is only one mode of transport, used by all users, with a price $p = 100$ and a travel time of $t = 1$. Suppose that a second mode of transport is introduced, which is faster but more expensive, with price, $p' = 200$ and travel time $t' = 0.3$. The cost for users in the first category is given by:

$$100 + 1 \times 100 = 200 \text{ for the old mode}$$
$$200 + 0.3 \times 100 = 230 \text{ for the new mode}$$

Thus users in category 1 do not change mode.

Costs for users in the second group are not known with certainty. For the old mode they will be between:

$$100 + 1 \times 200 = 300 \text{ and } 100 + 1 \times 300 = 400$$

and for the new mode between:

$$200 + 0.3 \times 200 = 260 \text{ and } 200 + 0.3 \times 300 = 290.$$

Thus the uncertainty over the value of time for users in the second category has no effect in the traffic model; in all cases the users will change mode. However, if we calculate the user benefit, this varies, by user, between:

$$300 - 260 = 40 \text{ and } 400 - 290 = 110$$

A particular consideration needs to be given to safety. This relates to uncertainty over the likelihood of accidents. Individuals may be ready to pay in order to reduce the risk of accidents, but they typically may not know these risks accurately. Only if they do know the risks is it legitimate to introduce a safety element into the generalised cost of the individual, if they do not know the risks accurately it should not be included in the generalised cost, but a measure of the change in the total cost of safety would need to be introduced in any valuation of the investment.

3.1.2 Environmental externalities

Taking environmental costs into account does not pose any particular problem in principle once the range of relevant costs has been identified. It is sufficient to evaluate these impacts in the initial and final situations (quantity of pollutants emitted, decibels of noise, etc), and to multiply these physical quantities by the unit costs of the damage. However, there remain some environmental effects where both the measurement of the physical impacts and their evaluation continue to present some difficulties, for example the effects of segregation, water and soil pollution and the impact of intrusion and aesthetic effects on landscapes.

3.1.3 The organisations managing transport

Those responsible for the management of infrastructure expect both their costs and their revenues to change if they invest in developing the infrastructure. If the operators face constant returns and charge prices according to marginal cost (i.e. equal to average cost) the costs and the additional revenues will cancel out. If, as is more likely, they face increasing returns, and/or do not charge prices for the use of infrastructure at marginal cost, it will be necessary to include in the calculation of net benefit any increases in their profits/economic rents (see Box 7.1).

3.1.4 The state and taxpayers

The net benefit is measured at market prices and thus includes all indirect taxes. In a situation where the government runs a balanced budget (which is typically assumed for comparative static analysis) any change in the tax revenues of the State following the development of the new infrastructure requires an equal, but opposite in sign, change in the taxes paid by general taxpayers.

   If all indirect taxes are at the same rate, this would only have the effect of multiplying the individual benefits by the same coefficient. But the goods not affected by this tax rate, for example those with higher taxes such as fuel, will be affected differentially and this will require an adjustment to the benefits to allow for this (see Box 7.8).

BOX 7.8

Taking fuel taxes into account

If a good a, for example fuel, is taxed at a different rate from the normal rate of indirect taxes θ, the equilibrium of the firm which produces it, assuming a competitive market where the good is sold at marginal cost, can be written thus (using the index i for all other goods in the economy, and writing as p_i the tax inclusive price):

$$\sum_i p_i(1-\theta)dq_i + p_a(1-\theta_a)dq_a = 0$$

If the road investment leads to a change dq_a in the consumption of good a, the final benefit would be, with the same rate of tax applied to all goods;

$$dU = \sum p_i dq_i = -p_a dq_a$$

Taking account of the different rate of tax, it becomes:

$$dU = -\frac{\theta-\theta_a}{1-\theta} p_a dq_a$$

In comparison with a common tax rate θ, the existence of a differential tax gives the State a bonus of revenue equal to $(\theta-\theta_a)$ times the price before tax, thus $\dfrac{\theta-\theta_a}{1-\theta} p_a$ per unit of good consumed (or saved).

3.1.5 Summary

The total of these elements which have to be disentangled must now be combined with the process of realising the investment. The same good considered at two points in time is in effect two goods with different values, with the current good having in general a higher value than one which is only available later (Varian 1992). The preference for consumption now rather than later (time-preference) is given by the real rate of interest (after removing the effects of inflation).

Each element in the net benefit calculation has to be evaluated in terms of its present value and not at the date that it is actually incurred in order to make a sensible comparison. If, at the end of its useful life, the investment still has a residual value, this must also be integrated into the final calculation. This is expressed as the net present value of the project in the form:

$$B = -\frac{I}{(1+i)^t} + \sum_{t=t_0+1}^{t=T} \frac{A(t)-r(t)}{(1+i)^t} + VR/(1+i)^{T+1}$$

where:

i is the rate of interest /discount

I   is the cost of the investment, allowing for the fact that the expenditure
       may be incurred over several years and may involve changes in
       investments in other operations
t_o is the year in which operation begins
r(t) represents the changes in the costs of maintenance and annual
       operational costs in year *t*
VR   is the residual value of the investment
A(t) is the sum of the various changes in benefits accruing to the various
       groups discussed above:
- user benefits
- property owner benefits
- benefits to infrastructure operators
- benefits to the State (taxpayers).

3.1.6 Using the investment rule for decision making

How can we use this criterion in order to select projects and develop
investment?

The use of the net present value concept enables us first of all to identify
the optimal date to undertake a project. This is the time t_0 which maximises
the net present value $B(t_0)$ (Box 7.9). This maximisation depends on all the
various parameters in the equation. But there can be situations, found fairly
frequently, where this produces an interesting outcome: this is where the life
of the investment is infinite and the benefits increase through time (for
example because traffic is growing). Then the optimal date for the
investment is year t_0 which (according to Box 7.9) will be:

$$\frac{A(t_0)}{I} = i$$

thus the immediate net benefit of the project is equal to the discount rate.

BOX 7.9

Determining the optimal timing of an investment

Assuming continuous time and calling:

θ the year of initial operation
t   the current year
$a(t,\theta)$ benefits accruing in year *t* given initial operation in year θ
I   the cost of the investment
r   the discount rate
B   net present value

we obtain:

$$B(\theta) = \int_{t=\theta}^{\infty} a(t,\theta)\exp(-rt)dt - I\exp(-r\theta)$$

If the function $a(\ )$ does not depend on θ and is increasing with t, then the maximum of B is obtained for θ as shown by:

$$a(\theta) = rI$$

The net present value of benefits criterion also enables us to compare mutually exclusive projects, for example two alternative routes for the same project. The optimal date can be obtained for each and a choice between the two projects made on the basis of the greater net present value at that date. Decisions concerning independent projects (those where the returns from one project are not affected by the existence of the other project) are equally straightforward: each project is undertaken at its optimal date. When projects are not completely independent it is necessary to identify the possible sequences of investments in order to determine the optimal date for realising each project, and the net present value at that date in order to identify the optimal sequence as that which produces the greatest total net present values.

It is necessary to understand the limits of the net present value criterion. It is not a process of optimisation, simply a comparison between a proposed project and a reference situation. The fact that the net present value is positive only shows that the project is preferred to the reference situation. It is thus particularly important to ensure that the reference situation is chosen with care, and to identify a wide range of possible alternative projects for comparison. The reference situation should ideally be the best possible alternative to the project which is being evaluated. One can never be sure exactly what this will be, since it requires that all the possible hierarchies of projects have been identified. However, there is a tendency for analysts to choose an inappropriate reference situation in order to bias the evaluation in favour of the chosen project. It is also important to ensure the inclusion of as wide a set of alternatives as possible, not forgetting that an appropriate alternative to an infrastructure investment project could involve a management or pricing option for existing infrastructure, an investment in an alternative mode, or even a change of policy in a sector other than transport which would have transport repercussions.

3.1.7 Validity conditions of net present value criterion

The essential conditions to ensure the validity of the net present value criterion are that:

- the change being made is essentially marginal in character,
- the rest of the economy is optimal (that is firms are price-takers),
- we ignore problems of distribution, justified on the basis that we assume that the initial distribution is optimal and that any lump sum transfers to correct specific incidences of benefits are made.

We can illustrate through some examples the problems caused by these assumptions not holding.

Non marginal changes

As we have already seen, consumers' surplus in the sense developed by Dupuit and Marshall is essentially arbitrary. More appropriate measures are the equivalent or compensating variations in income which are defined with reference to the compensated or Hicksian demand curves. Kanemoto and Mera (1985) have shown how the conventional approach for marginal changes can be modified to suit discrete changes. Morisugi and Hayashiyama (1997) have calculated both the conventional consumers' surplus and the equivalent variation attributable to the development of the Japanese railway network over around a century showing that the difference between the two measures is small, and certainly smaller than the measurement errors affecting such a calculation.

Effect of non-optimal pricing in transport

The assumption that the rest of the economy is in a first best optimum implies that the new infrastructure should be priced at marginal social cost. If this is not the situation the investment choice rule does not apply and has to be modified as shown in Box 7.10, based on a simple example (see Nilsson 1992 for a more complete analysis in the case of several substitute modes and SACTRA, 1999, for the implications for the evaluation of projects).

BOX 7.10

Investment rules in the case of non-optimal pricing
(after Small 1992)

Assume a road on which each user takes time $t(q, k)$ which depends on traffic q and the length of the road K; the value of time, common to all users, is h; the annual cost of the road is ρK (depreciation + maintenance). Demand is given by $p(q)$. Social benefit is given by:

$$CS(q,K) = \int_0^q p(u)du - hqt(q,K) - \rho K$$

It can easily be seen that maximisation with respect to q and K depends on the usual rules relating to:

- price:

$$p(q) = ht(q,K) + hq\frac{\partial t}{\partial q}$$

- and investment choice:

$$\rho = -hq\frac{\partial t}{\partial K}$$

Suppose now that the price is sub-optimal. This is represented by a constraint:

$$p(q) - ht(q,K) - p_0 \le 0$$

where p_0 is the price imposed, below the optimum price. If λ is the dual variable associated with this constraint, it can be seen that:

$$\rho = -h\frac{\partial t}{\partial K}(q - \lambda)$$

Thus the investment choice rule has to be modified: the rate of return is calculated applying the time saving allowed by the investment, not to traffic q, but to traffic $(q - \lambda)$.

It can be seen that where prices below the optimum are charged the usual investment choice rule tends to overestimate the rate of return on investments. The distortion occasioned by investment decisions based on incorrect pricing are profound and can be illustrated by the Braess paradox met in Chapter 4, which shows an example where even a costless investment could be erroneous.

Another example is that where the demand for transport on a particular route is very elastic. Thus in Figure 7.6 we see that an increase in capacity leads to a very small reduction in the generalised cost of its use and the investment will give a low rate of return.

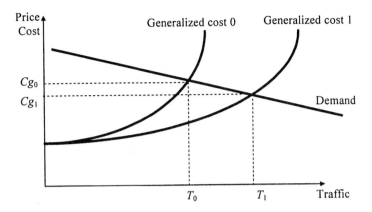

Figure 7.6 Consequences of an elastic demand for transport

Alternatively the imposition of a congestion charge would have much greater effects on generalised cost, on traffic and on social welfare. These considerations show the importance of accurate traffic modelling, particularly with respect to induced traffic. Figure 7.7 shows two different situations, that on the left is more likely to represent interurban conditions and that on the right urban conditions (Jansson, 1993).

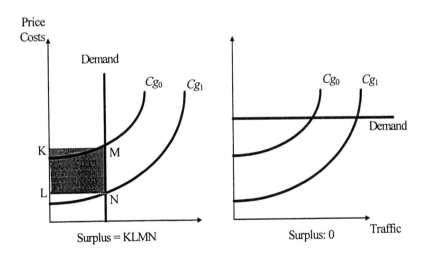

Figure 7.7 Consequences of different approaches to dealing with induced traffic

Goodwin (1996) develops this point, using before and after studies to show that in general induced traffic is underestimated in urban conditions and deduced that rates of return are usually over-estimated. This point was discussed in detail in SACTRA (1994) and a more formal analysis has been developed by Venables (1999).

Non-optimalities outside the transport system
Non-optimalities outside the transport system can also be relevant. Box 7.11 provides an example of the errors which can arise in the presence of a monopoly which aims to maximise profit.

BOX 7.11

The calculation of rate of return in the presence of monopoly

Assume an economy consisting of:

- a consumption good q: produced in competitive conditions, which only employs natural resources in the quantity q
- a good s: produced by a monopolist at constant unit cost c, sold at unit price p.

Transport between the residential location and the monopolist t is produced by each household at a constant unit cost, each unit of transport moves one unit of good s produced by the monopolist. Traffic on the road is s. Individuals have a utility function: $U(q,s) = q + u(s)$. The natural resource used in production is available in a limited quantity r and thus:

$$q + cs + ts = r$$

The behaviour of consumers is described by:

$$t + p = u'(s)$$

That of the monopolist by:

$$Max_s[(u'(s) - t - c)s]$$

The monopolist will produce the quantity, s^*, such that:

$$u' - t - c + su'' = 0$$

Suppose that the cost of transport changes from t to $t + dt$. By the usual calculation of the welfare effect of this change we obtain the value:

$$dCS_u = -sdt$$

which is the consumer's surplus of the user. This has to be modified to take into account the fact that there is only a limited quantity of natural resources r which does not change, thus:

$$dr = dq + cds + tds + sdt$$

From this it can be seen that:

$$dSC_u = dq + (c + t)ds$$

In fact the true change in welfare is equal to the change in utility of the households:

$$dSC = \frac{\partial U}{\partial q} dq + \frac{\partial U}{\partial s} ds = dq + u'(s)ds = dq + (p + t)ds$$

Since p differs from c, dSC differs from dSC_u

It can thus be seen that the exact value of the change in welfare is obtained by adding to the user benefit dSC_u the change in profit at a constant price of the monopolist:

$$d\Pi = d[(p - c)s] = (p - c)ds + sdp = \delta\Pi + sdp.$$

In effect:

$$\delta\Pi = (p - c)ds$$

and:

$$dSC = dSC_u + \delta\Pi$$

Macro-economic disequilibrium

In situations where full employment does not hold there will also be a divergence from the social optimum. In effect the theorem establishing the equivalence between the partial and general equilibrium analysis is no longer valid (see Box 7.1). There are two possible ways of taking into account the existence of unemployment. The first consists effectively of calculating the benefits using a price of labour which is below the market price in order to reflect that the market price does not reflect the true social cost of labour: this is to use a so-called shadow price of labour. The second method consists of estimating the amount of employment which would be created by the proposal and adding this to the conventional benefit estimate. The difficulty of this method is that of estimating the employment which will be created which can be genuinely ascribed to the project, not just the directly created employment but any induced by the initial boost to employment. As we have seen in earlier chapters there is a tendency to try and inflate the employment creating impacts of large projects and it is often difficult to obtain unambiguous estimates.

Cost of public funds.
It is often assumed that public funds have a cost different from that of private funds to the extent that the taxes which provide them are not optimal. Thus one public euro is not equal to one private euro but rather to $(1 + \lambda)$ private euro. If the use of public funds is thus translated by this factor $(1 + \lambda)$ it can be shown that an optimal investment decision rule is obtained. This is the same as allowing for an externally imposed constraint on the availability of credit.

3.1.8 Gaps in the net present value criterion
The net present value criterion does have some gaps in its coverage which pose problems for the decision maker in making a choice of investments. It is restricted to the purely financial aspects, or at least to those aspects which can easily be monetised, and thus ignores impacts on the ecological balance, aesthetic concerns, wider impacts on economic development, constraints on financing, distributional impacts and the existence of uncertainty.

Impacts on ecological balance and aesthetic concerns
These two issues have similar characteristics which make it difficult, on the basis of current knowledge to be translated into monetary terms.

Impacts on ecological balance can be measured simply as the change in biodiversity. A new infrastructure will, by disturbing the local ecology, lead to the dispersion of certain species, or their complete destruction, initially locally and potentially globally. This is the basis of much ecological opposition to new infrastructure, but how can this be quantified in monetary terms against the identifiable benefits? Biodiversity impacts bring together all of the problems encountered in trying to evaluate non-marketed goods: long-term impacts affecting future generations, considerable uncertainty over the precise impacts, how to measure the option or existence values of resources, which are probably rather higher than the resources current value in use. Contingent valuation methods provide an approach, but the results are often unreliable due to lack of information on the part of those interviewed or failure to conduct interviews carefully. Reliable evaluation on the basis of damage costs is extremely difficult due to the lack of sufficient long-run information.

Similar considerations apply to the consideration of aesthetics, the issue of how new infrastructures look, how they affect the landscape and impact on the existing built-up environment. It is again possible to conduct interviews to obtain the views of the public, from which contingent valuations can be derived which can be used in net present value calculations. But again these are costly and unreliable.

Taking into account these two types of impact cannot easily be achieved in terms of monetary measures. All that can be done safely is to describe the impacts and provide this information to the decision-makers to be taken into account alongside the net present value calculation. Some countries use a multi-criteria analysis procedure which enables decision-makers to establish a consistent framework within which such decisions can be taken, using past weightings on each element as a guide. Even without such a formal approach, it is possible to present all the information in a common way to decision makers so there is at least a consistent view taken of all projects, as for example in the New Approach to Appraisal in the UK which uses an Assessment Summary Table to bring all the factors together (see Vickerman, 2000b).

Uncertainty
Two categories of uncertainty are relevant to the analysis. The first does not reduce through time, for example there may be uncertainty over construction costs even where all necessary studies have been carried out to reduce the uncertainty. The other category is that which can, at least partially, be reduced in the future, for example uncertainty over future economic growth. We can analyse these two types of uncertainty using the classic tools of risk analysis, in particular taking account of attitudes to risk. The simplest way of representing this is to assume an agent facing a lottery in which the outcome is an average sum of $\overline{g}$ with probability σ which is associated with a utility not equal to $\overline{g}$, but to $(\overline{g} - r\sigma^2/2)$. In this expression r is a coefficient which represents the agent's degree of aversion to risk ($r = 0$ represents a situation where the individual is risk-neutral).

Irreducible uncertainty
Given these analytical tools it is relatively easy in principle to introduce uncertainty into the calculation of rates of return as long as it is possible to define the probabilities of possible events. When there is neither aversion to, nor preference for, risk (risk–neutrality) and the outcome is linear in the probabilities, it is relatively easy to define the rate of return. Where there is risk aversion or non-linear probabilities, errors are more likely. Two specific cases can be used to illustrate these differences. The first concerns the calculation of the benefits from an investment when there is an irreducible uncertainty in forecast traffic T. The benefit is then calculated in the form:

$$A = hTt(T)$$

where h is the value of time, T is traffic and $t(T)$ is the travel time, which displays a strong curvature as traffic approaches saturation levels. Because of this curvature, if T is a probabilistic variable $E(A)$ can be very different from $A(T^*)$, and the method for calculating the rate of return on the investment will in general correct for this effect.

The second example relates to risk aversion, which can differ substantially from one individual to another depending both on attitude and on wealth. For example, a lottery where there is a 50 per cent chance of losing 100 and a 50 per cent chance of gaining 100 has an expected value of 0 to an individual with a wealth of 1 million, large relative to the risk involved. On the other hand, for an individual with a wealth of 100, the gamble would be very dangerous since it implies a risk of complete ruin, and hence risk aversion is likely to be much greater. Thus for investment decisions, public authorities will have a degree of risk aversion which is much less than that of private investors. This translates into the practicalities of choice, public sector decision makers are more likely to concern themselves with the average rate of return without so much concern over risk whereas private investors, and particularly banks which traditionally have a strong degree of risk aversion, pay more attention to risk. Both may be likely to make inappropriate decisions because of their extreme attitudes to risk.

Reducible uncertainty and irreversibility
The previous examples of uncertainties which can not be reduced are extreme cases. In the majority of cases, uncertainty can be expected to be reduced through time; as our knowledge improves so can our decisions. However, this can still give rise to problems when decisions cannot be reversed, as is often the case with investment in infrastructure where, once the infrastructure has been built it is not possible to change its use if, for example, it proves to be unprofitable. The investment constitutes a sunk cost.

This can be illustrated by reference to a simple example, based on Pindyck (1991). Assume an investment costing 800 which will produce a certain revenue in the first year of 100 and then in every subsequent year to infinity either 50 with a probability of 0.5 or 150 with a probability of 0.5. In the case of irreducible uncertainty analysed above the net present value of the investment can be calculated as:

$$NPV = -800 + \sum_{t=0}^{\infty} \frac{100}{(1.1)^t} = 300$$

assuming that the discount rate is 10 per cent and the investment can be realised immediately.

It is different if in a year more is known than today. In this case should we wait a year before taking the decision ? To see this calculate the NPV in $t=1$ and if the sum received is 50, it is easy to see that there is no interest in investing because then the NPV is:

$$NPV(p = 50) = -\frac{800}{1.1} + \sum_{t=1}^{\infty} \frac{50}{(1.1)^t} < 0$$

If on the other hand the annual profit in $t = 1$ is 150, it will be worth investing since the NPV is:

$$NPV(p = 150) = -\frac{800}{1.1} + \sum_{t=1}^{\infty} \frac{150}{(1.1)^t} = 772$$

Thus the expected NPV in case of a decision at $t = 1$ is:

$$\tfrac{1}{2}(0) + \tfrac{1}{2}(772) = 386$$

which is greater than the NPV of the decision to invest immediately. Thus it will be better to wait a year and the acquisition of information increases the value of the future decisions. The difference between the NPV of the optimally timed decision and that of the immediate investment is called the (option value) of the investment, it is the supplement which an investor is ready to pay for the right to wait in order to make better informed decisions, a sort of value of flexibility.

The model presented above is simplistic to the extent that uncertainty is removed totally at a specific date. Reality is better represented in a model where uncertainty is reduced little by little (see Pindyck, 1991). In such a situation the rule by which the immediate profitability of an investment is equated to the discount rate has to be modified: the investment must be realised for a higher value than the discount rate, the extent of this depends on the probabilities.

Distributional impacts

In principle, compensation should resolve the distributional objectives desired by society at large. In practice, however, this does not happen and the compensation implied by the theory is rarely if ever carried out. Moreover, the tools which would allow the calculation of such compensation are not available. In effect, in the usual calculation of benefit, the user surplus is only an intermediate stage in the calculation as shown in Box 7.1. The benefit created by the investment does not remain with the users, but is dispersed through the economy. To determine the true beneficiaries of the investment it would be necessary to develop a complete model of the economy. Some land-use transport models attempt to do this, but these tend only to provide an effective estimate of the geographical distribution of any change in the regional product. Computable general equilibrium models can do this between sectors, but less easily between individuals as they usually work with the assumption of a representative individual.

In any case compensation criteria are not complete and unambiguous, especially when the changes are not marginal. Finally, redistribution has impacts on efficiency and in practice it is not possible to separate the two problems: first aim to achieve efficiency and then distribute the product.

Impacts on economic development
The impact of transport improvements on economic development can be viewed at both the national and regional levels.

At the regional level the typical overriding concern is one of redistribution between regions in the interest of achieving greater convergence or cohesion. This applies both in national policy and, for example, as part of the development of EU policy. Frequently the political desire for a visible policy instrument such as transport infrastructure takes precedence over the accurate calculation of economic benefit. As we have seen in Chapters 2 and 3, the improvement of communications does not give such an unambiguous impact on the regional economy and it is just as possible that improvements can induce polarisation in economic activity and divergence rather than convergence in regional performance.

Besides these spatial effects improvements in transport infrastructure will have a wider macroeconomic effect through an impact on productivity, as seen in Chapter 1. The question here is whether it is reasonable or feasible to take these effects into account in project evaluation. Essentially it is not possible to give an unambiguous answer; some ex-post calculations suggest a systematically higher rate of return than ex-ante analyses. However, these effects vary considerably from project to project and it is not possible to generate a simple multiplier effect which could be applied to all evaluations.

Which community is relevant for the evaluation?
Whereas it is frequently obvious that a particular investment affects just a single community, both in terms of its costs and its benefits, transport infrastructure increasingly affects more than one community. Thus defining the appropriate community becomes a key question. This is particularly relevant for investments at the EU level which, even when not international infrastructures, can have impacts on other member states. This can be through the direct creation of externalities such as congestion and environmental effects by transit traffic, but also by changing the balance of economic activity between member states. Where European Union funds are used to finance the investment there is also an element of transfer involved.

Courcelle *et al.* (1998) have studied this from a theoretical point of view using a model of two countries within which there is both national and international traffic. This reveals a number of interdependences. For example a change in the price of transport in country 1 has a direct effect on the utility of consumers in that country, but also through local external effects and changes in government tax revenues. For consumers in country 2 there are effects through cross-border pollution and through public finances. According to the degree of cooperation between the countries there can be different investment and pricing policies in the two countries, and this may differ according to the extent to which it is possible to discriminate between the residents of the different countries. Without cooperation, if each country can discriminate there will be a tendency to try and impose a higher tax on foreign traffic. This has been the basis of Swiss policy towards transit traffic. Non-cooperative behaviour can produce solutions which are not globally efficient.

In a different analysis, using a computable general equilibrium model, Bröcker (1998, 2000) has shown how the benefits of different key EU infrastructure are distributed between the member states. Some projects have relatively small benefits accruing to the member states directly affected, and thus a relatively large Community-wide benefit for the EU. On the other hand there are projects which imply a redistribution from the EU as a whole to the individual member states.

3.2 Putting Investment Choice into Practice

There are two basic issues in implementation: the experience gained from studies and the extent to which these have weight in decision-making. We deal with each of these issues before discussing the impact of different modes of financing projects.

3.2.1 Practical experience of evaluation studies

There is an enormous wealth of experience of different types of study which have been carried out in different countries and for different modes of transport. Studies of road investment have been most widely developed, and show the greatest uniformity. This has led to the development of manuals which specify in precise detail how to carry out such studies in order to obtain a degree of uniformity in evaluation and allow for comparison.

Thus we find for example, in France a general report (Boiteux, 2000), which defines the main principles of implementation of economic methods from which the Ministry of Transport has developed precise evaluations procedures (Quinet, 2000). In the UK, following the original report of the Leitch Committee in 1977 (ACTRA, 1977), there have been successive revisions to the Cost–Benefit Analysis procedure (COBA) incorporating recommendations of successive reports by the Standing Advisory Committee on Trunk Road Assessment (SACTRA, 1986, 1992, 1994, 1999). This has been made more general in the New Approach to Appraisal which incorporates a number of elements not included in the strict economic evaluation of COBA. This has now been extended to apply to modes other than road in the Guidance on Methods for Multi-Modal Studies (GOMMMS) (Department for Transport, 2003; Vickerman, 2000b). In Germany, evaluation is based on a cost–benefit analysis, but one in which a rather wider range of impacts is formally included than in the UK COBA model, particularly environmental and regional economic impacts (Rothengatter, 2000; Bundesministerium für Verkehr, 2003). It is impossible to review all the national approaches in detail, but a valuable comparative exercise is contained in Bristow and Nellthorp (2000).

Table 7.1 summarizes some basic differences in the key values for France, Germany and the UK.

Table 7. 1 Key values for road project evaluation

Value	France	Germany	UK
Value of working time, car users €/hr	21	20	18
Value of human life, €mn	0.56	0.79	1.0
Discount rate, %	8	3	6–8*
Project life, years	20	40	30

Note: * In the latest Treasury Green Book (HM Treasury, 2003) this value is reduced to 3.5% and it is recommended that a declining schedule of rates should be used for very long-term projects (over 30 years life)

Source: Hayashi and Morisugi (2000)

The key issues which arise in these procedures, and which receive different emphasis or different values are:

- the inclusion of non-monetised factors, and if so how (e.g. formal multi-criteria analysis, informal summarising);
- the parameters of cost reduction included (time savings, accident reduction, maintenance costs, etc);
- the values attached to these parameters (how they are derived, whether standard values or a range of values are used);
- the treatment of induced demand;
- the inclusion of wider economic impacts, either local or national, and whether based on a single indicator such as employment or a more general measure of economic welfare;
- the appropriate discount rate;
- the assumption about project life.

As well as the precise criteria which are used to carry out an evaluation there are differences according to the relevant stage in the process at which the evaluation is undertaken. Traditionally there are three stages to this process:

- long-term planning: most countries have some form of overall strategic plan for transport infrastructure development, such as the various Schémas Directeurs in France or the Bundesverkehrswegeplan (BVWP) in Germany. These provide a framework for the main axes of development rather than precise projects or defined final routes. They establish the relative importance of different modes, the strategic priorities for geographical development and a broad indicator of the financial cost. They are not typically based on detailed project evaluations and rates of return, if given, are indicative and more related to the macroeconomic importance of the schemes, long-run budgetary considerations and long-run environmental commitments.
- medium-term planning: within the strategic planning framework medium-term plans are concerned with fixing details of more precise routes, scheduling projects in budgets, etc. It is at this stage that more precise economic evaluation is needed, although until final decisions are taken it is often difficult to perform complete evaluations. This leads to difficulties in that evaluations tend to be based on a comparison of a defined project with a do-nothing situation rather than on a comparison of a range of alternative projects, especially on a range of projects using alternative modes.
- implementation: this is concerned with the detailed final planning of project design, usually requiring a decision to have been taken to proceed with the project, but here dealing with the planning inquiry and legal procedures to implement the project. Economic evaluation is again less important at this stage since the key decisions will have been taken, even though detailed changes made at this stage may have substantial impacts on both net benefits and rates of return.

It will be noted that the window within which serious economic evaluation is undertaken is quite narrow and often has to be undertaken before detailed plans are finalised. The latter, including modifications to accommodate specific environmental or human interests, or to allow for changing government priorities can be very costly and fundamentally change the nature of a project. This leads to the observation that many large projects appear to face enormous cost overruns after they have been evaluated (Flyvbjerg *et al.* 2003). In these cases it is not always an error in evaluation which causes the problem, but in effect a fundamental change in the project itself. As an example, the Channel Tunnel between the UK and France experienced an effective doubling in the total cost of development, but a considerable proportion of this was due to the need to revise the project to allow for changing governmental safety requirements during the period of construction (Holliday *et al.*, 1991).

We have discussed above the use of economic evaluation tools in the context of new infrastructure investment, since this is where they are most frequently used. However, there is no need to restrict their use solely to this type of evaluation; indeed efficiency suggests that the same approach to evaluation should be applied to all policy measures. These could include investment in traffic management systems to improve efficiency in the management of infrastructure, or the introduction of pricing systems (see SACTRA, 1999, for a fuller discussion). Frybourg and Orselli (1997) have evaluated the Sirius project, a real-time traffic information system for the Paris freeways, demonstrating that the time savings to traffic (even that which did not use the information to change route) led to a rate of return of the order of 100 per cent. Similar returns have been identified by Perrett and Stevens (1996), much greater than the typical returns on infrastructure investment. This suggests strongly the need to ensure that there is a level playing field within which all transport projects are evaluated on the same basis.

3.2.2 Using evaluations in decision-making

In most countries evaluation procedures are applied in rather different ways in different modes and, within modes, in different situations. Thus, for example, in the UK whilst all road developments have been subject to the COBA procedure, rail investment has typically required a narrower financial rate of return except where there were some identifiable regional economic benefits. In France, rather different criteria are applied according to whether the project is an inter-urban project, a metropolitan project or a local provincial project. This means that rather different rates of return are sought in different cases. Where wider impacts are included, the criterion for acceptance can often be rather weaker.

Nilsson (1991) analyses the use made of cost-benefit analysis in Sweden. By comparing ex-ante and ex-post results from more than 200 road projects he concluded that CBA had had very weak impact on the ranking of projects, but that other, often non-quantified impacts, such as the expected impact on employment had been rather more important in reaching decisions on projects and that costs of construction had been strongly under-estimated. Flyvbjerg *et al.* (2003) argue that under-estimation of costs and over-estimation of traffic or revenues arise as a result of the typical authorisation procedures used for such projects, characterised by:

- the absence of a sufficiently well-defined study prior to the decision leading to premature commitments which became irreversible;
- excessive concentration on the technical aspects of projects to the exclusion of the economic aspects;
- delay in the recognition of external effects;
- individuals and groups affected by a project brought into the process too late;
- no analysis of risk;
- the institutional arrangements for project control and ownership are not sufficiently considered in the preparation of a project so that there is no clear client–contractor relationship.

This results in both confusion and conflict between project promoters, project financers, those affected directly and indirectly by the project and the public authorities with ultimate responsibility for taking the decision and coping with the consequences of success or failure. It is thus necessary to develop much clearer mechanisms to identify roles and responsibilities; this implies clearer objectives, clear penalties for failure and mechanisms for their enforcement. This applies whether the project is a public sector project undertaken by the public sector, or a project for which both the management and the implementation is ceded to the private sector.

3.2.3 Private finance of infrastructure

Private finance of infrastructure is used for several different reasons. One of the main arguments advanced in favour of private finance is that it solves some of the problems outlined in the preceding section by introducing a much clearer set of contractual relationships which can ensure better decision-making. However, the most frequent reasons for using private finance are less to do with these efficiency arguments than to increase the available resources for infrastructure investment, make these available earlier than would be possible from public budgets, and to reduce the pressure on public budgets. The basic principle is a simple one: the right to build and operate an infrastructure is conceded to a private sector operator who provides the finance and manages the project for a defined period, after which it is returned to the public sector. The principle of a concession or franchise requires a contractual obligation to carry out the defined works, maintain the infrastructure and provide a minimum level of service for a set period (typically between 20 and 50 years). The degree of regulation over the operation can vary. From the public sector's point of view there is the perceived benefit of a transfer of some of the risk to the private sector, which in turn has an incentive to reduce that risk for which it will be rewarded by a higher return on the assets invested.

Within the broad principle there are many variations on the private finance model. These relate to the legal status of the operator, to the degree of risk transfer, to the degree and nature of regulation.

Private sector infrastructure operators can be fully independent private companies (such as Eurotunnel, the Channel Tunnel operator), privatised companies subject to regulation (such as Railtrack, the privatised British rail infrastructure operator, or joint public–private ventures (such as the majority of Sociétés d'Autoroutes, the French motorway operators). In some cases the private operator is a single company, which can be either an existing company or one set up for the specific purpose of developing a specific infrastructure. In many cases the range of expertise required to plan, build and operate an infrastructure leads to joint ventures, often between construction firms and banks, both if which have particular interests in the development of infrastructure. Notably in these cases the focus is again on the finance and construction of the infrastructure rather than its efficient operation, although the development of new urban transit systems has often involved experienced public transport operators in the consortia. In many cases the private operator only assumes a portion of the risk, since the public sector continues to be involved. This involvement may be in the form of a public–private partnership, a route also found in urban public transit developments where the public sector retains a degree of management control in return for substantial subsidy, but the private sector has to accept a share of the risk, particularly in the construction phase in return for a share in the profit. More often the involvement is through direct subsidy to a private operator, or the provision of public sector guarantees or through regulation.

Subsidies and guarantees enable the private operator to obtain finance at a lower cost than might otherwise be possible, since it provides a degree of government backing. However, this implies the retention of a degree of risk by the public sector. The collapse of Railtrack in the UK was occasioned by the ultimate refusal of the government to continue paying increasing subsidies and to have to accept the implicit risk in its operations. Its subsequent replacement by Network Rail, a not-for-profit company, showed, however, the limit of this risk sharing since the government did have in effect to provide some compensation for shareholders, the argument being that government controls the regulatory framework (including access charges and subsidies for public-interest investments) which set the financial environment within which the private sector operator has to work. In the limit it is not clear that, even where no guarantees are given, there is any real transfer of risk to the private sector since large-scale infrastructure projects by their nature, once authorised, acquire a degree of public sector interest.

Regulation can be a fairly light quality control (for example, Eurotunnel is required to provide a minimum level of service at all times of the day and year), but more frequently involves either price or rate of return regulation. Price regulation has been widely used for tolled roads, bridges and tunnels, but has also been used with respect to rail track access charges. This is similar to the price regulation which is common in other privately provided public utilities where there is effectively the replacement of a public monopoly with a private monopoly. The tendency is to use price regulation as a means of forcing the private sector to continue to seek greater efficiency through the use of price limit fixed in relation to the rate of price inflation (RPI – X, where X is the percentage below the retail price index below which price increases must fall). In the UK it has been announced in 2003 that rail fares will rise at a rate above inflation for a period as the efficiency gains have not been sufficient to generate the revenue needed for continued investment. Rate of return regulation has not been so widely used in transport, but involves the government setting a limit to the effective rate of return on assets rather than a direct control on price.

From this it can be seen that private finance raises two broad sorts of issue which need to be explored further: the impact on the cost of provision of infrastructure; and the impact on the infrastructure investment programme itself.

Impacts on the provision of infrastructure
A concession gives rise to a series of contracts. The principal contract is between the authority ceding the concession (usually the government) and the concessionaire (who secures the right to develop and operate the infrastructure). Other contracts link the concessionaire to the banks, insurance companies, construction firms and regulatory authorities responsible for certifying and authorising the infrastructure. Wherever such a contract is signed there is the possibility of shifting risk; such contracts are typically signed under conditions of asymmetric information. In comparison with the typical vertically integrated public sector transport provider, the transaction costs, the costs involved in the provision of an intermediate good or service to another part of the production process, become open and transparent and thus susceptible to competition and market forces leading to greater efficiency. However, the contractual nature of these open relationships also renders them susceptible to greater costs.

We can distinguish three sorts of risk against which contracts cannot be fully protected and thus become incomplete:

- political risk, essentially the problem that the government's future decisions are unknown, can not be fully contractually controlled, for example, regulatory change affecting prices, environmental protection etc., decisions concerning potentially competing infrastructure, tax regimes, general macroeconomic policy.;

- technical risk: affecting the cost of construction, given the unique character of most infrastructure projects, all the technical detail can rarely if ever be known before construction commences;
- commercial risk: affected by the achieved levels of traffic, which can never be known accurately, especially given the character of much new infrastructure leading to the expected development of new markets, and the impact of this on revenues in markets where the exact nature of the demand function is rarely known accurately ex-ante.

All of these risks exist in the case of public sector development of infrastructure, but tend to be hidden in the integration of the various parts of the development process; planning, finance, construction and operation which leads to a difficulty in identifying where projects which fail to achieve forecast rates of return have gone wrong.

The hope is that private management of infrastructure would enable the exercise of a greater degree of control over each separate stage and therefore over the operation as a whole. Where this was not being provided by an integrated operation, the market would ensure greater efficiency directly, but even in the case of an integrated infrastructure operator, shareholders would exert more direct pressure on managers to achieve greater profitability and hence, it was believed, greater efficiency, than would the voter, via the government, on the public sector. Ultimately the enforcing of contracts would provide a legal constraint on the private sector operator.

The governmental risk would remain with the government under this model; public authorities would be contractually bound to honour certain agreements. Technical construction risks would remain with the construction companies. Market risks would be the concern of the infrastructure operator. If each of these risks were genuinely in the domain of each of the identified agent it would be logical for each to accept this risk in its entirety; this would be the solution which provided most incentive for effort to minimise that risk. However, each agent accepting this risk burden will require the payment of a risk premium to cover that risk, depending on the degree of risk aversion (see Box 7.12).

BOX 7.12

A simple model of reward for effort and risk coverage

Assume a firm (the agent), which responds to a public invitation to provide a service under contract to another party (the principal), of which the cost of provision is given by:

$$C = Cp - e + \varepsilon$$

where:

- ε is a probabilistic variable distributed with zero mean and standard deviation σ, whose value is unknown to both parties to the contract;
- e is the effort of the agent, which the principal is not able to observe;
- Cp is a constant.

The principal can only observe C and cannot distinguish either e or ε. The agent is paid by the principal according to:

$$R = \delta + \gamma C$$

The objective of the agent is to maximise utility U:

$$U = R - C - \psi(e)$$

$\psi(e)$ is the cost of effort to the agent.

Assume that $\psi' > 0$ and that ψ'' is a positive constant. The utility is then probabilistic, depending on the value of ε, with the mean:

$$U = \delta + (\gamma - 1)(Cp - e) - \psi(e)$$

If the agent is assumed to be risk averse, with a degree aversion r, the expected utility is not $\bar{U}$, but:

$$E(U) = \delta + (\gamma - 1)(Cp - e) - \psi(e) - (\gamma - 1)r^2\sigma^2/2$$

And the utility of the principal is:

$$Up = W - R$$

where W is the value attached to the service. If the principal is not risk averse, then:

$$E(Up) = W - R$$

The agent's behaviour is to maximise expected utility, which leads to:

$$\psi'(e) = 1 - \gamma$$

and thus fixes e when the principal has fixed γ.

The principal's behaviour is to maximise utility, taking account of the behaviour of the agent, thus:

$$\text{Max } E(Up) = \text{Max } (W - \delta - \gamma(Cp - e))$$

The principal can set the variables δ and γ, e is determined by: $\psi'(e) = 1 - \gamma$ and faces the constraint:

$$E(U) \geq 0$$

which requires that the agent is disposed to participate in the contract. The principal is interested in this utility not being zero, and hence the inequality can be replaced by an equality.

The result of this optimisation is:

$$\gamma = 1 - 1/(1 + \sigma^2 r^2 \psi'')$$

$$\delta = (1 - \gamma)(Cp - e) + \psi(e) + (\gamma - 1)^2 r^2 \sigma^2/2$$

and:

$$\psi'(e) = 1 - \gamma$$

Taking the particular case where the agent is risk neutral: $r=0$. Then,

$$\gamma = 0$$

$$\psi''(e) = 1$$

$$E(Up) = W - (Cp - e) - \psi(e)$$

And this shows that the agent would assume all the risk. The agent's effort is optimal from a social point of view, it is achieved by maximising: $(E(U)+E(Up))$. The expected utility of the agent is zero.

In comparison, if the agent is risk averse, the effort exercised in below the optimum and the principal has to support part of the risk, the share rising as the agent becomes more risk averse, but the expected utility of the agent remains zero

The principal can reduce the variance with respect to the optimum if it knows a quantity y correlated with the probability of risk. Thus R is replaced by:

$$\delta + \gamma C + \alpha y$$

and α is chosen to minimise the variance of this new remuneration stream which leads to:

$$\alpha = -\rho \sigma / \sigma_y$$

where:

σ_y is the standard deviation of y
ρ is the correlation coefficient between y and ε.

Concerning construction costs, for instance, certain risks can be almost totally controlled by a firm devoting sufficient effort, but others, for example problems with foundations which may only become apparent after construction has started however much advanced work has been committed, will always retain an element of uncertainty, overcoming which would be prohibitively costly. For this reason, the former can be legitimately the responsibility of the contractor, but the latter will normally require the infrastructure operator to agree to share the risk burden and thus face an uncertainty in its costs.

For reasons associated with the incompleteness of contracts (the impossibility of knowing all eventualities in advance) the total coverage of political risk is not possible.

Commercial risk presents even more difficult problems. We have seen the sources of error in traffic studies, private concessionaires should not be less well placed than public authorities to understand these, and given that the public authorities will typically have conducted their own feasibility studies they should be equally well informed. Furthermore, it is rarely possible to insure against this risk. In the case of, for example, electricity supply, it is possible to achieve a measure of this through the use of long-term contracts, and such contracts are being found in the segregated railway and in the case of, for example, the Channel Tunnel, but in road transport, where each user of the infrastructure has a relatively small demand for infrastructure use, the signing of contracts with individual users is less likely.

The expected benefits from private financing in terms of the management and operation of infrastructure can diminish or disappear if the contracts are badly drawn up and either do not take adequate account of risk or fail to put in place an adequate system of compensation for failure to meet the intended contract terms.

Public–private partnerships are not without danger if they are badly organized. Similarly, if a private owner of an infrastructure concession sub-contracts the operation of the infrastructure to another party it may be possible to achieve a better coordination with the rest of the network, but at the cost of an increased confusion of responsibilities which can generate inefficiency. The original promoters of a project may seek to limit their exposure to the commercial risk and seek to withdraw as soon as possible. Often these promoters, who tend to be construction companies and banks, seek to offset potential losses from the sale of their equity in the project against the profits from the initial construction. This leads to the speculation that it would be desirable from the perspective of the project as a whole if promoters were to remain fully engaged for the entire lifetime with a significant share of the equity.

The presence of these risks leads to the cost of private finance being higher than that of public finance. In the latter case government guarantees enable loans to be raised at the lowest possible rates of interest. In the case of private finance, the rate of interest on loans is higher and equity capital requires a higher rate of remuneration to cover the risks.

BOX 7.14

Mechanisms of private finance

Private finance brings together a range of partners who are distinguished by the priorities accorded to the return on their funding and by the nature of this return. To simplify, we can distinguish between banks as providers of loan funds, bearing a fixed rate of interest and repaid according to a set pattern, and equity shareholders, who provide capital on which the remuneration is variable and repayment depends on the banks having been repaid first.

To provide against risk, banks require that the expected revenue stream is greater than the loans provided by a factor (typically a value between 1.5 and 2) which depends on the degree of uncertainty they attach to the project. The key ratios which determine this factor are:

- The *(Debt-Service Cover Ratio)* (DSCR):
  (Cash-flow in year t)/(Repayment due in year t)
- The *(Loan Life Service Cover Ratio)* (LLSCR) calculated over the length of the loans:
  (Present value of future cash-flow)/(Present value of future repayments)
- The *(Project Life Service Cover Ratio)* (PLSCR), similar to the LLSCR but calculated over the duration of the concession.

These constraints *imposed* by bank loans influence the structure of the finance, limiting the use of loans and making the return on capital very sensitive to the revenue stream.

Private concessionaires do seem to display some greater efficiency in terms of construction costs. French evidence suggests such costs are of the order of 5 to 10 per cent lower than those of public sector projects, coming mainly from savings in administration costs, although offset by higher maintenance costs. The National Audit Office (1988, 2003) in the UK has also reported savings from the private finance provision of roads and their maintenance.

In effect infrastructure concessions can be characterised by an initially very difficult financial situation which becomes easier through the life of the concession as the project tends to become cash rich toward the end and risks much lower, as shown in Figure 7.8. Receipts grow through time due to the growth in traffic, but costs tend to be fairly stable and then fall dramatically at the end of the life of the loans when only maintenance costs remain.

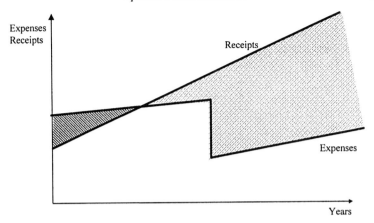

Figure 7.8 Evolution of the financial situation of a concession

Risks are substantial at the start of the concession, but costs become more reliably known during the course of construction and during the early years of operation. Similarly, although traffic may take some time to adjust to a new infrastructure, after an initial period it also becomes more stable and predictable. There is thus a period of a few years around the start of operation where both costs and revenues become progressively better known. This leads to a changing game structure between the concessionaire, the banks and the government authorities. In the early years the concessionaire has a great need of finance and neither banks nor governments can refuse this without risking the collapse of the project. For the banks, failure of the project is likely to be more costly than the cost of refinancing it. For the government there are both loss of potential welfare benefits and the more difficult to calculate political costs from allowing a project to fail. Typically a response is to extend the length of the concession to try and increase the net present value of the project, although an extension such as that of Eurotunnel from an original 55 years to 99 years has more of a symbolic than a real financial value once discounted. Ultimately governments have the power to nationalise concessions which become too costly, or, as in the case of Railtrack in the UK, to force the concessionaire into effective bankruptcy.

Private finance and investment programmes
The use of private finance has a number of effects on the development of an investment programme in transport. First, there is a sense in which it is anti-economic, new privately financed roads for example are built to alleviate the situation on congested existing roads which are under-priced, and prevent the move to a more efficient overall solution. In addition, we should not ignore the cost of direct toll collection: it has been shown in France, where the use

of toll road concessions is widespread, that the cost of collection amounts to about 15 per cent of the toll revenues. An alternative approach, that of shadow tolls, as used in privately financed roads in the UK where the government pays the concessionaire according to the volume of traffic using the road out of general revenues, avoids this cost but fails to confront the user with the direct cost of road use.

Private finance initiatives can have further effects through the way they change the relationship between potential private investors and the government. Private finance may change the date at which a project is realized since the private funder will propose a timing which maximises the net present private value of the project, which is not necessarily the same as the net social benefit (Szymanski, 1991). If we consider several competing private interests, the expectation would again be that the date would be advanced, but, in the limit, to the point where the private net benefit is competed away to zero. Earlier completion of new infrastructure is often seen as one of the main advantages of private finance, but that assumes that the only issue in timing is that of the budget constraint.

Finally, and most importantly, private finance can affect the whole programme of infrastructure development. The success of some early privately financed projects has led to an expectation that all future projects can be successful. Furthermore the cash flow from the early projects provides the means by which further projects can be started. There is a tendency for investors to be less risk averse in these cases and thus commit funds to projects for reasons other than their rate of return. This may mean that funds are transferred into less worthwhile projects, which are similar to the initially successful ones, and have the effect of crowding out more worthwhile, but different, projects.

4. CONCLUSION: PUBLIC DECISIONS IN PRACTICE

The theoretical framework concerned with optimal public decisions is comprehensive, coherent and elegant. However, its use in practice is far from complete. In the two main areas at which we have looked, pricing and investment, it is clear that the reality of decision taking is often far from the recommendations of theory.

A first reason for this gap is the difficulty of putting recommendations into practice, notably those on pricing. Marginal social costs vary so much through both time and space that their rigorous application for roads is almost impracticable without the full availability (and acceptability) of a system of electronic pricing. Such systems exist, but require political will and considerable development to make them work in such a way as to have the desired effect on user behaviour.

The definition of an economic optimum has recourse to concepts and calculations which are often difficult to understand or interpret for those making the final decisions, which are just as likely to be influenced by the views of voters or specific interest groups.

Furthermore it has to be recognised that the results of technical studies can be manipulated by the analyst. Results depend on large numbers of parameters which are not known with certainty (value of time, value of life, cost of externalities) and which raise prejudices in the minds of many users.

This ability to manipulate results is most frequently found in the tendency to use arguments concerning local economic development as a justification for projects. We have seen the limits to this argument, whilst there is evidence that globally infrastructure investment does have an impact, this is not always as strongly positive as claimed and clearly varies substantially from project to project in terms of its local impacts. Moreover, it combines two effects, the effectiveness of the announcement of a project on the behaviour of other investors in an area (the announcement effect) and the reality which is often that the major impact is distortional. Unfortunately insufficient ex-post studies are carried out to demonstrate the actual effects and there is a continuing tendency, reinforced by the distributional effect that every region wants new infrastructure to keep up with its neighbours; a factor which accelerates the diminishing returns to infrastructure globally.

Finally, the decision-making process concerning infrastructure is becoming less and less that of the 'benevolent dictator' taking decisions on the basis of full knowledge of all the relevant factors in the interests of maximising social welfare and more and more a complex game of decision-making involving many actors negotiating a result. The final decision may thus say more about the negotiating skills of the actors than about rational decision-making.

It is no longer sufficient to know simply that a project overall meets an adequate rate of return, assuming that gainers can compensate losers. It must also be capable of identifying the losers in order to ensure that they will be compensated in an acceptable way in order to remove their opposition and ensure the social acceptability of a project. As well as these purely instrumental issues of compensation it has become more important to identify equity considerations clearly as a supplementary objective in the project itself. Verhoef *et al.* (1997), in studying the trade-off between efficiency and social acceptability have suggested that, given the conflict between the two, tradable permits could be used in order to identify a second-best solution.

The games played between different interest groups are not just those between groups directly affected by a given proposal, such as the users against those suffering from the disbenefits of increased traffic, but also between the particular interests of those representing different modes. Each of these has a vested interest in ensuring the protection of the interests of their own mode and advancing its case, and each is prepared to use economic analysis in a particular way to justify this, leading away from the development of an accepted common methodology. Given that different modes may also have recourse to different sources of funding there is no opportunity for banks, etc to impose a common method of evaluation and hence it is difficult to achieve a common method for ranking projects.

The second reason is more serious in its consequences: wrong choices over the form of any intervention. This is dominated by the tendency to avoid pricing as a solution to both congestion and external effects. The need is to present the approach as more transparent to the decision-maker, less certain, with more emphasis on identifying losers and gainers, rather than as some form of black box. It would then be more feasible to insist on greater auditability of decisions, both before and after.

Above all, public decisions on infrastructure embody a fundamental contradiction, they have an irreversible character and permanent effects, but decisions are based essentially on their immediate short-term impacts.

8. Forms and Effects of Competition between Operators

Transport markets present a wide variety of situations of competition between operators and produce a wide variety of effects in terms of both efficiency and equity.

1. FORMS OF COMPETITION

Competition occurs, in differing degrees, at all stages of transport activity. However, it is especially important at stages of activity which occur downstream from the management of infrastructure, the provision of transport services on which we concentrate here. Following the outline structure of Chapter 6, the process of production in transport can be likened to chains, involving a multiplicity of markets, developed to a different degree in different sectors, as shown in Figure 8.1:

- the most important is that which relates transport operators to their final consumers, passengers or the shippers of goods;
- that which relates operators to the providers of vehicles and rolling stock;
- the links between operators and customers can be either direct or undertaken through a range of intermediaries.

We analyse these in turn, starting with the market for vehicles and rolling stock and then that of intermediaries, before concentrating on the main market which links operators and the final consumers of transport.

1.1 The Market for Vehicles and Rolling Stock

The vehicle production market is only at all competitive for cars and trucks. For most other modes of transport there is only limited competition and the market has often involved considerable public sector involvement.

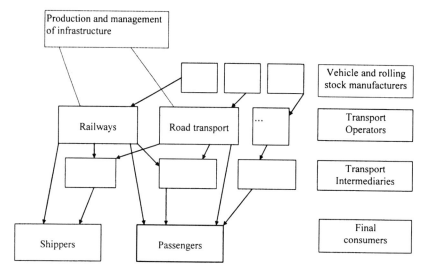

Figure 8.1 Outline of the process of production of transport services

In aircraft construction there are only two main global firms making commercial aircraft, one US, Boeing and the other European, Airbus. Increasing returns, due in the main to the huge costs of research and development, make entry to the market difficult. Aircraft manufacturers also need to invest heavily in marketing and after-sales service. This contributes to their need to protect markets and provide a wide range of products so as to be represented in all market sectors and provide a complete fleet of differing aircraft types to the major airline customers, which in turn leads to the growth of economies of scope. The fragility of the former third main firm, McDonnell-Douglas, was due in part to its smaller scale and the more limited range of products. The relative success of Airbus has depended in part on its ability to identify and exploit sectors of the markets which Boeing had left open and on the choice of technologies which Boeing had regarded as too risky (Haudeville, 1994). However, it is clear that the political support for Airbus as a joint European venture has also played a major role in its success.

All the manufacturers have developed partnerships with a wide range of firms in order to spread the fixed costs of development. These links allow technology transfer to play a major strategic role in securing an advantage over competitors, although this bears a risk of allowing potential new entrants into the market.

Aircraft manufacturers have needed to respond to the effects of deregulation in the airline industry. Golob (1995) concluded that manufacturers had responded to the new and rapidly changing needs of the airlines through the development of new financial procedures, such as the growth of leasing, which leads to a sharing of risks in both markets.

Despite the involvement of the State in rail operation, rail rolling stock manufacture is largely independent of government control. However, the market is different in the various parts of the world and it is interesting to compare the features of North American markets with those in Europe.

In North America, there are large numbers of rail operators, both for freight (long distance transport) and for passengers (short distance transport). This is matched by a rather large number of rolling stock providers, apart from the two big ones, General Motors and General Electric. Thus the market is fairly close to being competitive, with large numbers of both suppliers and customers. Competition has led to substantial outsourcing and the two big makers subcontract about 80 per cent of their turnover.

The picture has been quite different in Europe, although there are signs that it is changing and becoming closer to the American situation. Up to the beginning of the 1990s, the railway operators of the main European countries were essentially independent of each other, were state monopolies, and had no obligation to use international competition for the provision of rolling stock. This led to a bilateral monopoly in each country between the rail operator (for example, DB in Germany, SNCF in France, FS in Italy) and the rolling stock provider (Siemens in Germany, Alsthom in France, Ansaldo in Italy). The connection between the rail operator and the rolling stock provider was very close within each country, but involved virtually no links between one country and another. Technical staff in manufacturer and operator cooperated very closely and this led to:

- rapid technical progress, leading to the various high speed trains (HST) of each country (ICE in Germany, TGV in France, Pendolino in Italy), which needed close cooperation between the future operator and the maker;
- but at the expense of small production runs, leading to high costs;
- and standards differing from one country to another, thus maintaining a long tradition of different standards: although the track gauge is the same, except in Spain, Portugal, Finland and Ireland, the loading gauges, the power and the signalling systems, differ from one country to another. Even inside one country large differences can be found on those grounds. This has made though operation, inter-operability, difficult and limited the ability of manufacturers to sell elsewhere.

On the contrary, the outcome of the American market structure was the reverse: low technical progress, long production runs, widely used standards, and interoperability of rolling stock over the whole continent.

Thus there is a basic dilemma. On the one hand there are benefits from constructing rolling stock for the specific needs of individual situations, on the other hand there are benefits from constructing universal rolling stock, possibly involving greater initial cost, but giving rise to longer production runs. Achieving this is necessary for the European Union's desire to see greater interoperability in the rail sector, not least in the area of high-speed rail which has a particular emphasis on international traffic. Increasingly manufacturers have been cooperating, establishing joint ventures or merging in the interests of serving more than one market. New technology is being used to create modular vehicles which can be adapted for use in specific situations whilst maintaining the basic cost advantages of a single set of research and development and longer production runs. This does require there to be greater uniformity in signalling and safety systems, but it is taking a long time to break down the traditional differences between different national railway operating cultures.

Under pressure from liberalisation and the European Commission's efforts to increase competition, tendering has been required to become international. The opening of the market to international competition has induced American providers to enter the market (Bombardier, for example) either through direct sales to European rail operators or through mergers and the absorption of European firms. Foreign makers are becoming active in each domestic market. European rail operators have started to pay more attention to their buying strategy and to the prices they pay and buying foreign made materials has become more frequent.

An interesting feature is the competition which has been evolving in the HST market. In overseas markets each of the three main providers (Siemens, Alsthom, Fiat) has acted as competitors (as for example in the case of Korea), while in European markets they have acted cooperatively, as in the development of trains for international links such as Thalys or Eurostar.

Due to the historically non-competitive nature of the markets, the economics of rail rolling stock has not been subject to much econometric study, nor to precise and detailed statistical information. In particular, there are no official comprehensive records of rail rolling stock investments and no data can be given on their evolution.

1.2 The Role of Intermediaries in the Transport Sector

Auxiliary firms, intermediaries, have a range of functions in the transport sector. For passengers, intermediaries are such organisations as travel agencies, which provide information on modes, times, prices, etc. to enable their clients to satisfy their travel needs. For goods transport, under various names, there is a diversity of types of auxiliary:

- groupage: organising the transport of consignments in vehicles;
- supply chain or logistics management: bringing together the transport needs of various stages of production and organising the best mode;
- the organisation of formalities for customs and other documentation in international transport.

These intermediaries can be transport operators which undertake these operations in addition to the direct provision of transport services in order to provide a total transport service. Thus road haulage firms offer integrated services to their clients. Increasingly large travel agents operate their own aircraft for holiday charter flights and airlines, and some rail operators, have adopted Internet technology for on-line booking.

Combined transport offers a particularly interesting case study where a number of operators have developed to provide a through service using a variety of modes, but particularly to exploit the possibilities of open access to the rail network proposed by EC directive 91/440. In a number of countries combined transport had been heavily controlled by the national rail company. The fear of open access was that foreign operators would enter national markets and effectively cream off the most profitable routes. Despite the hopes of combined transport offering a major market development, there have been a number of handicaps which have prevented it achieving all that had been hoped for. Technical differences between networks lead to higher costs for international operations which, coupled with organisational problems of dealing with many national rail operators and the problems of terminal locations, make it difficult to undercut direct road haulage operators. Combined transport has only been successful in relatively small markets, typically involving distances greater than 500 km involving regular and large consignments which can use complete trains, or large train blocks, and with origins and destinations close to terminals.

The use of intermediaries is neither necessary nor systematic. When transport needs are simple to satisfy, final consumers can easily deal directly with operators. It is when these needs become more complex that intermediaries have a role. There are three main factors which determine this: the management of uncertainty, the search for scale economies and the substitution of vertical integration for market forces in certain areas.

Intermediaries can manage risk and uncertainty. Travel agents deal with many different airlines ensuring greater protection against problems with any particular company. Where the agent secures a quota of seats on any particular flight for the exclusive use of its clients this provides a measure of protection against overbooking and other such problems facing the individual traveller. On the other side of the market, by guaranteeing a certain number of places on an operator's vehicle they are providing a greater degree of certainty in the operator's revenue stream, in return for which the agent typically receives a commission. Thus, for example, Non-Vessel-Operator-Common-Carriers in maritime transport fulfil the essential role of purchasing cargo space which they can sell on to shippers who can thus be guaranteed shipping space when they need it.

The second main function is to provide to shippers, who may only have infrequent needs for transport in particular markets, a specialist knowledge of transport operations. This covers both technical and organisational knowledge, types of vehicle available, border formalities and customs procedures, etc., the acquisition of which would require a substantial investment by the customer. Furthermore, professional transport intermediaries can exert greater influence on operators through their greater purchasing power.

Finally, transport intermediaries enable the achievement of a more optimal market situation, albeit it at a higher cost than a free market. This is particularly the case where the coordination of activities is of high importance (Box 8.1).

BOX 8.1

Coordination and optimisation

Assume a cost function to minimise, which depends on two factors, of the form $C(x_1, x_2)$, with a given proportionality between the two factors, such as $x_2 = \lambda x_1$. These could be, for example, vehicles and the fuel to operate them.

The minimum cost is attained, for example for x_1 and $x_2 = \lambda x_1$. Any error in the determination of these variables, for example, taking: $x_1 + dx_1$ and $x_2 + \lambda dx_1$, is of the second order in dx_1. But if the error depends on the relationship between the two factors, for example: $x_1 + dx_1$ and $x_2 = \lambda x_1$, the error is of the first order in dx_1.

Intermediaries play this coordinating role to the extent that, due to their knowledge of the market they can introduce clients to the best placed operator for the client's needs and can ensure a greater matching of demand and supply by achieving a more efficient grouping of demands with the availability of capacity. However, there is the possibility of using this information in a strategic way. Airlines have benefited from the way travel agents access information through computerised reservation systems, which can steer clients towards the use of particular airlines, in part through disguised commissions, and can thus act in an anti-competitive manner.

Intermediaries may also extend their interests either towards the operators or towards the clients. Large-scale road haulage operators and intermediaries may be involved in the setting up of small dedicated operators, for example, through providing start-up finance, in order to seek influence in particular markets and prevent new entrants. In the direction of serving clients there are attempts to seek activities outside the specific transport activity, in order to attract customer loyalty and seek economies of scope. Thus travel agencies have become integrated tourism suppliers providing travel, hotel, car rental and other services; freight operators have become total logistics suppliers.

1.3   The Direct Market for Transport

Even if certain markets look at first glance as if they are either perfectly competitive (road haulage) or monopolistic (rail transport) it is rare to find such clear-cut cases. Most markets are likely to be oligopolistic. A national rail operator is after all a competitor with other modes; even relatively small road hauliers have some power over individual geographical markets or routes and build up preferential dealings with certain clients. The basic analytical framework must therefore be one of oligopoly, albeit it in different forms and to different degrees. Therefore, we recall first the basic characteristics of oligopoly before applying the theory to transport.

1.3.1 Basic oligopoly theories

There are two basic approaches to the analysis of oligopoly. In the approach developed by Bertrand the basic decision variable is that of price, each firm sets price assuming that the other's price is fixed. The tendency therefore is for firms to compete prices downwards. The alternative, Cournot, approach uses quantity as the decision variable, each firm fixes output assuming that the other's output is given, and this determines the price each will charge.

The classic analysis of these two approaches searches to find the corresponding Nash equilibrium. Assume two firms, $i = 1, 2$, each seeking to maximise profit. The profit of each firm depends on the choice of the strategic variable x_i which is under its control, and the choice of the other firm for this strategic variable, x_j, which is under its control:

$$\Pi_1 = \Pi_1(x_1, x_2)$$
$$\Pi_2 = \Pi_2(x_1, x_2)$$

The Nash equilibrium is the situation where neither party regrets the decisions made:

$$\Pi_1(x_1^*, x_2^*) = \underset{x_1}{Max}\ \Pi_1(x_1, x_2^*)$$

$$\Pi_2(x_1^*, x_2^*) = \underset{x_2}{Max}\ \Pi_2(x_1^*, x_2)$$

In a Bertrand duopoly the strategic variable is price. The simplest exposition of this is that the two firms ($i = 1,2$) each has a constant marginal cost of production c_i (assuming that $c_1 \leq c_2$). Each chooses a price and the quantities they intend to sell are determined thus:

$$
\begin{aligned}
q_1 &= D(p_1) &&\text{if } p_1 < p_2 \\
&&&\text{or } p_1 = p_2 \text{ and } c_1 < c_2 \\
q_1 &= D(p_1)/2 &&\text{if } p_1 = p_2 \text{ and } c_1 = c_2 \\
q_1 &= 0 &&\text{otherwise}
\end{aligned}
$$

It can be shown that price will be set at the level of c_2, and the quantity sold by each firm can be deduced from the above relationships. Competition is severe and eliminates all profit from the less well performing firm.

In a Cournot duopoly the strategic variables are the quantities and the profits of firm 1 can be written as:

$$\Pi_1(q_1, q_2) = q_1 p(q_1 + q_2) - c_1(q_1)$$

and symmetrically for firm 2. If we assume that each firm fixes output independently of the other, the solution is given simply by the conditions for maximising profits (where we assume for simplicity: $q_1 + q_2 = Q$)

$$p(Q*) + q_1^* \frac{dp}{dQ} - \frac{dc_1}{dq_1} = 0$$

$$p(Q*) + q_2^* \frac{dp}{dQ} - \frac{dc_2}{dq_2} = 0$$

It can easily be seen that each firm makes a profit and competition is thus less abrasive than in the Bertrand case.

In transport, competition occurs most often in the domain of price, particularly if we interpret price as generalised price, including such elements as comfort, convenience, time spent, etc. The Bertrand analysis assumes that operators are not subject to capacity constraints. When firms enter the market, choosing an appropriate level of capacity, and subsequently compete solely on the basis of price, Kreps and Scheinkman (1983) showed that the resulting solution is equivalent to that of Cournot duopoly.

The general idea which emerges from the theoretical analysis is that when transport capacities are high, or can be enlarged through the transfer of capacity from other locations, and the services provided are not differentiated, then competition is likely to be of a Bertrand type, based on price. This is the case found, for example in road haulage or air transport. If, on the other hand, capacity is difficult to increase, then competition is likely to be of a Cournot type, based on quantities. This is the case found, for example, in rail, maritime or inland waterway transport.

1.3.2 Applications to transport

Rail–road competition

A primary concern is the conditions of competition which obtain in the transport of goods by road or rail. Competition between road haulage operators themselves tends towards perfect competition when the number of operators is large and each is small. As the number of firms reduces, competition tends towards a Bertrand-type oligopoly; the shipper will tend to switch towards the operator with the lowest price. It can be assumed that marginal costs are constant and that capacity is not limited, entry into the market is relatively easy, and in a particular location can be achieved simply by moving vehicles from one route to another. Thus the road haulage price will be fixed at the marginal cost of road haulage.

However, for rail there are two possible outcomes. If marginal cost is higher than that of the road haulier, rail will be excluded from the market. If marginal cost is lower, rail can operate in the market, but in practice at a price roughly equivalent to that of the marginal cost of road haulage. In other words it is likely that that the marginal cost of road haulage will be the determinant of price whichever operator finally dominates the market. This analysis assumes that price is the sole variable determining choice by the shipper. In fact, delays, reliability, etc. will also be relevant and the analysis should be based on generalised costs to the shipper not just price. Moreover, the services are not total substitutes which also reduces competition.

Competition between Eurotunnel and ferries

The second example is that of competition between the different operators on the cross-Channel route between Britain and France. Up to 1994 this involved competition between ferry companies, including conventional and fast ferries, since the completion of the Channel Tunnel this has included also competition from Eurotunnel. Both modes provide services for cars, trucks, buses and pedestrians. Ferries can provide a choice of routes serving a number of ports on both sides, but the principal link is that between Dover and Calais, effectively the same route as Eurotunnel.

An analysis of the market has been carried out by Szymanski (1993, 1996), dealing respectively with competition between the ferries before the tunnel and then between the ferries and Eurotunnel. For a long time the ferry market had been dominated by two main operators P and O European Ferries and Sealink, the former the result of a merger in the late 1980s and the latter the successor of the ferry services provided by the national rail companies. The behaviour of these two can be analysed as a duopoly. The ferries practised a form of price discrimination between different groups of travellers, but a comparison of fares suggests that these were very similar for the two operators and changed in the same way, and from 1986, when the Tunnel was announced, these fares converged even further and grew appreciably in anticipation of competition from the Eurotunnel.

The similarity of prices for each category of traffic conforms to the expectation of a theoretical analysis of competition, in particular that competition was on the basis of price and not quantity. This is not a pure Bertrand duopoly. Prices were fixed largely by reference to the marginal cost of each class of traffic, subject to covering fixed costs and making a (more than marginal) profit. This cannot be attributed to limits of capacity, available capacity was almost always some 2 to 3 times greater than demand. This capacity was necessary to meet certain seasonal peaks, but it also served a strategic purpose, as a means of dissuading potential entrants to the market by suggesting that the incumbent operators had low marginal costs and could therefore survive any price war.

In fact the existence of profit shows a certain form of mutual understanding between the operators. Complete collusion was not possible because if profits had risen too high other firms could have been encouraged to enter the market and secured a share of the profits before the incumbent firms were able to respond and force their withdrawal. Besides such actions would have drawn the attention of the regulatory authorities and encouraged intervention by the Monopolies and Mergers Commission in the UK (see Monopolies and Mergers Commission, 1989).

When the decision to build the tunnel was made the situation changed. The planning horizon became more finite such that the probabilities of collusion reduced, but the coming prospect of the tunnel and the prospective upheaval in the market made entry less attractive for any potential competitor. This has been modelled by Szymanski (1993) in a way which can be represented by assuming the duopolists face a regulator who can either intervene or not. If the regulator intervenes, this would impose a transaction cost of L and price would change from the ruling price, p, to a price close to marginal cost, *c*. Regulation is valid for *n* years; the regulator's objective function *F* depends on the relationship between *p* and *c*, which translates the gain in social welfare, from setting *n* and *L*, according to an equation of the form:

$$F = nF(p - c) - L$$

The regulator only intervenes if *F* is positive; and imposes a limit on the value of *p* = *p**, this is the effective limit price for the duopolists which triggers intervention. *P** is an increasing function of *n*, *n* gets smaller as we approach the entry into service of the tunnel since this would provide a natural regulation.

After the entry of Eurotunnel into the market the situation would change completely. There would be two categories of operator: one (Eurotunnel) with a low marginal cost, the other (assuming the ferries regroup into a single operator) with a high marginal cost. This has some similarities with the road-rail competition situation, but it is not possible to take account of the different qualities of service. At least for passengers and cars, delays, efficiency, quality of the crossing are all different and the ferries provide a range of different crossing routes whilst the tunnel provides only one. Szymanski (1996) models this in the following way, taking for example the market for cars:

Let *X* be the total number of passengers (cars), assumed given:
S_T, S_F are the market shares of the tunnel and the ferries
p_T, p_F are the prices
c_T, c_F are marginal costs
F_T, F_F are fixed costs
Π_T, Π_F are profits

Assume that:

$$S_T = A + elog(p_F/p_T)$$

From which can be derived the equilibrium of the game, maximising Π_T and Π_F respectively with respect to p_T and p_F:

$$-e(p_T - c_T)/p_T + logA + elog(p_F/p_T) = 0$$
$$-e(p_F - c_F)/p_F + 1 - logA - elog(p_F/p_T) = 0$$

Assuming marginal costs of the order of (c_T = £15, c_F = £75) a simulation based on possible values for *A* and *e* gives the range of optimal fares shown in Table 8.1.

Table 8.1 Simulated fares from Eurotunnel-Ferry competition

	Actual (1996)	Scenario 1 $A = 0.25$ $e = 0.8$	Scenario 2 $A = 0.25$ $e = 1.0$	Scenario 3 $A = 0.75$ $e = 0.8$	Scenario 4 $A = 0.75$ $e = 1.0$
Tunnel fare	120	81	60	126	85
Ferry fare	100	133	100	119	91

Source: Szymanski (1996)

It can be seen that the model provides values which for a wide range of parameters include the actual fares charged. The parameters which correspond most closely to the actual fares correspond to the situation which would imply a great attraction of the tunnel (*A* larger). The results suggest that the prices of both were perhaps a little on the high side, but this might present an understandable initial situation to the extent that it would be seen as easier for the operators to reduce prices subsequently than raise them.

After the entry into service of the tunnel, the situation changed to one of Bertrand-type competition with excessive price competition. The first issue is whether Eurotunnel had an interest in eliminating its competitors, given its much lower marginal costs. Two arguments can be put against this. First, entry into the ferry market is easy and any eliminated competitors could easily be replaced. Second, if competitors could effectively be eliminated, Eurotunnel would become a monopoly operator and susceptible to regulation. A more serious risk is one of collusion, from which the ferries would be the main winners since their margin over marginal cost is much smaller and risks not covering fixed costs. Rather surprisingly therefore the ferries entered into active price competition, increasing capacity and reducing fares. At best they might have been able to force Eurotunnel into liquidation, but the tunnel itself would not go away and a liquidated tunnel operator with all its capital costs written off would have been an even more difficult competitor for the ferries.

Competition between operators on the same route
The third example is that of competition between airlines on common routes. Brander and Zhang (1993) analysed the competition between American Airlines and United, calculating the reaction function of each firm, the relationship between a change in the quantity produced by the competitor and the change in output of the firm itself. The slope of the reaction function is −1 for a Bertrand duopoly, 0 for a Cournot duopoly and q_1/q_2 in the case of collusion between the two operators. The authors tested the strategy of a

dynamic game in which each company had the option of cooperating or not cooperating and of punishing the other company if it failed to cooperate. This produced values for the reaction function which were equal to -1 if one firm was punishing the other and if not between -1 and those of collusion (since, because of uncertainty, punishment could only be undertaken when a threshold of profit reduction was reached). In the case of Cournot duopoly the values of -1 were replaced by values of 0.

The results from this study show that if it is assumed that successive plays of the game are independent, the reaction functions indicate competition rather closer to Cournot than to Bertrand, the coefficients are of the order of 0.4. Their variation over a period, however, gives rise to the belief that phases of collusion alternate with phases of price wars. This is not dissimilar to the outcome of the previous example of competition between Eurotunnel and the ferries.

Competition on networks
Networks are an inherent feature of transport markets. Despite this, most of the traditional analysis of competition in these markets takes the case of single routes. In this section we try and extent these to allow for networks, albeit in some fairly simple models. Networks arise because operators find advantages in exploiting simultaneously various geographical markets which have interdependence both in demand and supply. The most comprehensive analysis of the network question and its implications has been carried out in air transport and hence we shall use this mode as the basis for the subsequent analysis.

Effect of network size. Network size affects the number and type of the links served. Different structures can be defined in terms of indicators which measure their properties in terms of connectivity, connectedness, etc. (Curien and Dupuy, 1996; Peeters *et al.*, 1998; Button, 2001). It can also involve the compatibility of timetables. Two links, between AB and BC, can be served by the same company, but if the timetables are not compatible, the availability of these two links is of no use to the potential user. Network size presents benefits to the user to the extent that it provides more destinations available without having to change operator, more consistent information, likelihood of more compatible timetables and more possibilities of making changes to times or rotates. The strategy of transport operators in extending their networks, or in increasing network compatibility is usually to provide for coordination of timetables, through ticketing, or reciprocal acceptance of tickets etc. The analysis in Box 8.2 shows that increasing coordination has global benefits, but these accrue disproportionately to the small operator.

BOX 8.2

Network compatibility

Assume two operators in competition on a given route, with networks of size x_A for operator A, x_B for operator B, and each has zero marginal cost. Assume that a network of size x provides a utility to the user of $u(x)$ and that each company charging a price p supplies a service with the generalised cost to user of:

$$P = p - u(x)$$

If the operators compete in terms of capacity q_i with equality in the generalised price, and if demand on the route is given by:

$$P_A = P_B = 1 - q_A - q_B$$

It follows that:

$$\Pi_I = q_i(1 - q_A - q_B + u(x_i))$$

and the equilibrium quantities are given by:

$$q_B = (1 + 2u_B - u_A)/3$$
$$q_A = (1 + 2u_A - u_B)/3$$

If network B is larger than network A:

$$q_B > q_A$$

and now the operators agree to open their networks to each other, the common network is:

$$x_A + x_B$$
$$u_{A+B} > u_A + u_B$$

and the new equilibrium traffic levels are:

$$q_A{}^* = q_B{}^* = (1 + u_{A+B})/3$$

It can be seen that:

$$q_B{}^* - q_B < q_A{}^* - q_A$$
$$\Pi_B > \Pi_A$$
$$\Pi_A{}^* = \Pi_B{}^*$$
$$\Pi_A{}^* > \Pi_A$$

but nothing can be said about Π_B and $\Pi_B{}^*$

The smaller operator gains from the opening, as do the users, but the result for the large operator is ambiguous.

Direct or hub-and-spoke networks. The structure of transport activities, combined with economies of scope in serving different routes and the economies of scale available, which depend on the traffic intensity on individual links, all contribute to determining the structure of supply.

In terms of providing networks, economies of scope translate into the serving of a range of destinations being achieved more economically by one operator than by several. Serving several routes in common enables the operator to use a larger fleet, manage it better, achieve higher rates of utilisation, deal with incidents, etc. Similarly, scale economies imply that, on any given link, costs will rise less rapidly than traffic. The cost per tonne-km of capacity or seat-km is much lower in larger trucks or jumbo jets than in smaller vehicles.

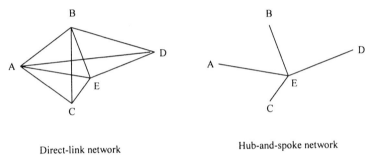

Direct-link network   Hub-and-spoke network

Figure 8.2 Direct-link and hub-and-spoke networks

These characteristics can be identified first in the structure of the networks themselves, in particular in the contrast between direct link networks and hub-and-spoke networks (Figure 8.2). In the absence of economies of scale and scope, direct-link networks, which provide a system with the shortest direct link between any two points, do so at minimum cost since they minimise the total number of passenger-km or tonne-km. With economies of scale and scope the situation is rather different. The link between A and B can be provided at a lower cost via E if the scale economies are sufficiently high and result in a lowering of unit costs on AE and EB due to the concentration of a higher level of traffic than on the direct link between A and B. The most advantageous structure in these circumstances is a so-called hub-and-spoke network where each point is connected to one other point which serves as the network hub, all traffic passes through the hub. This idea can be developed in a number of simple networks.

BOX 8.3

Economies of scale and hub-and-spoke networks
(after Encaoua and Perrot, 1992)

Assume three towns equidistant from one another which exchange traffic equal to q; this traffic is served by an operator which, for each origin-destination pair faces a cost function dependent on the level of traffic, of the form: $C(x)$.

The cost function is increasing and concave (due to returns to scale). We need to identify the condition under which the direct link AB is more economical than requiring traffic to pass through C. To see this it is necessary to compare:

$3C(q)$ the cost of transport corresponding to a network of direct links with

$2C(2q)$ – the cost of transport corresponding to a hub-and spoke network.

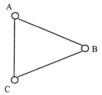

The condition for a hub-and-spoke network in terms of cost to the operator is:

$$3C(q) > 2C(2q)$$

The hub-and-spoke network is profitable if the returns to scale are sufficiently high: note that this is the solution of the analysis for the operator, but if the cost for the user is also taken into account we need to identify the increased time from the increased length of the travel, plus the time penalty for having to change at the hub, leading to additional costs.

It should be noted that when we move from a network of direct links to a hub-and-spoke network, despite the cost advantage to the operator, there are disadvantages to the user in terms of the loss of time and the cost of changing vehicles. Thus it is possible for social welfare to be reduced.

Interdependence between markets. One consequence of hub-and-spoke networks and non-constant returns is the interdependence between markets, which we can analyse in a simple model. Assume three towns, ABC, served by a network which only has the links AB and BC; traffic from A to C has to change in B. Let q_{ij} be the traffic between any two towns i and j; traffic on arc AB is given by:

$$Q_{AB} = q_{AB} + q_{AC}$$

and the cost for the operator will be:

$$C(Q_{AB}, Q_{BC})$$

And similarly for the arc BC. The markets will be independent even if this cost is separable between the two links, that is even if:

$$C(Q_{AB}, Q_{BC}) = C_1(Q_{AB}) + C_2(Q_{BC})$$

In effect an increase in the demand q_{AB} would lead to a fall in the unit cost on AB and hence (in most competitive situations) to a fall in the price on AB, and thus an increase in demand particularly q_{AC} and an effect on the market on link BC, probably a reduction in price, and an increase in price and demand q_{BC} and q_{AC}, due to the reduction in cost C_2.

The consequences of such situations can be studied from both a theoretical and an applied point of view. Encaoua and Perrot (1992) have analysed the equilibrium conditions in a market comprising a network of arcs served by operators facing cost functions displaying both scale and scope economies, but where demand on each origin-destination link is fixed. Users choose whichever operator offers the lowest generalised cost, taking into account fare, travel time and waiting time. A fixed number of operators compete on the basis of two factors: the network each chooses to serve and the price charged for journeys on that network. The social optimum is an equilibrium, but there are one or more other Nash equilibria which are not optimal. Using slightly different assumptions (including airport congestion) Hong and Harker (1992) have shown the existence of a unique equilibrium and explored the consequences of different ways of distributing slots on the social optimum.

In a more applied study, Nero (1996), models the impacts of European deregulation using a duopoly model representing the links between two countries. In Figure 8.3, HA and HB represent the links within country 1 and SZ and SY those in country 2. HS is the international link between the two countries. Demand is given by demand functions of the form:

$$P(Q_{ij}) = a - Q_{ij}/2$$

where i and j represent the O-D possibilities for each airline (AH, AS, AB, BH, BS, HS for airline 1), and where the cost function is:

$$C = \sum_l C_l(Q_l) = \sum_l (Q_l - \theta Q_l^2 / 2)$$

where Q_l is, for each airline, the traffic on each arc (for example 1, 2 and 3 for airline 1).

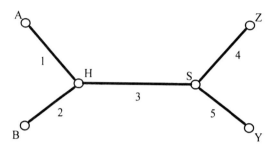

Figure 8.3 Hub-and-spoke links in international markets

Several situations can be analysed:

- monopoly on the internal links and collusion on the international link HS, roughly the European situation before deregulation;
- monopoly on the internal links and Cournot duopoly on HS: roughly the European situation after deregulation;
- merger of the two companies.

The results which depend essentially on the parameters α and θ, are to some extent counter-intuitive, because of the interdependence of costs in the different O-D markets. For reasonable values of the parameters (notably the existence of very strong scale economies) the following conclusions can be drawn:

- collusion leads to higher prices and lower traffic on HS than on internal links (this result derives from the existence of economies of density which are not fully exploited on HS because the traffic is split between two airlines, in contrast to what happens on the internal links);
- the competition on HS leads to an increase of traffic and a reduction of price, not just on HS, but also on the internal links. This leads to an increase of consumers' surplus of users and of social welfare;
- merger is preferable to collusion for all links because it allows full benefits from the scale economies on HS, which has positive effects on the internal links. It is equally better than competition on internal links, depending on the parameters related to the internal link HS: merger is better if scale economies, symbolised by θ, are sufficiently high.

Two policy conclusions can be drawn: competition is better than collusion, even on the internal links, and merger is not necessarily bad if the scale economies are sufficiently high.

Other simple models can be used to explore competitive situations. Take the case identified by Bruckner and Spiller (1991) and reanalysed by Encaoua and Perrot (1992). In the initial state the network is as shown in Figure 8.4a. Then another company enters the system and the situation changes to that shown in Figure 8.4b. What effects does this have on the market? The qualitative implications which follow, using the principles of Cournot duopoly, suggest that the arrival of company 2 has the effect of reducing the traffic between A and B. As a result the unit costs on the sections HA and HB will increase and the cost of travelling on HA and HB, CA and CB will increase with a corresponding fall in traffic. These consequences can be offset by a reduction in price depending on competition and the elasticity of demand. What clearly emerges is a network effect in which any change in the conditions on any one link will have repercussions on the other links of the network.

a.   b.

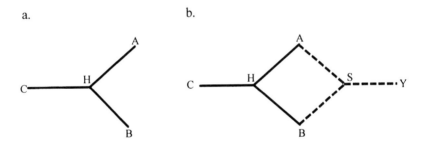

Figure 8.4 Effect of a new entrant in a network

The relationships between links on a network can also be analysed through a simple model of a feeder link: one company serves the link AB which has heavy traffic, where it finds itself in competition with other companies. The market price is P and the marginal cost, assumed constant, is Γ; unit profits are thus $P - \Gamma$ and strictly positive. If the company also serves link CA, a feeder link to AB, where unit costs are γ, it can bear losses on this link, and accept a price p less than γ, depending on the share π of traffic from the feeder link in the total traffic on AB. The condition is:

$$(1 - \pi)(p - \gamma) + \pi(p - \gamma + P - \Gamma) > 0$$

or :

$$p > \gamma - \pi(P - \Gamma)$$

Complementarity and substitution can also affect the choice of airport hubs by airlines. Pels *et al.* (1997) have analysed the choice policy of airlines as a function of the pricing policy (marginal cost or full cost) of airports. The impact on the choice of hub depends on the level of demand and the importance of scale economies.

Differentiation of products and services
A common form of competition in transport is product differentiation. This can be analysed by models similar to those used in Chapter 2 to study spatial competition. There the distance x could be interpreted as a parameter measuring the differentiation of agents' utilities, the products supplied by the two competing firms correspond to the different values of this parameter. For each consumer and each product a generalised price can be defined as $p' = p + f(x - x_0)$, where p is the product price, x_0 the value of the parameter for the product, x_i the value of the parameter for the consumer. The strategy of the firms is to choose the value of the parameter x_0 which will be the most favourable. If this is placed in the context of price competition, and if the users' utilities vary according to the variance between their parameter and that which characterises the product, we obtain the result that the firms will be interested in the maximum level of differentiation to exploit the possible monopolistic advantage. If on the other hand the utilities vary with the absolute value of the parameter, firms will be less interested in differentiation in order to retain some share of the competitor's market.

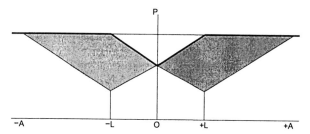

Figure 8.5 Competition between airports

A particular form of discrimination in transport is that which occurs on a single link served by modes of transport with different levels of performance, especially speed. This can also be found in a particularly interesting case, that of competition between airfreight companies (Bensimon, 1993). This is illustrated in Figure 8.5 (similar to Figure 2.1 in Chapter 2). The companies offer their clients an inclusive service which comprises collecting the goods by truck for delivery to the airport, its airfreighting and final delivery to the destination. Each company charges a price which includes the sum of these parts. Assume there are two companies, each based at an airport at a distance

$2L$ from each other and facing clients uniformly distributed along the axis between them. Each client wishes to send a consignment with a reservation price of P, the cost of air transport is equal for both companies and the cost of airport access is proportional to distance. It is easy to see that at each point the costs of the two airports are represented by the two cones defined by fine lines, that the price is represented by the upper part of these two cones (defined by thick lines), and that the profit of each company is represented by the shaded areas. The firms divide the market, and the price achieved depends on both competition and costs. It is at a minimum between these two locations where competition is the most active, but where costs are not at a minimum.

One aspect of product differentiation is that of the quality of service. The question is when an operator is using service quality as an objective, can this lead to a level which is socially optimal. We can examine this using a simple model adapted from Tirole (1988). Assuming a monopoly whose cost of production depends on quantity Q and the quality provided θ; demand takes the form:

$$p = p(q,\theta)$$

the monopolist's profit is:

$$\Pi = qp - C(q,\theta)$$

and is maximised where:

$$\frac{\partial \Pi}{\partial q} = pq + q\frac{\partial p}{\partial q} - \frac{\partial C}{\partial q} = 0$$

$$\frac{\partial \Pi}{\partial \theta} = q\frac{\partial p}{\partial \theta} - \frac{\partial C}{\partial \theta} = 0$$

Social welfare is given by:

$$CS = \int_0^q p(q,\theta)dq - C(q,\theta)$$

which is maximised where:

$$\frac{\partial C}{\partial q} = p$$

$$\frac{\partial C}{\partial \theta} = \int_0^q \frac{\partial p}{\partial \theta}dq$$

These two conditions are equivalent if $\dfrac{\partial p}{\partial \theta}$ is constant, implying:

$$p = f(q) - a\theta$$

or:

$$q = f(p + a\theta)$$

As we have seen in Chapter 4 most traffic models satisfy this condition where the principal parameters are time, safety, comfort. These results tend to suggest that operators themselves are interested in supplying the highest level of service quality as long as these factors do not create external effects and that users have access to accurate information.

A specific aspect of competition found in transport is that of competition over times of departure and arrival. We have already seen how this affects firms in a network situation. The effect of this competition on the timetables of regular operations in public transport has been analysed by a number of authors. Quinet (1991) assumes that the departure times desired by users are uniformly distributed and that the generalised price is a linear function of waiting time and shows that competition over the times of departure is then unstable. This corresponds to empirical observations, for example between competing bus companies. It would appear that a monopoly, which is one of the likely outcomes of this competition, would offer a level of service at only about half the socially optimum level. This is important to bear in mind in the context of comparing the behaviour of a private monopolist with that of a publicly provided service.

Price discrimination
Transport is a classic case for the application of price discrimination. This is usually classed in three categories.

First-degree price discrimination occurs where the operator knows the willingness to pay of each customer and can impose a different price on each one. This is approximately the situation in rail transport for complete trainloads. The operator has a small number of clients for whom there is very accurate information on their needs and what they are prepared to pay for each trainload (approximately the cost of sending the consignment by an alternative mode). It is therefore possible to establish a contract in which the operator can fix a price in order to appropriate the entire consumer's surplus of each client. In these conditions the level of traffic T_0 is optimal, the difference from the competitive optimum rests in the transfer of the surplus (Figure 8.6).

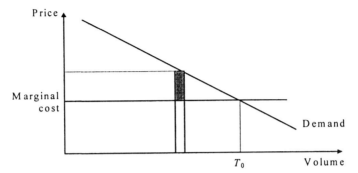

Figure 8.6 First degree price discrimination

Second-degree price discrimination arises when a firm is able to differentiate between different groups of customers according to a specific criterion. For example, customers could be identified by age (e.g. students or pensioners), by the time they wish to travel (e.g. weekend, off-peak, peak) or the period they wish to stay away. A different price is established for each group, and this can be maintained because it is not possible for clients to arbitrage between the categories. This can be analysed in a simple model. Assume a monopolist producing a good according to a cost $C(q)$. Different groups of clients are defined by their inverse demand functions, assumed to be independent of each other, $p_i = p_i(q_i)$.

The firm's profit is:

$$\Pi = \sum_i q_i p_i(q_i) - C(\sum_i q_i)$$

which is maximised when:

$$q_i \frac{dp_i}{dq_i} + p_i(q_i) - \frac{dC}{dq_i} = 0$$

From which it can easily be shown that price is defined by:

$$\frac{p_i - \dfrac{dC}{dq_i}}{p_i} = -\frac{1}{e_i}$$

where e is the elasticity of demand.

This Ramsey–Boiteux pricing leads to a higher price being paid by users with a low elasticity and less by those with a higher elasticity. This explains the differentiated price policies frequently used in transport, but does it lead to an increase in social welfare? There is no general result, but it can be shown that if discrimination leads to a reduction in quantity, social welfare will fall; but the inverse is not necessarily true (Mougeot and Naegelen, 1994).

Third-degree price discrimination arises when the population consists of two or more categories of users, but it is not possible to distinguish between them according to an unambiguous objective criterion. For example, consumers are characterised by a parameter θ which varies between $\underline{\theta}$ and $\overline{\theta}$ and is distributed as:

$$F(\theta) = Pr(\theta \leq \theta_0)$$

The indirect utility for the good is given by:

$$S(\theta, q) = \theta u(q) - T(q)$$

where $u(q)$ is such that $u' > 0$ and $u'' < 0$ and $T(q)$ is the price proposed by the monopolist for the purchase of quantity q. The monopolist's problem is to define a price $T(q)$ which will lead to a maximum profit (see Box 8.4).

BOX 8.4

Third degree discrimination and price structures

Consumers are characterized by a parameter θ varying between $\underline{\theta}$ and $\overline{\theta}$.

$$F(\theta) = Pr(\theta \leq \theta_0)$$

whose indirect utility for the good in question is given by:

$$S(\theta, q) = \theta u(q) - T(q)$$

where $u(q)$ is such that $u' > 0$; $u'' < 0$ and $T(q)$ is the price proposed by the monopolist for the purchase of quantity q. The monopolist needs to determine a price $T(q)$ which leads to a maximum profit.

The effect of this price is that quantity q will be bought by the user of characteristic θ. If $q = q(\theta)$ it can be shown that:

$$S(\theta, q(\theta)) > S(\theta, q(\theta'))   \theta \neq \theta'$$

or:

$$S(\theta, q(\theta)) = \theta u(q(\theta)) - T(q(\theta)) > \theta u(q(\theta')) - T(q(\theta'))   \forall \theta, \theta'$$

Taking account of this:

$$T(q(\theta')) = -S(\theta', q(\theta')) + \theta'u(q(\theta'))$$

it can be shown that:

$$S(\theta, q(\theta)) \geq S(\beta', q(\theta')) + u(q(\theta'))(\theta - \theta')$$

and by inversion:

$$S(\theta', q(\theta')) \geq S(\theta, q(\theta)) + u(q(\theta))(\theta' - \theta)$$

from which:

$$u(q(\theta))(\theta - \theta') \geq u(q(\theta'))(\theta - \theta')$$

such that if:

$$\theta > \theta'$$

then:

$$u(q(\theta)) > u(q(\theta'))$$

and:

$$q(\theta) > q(\theta')$$

It is also necessary that each agent wishes to buy; that is that:

$$\theta u(q(\theta)) - T(q(\theta)) \geq 0$$

But this last constraint is attained for all θ as it is for the user $\underline{\theta}$. In effect:

$$\theta u(q(\theta)) - T(q(\theta)) > \theta u(q(\underline{\theta})) - T(q(\underline{\theta})) \geq \underline{\theta} u(q(\underline{\theta})) - T(q(\underline{\theta}))$$

Moreover:

$$\frac{dS}{d\theta} = \frac{\partial S}{\partial \theta} + \frac{\partial S}{\partial q}\frac{dq}{d\theta}$$

But as S is a maximum in q,

$$\frac{dS}{d\theta} = \frac{\partial S}{\partial \theta} = u(q(\theta))$$

(this is the envelope theorem) and:

$$S(\theta) = \int\limits_{\underline{\theta}}^{\theta} u(q(y))dy + S_{\underline{\theta}}$$

Thus:

$$T(q(\theta)) = au(q(\theta)) - \int\limits_{\underline{\theta}}^{\theta} u(q(y))dy - S_{\underline{\theta}}$$

and the expected profit of the firm is:

$$E(\Pi) = \int\limits_{\underline{\theta}}^{\bar{\theta}} (T(q(y)) - cq(y)) f(y)dy$$

$$= \int\limits_{\underline{\theta}}^{\bar{\theta}} [(yu(q(y)) - cq(y)) f(y) - u(q(u))(1 - F(y))]dy - S_{\underline{\theta}}$$

The maximization of $E(\Pi)$ implies:

$$S_{\underline{\theta}} = 0$$

and

$$\theta u'(q(\theta)) = c + \frac{1 - F(\theta)}{f(\theta)} u'(q(\theta))$$

where:

$$\frac{u' - c}{u'} = \frac{1 - F}{\theta f(\theta)}$$

It can be seen, assuming $\theta' = \theta + d\theta$ that:

$$\theta u'(q(\theta)) = T_q'(q(\theta)) = p(q)$$

and calling $p(q)$ the cost of an additional unit with respect to the consumption of q. From which:

$$\frac{p(q) - c}{p(q)} = \frac{1 - F(\theta)}{\theta f(\theta)}$$

Several conclusions can be drawn. If $(1 - F)/\theta f$ is non increasing, it follows that $p(\theta)$ is also given by:

$$dp/d\theta < 0$$

and then as has been seen:

$$dq/d\theta < 0$$

then:

$$T''_q = dp/dq = (dp/d\theta) : (dq/d\theta)$$

is negative.

Summarising the characteristics of the solution shown in detail in Box 8.4

- the utility of the user with the lowest value of the parameter is zero;
- the quantity consumed is larger as θ increases;
- the price paid increases with quantity, but less quickly;
- the marginal price is above marginal cost and decreases with θ (with the taste of the consumer for the good); it becomes equal to marginal cost for $\bar{\theta}$. Only the corresponding user (the one finding it most attractive) is served in an optimal manner.

This type of discrimination explains the use of 'carnets' of tickets, less expensive than single ones; and various types of season tickets which are cheaper than an equivalent number of single tickets. This last mechanism is related to the idea of a two-part tariff of which the principle is presented in Box 8.5.

BOX 8.5

Two-part tariffs

Assume that the clientele of a monopolist, for which the marginal cost of production is zero, is composed of two groups of users; each group is composed of identical users, but the monopolist is unable to distinguish the two groups. For the two groups the inverse demand curves are given, respectively, by:

$$p(q_1) = (a - q_1) \quad \text{from where: } q_1 = a - p,$$
$$\text{and } p(q_2) = k(a - q_2) \quad \text{from where: } q_2 = ka - kp$$

With these characteristics, the second group demands more than the first. If the monopolist fixes a single price, its profit, given fixed costs, is given by:

$$B = p(a - p)(1 + k)/2$$

and thus:

$$B = a^2(1 + k)/8$$

with a price:

$$p = a/2$$

The monopolist can increased its gain with a two-part tariff of the form:

$$p(q) = A + bq$$

If b is fixed, the maximum subscription (A) which prevents customers in the group with weak demand from leaving the market is:

$$A = (a - b)^2/2$$

Then all the surplus of this group can be secured by the monopolist and the profit becomes:

$$B = (a - b)^2/2 + b(a - b)(1 + k)/2$$

which is maximized where:

$$b = a(k - 1)/(2k) \quad \text{and thus:} \quad B = a^2(k + 1)/4$$

It can easily be seen that social welfare has increased.

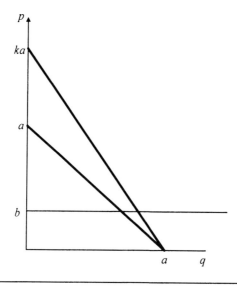

If the parameter θ is interpreted as a quality indicator, this mechanism explains the existence of different classes in public transport, with the paradox that the users of economy class pay an amount exactly equal to the value of the service whereas those of business or first class benefit from a surplus.

Yield management combines price discrimination and the management of contingent demand in order to optimise revenue in systems where the sale of transport services is through reservation, such as used in air transport and increasingly in rail transport.

Price discrimination can be of the second degree, reduced tariffs for certain people such as the elderly, supplements at peak times, etc. This can involve not just different prices but also specific quotas by category. These quotas, fixed initially on the basis of past experience, can be changed during the reservation period to take account of the way that demand develops during this period. If demand is stronger than expected the quotas available at lower prices will be reduced.

The system also allows the possibility of reductions for purchases in advance, which are non-changeable and non-reimbursable. The reductions can be justified because they make a contribution to the revenues of the company and are an insurance against the vagaries of demand, depending on the degree of risk aversion of the firm (Caillaud and Quinet, 1993b). These reductions for purchase in advance are also found in the setting of quotas which can vary over the reservation period as a function of the evolution of demand.

For all these categories, the firm seeks to vary prices. This rarely happens overtly, in order to avoid negative reactions of customers, but there is a bias towards the creation of new categories which appear to be different from the old, and thus to reduce the effective quota. Thus in the case of air transport the quotas available at low tariffs may disappear when the demand at full fare is sufficient, or, on the other hand, a few days before departure new offers at low prices can emerge.

All this is led by optimisation programmes based on future probabilities in order to maximise revenue on the basis of achieving the highest possible load factors in the most efficient way (see Sauvant, 1996).

Destructive competition.
Transport is frequently held to be a market in which there is strong evidence of destructive competition. This is best analysed in terms of the theory of cooperative games and the existence of a core as described in more detail in Box 8.6 (Sharkey (1982).

BOX 8.6

Analysis of the stability of a market

A cooperative game is defined by N players who receive utilities u_i. A coalition S of players can receive a set of utilities defined as a vector $\bar{u}$. The core of the game, if it exists (not all games have a core), is the set of attainable utilities v_i (i taking values from 0 to N) such that no coalition of participants j can obtain utilities $\bar{u}$ such that: $u_j > v_j$.

If utilities are transferable from one individual to another, the vectors $\bar{u}$ and $\bar{v}$ can be replaced by the numbers: $v = \Sigma v_i$ and $u = \Sigma u_i$.

If there is an infinite number of players, they can be represented by points on the segment $(0, t)$. A coalition is a set of points, and the game is defined by a characteristic utility function such that the coalition of players consists of between 0 and s which can be guaranteed as $V(s)$.

It can be shown that such a game has a core if, and only if:

$$V(s)/s \le V(t)/t$$

Consider a market comprising a finite number of firms, all with the same average cost function $CM(q)$ (where $CM(q)$ has a U-shape) and an infinite number of consumers each with identical utility u for the good in question.

The number of firms producing a given quantity q at a minimum average cost such that the minimum average costs $K(q)$ looks like that in the accompanying diagram; this cost $K(q)$ is defined by:

$$K(q) = \underset{n}{\mathrm{Min}}(CM(q/n))$$

If, as is often assumed, the curve $CM(q)$ is U-shaped and is flat in the neighbourhood of q_0, $K(q)$ is a set of succeeding U-shapes, becoming flatter and flatter until in the limit, when q is very large, it becomes the situation of perfect competition where each firm, very small in relation to the market, operates at its minimum average cost. The utility of a group of consumers is then the inverse of the minimum cost. In these conditions the market can be represented as a game between the consumers which has a characteristic function:

$$V(s)=sK(s)$$

The stability condition for this is only fulfilled if: $q = nq_0$. This is achieved when n is very large or when n is small, for specific values of output ($q = nq_0$). This can be explained as follows: when the capacity of the industry (defined as the output associated with a minimum average cost) is not equal to demand at this price, then market equilibrium requires that price is greater than minimum average cost; but if a group of consumers seeks to collude with one or more firms to try and secure output at minimum average cost, this will result in instability in the market.

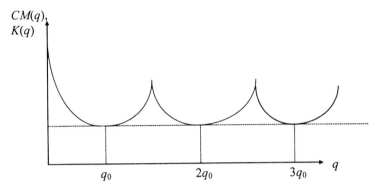

The cost curves considered here are average cost curves, they provide a guide to the firm in the context of long-run equilibrium, they are useful when both demand and supply conditions are likely to remain fairly stable.

When this is not the case, when market conditions are variable, the curves shown must be seen as representing average variable costs, excluding fixed costs. If, for example, the level of demand falls (this is the source of the strongest form of short-tem variation) market equilibrium requires that one or more firms leave the market in order to restore the equality between price and minimum average cost. But the firms which should leave can, in the interest in waiting for better conditions, cut prices below minimum average cost as long as they cover average variable costs and make some contribution to fixed costs.

The general idea is that when production capacities are not adjusted to the level of demand, instability will arise and the competitive market will not function correctly. Such situations are common in transport; instability arises from the nature of both demand and supply. Demand is variable, it is subject to seasonal and cyclical variations. Supply varies because of the non-regular character of transport flows, the need for empty return trips. Overall situations where capacity is exceeded tend to be the most common. Capital equipment in transport forms an important part of operators' costs, but has a long life and a long lead time to add new capacity. It is easy to see that there is likely to be instability in markets for non-regular traffic, here operators are likely to have to exist in a constant situation of price war and prices fluctuate widely.

Another market where this instability has been observed is that following bus deregulation in the UK. Rapid entry of new firms competing on more profitable routes led to severe price and service competition, followed by a period of retrenchment and regrouping. One means of combating this instability is through collusion between firms. Collusion can equally well arise without any instability simply because of the interest of the competitors in rent seeking through building a more durable stable relationship.

Table 8.2 Probability of collusion

Condition	Rent seeking	Combating instability
Heterogeneous supply	Weak	Weak
Inelastic demand	Weak	High
Few firms	High	High
Recession	Not Clear	High
Variable supply or demand	Weak	High
Legal restriction	High	Weak

Source: Button (1991)

Button (1991) has analysed the conditions under which these two types of collusion, rent seeking and combating instability, appear (Table 8.2) suggesting that, in general, in transport, there are relatively low risks of collusion for rent-seeking purposes, but those to guard against instability are much stronger.

2. THE EFFECTS OF COMPETITION

In transport competition can be used in diverse ways, but can often be ruinous and destructive. For this reason governments in most countries, to a greater or lesser degree, seek to intervene variously to preserve competition from excessive monopoly, to protect consumers from destructive competition, or at the least to maintain a degree of surveillance over the market.

2.1   Government Intervention in Competitive Markets

Governments are almost never totally absent from transport markets. Here we concentrate on their involvement in competitive markets, leaving the case of intervention in monopolistic markets to the following chapter. The distinction is often a difficult one to make since the same market can at some times be competitive and at other times monopolistic. It is possible to have a monopolist in control of a specific product, but for there to be a close substitute available. Government intervention can at various times be seen to be on the one hand promoting competition whilst in other areas legalising a monopoly.

The extent, and intensity, of intervention varies through time. In the immediate post-Second World War period there was strong pressure in many countries to regulate and nationalise major transport suppliers. In the 1970s and 1980s, earlier in some countries, later in others, came a period of liberalisation, deregulation and privatisation. More recently there has been an increasing reappraisal of the role of government intervention and public sector involvement more generally as an aid to the functioning of markets.

First of all government intervention has a general role in the oversight of all economic activity, verifying that laws and regulations are being observed, ensuring the quality and safety of products, protecting the rights of workers. In transport there is a particular need to ensure meeting obligations to provide public services, often through the protection of a monopoly provider. This is done both through the granting of exclusive rights to a specific market and through the protection of the rights to cross-subsidise. Thus, in granting airline routes, the US Civil Aeronautics Board arranges that companies should have access to both profitable and non-profitable routes in order to ensure local public service provision despite routes being loss-making. Urban and regional public transport in France is operated under exclusive rights in the belief that competition would not ensure the frequency or the fare levels which could meet public service obligations. We develop these aspects in more detail in the following chapter.

Intervention also fulfils an efficiency function in correcting the negative impacts of external effects through regulation and taxation as seen in Chapter 7. Most of all, however, is the role of government as regulator, ensuring the stability of markets against the fear that free markets will lead to disorder which is to be avoided.

Thus, as early as the nineteenth century, the United States had put in place railway regulation to prevent railway companies using their power against the interests of their customers, especially farmers. Later the regulation of truckers fulfilled an equivalent role, preventing competition which would affect the railways and thus have wider consequences. This was a particularly constraining regulatory structure which affected both entry to the market and prices. It was necessary to obtain a licence, available only in limited numbers, which defined the nature of the product to be carried, the quantity authorised and the origin and destination. Air transport was also heavily regulated in the US from its birth up to the end of the 1970s to avoid competition between firms enjoying increasing returns whilst preventing monopolies which could abuse their market power.

In France, State intervention has had two motives, the protection of threatened activities and the belief that a totally free market would lead to damaging instability. To protect the railways, road haulage was regulated in 1947, requiring licences and forked tariffs (where both maximum and minimum prices are set for a particular route, the maximum to avoid monopoly power and the minimum to protect against destructive competition through price wars). This was not sufficient to prevent a continuing loss of markets by SNCF, the national rail operator. Similarly shipping was protected by the use of licences, obligatory tariffs and by a system of 'tour de role' through which suppliers had to take it in turn to offer services in a particular market.

Germany similarly regulated road haulage in two main markets, short- and long-distance to protect both the railways and inland shipping.

In the UK, strict regulation of road haulage also existed up to 1968, with a strict control on the quantity of licences available. A large part of the truck fleet was nationalised for much of this time. This was replaced by a system of quality licensing, but relative freedom of operation. Long-distance coach services were regulated by a strict quantity licensing system until 1980. Local bus services were similarly strictly regulated (and also largely provided by nationalised or municipal operators) until 1986, when they became largely deregulated except for a residual system of notification of entry and exit and the need to deposit published timetables.

All European countries also regulated aviation for similar reasons to the US, except in Europe the situation was rather different because of the greater share of international traffic. Thus most routes had to be regulated reciprocally by both countries and there were regulations preventing non national carriers from operating within or between third countries. Since most major carriers were also seen as (typically nationally-owned) flag carriers this was a case of protecting the monopoly interests of the State against both new entrants and the flag-carriers of other States.

Those arguing for deregulation identify the negative effects of government intervention as obstacles to technical progress, as a distortion of productivity gains, as a means of creating rents liable to be dissipated in wastage, as the reason for poor levels of service and failure to satisfy consumers' needs.

2.2   Liberalisation and its Consequences.

During the 1980s a strong liberalising trend was established in the US, affecting aviation, inter-State goods and passenger transport by road, and rail transport. In all these areas controls were removed on entry to the market and the regulation of prices.

This new spirit of liberalisation was also felt in Europe, most particularly in Britain where the removal of regulatory control was accompanied by a push to privatise the remaining State-owned enterprises. Liberalisation was also prevalent in the Netherlands and in the Nordic countries. Germany took a more circumspect view, generally in favour of liberalisation but in a measured way. France moved much less quickly in this direction, only road haulage was completely liberalised, although changes in both aviation and road passenger transport followed European Union pressure. This latter factor has played an important role in championing the cause of liberalisation as part of the push towards the creation of single European transport market.

BOX 8.7

European Transport Policy

Transport is one of the three sectors which, according to the Treaty of Rome, 1958, the founding treaty of the European Union, should have a common policy. Since 1958 the measures taken in support of such a policy have been extremely limited. Initially they were restricted to land transport due to a very restrictive interpretation of the Treaty. Air and sea transport were only added later. The first effective measures were not taken until after 1972 when the Council of Ministers initiated a policy aimed towards achieving a greater uniformity and harmonisation between modes and countries. These measures did not attain a situation of harmonised charges for infrastructure or procedures for investment, the first stated objective, but some significant progress was made on conditions of work, technical norms, agreement on fiscal treatment of cross-border traffic and the harmonisation of railway accounts.

It is from 1985 that the Common Transport Policy began to develop. The main impulse for this came from the Court of Justice which condemned the Commission for its failure to make progress. Moreover, following the 'Nouvelles Frontières' case in air transport, the decision required the inclusion of this mode in the policy. The Single European Act of 1987 confirmed this general direction with the move to create a single market for the free movement of goods, services, capital and persons. This assured a double need for transport, a single European market in the transport sectors and the role of transport in achieving a single European market for all other activities.

The Commission has subsequently taken a number of measures with priority given to liberalisation through the harmonisation of the conditions of competition, progressive removal of licensing systems for road haulage and the need for bilateral authorisation for air transport, and defining the conditions for access to the sector. Road haulage was completely liberalised in 1998 with the authorisation of cabotage (the carriage of goods entirely within another Member State); air transport liberalisation was complete in 1997.

At the same time there has been considerable progress in the harmonisation of technical standards and conditions of work in the sector. A number of important directives have been made towards fiscal harmonisation: taxes on fuel, adoption of the 'principle of territoriality' for infrastructure charging, leading to the imposition of a system of vignettes (licences) for heavy goods vehicles using highways in a group of countries where there are no tolled highways. There have also been directives regarding the allocation of slots in air transport (giving a degree of priority to new entrants) and the use of computerised reservation systems.

Action by the Commission has been much more limited as far as other modes are concerned. In inland waterways decisions have been above all concerned with the reductions in capacity necessary to meet a fall in demand. In railways (see Chapter 9 for more detail) the Commission's actions to liberalise the market started in 1991 with a directive (91/440) requiring the separation, at least in terms of accounting practices, of the management of infrastructure and other activities, and through the liberalisation of certain markets: international combined transport and international transit traffic. At the same time directives were made regarding rules on access to markets and on the allocation and pricing of timetable slots.

Besides these essentially regulatory measures designed to liberalise markets, the EU has promoted an infrastructure policy through the definition of a series of Trans European Networks (TENs) covering, highways, high-speed and conventional rail, inland waterways, seaports and airports, supported by a wide range of subsidies, albeit these contribute only a tiny fraction of the total cost of the TENs programme which approaches €500 billion. Parallel to the definition of infrastructure networks and the need to invest in these, the Commission has promoted the concept of 'fair and efficient' pricing for the use of infrastructure with the emphasis on achieving a greater degree of consistency in charging across modes and Member States. This also serves the interests of achieving a more sustainable transport policy with regard to meeting growing transport needs with due regard to the environmental consequences.

In 2001 the Commission introduced a new Transport White Paper entitled 'European Transport Policy for 2010: The time to decide', designed to promote a much more pro–active period of policy. The White Paper has four main themes:

- shifting the balance between modes (essentially the road-rail balance, but also raising concerns about the impacts of the growth in air travel);
- eliminating bottlenecks (essentially looking to the completion of the TENs, a continuing emphasis on infrastructure);
- placing users at the heart of policy (a rather misleading theme which consists of safety issues and, on the pretext of making costs more transparent, proposals for wider use of direct user charges);
- enlargement and globalisation (recognising that transport within the EU is not independent of wider pressures, not least those of EU enlargement).

Much of this carried forward the basic themes of harmonisation and liberalisation already identified during the 1990s, but still requiring a great political will in the Member States to ensure any real achievement.

The experience of deregulation can be associated with a number of common characteristics which we shall discuss briefly before looking in more detail at the particular cases: the deregulation of air transport in the US; of road haulage in Europe; and of coach services in Britain.

2.2.1 Common elements in deregulation
The most striking characteristic is perhaps the transformation of the way networks are used. Publicly-owned transport undertakings had tended to impose network structures which ensured as many direct links as possible whilst private sector firms, given free choice in the network structure, have moved towards a hub-and-spoke structure. This has enabled them to benefit from the economies of scale present in larger traffic flows.

One consequence of this has been a reduction in costs, also resulting from increased competition between firms. Productivity gains have combined with reductions in unit costs, notably in wage costs. Glaister (2002b) estimates that cost reductions in public passenger transport in Britain are mainly due to reductions in wage costs, about one-third due to reductions in the number of workers and about two-thirds due to a reduction in effective wages. Restructuring has also led to changes in the products provided. Diversity has increased with increased frequencies, greater variety in types of vehicles used (minibuses, regional jets, etc.), services adapted to the need of individual client groups, a greater range of tariffs (especially in air transport, but increasingly in rail transport as well), and the increased use of yield management to obtain the maximum revenue for each unit of capacity on offer. As a result some links have seen a substantial growth in traffic. Others, notably those which are less profitable, have been closed except where the public sector has been prepared to subsidise them to keep them in operation.

The process of adaptation to new conditions of competition tends to take a number of years and often is marked by failures on the way, mergers, the entry of new operators and the departure of others, some coming and going very quickly. However, the general result is that the search by operators for some degree of monopoly power has led, following an initial increase in the number of competitors, to a gradual reduction, often to a level below the starting level. Similarly prices, which tended to fall immediately following liberalisation have then tended to rise again and stabilized.

Winston (1993) has attempted to measure the change in surplus resulting from deregulation for the United States (Table 8.3).

Table 8.3 The gains from deregulation in the USA ($mn/ year, 1990 prices)

	Consumer surplus	Producer Surplus	Total
Airlines	8.8 to 14.8	4.9	13.7 to 19.7
Railways	7.2 to 9.7	3.2	10.4 to 12.9
Road haulage	15.4	−4.8	10.6

Source: Winston (1993)

2.2.2 The deregulation of air transport in the United States

Up to the mid-1970s air transport in the US was very tightly regulated. In addition to technical and social regulation, there was complete administrative control on the allocation of routes, frequencies and fares. However, the Civil Aeronautics Board was becoming much more liberal up to the Airline Deregulation Act of 1978 which confirmed this practice and allowed it to accelerate. Now entry and exit as well as fares are completely free.

There have been numerous consequences of this change. They are seen particularly in an increasing differentiation of fares and services, and also changes in the structure of production: reductions in the number of direct flights and the transformation of networks into hub-and-spoke structures where each airline has one or more hubs on which flights from a range of origins converge. This has allowed an increase in aircraft size leading to scale economies and the achievement of a better position to cope with variations in traffic. This has led to an increase in the number of stopovers necessary on any given journey, though not necessarily of plane, and generally a reduction in the need to change airline, from 11.2 per cent of journeys in 1978 to only 1.2 per cent in 1990. Moreover frequencies have increased, but airlines have abandoned unprofitable routes which they had previously been required to operate for public service reasons. Only those routes which the public authorities are prepared to subsidise have been spared.

A more efficient structuring of supply, lower prices and costs, better adaptation to demand, all suggest an enormous increase in benefits. It would seem that, despite some incidents, there has not been a sacrifice of safety to achieve these benefits.

However the dynamic created by these changes had slowed to a stop before the upheaval occasioned by the 11 September 2001 terrorist attacks. This was largely due to the action of the airlines and their largely successful efforts to prevent competition. After a period of change with new entries, mergers, failures, there has been a tendency towards reconcentration and the market became more concentrated than before deregulation. The eight largest companies moved to control more than 60 per cent of the market in comparison with 56 per cent before deregulation. Additionally the merger of operators sharing a hub has not been prohibited, and logically such mergers lead to a growth in profits although the impact on consumers is not fully clear as costs fall.

Besides the classic actions of the airlines to differentiate tariffs and services or promote customer loyalty through frequent flyer programmes, other strategies have been very successful in reducing competition, most notably the use of computerised reservation systems. These systems are slow and costly to develop, only large companies can create them and those who do clearly bias the system in their favour and charge high prices to others to access the system. It is hardly surprising that these systems have led to a number of legal actions on the basis of their anti-competitiveness.

A further factor restricting competition results directly from the organisation of hubs. At its hub airport an airline can create monopoly power through its exclusive use of terminals and departure gates and through its ability to use grandfather rights on slots to frustrate new entrants and periodic attempts to reallocate landing and take-off slots on the market. Attempts to regulate fares have only very rarely been used. Some airports have tried to introduce auction systems for slot allocation, but this is severely handicapped by the separation of the market into short-haul and long-haul sectors (Starkie, 1994).

A particular interest is in the effects of potential competition. The theory of contestable markets assumes that, when entry or exit to or from the market is costless, the potential competition which results is just as effective as real competition. This has been one of the principal arguments in favour of deregulation. It is argued that it is not necessary to regulate monopoly power in the airline market since potential competition will have the same effect. However, the evidence is not so convincing. Studies of fares and costs have shown that profits depend strictly on the number of real competitors and that potential competition has only a limited effect, which is perceptible only if the potential entrant to a market already has a presence at the extremities of the route in question.

If the deregulation of the air transport market has in general had positive effects, it has been accompanied by some unanticipated consequences. The market, which had previously been paralysed by public sector intervention, has now been affected by the capacity the large operators have shown to develop monopoly powers, which have not been able to be curbed by active policies of the government. There is scope for intervention in the organisation and management of scarce resources, such as airports, where saturation has been reached, or on the question of computerised reservation systems (CRS), where high fixed costs preclude new entrants. It is necessary to establish codes of conduct for the usage of CRS; to establish procedures for the allocation of terminal slots and take-off and landing slots at airports, for example by auction, and that such allocation should be for a strictly limited duration and in a way which does not ensure the persistent domination by one operator. Finally there needs to be an explicit policy towards the extension of airport infrastructure.

Some of these possible actions imply a return to the traditional role of the public sector through regulation or the construction of infrastructure. Others are less common, for example the allocation of scarce resources through the use of auctions. All cases require the public sector to maintain an attentive and active vigilance, to be prepared to anticipate the need for intervention, and to do this within an established private sector market. This requires the authorities to be prepared to change the accepted systems of rights acquired through habitual use and to be prepared to expropriate certain agents of their exclusive property rights.

2.2.3 The deregulation of road haulage in Europe
Although a number of countries had deregulated road haulage earlier, notably the UK in 1968, until the early 1980s there was not much interest across Europe in what was regarded as a much less significant area of concern. There had been directives concerning the harmonisation of working conditions, principally to ensure the respecting of drivers' hours regulations largely on safety grounds; technical characteristics of vehicles (again with a safety concern in mind); and not altogether successful attempts to harmonise taxes on fuels and charges for the use of infrastructure. However, access to the market (through some form of operating licence) was still strictly regulated in most countries, although in a way which was not harmonised between countries. In France, for example, regulation was established in 1949 largely to protect SNCF and to prevent excessive competition in times

of weak demand. Access to international markets was regulated by bilateral agreements defining quotas of licences, plus a relatively meagre quota of multilateral European licences. Cabotage (carrying loads with both an origin and a destination within a foreign country) was prohibited. Hence a high proportion of all truck movements in Europe were empty, an inefficient use of capacity.

The situation changed after 1985, following the Court of Justice decision requiring the Commission to implement the provisions of the Treaty to ensure the free circulation of goods and people and to define a common policy for transport. There was a gradual enlargement of quotas until they were finally abolished in 1993, the creation of cabotage licences and then full freedom for cabotage from 1998 and the EU defined the rules of access to the haulage profession.

Road haulage traffic increased substantially over this period, especially in relation to other modes. The average annual growth of road transport (in terms of tonne-km) was around 4 per cent over the period 1970–99, against a total annual increase of traffic by all modes of around 3 per cent. The modal share of road in total freight transport rose from 31 per cent in 1970 to 44.5 per cent in 1999, whilst that of rail slumped from 21 per cent to 8 per cent. In inland transport the share of road went up from 48 per cent to 75 per cent over the same period, that of rail down from 33 per cent to 13 per cent. Although there are some differences between EU countries in the share of road, from 98 per cent in Greece to 40 per cent for Austria, for the big countries this range was narrower from 70 per cent in Germany to 87 per cent in Italy, with France at 76 per cent and the UK at 83 per cent.

The liberalisation of international transport has played an important role in the considerable acceleration of liberalisation in the single market. Germany was the most reluctant to abandon a licensing system. In France liberalisation involved suppressing the obligatory tariff and a major increase in the number of licences. Liberalization interacted with industrial restructuring and relocation, with firms seeking new sources of supply, new markets, and new types of production in different locations, as well as the use of just-in-time production techniques. This required transport enterprises which were flexible, able to fit in with new structures and offer quality. The number of firms in France increased by 10 per cent indicating new entry, but more significantly the number of firms of more than 100 employees went from 11 in 1986 to 170 in 1991, whilst the incidence of sub-contacting also increased; the share increased from 16 per cent to 19 per cent over the same period.

All of these changes had beneficial effects: costs fell, there was better adaptation to the needs of transport users, and a consequent increase in activity and employment. One report (OEST, 1994) estimated these gains for France at FRF9 billion (€1.4 billion) in 1991, from which need to be deducted the additional external costs resulting from increased traffic, net of additional tax receipts, of FRF3.6billion (€0.56 billion). Freedom in pricing and the lack of need for licences contributed to an increase in competition and new initiatives. But these beneficial effects need to be set against other consequences, not all so advantageous.

First, there has been an enormous growth in road freight traffic which has effectively doubled in a decade, at the expense of rail and inland waterways. Vehicle movements (vehicle-km) have in some cases risen more rapidly than total goods movements (tonne-km) because of the general reduction in the volume of consignments. This is the cause of what is seen as an increase in the traffic intensity of the economy, the amount of transport generated by a unit of output. Although wider changes in trade patterns and concentration within the EU single market have had a role in this, transport has had a major contribution. This is a direct result of increased competition and has serious consequences for both congestion and pollution.

On the other hand, the competitive pressures have caused haulage firms to seek greater efficiently in working practices. This has had serious consequences for workers within industry, increased working hours (as drivers struggle to meet demanding schedules in a situation of increased congestion) downward pressure on wage rates as firms seeks to meet competition, and the possibility of overloading vehicles as a means of cutting costs adding to both safety risks and the cost of degradation to the highway. But it has also led to increasing efficiency in the use of fleets such that the upward pressure on vehicles-km has been countered in much of the EU (Vickerman, 2003a; McKinnon, 2003).

The effect in all countries has also been increased pressure on the financial position of the railways, which in many cases leads to continuing pressure on public budgets. Conditions in the road sector, with very tight margins on operations, have led both to industrial disputes over hours and wages (most notably in France with strikes and blockades) and to confrontations over rising fuel costs, given what is perceived to be the high tax take by governments (demonstrations in several EU countries including a blockade of oil terminals and strikes by fuel tanker drivers in the UK). Thus far these problems have not been fully resolved through a consistent policy towards the sector.

Underlying the problem, for which the above external problems are often cited as a cause, is the essentially destructive nature of competition within the road haulage sector. This arises for two main reasons. First, is the ease of entry into the market: the cost of a vehicle is relatively low, loans are easily secured against the value of a real asset, the technical competence for entry is relatively modest and this has led to oversupply. The second factor is the permanent disequilibrium between supply and demand on many routes, due to demand fluctuations, the ease with which supply can be moved to other locations, imbalances between flows in different directions (making it difficult for firms to find return loads easily). This has led to downward pressure on freight prices and hence on rates of return. The primary need would appear to be to address the issue of the cost of entry to the market to ensure that those setting up haulage firms are better prepared in terms of both financial and organisational matters. This raises particular problems when, in the context of the single market and free entry to foreign hauliers, many see their livelihoods threatened by what are perceived to be less well regulated (in terms of meeting technical and social standard) firms from other countries.

Liberalisation does not means the total abnegation of interest by the State, for an efficient market to work it is essential that governments put in place, and enforce, regulations which can ensure that the market is able to function effectively. It also has a responsibility to ensure that external effects are adequately identified and corrected. This message is often inadequately expressed, any State involvement is perceived as interference with the free market. It needs to be identified as the key to ensuring that the benefits from competition can be attained, whereas at the moment they are all too frequently being lost.

2.2.4 Deregulation of coach and bus services in the UK

Scheduled express coach services in Britain were characterised before 1980 by an apparent openness to competition, but in fact a rather restrictive system of public control. In theory it was sufficient for a coach operator to show that there was a need for a service which would be in the public interest to obtain a licence to operate it. However, the right to object by incumbent operators, including British Rail, were usually sufficient to prevent this and very few new licences were issued each year. The market for express coach services was dominated by two publicly owned operators, the National Bus Company which controlled most local bus services outside the major urban areas in England and Wales, which marketed its coach services as 'National Express' and the Scottish Bus Group, which had a similar role in Scotland, and operated the Anglo-Scottish routes.

Liberalisation was effected in two stages (Mackie, 1997; Glaister, 2002a). In 1980 the express coach market was deregulated, that is any operator possessing an operator's licence (which was designed to control quality and safety issues), could publish its intention to operate a route at fares which it was free to fix. Generally routes shorter than 50 km were excluded. The Traffic Commissioners, who previously had the role of issuing licences, retained the residual role of policing operations in the public interest to ensure that published services were operated according to timetables etc. and had the power to rescind operators' licences.

In the second stage, the remainder of bus services outside London were similarly deregulated along with the break up of National Bus Company and Scottish Bus Group into local companies which were then progressively privatised, mainly by management buy-outs. The National Express branding was also privatised and the new 'operator' maintained a national coach network largely by franchising out routes to individual operators. As in the case of US airline deregulation, the public sector, in the form of local authorities, could subsidise the provision of socially desirable services which private operators were not prepared to supply on a commercial basis.

The initial response to deregulation in 1980 was for a number of new operators to enter the market (including existing small operators previously unable to operate in the scheduled routes market). Various different strategies were tried. Some tried to enter on the main existing routes where frequencies and expected profits were high, by competing on price. Others decided to compete on quality, offering various premium services.

The response of National Express was first to restructure the network to eliminate unprofitable routes and to create a hub-and-spoke network with a number of key hubs. Second, it responded directly to the competition by creating a second network of higher quality services linking the main centres and lowering prices where necessary, revealing a great capacity to respond rapidly to fare or service level changes. Both of these reduced the effective room for entrant to make gains. National Express benefited from the sheer size of its network, which provided large publicity, and through its links to the local bus operators, a large established network of ticket agents. It also resorted to other tactics, preventing access of other operators to key coach stations which it controlled, and introducing a computerised reservation system which gave priority to its services.

National Express resisted the attempted entry of new operators and succeeded in regaining those parts of the network which it lost initially, only a few small operators remained in niche markets. Interestingly, the Scottish Bus Group was less successful and its major routes were eventually absorbed by National Express which controls around 80 per cent of the market.

In a 1994 Report the Monopolies and Mergers Commission judged that, taking account of the network, entry to the market would be very difficult, competition can only exist at the margin. They estimated that this competition, including that by rail, was, however, sufficient to exercise control over National Express and to avoid it being able to benefit from its monopoly and render any attempted regulation of price ineffective. Interestingly since that date National Express has grown to become not only the owner of a number of privatised local bus companies, but also the largest holder of rail franchises, with 9 of the 25 franchises, including one inter-city route.

In sum, liberalisation has had beneficial effects for travellers: diversification of services, lowering of fares, improvements in quality and a growth in traffic, all following a reduction in costs and increasing productivity. Arguably this arises from a transfer of surplus from the employees of the publicly-owned company to the users of a privately-owned company. It is a little more complicated than that, however, since National Express is not the direct operator of almost all of its services, it franchises routes and is thus able to pass on the squeeze on margins to the franchisees, who of course can only get access to the market via National Express.

The second stage of liberalisation, which occurred in 1986, affecting all local bus services outside London, has not been as successful in terms of the main indicators used above. Essentially ridership fell dramatically, and has continued to fall, whilst vehicle-km supplied increased. Fares also rose, although again wage costs were squeezed. The original idea of smaller local companies servicing locally identified needs was soon undermined by mergers as five main groups emerged, three large and two somewhat smaller. These now control most local bus service provision. The evolution of the market was characterised by a substantial amount of asset stripping as the new groups, working on tight margins, sought to dispose of depots and bus stations for which there was a ready property market. Some areas faced substantial bus wars as new entrants sought to gain a share of the market, the main characteristic was the classic destructive competition effect of excessive capacity pushing down fares to an unsustainable level from which a dominant firm emerged with monopoly power. Some of the emerging winners could use their previous success as an effective way of discouraging potential entrants in other markets.

Although the British experiment went further than most moves towards liberalisation of coach and local bus services in Europe, Banister *et al.* (1992) have compared the British experience with various alternative approaches in other countries. They placed the emphasis on the strategies used by firms to dissuade potential competitors from entry and on developments in service quality. They also examined the scope for predatory attacks on markets, which had not been found to be particularly successful in Britain, noting that the general effect was for fares to increase on deregulation, and the strong network economies which appear to exist. The general conclusion was of a negative impact on passengers, principally through increased service instability as operators continually tried to adjust services, and the resulting poor quality of information.

This example illustrates a number of points which recur in the discussion of the experiences of liberalisation:

- the virtue of competition, even if it is rather attenuated, for example simply occurring at the margins as in the National Express case, or through the existence of other modes;
- the advantages of ensuring that it can take place, even if this means the loss of some scale or network economies;
- the tendency to the reconcentration of firms after an initially unstable period;
- the necessity for continued vigilance and action by government to ensure that the benefits are not being lost through inaction.

3. CONCLUSIONS

The examples used above allow us to make some general comparison of the impacts of deregulation in transport markets and to take a view of the competitive conditions in the sector.

Generally speaking deregulation has been beneficial to users. Prices have been lower, at least initially, services have expanded and diversified and become better adapted to users' needs. The fears of many of adverse effects, particularly for example with regard to safety, have by and large not occurred. The effects on employment in the sector have also been generally positive, largely due to the growth in traffic consequent on lower prices compensating the downward pressure on unit wage costs as a result of competition. Deregulation has also provided a better environment for the introduction of new techniques and new technologies better capable of serving diversified markets: hub-and-spoke networks, a range of vehicle sizes, new types of urban public transport, etc. Generally transport costs have fallen with deregulation, mostly due to falling wage costs through both lower wages rates and increased productivity. In general, therefore the broadest conclusion is of a transfer from employees of transport firms to their users.

However, with the exception of the case of road haulage, competition has been difficult to maintain, collusion occurs frequently, the tendency for oligopoly to emerge leads to less pressure for price competition although it occurs in terms of frequency or service quality. The tendency towards concentration is quite general, demonstrating the role of scale economies and the effects of networks, but also the ability to exploit monopoly power over certain scarce resource, such as airports, bus stations, reservation systems.

There is therefore a sense in which the disengagement of governments has achieved its objectives in liberalising transport activities and allowing them to respond more easily and rapidly to the needs of users. However, it has also allowed the firms providing these activities privileged access to scarce resources. Whilst it may have been necessary as a means of increasing efficiency, the way in which it has been achieved has certain downsides.

Paradoxically, the greatest need for intervention and re-regulation has come from the excesses of competition in road haulage and in the early stages of bus deregulation in Britain. Destructive competition has been shown not to be just a theoretical curiosity, but a very real problem. Whilst much of the sector is dominated by the existence of scale and network economies, and the access to key scarce resources, which give an advantage to the incumbent, this can also be potentially fragile.

The impact of the 11 September 2001 terrorist attacks in New York and Washington has had repercussions on the airline industry in which the stability of the main incumbent operators in both the US and Europe was disturbed. This has allowed low-cost carriers exactly the opportunity they needed to attack not just marginal traffic as previously, but also the core traffic of the major airlines. Low-cost carriers have shown how by building a route structure on the densest traffic routes from secondary hubs and concentrating on the simplest level of service, with much lower overheads and working their fleet much harder to keep costs down they have learnt from the earlier experiences of entry failures. But in such a situation the regulatory authorities have to keep an active vigilance to avoid the loss of public service provision.

Putting in place effective competition is in a sense the inverse of laisser-faire. The public sector needs to change from its traditional role as the provider and heavy regulator, to a watchful knowledge of developments in the sector, able to respond swiftly and effectively to any situation in which there could be a serious loss of social welfare. Liberalisation and deregulation have thus refocused the context and means of public intervention in transport.

9. Monopoly and Public Service in Transport

Monopolies have always been a concern for both economists and politicians. The removal of monopoly influences was one of the primary objectives of the movement towards liberalisation. This was especially relevant in transport where the most obvious examples of natural monopolies can be found. With the possible exception of road haulage, most modes of transport display, at least to some extent, economies of scale and scope, network economies and the need for expensive and lumpy infrastructure – the basis of natural monopoly.

Natural monopoly is often accompanied by public service obligations which provide additional specific characteristics. The most obvious example of these characteristics and the problems they pose is railways, and we shall use this sector to discuss the many different approaches to reform which have been introduced in almost all countries in recent years. This will allow us to assess the different ways of controlling and managing monopolies, the choice between fragmentation and integration, problems of access to the network, alternatives to competition and methods of State control. This leads to a discussion of how to exercise public service obligations: through public or private ownership, concessions or franchises, or regulated competition.

1. RAILWAY REFORMS

Until the 1980s almost all European railways were organised at a national level as integrated public enterprises. Such organisation enabled them to profit from scale economies and avoided the potential for abuse by a private monopolist whilst ensuring more easily the meeting of public service obligations. However, it was becoming increasingly clear that there were many disadvantages to such a system. Above all, management appeared incoherent and ineffective as result of the frequent, and often contradictory, interference of government and of the essentially bureaucratic nature of publicly-owned companies. Decisions, particularly on investment, were more often subordinated to the needs of the political calendar and government budgets, than to the needs of the market. The organisation was insufficiently responsive to the needs created by waste and financial losses.

These problems were recognised and various solutions were tried in different countries to overcome them, but generally without success in curbing increasing deficits. These reforms had a certain number of common features, in terms of both objectives and means. They involved introducing competitive pressures to reduce costs and ensure more flexible adaptation to changing demand, the severing, or at least reduction, of direct links with government and reduction of the size of the bureaucratic structures associated with railway administration. We look at a number of these approaches, both in Europe and elsewhere.

1.1 Railways Outside Europe

In Japan, reform involved splitting Japan National Railways (JNR) into seven separate companies, defined on a regional basis, to provide passenger services and manage infrastructure (Mituzani and Nakamura 1997). An eighth company was in charge of freight and had to buy track capacity from the other companies. The passenger companies were thus not in competition with each other, except to a limited degree at the boundaries of their respective territories and through comparison of their respective performance ('yardstick competition'). The effect of the reform was a reduction in costs, associated with a substantial reduction in the labour force, of the order of 30 per cent, an increase in passengers and a return to profit. The new companies were then privatised. The main motive of the reform was not to introduce competition, but rather to reduce the power of trades unions and to transfer their surplus to users and to transform structures which were seen to be rigid and incapable of adaptation.

BOX 9.1

The reform of Japanese railways

Before the 1989 reform, the publicly-owned Japan National Railways (JNR), founded in 1949, provided almost all long-distance railway services in Japan. There are in addition many traditionally private companies providing more local services. JNR had seen its share of the inter-urban passenger market fall (from 45 per cent in 1965 to 23 per cent in 1985 in terms of passenger-km). Moreover profitability fell from 1964, losses grew steadily, reaching Yen 1000 billion (around €8 billion) by 1980. The State enterprise was costing as much as the budget of the State itself. It was seen that much of this stemmed from the way in which the enterprise was

---

managed with too much interference by government in management, from tariffs which did not reflect the costs of providing the service, from political intervention to maintain unprofitable routes and from conflicts between management and unions.

The enterprise reform of 1987 consisted of splitting JNR into 7 area companies with responsibility for managing infrastructure and providing passenger services in that area and for supplying track capacity to the eighth company responsible for freight. Furthermore these new companies were freed from State control and given freedom to fix fares and service levels, to manage in their own way and to diversify. Their private status did not involve an immediate floating of their stock for public purchase, initially they were owned by a public holding company, and were only later quoted on the stock market.

The result was a much better response to the needs of passengers, there was growth in the services offered, improvement of times and frequencies, a relatively small rise in fares, leading to a growth in traffic of close to 20 per cent between 1987 and 1991. Productivity increased considerably, especially in the first few years after privatisation: productivity of labour per vehicle-km rose 15.5 per cent per year between 1985 and 1989 and thereafter at 7.8 per cent compared with 4.5 per cent before.

This improvement arose in large measure from the reduction in staff, from 280 000 before privatisation to 160 000 in 1996. Now the productivity of the privatised Japanese railway companies compares more closely with that of the private companies, even if they are still about 20 per cent poorer.

Furthermore, the companies have diversified considerably into commercial developments around stations, tourism and the sale of land. The State budget situation has been improved as deficits have been turned into surpluses. The drivers of this transformation have been the relaxation of State control and greater autonomy for management, the development of competition, especially with airlines, and yardstick competition with the old private railway companies. Real competition only occurs on the fringes of each network, on the few links served by more than company.

The negative aspects lie in the less frequented routes where fares have risen and levels of service fallen, and in the consequences for the labour force. Furthermore the accumulated debt from the old JNR has not been reduced substantially: the policy depended on the sale of surplus land and the sale of equity in the companies, but the recent poor economic situation has not allowed the fulfilment of all the hopes in this area.

In South America, Argentina, Brazil and Chile either have, or are in the process of, reforming railways in a similar way, but are basing their reforms more fully on the introduction of competition.

In Argentina, the network, which is primarily a freight network, was in a very bad technical state, in deficit and performing poorly. The reform consisted of splitting the network into four geographical entities, each let as a concession following a general invitation to bid. For the 30 years of the contract, the concessionaire manages the infrastructure, provides freight transport services and provides access to the infrastructure for passenger operators (in general small-scale suburban operators, which are also operated as concessions). Competition is provided by an ex-ante competition for the market, the bids of the potential concessionaires are judged by a marking system which takes account of the subsidies required, the business plan, proposed tariffs and services, technical improvements proposed and especially the proposed investment programme.

As in Japan there have been significant effects of the reform, marked by an improvement in technology, a reduction in costs and a large reduction in staffing levels of the order of 75 per cent – the number of employees fell from 92 000 to around 20 000. The losses of the railways, which had reached $800 million in 1989, were only around $200 million by the mid-1990s.

1.2   European Railways

Changes in Europe were prompted, as in other countries, by the coincidence of the relative decline of traffic on the railways and the growing burden which this was imposing on the public sector budget (Table 9.1). The wish was to use the opportunity to breathe new life into rail as a way of promoting a mode which would be a substitute for increasingly congested roads and more environmentally friendly.

Table 9.1 Burden on public budgets, as percentage of rail revenues (1994)

Railway	Deficit as % revenue
RENFE (Spain)	61.6
SNCB (Belgium)	46.0
SNCF (France)	31.8
CFF (Switzerland)	36.0
NSB (Norway)	61.8
DB (Germany)	36.3
FS (Italy)	36.7

Source: UIC Statistical Yearbook

1.2.1 Directive 91-440 and its consequences

At a European level the first tangible effect of this new pressure was in terms of EU Directive 91-440 of 1991. This established a general principle that railway operating companies should be independent of the State, commercially viable and directed towards satisfying the needs of the market. In order to achieve this, a certain number of organisational changes were required. The most important of these was the necessity of a separation between the management of the infrastructure and the provision of railway services. A measure of competition should be introduced into the provision of services, initially in terms of opening access to international rail operators for transit traffic or to promote international combined transport. This was seen as a first step towards the eventual general open access of rail infrastructure to competing operators, but this required agreement on the rules governing the organisation of the market – these rules are largely contained in two further directives 95-18 and 95-19.

The first of these dealt with the conditions which a potential operator of trains must satisfy in order to enable entry to the market: professional, financial and technical conditions and the role of each State in determining these. Directive 95-19 defined the procedures by which track usage slots should be allocated and charged for. There should be an appropriate body defined in each State charged with these tasks, subject to non-discriminatory rules and seeking to achieve an optimal usage of the infrastructure. In the allocation of slots, priority should be given to public interest services, such as commuter services, or those for which infrastructure had been specifically provided (e.g. high-speed trains). Charges for infrastructure use should be fixed in consultation with the infrastructure management as a function of the nature of the service provided, the time of use, the expenditure imposed and the market situation.

Finally, a White Paper 'A Strategy for Revitalising the Community's Railways' appeared in 1996, which focused the debate on a number of measures needed to complete and reinforce the process started with Directive 91-440:

- financial arrangements: Member States should free the railways from the burden of their debts and regularise their finances in accordance with Community rules on State aid;
- market organisation: separation of the management of infrastructure from the provision of railway services in distinct units; the establishing of 'freight freeways', major corridors where access would be open and the conditions of use simplified;
- public service obligations: should be fulfilled through specific contracts between governments and operators;

- interoperability of networks in different countries: through harmonisation of technical standards;
- social measures: to allow retraining and restructuring of the workforce.

This need to act on the railways was reinforced in the 2001 Transport White Paper 'European Transport Policy for 2010: time to decide' with two principal objectives. First, there is the need to ensure that the railways carried a share of traffic more appropriate to their capacity, particularly their role in taking freight off the roads. Second, enlargement brings particular challenges to the rail sector of the new member states, which have enormous investment requirements to bring them up to international standards.

1.2.2 Implementation

The Directives and recommendations of the European Commission have been implemented in very different ways in different countries.

The United Kingdom had already embarked on a reform of the railways which went well beyond the requirements of the European directives. Sweden had also anticipated the changes, although without undertaking such comprehensive reforms. Germany and the Netherlands followed the recommendations and timescale of the directives, but France and a number of other countries moved much more slowly and reluctantly along the reform route laid down (see Box 9.2 for two contrasting examples).

BOX 9.2

Railway reforms in Sweden and Germany

Sweden
Swedish reform was motivated by the poor performance of the railway company Statens Järnväger (SJ). It has a large deficit, slow and cumbersome decision processes, overlaps and conflicts between its commercial functions and its public service obligations. In 1988 the Swedish government decided to effect a separation between infrastructure and railway services.

Infrastructure was transferred to a new firm Banverket (BV) which would be responsible for planning infrastructure investment according to social rate of return criteria, taking account of external effects. Finance would be guaranteed by the State, users would pay user charges calculated to take account of the non-optimal charges made for road use.

The operation of trains was essentially charged to SJ, a publicly-owned company, but one which had to operate on a purely commercial basis, without public subsidy, but with freedom to fix fares and service levels. SJ

---

has a quasi-monopoly over main lines, regional routes are under the control of local transport authorities, which define the services to be operated and can contract operators, including those other than SJ, to run services.

Financial supports from the State to the railways increased from SEK2 277 million (€248 mn) in 1987 to SEK 7 281 million (€792 mn) in 1993, although during this period infrastructure investment rose considerably from SEK 882 million (€96 mn) to SEK 7 213 million (€785 mn). Subsidies for train operation fell from SEK 1 400 million (€152 mn) to just SEK 700 million (€76 mn), covering just regional lines and certain unprofitable national lines which were the subject of specific contracts. Access charges rose from zero in 1987 to SEK 659 million (€71 mn) by 1993. Finally the reforms were accompanied by a restructuring of SJ, including a reduction of the workforce from 29 000 to 14 000 and an organisation into business units aimed at meeting customers' needs.

The reform did not reduce the total claim on the public budget, but did achieve an improvement in quality, efficiency and frequency of service: rail traffic grew by around 30 per cent and air traffic fell by about 15 per cent. But the future development of the system depends on cooperation between BV and SJ, leading to question about BV's investment criteria, taking account of external effects, but dependent on forecast use by SJ. Is this less effective than if the system were integrated? How do BV and SJ plan investments which require new rolling stock and new infrastructure, for example the choice between new lines or tilting trains for high-speed operation? In the event it appears that the separation of infrastructure and operation has not posed operational problems, but there is effectively only one operator. The situation could be different in the future if competition develops, since 1996 the regions have been able to provide services over the main lines and freight traffic is deregulated.

Germany
In Germany the reform is more recent and on-going and has followed the requirements of the EU Directives quite closely. The relations between the State and Deutsche Bahn AG (DBAG) have been normalised in the sense of a reduction in the possibilities of intervention in the management decisions of DBAG. Furthermore there has been a major restructuring of the internal organisation of the company, founded from the fusion of the former Deutsche Bundesbahn and the Deutsche Reichsbahn, after German unification. This has involved separation into four divisions: regional passenger traffic, national passenger traffic, freight and infrastructure. In 1998 these divisions became subsidiaries of DBAG with a view to eventual privatisation. The re-organisation was accompanied by a

substantial and rapid reduction in the workforce from 350 000 in 1993 to around 250 000 in 1996. The State took responsibility for infrastructure investment in the form of interest-free loans, but the changes were expected to reduce the overall claim on the public budget by around DEM100 billion (€51 billion) in 10 years. Competition has been introduced through the franchising of regional services by the *Länder*, which operators other than DB have won, and through free entry to the freight market. These operators pay a track usage charge for infrastructure and although the number of operators has increased rapidly, they still have only a relatively small share of the market.

The British experience
The reform of railways has gone much further in the UK than elsewhere in Europe. For a long period from the early 1980s the state-owned British Rail (BR) was reorganised and restructured (Gourvish, 2002). Initially this involved the formation of various profit centres: Inter City, Network South East (in and around London), Regional Railways, Scot Rail and various operators for different types of freight traffic. These changes brought a number of improvements in performance, the level of subsidy fell from GBP1 430 million (€2 200 million) in 1983 to GBP1 035 (€1 600 million) in 1992, whilst traffic grew slightly and productivity was much improved (Nash 1997b).

From 1994 a much more radical reform was set in train (becoming fully effective in 1996) which involved fragmentation and privatisation. An overview of the complex structure which emerged from this reform is summarised in Figure 9.1, relating to the situation at the end of 2001. The organisations in this structure have a range of different statuses and ownership:

- Some are independent private sector companies: various freight operators, the rolling stock leasing companies, the companies responsible for the management and renewal of infrastructure and various ancillary companies – these all operate in a commercial and competitive environment.
- Some are private Train Operating Companies (TOCs) companies operating franchises awarded by the Office of Passenger Rail Franchising (OPRAF, now part of the Strategic Rail Authority). There were initially 25 separate passenger franchises operating a mix of Inter City main routes and regional local services. Franchises were granted for varying periods from 5 to 15 years, with contracts which specified certain minimum levels of service and required an agreed reduction in subsidy/increasing franchise payment. The period reflected the time

period necessary to invest and improve a particular franchise. TOCs have to achieve certain performance targets (involving penalty payments) and their fares are subject to regulation. In 2003 the first TOC to have its franchise terminated, after previously having agreed a shortening of the franchise period, was given six months' notice, and actually relinquished the franchise almost two months earlier than that deadline. Major costs involve track access charges paid to Railtrack, rolling stock leasing charges paid to ROSCOs and direct investment in service enhancement.

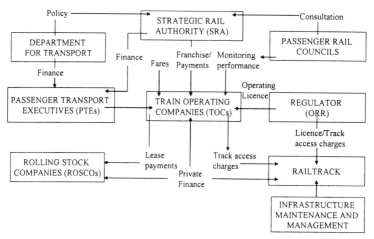

Figure 9.1 Organisational structure of British railways, 2001

- Railtrack, the initial infrastructure owner and operator was privatised from the former British Rail in 1996. It owned all the track and signalling and the major stations (minor stations being operated by the relevant franchised TOCs). Its income derived from track access charges and income from its property assets (such as commercial concessions on stations). Track access charges, and the allocation of track access, are regulated by the ORR and fixed according to the RPI-X formula used for all privatised utilities in the UK, here X was fixed at 2 per cent. Also, like other privatisations, the initial share offering was at a substantial discount: the flotation valued the company at GBP1 950 million (€2 750 million) against an estimated asset value of GBP5 600 million (€7 900 million) (Bradshaw, 1996). This enabled the company to appear more profitable in the early years. Railtrack essentially operated as a management company, most track maintenance and renewal was sub-contracted to private sector companies and major investment involved setting up joint ventures with private engineering and construction firms. Railtrack's management of these contracts has been the focus of much concern following a series of serious accidents where the condition of the infrastructure was a critical factor. This, coupled with the inability to meet investment needs from revenue streams led to Railtrack's demise. As discussed in Chapter 8, Railtrack was ultimately placed into administration in October 2001 and its assets transferred to a new not-for-profit company, Network Rail, in mid 2002.

- A variety of public sector agencies are responsible for the regulation and provision of subsidy to ensure the maintenance of public service obligation. Initially this involved just OPRAF and the Office of the Rail Regulator (ORR), plus the Passenger Transport Executives, which have responsibility for all local transport in the main urban areas outside London. Subsequently a Strategic Rail Authority was created to provide a degree of overall planning and direction, especially for strategic investment decisions which Railtrack had proved unable to develop effectively. The SRA subsumed OPRAF. The Health and Safety Executive is also responsible for ensuring compliance with safety rules and incorporates the Railway Inspectorate responsible for approving the safety of new systems and the investigation of accidents.

The network has seen an unprecedented rise in passengers and in investment following after a long period of relative decline. However, this has also been the main problem with the system since the previous lack of investment (not so much in terms of the level of expenditure, but in its effectiveness, made the system inherently incapable of coping with the stress of such change. The other main problem is the sheer complexity of the contractual system inherent in the organisation in Figure 9.1. The attribution of costs for interruption in the system is a major additional transaction cost for all participants. The desire to insure against failure means that, for example, the introduction of new rolling stock has been slow as there is reluctance to grant operating licenses until systems are proved to be failsafe, whilst the fragmentation of train operators, rolling stock providers and infrastructure operators has made it difficult to agree on solutions to technical difficulties and to plan complementary essential infrastructure to meet the needs of new rolling stock. In short the attempt to improve efficiency by making the internal transactions costs of the old fully integrated BR transparent and hence subject to efficiency gain though competition, appears to have increased transactions costs through the cost of the contractual relationships necessary. At the same time the lack of any real competition on all but a few routes has protected the TOCs from pressures to improve efficiency and generally operating performance has been poor.

It could be argued that the British reform essentially finished up with the worst aspects of all systems, it lost the potential benefits of an integrated system and replaced it with one which was over-regulated and over-complex and which did not allow any of the potential benefits of competition. Current developments, following the demise of Railtrack, involve a move to reduce the number of franchises to create more viable regional groupings, from the perspective both of satisfying demand and simplifying operation. Although there was some discussion of increasing the length of franchises to allow for longer-term planning and investment, the current move is towards shorter and much more specific franchises in terms of service delivery objectives. However, there remain issues about the level of fares and track access charges. Fares are already high by European standards, but the RPI-X cap has been relaxed into an RPI+X formula on the basis of users paying for service improvements. This also affects the potential of operators to pay enhanced track access charges seen as essential to secure long-term investment in infrastructure.

The French experience
In France, reform has been much more limited. The French national railway company (SNCF) has undergone an internal reform with the objective of separating infrastructure, passenger services and freight operations. This has had repercussions throughout the organisation. A new public agency, Réseau Ferré de France (RFF), was created in 1997 to take over part of the accumulated debt of SNCF and assume responsibility for management of the infrastructure. However, RFF is a relatively lightweight organisation which appears to be more a regulator than a manager. It defines investment policies and maintenance of infrastructure, but effective control lies with SNCF which RFF contracts to undertake work. RFF is financed by loans, together with State subsidies and access charges paid by SNCF and other rail operators.

2. ISSUES IN THE MANAGEMENT OF MONOPOLIES

The precise solutions selected by different countries have been diverse, but they have one main aspect in common, the desire to inject a degree of dynamism into the railways, improve their productivity, improve the level of service to rail users and to achieve a more flexible workforce. To achieve this, a variety of mechanisms have been introduced, the advantages and disadvantages of which we now examine: fragmentation, means of access to networks, introduction of competition and the nature of public control.

2.1 Fragmentation

Fragmentation is a feature of the majority of railway reforms. It is a response to two objectives. In almost all cases, it is a means of reducing the size of an organisation which is cumbersome and difficult to manage, in order to develop a more flexible and manageable system which is more reactive to change. Fragmentation is often also a precursor to the introduction of competition on part of the system. However, fragmentation can take different forms.

2.1.1 Geographical fragmentation

Geographical separation is justified by the limits of economies of scope. Econometric studies (Jara-Diaz and Munizaga, 1992; Preston, 1994) tend to show that in the large European networks such as Germany, France or the UK, the cost function displays diseconomies of scope implying that separation into smaller geographically distinct networks could lead to a reduction in costs. This reasoning can be countered by the consideration that, if the networks were effectively separated, additional costs would be incurred. For example, the provision of rolling stock and other material might be more costly due to the loss of scale economies and advantages of coordinating larger orders. The benefits of a complete network on demand may also be lost. It is necessary, in order to alleviate this problem, to ensure a system-wide ticketing system and information is in place – this has been retained for example in the British case.

Geographical fragmentation can also have negative effects on efficiency when the separated organisations provide complementary services for which pricing and the quantity and quality of supply have to be coordinated. This arises, for example, between main and feeder routes in a hub-and-spoke system, as shown in the case of air services by Oum *et al.*(1996).

2.1.2 Horizontal separation

Horizontal separation involves separating the organisation of different types of activity, for example those of passenger and freight services. The integration of the two has both advantages and disadvantages. It allows for economies in the use of both labour and rolling stock, but this can carry a cost since less specialised staff and rolling stock can be more costly (Henry and Quinet, 1996).

2.1.3 Vertical separation

Vertical separation is, in the case of railways, the separation of infrastructure and operation. It leads to the abolition of a hierarchical coordination of activities within an organisation and to substitute for it coordination through the market, usually with some intervention by a regulator.

It is clear that separation leads to an increase in transaction costs. Establishing timetables and priorities between services cannot be achieved simply through an internal conference, but requires not just negotiation, but substantial and complex contracts detailing responses to problems of disruption. It is expected, however, that any decisions which result from an open and transparent system will be based on a clear confrontation of the various interests involved. Thus any tendency for transactions costs to increase will be countered by increasing transparency in those costs and the pressure for greater efficiency through competition. But this argument does not apply so clearly when dealing with long-term decisions such as that of investment. Infrastructure and rolling stock investments are very closely related in terms of technical specifications (speeds, axle loads, etc.) and through the interaction of signalling and safety systems. Each partner will be uncertain of the preferences and decisions of the other, except where a long–term contract has been concluded, and this may lead to a tendency to under–investment.

2.2   Competition as a Means of Control of Monopoly

One of the intended objectives of reform, and one of the main possibilities offered by fragmentation, is the introduction of competition between operators. Competition offers a way of reducing inefficiency, both static (sub-optimal levels of production) and dynamic (waste). However, the social optimum involves a duplication of some fixed costs, the existence of which acts as an obstacle to the introduction of competition.

2.2.1 Fringe competition and comparison competition
Competition in its normal sense of separate firms providing essentially the same product in the same market is virtually non-existent in railways. The most usual form of direct competition is that which occurs on the fringes, where alongside a principal operator which occupies the major part of the market, one or more small operators can be found. This type of competition exists in the rail freight market and can also be found in the passenger market as a result of the reforms in, for example, Germany and Sweden. Similar competition can also be found in Japan at the geographical fringes of the main railway companies' areas of operation. There are also a small number of cases in Britain where different franchised operators provide services between two cities via different routes.

Japan also provides examples of comparison competition. Comparison here results from the analysis of the accounts and performance of the different operators. Such comparison can also be made between the various franchised companies in the UK, although the rather different nature of the types of operation here makes some comparisons unrealistic. More interesting in some respects has been the comparison between railway performance in different countries. Remy (1996) analyses the performance of the principal railway operators of OECD countries in terms of indicators such as productivity or financial performance. Oum and Yu (1994) use econometric methods to determine the production frontier and identify the distance from this frontier of each operator as a measure of inefficiency. These two studies both suggest that greater efficiency is gained by those operators which are in private ownership, have autonomy from State interference and an absence of public subsidy.

2.2.2 Potential competition and incumbent response

Competition can be effected by the presence of more than one operator in a market, but it can also be effective where there is the potential for competition from new entrants; this is the case of the contestable market (Baumol *et al.*, 1982).

The concept of contestable markets rests on the proposition that a monopoly cannot exercise its power in full to gain the maximum theoretical profit because of the fear of potential competition, attracted by the high profits. This assumes that entry to the market is costless and that the monopoly cannot react immediately to the entry. Thus an entrant could enter the market, cream off profits from the monopoly, and then leave the market, having weakened the monopoly's long-term financial return.

The absence of costs of entry and exit does not necessarily mean that there are no fixed costs or capital costs. It is sufficient that they can be covered, for example through the existence of a leasing market, which has been important in the aircraft market and is the basis for rolling stock investment in the UK's franchised railway. Entry costs exist essentially where sunk costs are not recoverable, as for example in the case of specific infrastructure investment which cannot be reused in any other market or any other way if they turn out not to yield an adequate rate of return.

It has been thought that a number of transport markets are contestable. Deregulation of transport markets in the US, especially of airlines, was based on this belief. Potential competition would control activities in a market more effectively and efficiently than regulation. In practice, however, entry and exit without some costs is rare. Contestability is thus not an all-or-nothing phenomenon, but can be found operating in a limited way (Morrison and Winston, 1987).

Moreover the existing firm, which seeks to reduce the possibilities of competition, has an interest in trying to prevent entry to the market by potential competitors. Tirole (1988) has developed a typology of possible strategies for the existing firms, strategies of dissuasion or accommodation according to whether or not it perceives it serves its own interest in allowing entry to take place. There are various methods which can be used to prevent entry:

- excess capacity which allows production at marginal cost and/or to increase the quantities sold in the market, provoking a fall in price and hence the rate of return to market entry;
- development of research expenditure signalling a potential future reduction in costs of production;
- a high level of production, providing the existing firm with a high level of experience;
- the acquisition of licences and patents to protect production;
- diversification of product range to cover the possible niche markets which could be exploited by entrants;
- the use of price as a signal to the potential entrant about the conditions of supply or demand. A low price could be used to make the potential entrant believe that the costs of the existing firm are lower than they actually are;
- reputation – not just the reputation that a firm may have with its customers, but also its reputation for reaction to potential entrants: an aggressive strategy towards any initial entrant may well dissuade others.

Among these various methods it would seem that excess capacity and research and development expenditure are the most widely used in transport to create barriers to entry although reputation, particularly aggressive behaviour to entrants, was a tactic used quite widely in the post-deregulation period in local bus operations in the UK.

2.3   Access to the Network

Implementing competition in the market, even in the limited forms described, poses particular problems of determining the conditions of access to the network and the charges to be made.

2.3.1 Conditions of access
Conditions of access are only defined in a very general manner by the Directives of the European Commission relating to railways. They concern first of all the certification of firms approved for access. This usually depends on their meeting specific financial and technical criteria so that they are

deemed to have the capacity to run a specified level of service safely without causing interference to the trains of other operators.

Second, general rules for the allocation of track slots are proposed. In practice this depends on establishing certain rules of priority. In general priority goes first to suburban passenger trains (largely because of the need to maintain regular services and the short journey times over which the recovery of any delay is possible), then to long-distance passenger trains and finally to freight. Responsibility for the allocation of slots is different each country. In France SNCF is responsible, in the UK it is Network Rail (as successor to Railtrack), but in each case this is under the authority of a regulator to whom operators have recourse in case of dispute.

One efficient way of allocating slots would be through the use of an auction system in which unused slots are allocated to the highest bidder. Such a system will ensure that each bidder will be induced to declare the true price that they are is prepared to pay. Nilsson (1995) has shown on the basis of fictitious auctions that such a system is practicable and would lead in most cases to a more efficient allocation. The principle is that each potential bidder defines the slots that bidder wishes to use and the value placed on each; this value will decline for slots further away from the time most preferred. The planner then optimises by allocating slots so as to maximise the total value of the bids. The result is the same as an auction system in which bidders behave by declaring the true value. It is however experimental to the extent of its complexity due to conflicts between services of different speeds (faster services occupy more slots) and the complementarities which occur in the allocation of neighbouring slots. Brewer and Plott (1996) have described an alternative system using ascending and simultaneous bids for all slots.

Such systems are only experimental at the moment (see Quinet, 2003, for a discussion of the possible roles of central planning and auctions). It is interesting to note that the equivalent is not used within integrated organisations to select between different types of service in the most rational way. In the UK there has been use of a system which comes close: every six months any additional slots are identified and then allocated by negotiation, which approaches a sort of informal auction. However, the quality of the outcome depends crucially on the degree of symmetry of information possessed by all parties, where the regulator often has the poorest information. The allocation of slots in some cases still depends critically on the rules established over train priorities, which tend to be based on the type of train rather than on its economic value. Charges are then based as much on the cost of that type of train as on the demand characteristics and willingness to pay of its users.

2.3.2 Charging for access

Within an auction system, the allocation of a slot implies the payment of a charge. From the perspective of a first-best optimum, the optimal charge imputes to each slot user the marginal costs of using that slot (the marginal costs of maintenance and management for the infrastructure manager), adjusted by the opportunity costs (the loss to other users of not being able to use the precise slots they would wish. We have already seen in Chapter 7 the difficulty of determining this given certain particular characteristics of rail congestion.

Marginal cost pricing is only useful in a first-best optimum. When public funds have a cost and when the competing mode is not priced at marginal cost it may be desirable to recover a certain amount of fixed costs. Two ways may be envisaged.

The first is that of a two-part tariff (see Box 8.5 in Chapter 8). Caillaud and Quinet (1993b), also identify other justifications for a regressive tariff for rail slots, for example the regressiveness of avoidable costs with the volume of traffic and the length of contract. It can also be a means of correcting imperfections in the market such as the double monopoly situation found in a number of cases. Finally a regressive tariff can serve as a sort of insurance policy for the infrastructure manager against risk.

A two-part tariff is, however, a major disadvantage to new firms seeking to enter a market. This suggests that Ramsey–Boiteux pricing may be preferable, as shown in Chapter 7.

2.3.3 Third-party access to the network

A particular problem arises if, as is often the case, the manager of the infrastructure is one of the users and hence finds itself in the position of providing its own competition. Laffont and Tirole (1993, 1994) have provided an analysis of this problem, the main lines of which are shown in Box 9.3, and which leads to a form of Ramsey–Boiteux pricing.

BOX 9.3

Problems of pricing third-party access to the network

Assume a rail operator with fixed costs k and that the marginal cost of managing the infrastructure is c_0. As an operator it provides two sorts of traffic q_1 and q_2, and the marginal cost of operation is c. Other operators compete on the network by buying slots at a price a and face a cost of operation of γ for traffic q_3 which is a substitute for q_2.

Total traffic is thus:

$$Q = q_1 + q_2 + q_3$$

The first-best optimum leads to a cost of access being fixed equal to c_0, but this leads to a deficit of k. If public funds incur a cost λ, its finance can possibly be recovered on the final output using Ramsey–Boiteux pricing (or a two-part tariff):

$$\frac{p_1 - c - c_0}{p_1} = \frac{\lambda}{1 + \lambda} \frac{1}{\varepsilon}$$

$$\frac{p_2 - c - c_0}{p_2} = \frac{\lambda}{1 + \lambda} \frac{1}{\eta_2}$$

$$\frac{p_3 - \gamma - c_0}{p_3} = \frac{\lambda}{1 + \lambda} \frac{1}{\eta_3}$$

The η are the super-elasticities defined in Chapter 7 (Box 7.6). If we recall that, for substitutes, the super-elasticities are smaller than the direct elasticities, it can be seen that the two goods in competition are more affected than good 1, which does not have a substitute.

The recovery of fixed costs can be made through a tax on output, differentiated by reference to a simple Ramsey–Boiteux tax, and impacting proportionately more strongly on the larger operator, and moreover the stronger are the goods substitutes.

If the state can impose the prices p_1 and p_2 on the monopoly, but not the tax on the competing operator, the optimum can be achieved by imposing differentiated access prices:

$$c_0 + \frac{\lambda p_3}{(1 + \lambda)\eta_3} \quad \text{on the competing operator}$$

$$c_0 + \frac{\lambda p_2}{(1 + \lambda)\eta_2} \quad \text{on the monopoly for traffic } q_2$$

$$c_0 + \frac{\lambda p_1}{(1 + \lambda)\varepsilon_1} \quad \text{on the monopoly for traffic } q_1$$

This type of result can be compared with the rule often used for pricing access, that of 'efficient component pricing' (Laffont and Tirole, 1994), which imputes to the competitor the loss which its presence imposes on the monopolist, that is:

$$a = p_2 - c$$

or:

$$a = c_0 + \lambda/(1 + \lambda)p_2/\eta_2$$

It can be seen that the rules are equivalent if the two substitute goods have the same demand and supply characteristics (identical demand elasticities and marginal costs). In other cases it can constitute a first approximation or reference point.

2.3.4 Practical considerations

The preceding considerations can be extended in two ways. The first concerns extension to the situation where it is necessary to make a contribution towards fixed costs. Nothing in what has been presented so far leads to limiting this contribution to operators who benefit from access to the infrastructure. The development of the argument which leads to the conclusion of Ramsey–Boiteux pricing shows on the contrary that it is beneficial to extend this to substitute products and particularly to those where the degree of substitution is strongest. That would imply attaining a greater efficiency if it were possible for road traffic to contribute to the fixed costs of railways, and vice–versa.

The second reflection, can lead to modification of the results. These have been established on the basis of a number of implicit assumptions, essentially that the manager of the infrastructure is a docile agent in the hands of public sector power whose objectives and constraints it embraces; that the public agency has perfect knowledge of all the conditions of supply and demand in the market; and that the monopoly is passive with respect to competitors, and does nothing to oppose their actions. These assumptions are self-evidently rather simple: the monopoly has its own objectives, different from the government, and it is going to try and achieve these using its superior level of information, leading to higher levels of profit and an elimination of undesirable competition. This can lead to the government agent reducing access charges in order to facilitate entry to the market. These considerations of incentives or asymmetry of information can work in a perverse way (Laffont and Tirole 1993), which lead to pricing structures which, for the large users comprise a large fixed charge and a much smaller variable charge.

Faced with these complex considerations the practicalities become very frustrating. Pricing structures in general use formulas assuming intervention for a fixed period, based on timetable slots which take account of congestion, which depend on the type of train, which takes account of the capacity allocated to each time of train and which allows for the costs of maintenance and management. There is in practice a period of bargaining in which the charges are progressively adjusted and change very quickly. It is only possible to identify certain major trends and issues in a number of different countries:

- In the Netherlands infrastructure is financed and managed by the State and charges are low, reflecting the policy of maintaining the advantages of access to the major ports.
- Sweden has established a system where infrastructure charges are equally low, based on marginal costs, but amended and reduced to balance the under-charging for roads in terms of externalities.
- In France the initial system, prior to 1999, was based on similar principles, but including congestion costs, and more or less similar to a Ramsey–Boiteux pricing formula.
- In Germany, infrastructure charges are fixed at a relatively high level to recover the total costs of infrastructure used by the operator, but the operator is heavily subsidised.

In all countries there is a system of penalties for failures and delays. These are used in practice in Britain and Sweden. In France, although the possibility is enacted it was not actually used in the provisional charging structure in place up to 2002.

It can be imagined just how difficult it would be to try and harmonise the charges for European infrastructure, but this is a central plank of the European Commission's desire to reinvigorate European railways and harmonise conditions of competition between Member States.

2.4 The Control of Monopolies

The alternative to the imposition of competition is the direct control of monopoly by the government. Such control is particularly important when the monopoly is invested with a public service obligation because the external effectiveness is in direct contradiction to the profit motive.

2.4.1 The organisation of control

Control can take many forms which differ according to the ownership of the monopoly. In a centrally planned state, control is direct and hierarchical, the monopoly firms are direct services of the government administration. More common in the public enterprise structure of most European Union countries, has been a system in which the relevant government ministry, which determined the public service obligation, exercised control through a very close relationship. Often some tasks were delegated to the operator, in many cases national rail companies defined their own technical standards for example.

In some countries, notably the United Kingdom, a more arm's length relationship between State and enterprise, regulator and operator, emerged recognising the divergence of objectives. Agencies were established between State and operator to effect such matters as safety. Even where the government effectively held the financial controls over major expenditures there was always a pretence that the publicly-owned company had independence in day-to-day operations.

For the regulator the main motive is to protect the integrity of the regulation from external influences, such as political pressure determined by electoral calendars, in order to give the regulatory regime stability and a continuity sufficient to render its actions effective and its policies credible. The regulator is essentially invested with a number of missions: to promote effective and equitable competition, to ensure the development of the industry, the satisfaction of the consumer and the fulfilment of the public service obligation. Thus, for example the Rail Regulator in the UK has the right to intervene on (and refuse) contracts between Railtrack (now Network Rail) and the rail operators, on fares and conditions of access, on passenger franchises in terms of their consequences for competition and for the development of the rail network. In fact the Rail Regulator perceived the intervention of the Government to place Railtrack in administration a potential interference with his duties and potentially detrimental to the future development of the rail industry. The Regulator, as the monitor of value for money, has also suggested that the current investment plans of Network Rail are untenable and that a delay could see a reduction in total cost by looking for greater efficiency. However, the Regulator only monitors the competitive situation, he does not select operators, grant franchises, or determine investment, that is the responsibility of the Strategic Rail Authority.

The difficulties are numerous. First, comes the choice of the regulator, who has to have qualities of honesty, independence, and devotion to the public interest, but must also command respect and trust from all parties. Above all there is the problem of dealing with different parties in a situation of asymmetric information without always knowing all the conditions of the market, costs, demand details, etc.

The effectiveness of control can be reduced by two phenomena, collusion and capture, which we shall discuss in more detail below. The relative importance of these depends on the way regulators are selected, the length of their mandate and the degree of precision with which their objectives have been defined in advance. It also depends on the extent to which the agents in the market being regulated, lobby the regulator and/or secure the attention of the government over the developing situation in the market.

2.4.2 Regulation of prices

Price regulation has the objective of removing a situation in which the monopoly holds the consumer to ransom, and produces a sub-optimal level of output. A number of alternative ways of effecting price regulation to overcome this situation have been proposed:

- cost plus regulation: the regulator fixes a price which is slightly above the monopoly's costs, sufficient to allow a profit to the operator;
- price-cap or RPI-X regulation: the regulator fixes the maximum growth in prices which can occur taking into account the general level of price inflation (Retail Price Index, RPI) but requiring the operator to achieve a certain percentage improvement in productivity relative to the general level of inflation;
- rate of return regulation: in which the rate of return on capital employed is the object of the regulation.

Both theoretical analysis and experience reveal the advantages and disadvantages of these different systems:

- cost plus does not provide any incentive to improve effort since costs are covered;
- price-cap has the opposite effect, it provides strong incentive to improve efficiency since all the gains are attributed to the enterprise, but it has a cost to the public sector since where there is asymmetric information or risk it may be necessary to allow a premium on the desired price level in order to persuade operators into the system, thus providing a degree of insurance against risk (Box 9.4).
- rate of return control can have an impact on the investment policy of the monopoly. The so-called Averch-Johnson effect means that the monopoly has an interest in over-investing to increase its profit (Box 9.5)

BOX 9.4

Adaptation of price-cap regulation in the case of multi-product firms

The case of multi-product firms is different. The condition for maximising social welfare requires, in addition to the traditional social surplus, the additional cost of public funds which leads to a Ramsey–Boiteux pricing solution. It can be shown that a system of price control can approach this pricing (Vogelsang and Finsinger, 1979), in which the constraint depends on a weighted sum of the prices of the different outputs:

$$S = \sum_i w_i P_i$$

where the weights are equal to the quantities produced in the preceding period and the value of S is equal to the total expenditure in the preceding period (if there is only one product this means that the price must not exceed the average cost in the previous period). The mechanism supposes that the firm is myopic; in the contrary case it could plan future profits by increasing current costs.

Similar strategies can appear in the dynamic case of cost plus or price cap regulation: the firm moderates it efforts under price-cap regulation believing that the regulator will acquire information on its costs and efficiency in time and then would use this as a basis for reducing prices. The result depends on the revelation of its long-term strategy and the credibility of the stance take by the regulator.

BOX 9.5

The Averch–Johnson effect

Given a monopoly producing a good q at price p, with capital K, for which the annual unit cost is I, and labour L at wage w, the production function is:

$$q=f(K,L)$$

If the regulator imposes a maximum profit rate of r, the monopoly has to solve the problems:

$$Max(pq - (iK + wL))$$

$$q - f(K,L) \le 0$$

$$pq - (iK + wL) - rK \le 0$$

The solution of which gives (with the usual Lagrangian multipliers):

$$-i + \lambda f'_K + \mu(r + i) = 0$$

$$-w + \lambda f'_L + \mu w = 0$$

$$p - \lambda - \mu p = 0$$

From which: $\lambda = p(1 - \mu)$ and as: $\lambda \ge 0; 1 - \mu \ge 0$
and:

$$\frac{f'_K}{f'_L} = \frac{i - \mu(r + i)}{w - \mu w} = \frac{i}{w} - \frac{\mu r}{w(1 - \mu)}$$

If $\mu = 0$, the constraint does not hold, and one obtains the classic equality:

$$\frac{f'_K}{f'_L} = \frac{i}{w}$$

If $\mu \neq 0$, the constraint holds and:

$$\frac{f'_K}{f'_L} < \frac{i}{w}$$

The marginal productivity of capital is below the optimum and there is over-investment.

An analysis of the dynamic between the monopoly and the regulator can lead, on the contrary, to the monopolist under-investing. That happens in the case of specific, non-reusable investments and given that these investments have been undertaken, the monopoly believes that the regulator will fix prices too low putting their profitability in question. The key to this question is in the stances taken by the regulator and its credibility. Helm and Thompson (1991) have analysed the effect of the control system on the incentive for the operator to invest.

Price regulation in transport is essentially price–cap regulation. For example, the regulation by the ORR in Britain deals with the pricing of slots and that by the SRA fares for passengers. In France, autoroute tolls are fixed by the Ministry of Finance by reference to the rate of inflation, although the exact relationship to the inflation rate is not fixed by statute. However, there is often an implicit rate of return regulation in which higher profits may risk stricter future price regulation; this induces additional investment as a means of holding off this threat. Cost–plus regulation is used for some public transport operators, for example RATP, the Paris transport authority, is compensated for increases in costs which are not covered by fare increases.

3. PUBLIC SERVICE OBLIGATIONS

In its widest sense a large number of transport activities have the character of providing a public service. This can either be very specific in terms of identifying individual services which are not otherwise profitable and for which the public sector takes responsibility, or can be attached to the entire sector as in the case of the Loi d'Orientation des Transports Intérieurs (LOTI) of 1982 in France.

The identification of a public service character does not imply that a service has to be operated directly by the public sector, nor by a monopoly operator. Taxis, for example, are in almost all countries run by private operators, display considerable competition both within the mode and with other modes, but do have a public service character and are in most cases fairly strictly regulated. Intervention is stronger when the public service obligation places constraints on what would happen under private sector management, in terms of the operation of unprofitable services and a fare structure different from that implied by profit maximisation.

In such situations intervention is needed to ensure the operator complies with the constraints required, to compensate if the constraint implies a deficit, and to protect from potential competition if the provision of unprofitable services is to be financed by cross-subsidies. However, this intervention can take a number of different forms.

3.1 Public Management

A simple means of ensuring that an operator complies with social objectives is to integrate the provision fully into the public sector as a full part of the administration. This could involve simply operating the service from the central administration, as in most communist countries of Europe in the second half of the twentieth century, or setting up a publicly-owned and managed enterprise at arm's length from the administration, as in the case of most of the national rail companies in western Europe. Whatever the legal status, the basic characteristics were the same, the operator fulfilled the basic objectives laid down by the relevant government authority. Although such a means of organising transport, and other public utilities has its merits (and arguably was the only way of ensuring their continued operation and development in the circumstances of the time), increasingly it has been shown to have a number of major drawbacks.

The main problem with State control is that the State has several, often contradictory roles: it determines the level of public service, it imposes obligations on fares, unprofitable routes, but it does not typically want to assume the financial consequences of these actions for reasons of its overall budgetary position. Moreover, since it can be involved in several different modes and other competing activities it is frequently the case that the State is having to compete against itself and make decisions in one sector which respond to decisions already made in another.

Managers in a public enterprise follow their own objectives in the context of a bureaucratic function rather than a genuinely managerial function (see Box 9.6), which often determines promotion by seniority rather than performance, using incremental salary scales rather than performance-related pay and tends to reward compliance with norms rather than innovation; communication tends to be horizontal rather than vertical and decisions are simply handed down from higher levels.

BOX 9.6

Bureaucratic management

This form of management, characteristic of public administration, is largely contrary to the main features of private sector organisation and the market:

- in terms of the origin of resources used: budgets are derived from a higher level authority rather than from operations in a market;
- in terms of the provision of stable and lifetime employment, with regular advancement, to those employed rather than insecurity and promotion on the basis of merit and results;
- in terms of the use of rules and norms as a measure of efficiency;
- in terms of the way control depends on the means and organisational structure, rather than on the inefficiency of individuals;
- communications and information passes from high to low and circulates badly between different levels in the hierarchy; whereas in the private sector communication is much more active between levels;
- the objective is biased towards the maximisation of budgets and staffing levels rather than towards the overall performance of the organisation.

The public enterprise typically has an objective of maximising social welfare reflecting both profit and external effects as well as distributional effects as shown by the theory of public choice. But the extent to which such an objective is effectively pursued has to be examined through comparing the divergent interests of the main actors: electors, politicians, civil servants and managers of the public enterprise, plus users (who may have different views as users than they do as electors). It is not clear that electors have the ability to ensure the achievement of maximum social welfare. Electors are usually offered a wide range of choices on which to make decisions, but typically only in collections of decisions according to politicians' manifestos. Elections occur at infrequent intervals and are not directly related to a specific set of choices for individual public enterprises. Moreover the gap between setting a target and the way it is delivered makes it difficult for the elector to see how individual decisions are carried through to actions. This results in a generally poor level of control which is reflected in the quality of the management.

As a result there has been a tendency for poorly performing public enterprises to begin to incur increasingly large deficits and to become a larger burden on the State. A range of reforms have been proposed in various countries to tackle this problem:

- clarification of the public sector accounting to make clearer the costs of meeting public service obligations and to identify the specific subsidies required to finance them;
- separation of commercially provided, market, activities and public service obligations within public enterprises so that each can be managed according to the appropriate principles for that market;
- giving enterprises a greater autonomy in their management to free them from excessive administrative control.

In France there was an attempt to provide a more contractual relationship between SNCF and the State, although this was found difficult to enforce in practice as SNCF found various of the measures difficult to implement (for example, public service obligations on minor routes) and the government frequently reneged on its responsibilities if macroeconomic or other budgetary priorities came to the fore. In the UK similar difficulties were encountered over government inconsistency in terms of, for example, British Rail's investment programme. In the 1980s there was an attempt to place British Rail on a more commercial footing through 'sectorisation' in which separate divisions for the main markets could be set their own objectives and this was found to be generally successful in, for example, creating an effective InterCity brand which was profitable (Gourvish, 2002). The benefits were however lost in later reorganisation and completely in the eventual break up of British Rail on privatisation.

3.2   The Concession or Franchise

Franchising, or the concession, is a frequently used vehicle in transport. We have already seen its use in infrastructure in Chapter 7, where its use is essentially one of financing investment. Here we look at its use in transport operations. We use the terms 'franchise' and 'concession' interchangeably, although it is possible to make some distinctions on legal grounds.

The concept is particularly attractive since the government or regulator is able to impose public service conditions as part of the granting of monopoly rights to the franchisee or concessionaire. The granting of the franchise takes place after a public call for bids. Often a two-stage process in used in which potential bidders pre-qualify and are then invited to submit a full bid. In some cases only one bidder is selected after pre-qualification and detailed contractual negotiations take place which may or may not result in the final granting of the concession. Variations on this system are used in different countries and for different modes. In some cases entire networks are franchised, in others individual routes or groups of routes can be franchised. Those countries which have begun to fragment their railway systems have made particular use of the method. In the UK all the former BR passenger railways are franchised. In Sweden regional railways are franchised. New urban light rail systems have been franchised in the UK, as have local bus services in London.

The system is not without difficulties, however. There is a risk of collusion between bidders, a risk of corruption, especially where there are subjective elements in the decision, problems of incomplete contracts and difficulties of controlling the franchisee to deliver contractual obligations.

Renewal of concessions is a particularly difficult issue, as has been seen as the first rail franchises have come up for renewal in the UK. The incumbent operator has superior information, but where a new operator gains a service as a result of inaccurate evaluation on the basis of less good information, this leads to the condition known as 'the winner's curse'. Investments made by the concessionaire pose a particular problem. The regulator will typically wish to see investments made and that there should not be an investment hiatus in the changeover period. This suggests that investments should be transferred between franchisees, but determining the value of, often specific, investments is difficult. Achieved investment is, on the other hand, an indicator of success in a franchise. The desire to see investment and for that investment to be allowed the opportunity to repay the investor is one argument in favour of longer franchises. For example, the first UK rail franchises were for periods between 3 to 5 and 15 years, most for about 7 years, according to the amount of investment necessary and the time estimated likely to be needed to return the franchisee to profitability. Later thought had been that rather longer franchises, perhaps as long as 20 years, might be necessary to involve the operator in taking long-term decisions of benefit to the network as a whole. However, there has now been a return to shorter, probably five-year, franchises as a means of keeping greater control over the operators.

Concessions are granted through a contract which transfers a larger or smaller amount of information rent to the operator and provides a more or less strong incentive to effort, according to the degree of asymmetry between the concessionaire and the organisations granting the concession.

Asymmetry of information can arise ex ante because the regulator understands the market situation and costs less well than the operator. A contract at a fixed price transfers to the operator a rent which can be modelled rather like the price discrimination model of the monopolist discussed in Chapter 8 (Box 8.5). The efficient operator receives a substantial rent, just as the most important customer receives a larger surplus. It can also arise ex-post due to the impossibility of the regulator observing the amount of effort put in by the operator.

Concessions are common in urban transport and Costa (1996) provides a survey of different models of management found in Europe. He identifies four models characterised by the extent to which the organising authority and operator are integrated or not and by the freedom of entry to the market (Table 9.2).

BOX 9.7

Uncertainty, hidden effort and risk

Consider a regulatory authority, referred to as the 'principal', who wishes to see a transport service developed by an operator, the 'agent'. The result of this is measurable afterward in terms of profit π. It depends on the effort exercised by the agent, e, which cannot be observed and a random effect ε, which for example could depend on macro-economic conditions or a change of preferences by consumers. The random effect has zero mean and standard deviation σ :

$$\pi = e + \varepsilon$$

The effort e required of the agent has a cost $C(e)$ which has first and second derivatives both positive. The agent is risk averse measured by the rate r, and requires a minimum utility u to operate.

Assume that the principal wishes to pay the agent relative to the profit π realised ex-post, through a linear function:

$$s(\pi) = \delta + \gamma\pi$$

How can the principal fix δ and γ? In order to see this, note that the agent derives a mean utility from the operation:

$$E(U_A) = \delta + \gamma e - r\gamma^2\sigma^2 / 2 - C(e)$$

Effort can be fixed, thus:

$$C'(e) = \gamma$$

The principal assumes risk aversion as follows:

$$E(U_p) = E(\pi) - s(\pi) = e - \delta - \gamma e$$

The problem is to maximise the utility, taking account of two constraints:

$$C'(e) = \gamma$$

$$E(U_A) \geq u$$

This gives:

$$\gamma = \frac{1}{1 + r\sigma^2 C''(e)}$$

$$\delta = u + C(e) + \frac{r\sigma 2C'(e)}{2} - eC''(e)$$

It is interesting to compare these results with the global optimum, which involves maximising:

$$E(U_A) + E(U_P) = e - C(e) - r\gamma^2\sigma^2 / 2$$

and leads to:

$$C'(e) = 1$$

The results and their implications can be seen in the following table:

Characteristics of the agent and the situation	No uncertainty ($\sigma=0$) or no aversion to risk ($r=0$)	Uncertainty and risk
$R\sigma$	0	$\neq 0$
$E(U_a)$	U	U
γ	1	$0 < \gamma < 1$
e	effort optimal: $C'(e) =$	effort sub-optimal: $C'(e) < 1$
δ	1	$u + C(e) - eC'(e) + r\gamma^2\sigma^2/2$
$E(U_P)$	$u + C(e) - e$	$e - C(e) - u - r\gamma^2\sigma^2/2$
	$e - C(e) - u$	

The 'participation in results', measured by γ is complete ($\gamma=1$) in the absence of uncertainty or of risk aversion, and it is that which ensures optimal effort. It is reduced in the presence of risk or risk aversion, and hence leads to a reduced effort and increased costs for the principal.

Table 9.2 *Models of organisation of urban transport and their consequences*

Models	Integrated regulator–operator	Separation regulator–single operator	Separation regulator–many operators	Freedom of entry and competition
Principal Characteristics				
Differentiated products	Weak	Weak	Weak	Yes
Barriers to entry	Yes	Yes	Medium	No
Functional integration	Yes	No	No	Yes
Vertical integration	Yes	Yes	Variable	Variable
Management strategy	Maximise size of network	Maximise size of network	Maximise size of network	Cost coverage
Price policy	Various objectives	Satisfactory rate of cost recovery	Satisfactory rate of cost recovery	Profit
Allocative and productive efficiency	Efficiency based on scale economies	Efficiency based on scale economies	Productive efficiency	Productive and dynamic efficiency
Technical progress	Slow	?	?	Quick

Source: Costa (1996)

3.2.1 Urban transport in France
In this scheme the main French urban areas are almost all in the second model, based on a separate regulator and a single monopoly operator with a concession contract. These contracts can be drawn up in a variety of ways (Box 9.8).

BOX 9.8

Alternative contractual arrangements in franchises

Given a price p fixed by the regulator, commercial effort, a, of the operator (e.g. marketing and communication) and structural parameters of demand θ_q, total traffic is given by:

$$q = D(p,a,\theta_q)$$

and effective revenues:

$$\tilde{r} = \overline{R}(pq)$$

Similarly given productivity effort of the operator, e, technological parameter, θ_c, production of output q implies effective costs:

$$\tilde{c}(q,e,\theta_c)$$

On the basis of the theory of contracts in the presence of incomplete information (Caillaud *et al.*, 1988) we can formalise the contractual process as follows. Negotiation and proposals by the potential operator define the revelation phase where $(\theta_c^a \theta_q^a)$ are announced to the regulator/franchiser. This determines the level of effort which it is desired to induce (a^0,e^0) which implicitly determine the revenue objectives (r^0) and the cost objectives (c^0), and the regulator determines the desired level of remuneration which he is prepared to allow the operators for the realisation of these objectives:

$$U^0 = t^0 + r^0 - c^0.$$

According to the type of contract used the effective remuneration will be determined as follows:

Risks and perils (RP): subsidy $t=t^0$

The operator supports all the (marginal) risk, but the regulator provides a fixed subsidy corresponding to the structural deficit desired for the transport sector given the defined objectives. The profit of the operator is:

$$u = U^0 + (\tilde{r} - r^0) - (\tilde{c} - c^0)$$

Guaranteed revenue (GR): subsidy: $t = t^0 + \max(0, r^0 - \tilde{r})$

The operator supports the marginal industrial risk and only the good commercial risks. Its profit is r^0.

Lump-sum price (LP): subsidy $t = t^0 + (r^0 - \tilde{r})$

The operator only takes the industrial risk, the regulator the commercial risk. The profit of the operator is:

$$U = U^0 - (\tilde{c} - c^0)$$

Management (M): subsidy $t = t^0 + (r^0 - \tilde{r}) - (c^0 - \tilde{c})$

The operator no longer takes any risk and the profit is $U = U^0$.

In all cases it is the regulator who fixes the price (fares); in fact the regulator fixes, as well as the price, the conditions of supply and demand (quality, length of network, frequency, etc.). But the operator can make suggestions so that the regulator can benefit from the operator's experience and the operator also retains a certain autonomy to fix special tariffs which could represent a significant proportion of total revenue.

The alternatives can be brought together into a single expression:

$$t = T + A(\tilde{r} - r^0) - B(\tilde{c} - c^0)$$

in which the following holds:
- management: $A = B = -1$
- risks and perils: $A = B = 0$
- lump-sum price: $A = -1, B = 0$
- guaranteed revenue: $B = 0, A = -1$ if $\tilde{r} \leq r^0$
                                  $A = 0$ if $\tilde{r} > r^0$

Econometric studies of the performance of these systems have been carried out by a number of authors (Croissant, 1996; Kerstens, 1996; Caillaud and Quinet, 1993a).

Croissant (1996) has considered the way in which urban transport in different cities has satisfied the objective on an economic optimum. Using a model which estimated cost functions, on the basis of traffic volumes, supply, and characteristics of the city and demand functions, he derived an expression for social welfare which depended on the fare structure and subsidy. His results suggested that achieving a first best optimum could involve an increase in subsidy. With the given level of subsidy an improvement of service quality accompanied by an increase in fares would be beneficial. Deregulation which led to fares closer to average costs would reduce costs, but would also reduce social welfare.

This analysis assumes that the efficiency of operators would not be affected by the mode of regulation, a hypothesis tested by Kerstens (1996), who analysed the effects of ownership and the type of contract on productive efficiency. Ownership had a slight influence on efficiency, private operators were more efficient, but more important was the form of contract. Three factors were important: the length of contract (longer contracts reduced efficiency); the amount of subsidy (larger amounts reduced efficiency); and the distribution of risk (the greater the risk supported by the operator, the greater was efficiency), but as important could be the rent implied in the contract (see Box 9.8).

Caillaud and Quinet (1993a) looked at the reasons for the choice of particular forms of contract seeking to explain the impact on the shares of receipts and costs. It appears that the share of receipts· is governed by asymmetry of information since the authority granting the concession often has less information about the details of demand and thus is more likely to allow the operator to receive rent through a fixed subsidy even if this means less effort on the art of the operator.

3.2.2 Urban transport in the United Kingdom
In the UK, outside London, the solution chosen, following deregulation in 1986, was based on market competition with free entry. After a period of, often destructive, competition, there has been a gradual return to monopoly operators subject only to a degree of fringe competition. The reductions in costs obtained during the transition period have now stopped and the efficiency gains which were achieved have to a large extent been at the expense of users: fares rose and service quality fell. Operators abandoned unprofitable routes leading to a need for local authorities to subsidise replacement services. The competitive gains have largely disappeared.

In London, a system of franchises was introduced for most of the bus network, initially route by route, but later more on an area basis. The impact of this has been judged to be successful, and certainly much more successful than in other cities in the UK (Glaister 2002a, 2002b; Mackie 1997). Costs have fallen, service quality has improved and these benefits have been maintained through a form of competition for the franchises. Although incumbent operators have advantages in the re-franchising, the number of different operators in London provides a better level of information allowing franchises to be let competitively, and a substantial amount of change in operators had taken place. The franchises have been let, according to their particular characteristics, on two different bases: gross and net. In the former case, the franchisee receives the right to run the route and keeps the revenue generated (fares are regulated on a standard basis). In the latter case, the operator does not take a risk on revenues, nor receives any benefit, but is in effect simply paid a fee for running the route.

3.3   Private Ownership

Private ownership is judged to be superior to public ownership due to internal efficiency which minimises costs, but inferior to public ownership on the basis of external efficiency, the pursuit of the public interest and social welfare.

The essential characteristic of private ownership depends on the fact that the firm is ultimately controlled by shareholders and not by government. The simplest hypothesis is that they are motivated by a profit maximising objective. But this rather general objective can be translated into different concrete proposals, for example, do we maximise profits in the short-term or long–term? Furthermore shareholder control can be lax for a number of reasons: if the shareholding is highly dispersed it is difficult for it to take a coherent set of decisions, the decisions of one shareholder can produce positive externalities for others from which he or she does not benefit; once again there is serious asymmetry of information. Efficiency can be improved by the existence of an intermediate level of control between the shareholders and the firm's management, constituted by the directors whose remuneration depends on the profits of the firm.

The problem which arises is that, on the one hand there is an incentive for profit for the firm and its managers, a low profit will cause a fall in the value of shares and induce shareholders to seek to change the management of the firm or to sell their shareholding, thus reducing the capital base of the company. Many shareholders are large institutions, who typically have better information than small shareholders, but their influence is important since if they decide to sell holdings this may prompt smaller shareholders to follow suit. This may lead to a degree of instability in which the managers become more concerned with share value than the underlying efficiency of the company.

A further incitement to effort is the risk of the company failing. Of course, in many cases the risk of failure may not be sensitive to the internal effort of the company, but rather driven by outside forces, but a major factor is the balance between equity and debt. Debt holders have priority in the call on the company's assets and hence high debt companies are at greater risk of failure if their debtors decide the future is not good. Good examples of this problem can be found in the transport sector. Eurotunnel has had a constant battle over the size of its debt, leading it to restructure its debt on a number of occasions through an equity for debt swap requiring former debtors to take an equity stake and thus be much more concerned about the long-term future of the company. Railtrack required an increasing amount of subsidy to support its operations, in this case typically guaranteed by government – again its increasing indebtedness was a major problem in the long-term viability of the company.

These theoretical considerations have been confirmed by a number of empirical studies (Gathon and Pestieau, 1995; Kerstens, 1996; Gomez-Ibanez and Meyer, 1993). Private enterprises are in the main more efficient than public enterprises. The main difference is that the former are more likely to work in a competitive market. How far they can achieve desired social welfare objectives depends on the size of any external effects.

We can illustrate these general points by a number of examples which show how private enterprise has worked in transport markets: most of these examples come from Britain which started earlier and has gone farther in encouraging the use of private sector operation in transport markets, mainly through the privatisation of former State-owned corporations.

BAA. The privatisation of the British Airports Authority as BAA plc took place in 1987. BAA operates the main London and Scottish airports and one or two regional airports and thus handles the vast bulk of UK air traffic. Competition exists from other major European hubs, mainly Paris, Amsterdam and Frankfurt, but London is dominant. Price control exists through the usual British price cap of (RPI − X), but this has not corrected the pre-existing problem of underpricing of traffic. A further complication is the sharing of implicit rents between BAA and the various commercial activities which operate concessions on the airport. Major investment is heavily controlled by government because of the external impacts of airport development, witness the long public inquiry into the development of a fifth terminal at London Heathrow. Although BAA is lobbying hard, it is the government which will finally decide if and where any new runway capacity will be developed.

British Airways was privatised in 1987, although the airline had already been turned from being a major loss maker in 1982 to profitability by 1984. The privatisation was motivated by the desire to introduce competition and certain routes were transferred from BA to other airlines on privatisation to effect this and access to Heathrow was allowed to other airlines, notably British

Midland. In the initial phase this attempt to introduce competition failed; BA took over a number of operators, including British Caledonian which had received some former BA routes, and maintained its dominant position at Heathrow. BA benefited against other major airlines from its network size and its control of the key European hub. However, it eventually has begun to suffer from the competition of new low-cost airlines which found it easier to develop in the less regulated British market. These were able to contest traditional BA routes at the same time as the lucrative inter-continental routes were becoming less profitable. BA tried to position itself initially as a quality airline in order to dominate the high yield markets, but the inroads on its short-haul traffic have proved to be larger than it expected and it initially performed less well than other major European airlines in the turmoil in intercontinental air markets after 11 September 2001. BA has now lost its position as the largest international airline to Lufthansa. BA's attempt to create its own low-cost airline, Go, to compete with the low-cost operators was not a great success and it was de-merged and eventually taken over by one of the main low-cost competitors, Easy-Jet. BA has had to shed a substantial part of its workforce and has retrenched to concentrate on routes which it can make profitable, including a radical overhaul of its pricing structure. BA has also tried to use the acquisition/merger route solve its problems, both with American Airlines (which fell foul of US regulators) and with KLM (which is likely to cause problems with EU merger rules), whilst it has seen its major European competitor, Lufthansa, take a stake in its major UK competitor, British Midland.

Railtrack. The privatisation of Railtrack has been discussed in some detail already. The main lesson from this has been the difficulty for a private enterprise to cope, first with the legacy of public neglect (the comparison with BAA and BA is interesting here, both of which performed much better in the early years), and second, where revenues are dependent entirely on strictly regulated markets, which are in the main contributed by government subsidy. Railtrack eventually lost the confidence both of the government, its main provider of finance, and the travelling public, because of what was perceived as having put profits (in order to try and maintain shareholder value) before safety and reliability.

Eurotunnel. The development of Eurotunnel has also been discussed in some detail above. This is perhaps the most interesting case of the genuinely private (as opposed to privatised) transport company, but which casts a degree of doubt on the merits of this approach. The main problems relate to the initial contractual situation, the changing regulatory structure imposed on the company and the problems of an initial phase of destructive competition.

What the example also shows is that private sector is not necessarily superior to the public sector in managing a large-scale infrastructure investment or in coping with a rapidly changing market.

The most complete synthesis on the effect of privatisation across the world is that of Gomez-Ibanez and Meyer (1993). They identify five conditions for a successful privatisation: the existence of competition, a range of possible gains in efficiency, low transfers, weak external effects and an adequate, but not excessive, financial rate of return. Generally speaking privatisation of operations is easier than that of infrastructure.

3. CONCLUSION

Our knowledge of the management of monopolies and the conditions under which the public service obligation is exercised has been considerably enriched from the experience of liberalisation and privatisation. The past century has seen a number of swings in the approach to public intervention and private initiative. Railways have been regrouped, nationalised and a start made on privatisation, more in some countries and less in others. Urban transport has been developed in different ways, but again there have been periods of direct public control and periods of movement towards a varying degree of deregulation under differing conditions.

The tendency towards a reduction in government intervention and the introduction of private sector management and market forces has become stronger in recent decades. This is to some extent due to a better understanding of the ways different economic mechanisms work, although it is also a lot to do with changing political views about liberal ideologies. This was largely motivated by the presidency of Ronald Reagan in the US and the premiership of Margaret Thatcher in the UK, who sought to push back the influence of the State on all aspects of life. The problem is that all too often rational theories become rigid doctrines and acts of faith. Within the general trend, it is also interesting to note that there has been a reduction in the power of national governments with the growth on the one hand of local government involvement (particularly at regional level) and on the other of European Union influence, largely in terms of setting a harmonised framework for action.

Within this ideological change, there has been a change in the notion of public service itself. Increasing standards of living have removed the basic reliance on public transport, but also raised people's expectation of the quality of service. Now the public service obligation is not so much about servicing the general population, but about ensuring continuing service to those otherwise excluded from transport and mobility: the old, the young, the less able-bodied, the poor. But these are exactly the groups who find it more difficult to express their preferences adequately and get them taken note of – in other words there has been an increasing gap between those who determine (and pay for) public service and those who benefit from it. Governments facing increasing constraint on their budgets have been reluctant to ensure the continuing development of the public service obligation.

10. From Economics to Transport Policy

The preceding chapters have demonstrated the range of accumulated knowledge of the economics of transport and the extent to which the implications of this has been implemented. Some theoretical concepts have been developed, or deepened, with particular reference to their application to transport: for example, the theory of public choice, the use of consumers' surplus, the concept of the values of time and life, the theory and models of discrete choice, aspects of production and cost theory, and the analysis of networks. It is in transport that applied studies of these concepts have been amongst the most frequent, supported by a substantial statistical base on traffic flows, costs and the choice of infrastructure.

However, we have also seen the degree of dissatisfaction with the way the sector has been organised from the economist's point of view: traffic management tools have been little, or badly, used, especially with respect to the use of pricing; recommendations have frequently not been followed, as in the cases of investment choice or the pricing of infrastructure; costs have remained too high, for example with respect to the production of certain public services; and the preoccupation with public opinion, especially the road lobby, has left a continuing burden of poor public transport and environmental damage.

These considerations lie behind our need to look more closely at the mismatch between the recommendations of economic theory and practice and the possibility of implementing a coherent policy towards the transport sector.

1. REDUCING THE GAP BETWEEN RECOMMENDATIONS AND PRACTICE

The existence of this gap between what theoretical models recommend and policy measures which are implemented depends on a number of factors. Here we look at two factors: how, and by whom, policy is implemented, and how policy can use the simple pricing and investment rules of pure theory in a world which does not comply with its requirements for optimality.

1.1 Policy Implementation – Who Takes the Decisions?

The first issue lies in the nature of the decision process which, in the case of transport, possibly more than in any other sector, is marked by the multiplicity of decision-makers. In the case of the public sector decision-makers, there has been a gradual transition from a situation where national governments, or state-controlled enterprises, were the dominant parties, to a situation where this power is shared more and more with both supra-national institutions and local government. In the case of private-sector decision-makers, all firms, and not just those firms within the transport sector strictly defined, are to some extent transport operators. At the same time, individuals are not just consumers of transport, but increasingly producers in terms both of their own time, and in the growth in the use of privately-owned vehicles.

This takes us a long way from a situation where a benevolent economic dictator can simply identify the required decisions and impose an optimal solution. For the economist trying to advise on an optimal transport policy, it is not sufficient to convince one person or a limited group of decision-makers, but instead a myriad of decision-makers with divergent interests is involved. This makes it different from say, macroeconomic policy advice or policies towards other sectors of the economy where, although there may be many divergent views, the number of key decision-makers whose decisions must be influenced by the policy is strictly limited.

In order to provide a convincing policy implementation process, it is necessary to put in place mechanisms which will provide assurance of its implementation. For the economist, the market and the market mechanism are the appropriate ways in which, under certain conditions, there exists a process which can provide a conciliation between various divergent interests, bringing competing self-interests towards the realisation of a social optimum.

However, it is difficult to find conditions under which these mechanisms can function well in the transport sector, due principally to the existence of two features: externalities and increasing returns. This makes the decentralisation of decisions a lot more complicated. Externalities pose problems both in relation to the costs of transport (as seen in Chapter 5) and in pricing and the choice of investment (as seen in Chapter 7). Similar problems arise in dealing with increasing returns, notably the difficulty of attributing fixed costs.

Moreover, the transport sector is, more than any other, a sector of diversity and differentiation (Winston, 1985). In transport all situations are specific, there is no unique user, there is no representative firm or standard cost. The sector is also one of mixed outcomes: most infrastructure is used by traffic which has both diverse motives for travel and diverse origins and destinations. Thus general rules and regulations are usually inappropriate for some or all users; they will typically fail to attain their objective completely, maybe sometimes more than others, but rarely exactly as expected. A similar problem faces the use of uniform taxes or prices, as seen in Chapter 7.

The inadequacy of economic instruments is accentuated by our insufficient knowledge of many of the situations which they are designed to influence. We have seen, for example, in analysing the interrelationship between transport and economic development, our lack of ability to predict long-term economic impacts or the spatial consequences which have assumed an important weight in such decisions. We have also seen, where we need to calculate the overall social welfare change from an investment, that we know very little about the way in such welfare may be distributed between different members of society.

However, it is possible to take an alternative view of the role of the economist. Up to now transport economists have concentrated on the idea of the social optimum. We have seen the limits of implementing this, uncertainty in estimation, the possibility of strategic manipulation and a character which is little understood by others and therefore difficult to convince them of its results. To this can be added that the economic calculus does not, of itself, enable the clarification of strategic choices, such as that between efficiency and public service, the choice of lifestyle, the weight given to considerations of sustainable development. From this point of view economics depends on politics and policy options and not the reverse.

1.2   Implementing Pricing Policy – the Problem of the Second-Best

Reference to the social optimum, which is indispensable for analysing optimal decisions, is no longer sufficient for their implementation. The theoretical discussion gives clear guidance as to the sort of pricing principles which should be applied, short–run marginal social costs provide the basis for a first–best pricing policy and the basis for optimal investment decisions using standard cost–benefit criteria. These are simple rules with clear information requirements which can form the basis of unambiguous policy recommendations. The problem for policy is that it is not being applied in a first-best world and hence this simplicity is lost.

Our theory shows clearly the way in which the basic rules should be modified to take account of this, but the modified rules require much more information, for example on elasticities and on the way in which transport is used differently in different activities. Once this additional information is required we encounter the problem that both the rule and the information required become open to interpretation. The simple rule of the first–best world has the advantage that it provides for us both the allocation rule and the basis for investment. The imperfect world leaves the decision-maker with a problem over whether to concentrate on the allocation problem or to worry about whether revenues will cover costs. In the reality of much public sector decision making this cost coverage issue will come to dominate and may lead to policies which perpetuate or exacerbate allocation problems, and hence long-run financial problems for perceived shorter-term gains. The fear of governments and regulators is that reliance on short-run marginal social cost leaves the likelihood of deficits which cause operators to seek subsidies and subsidies are seen as an incentive for inefficiency.

There is additionally the need to convince user groups, not just that charges are fair, but that the allocation of revenues is fair. Users are prepared to pay for what is seen as a fair return on their payment. At the crudest level this is the simple accounting of whether, for example, the user charges paid by motorists are returned in road expenditures. Charges are seen as a tax rather than a charge for the use of a resource (especially where that resource is something less immediately tangible such as environmental damage). Taxes have to be acceptable and tend to be viewed as unavoidable. Nevertheless, users have been prepared to accept a more general principle that charges raised within transport should be used within transport, but not necessarily on the same mode. Thus it is seen as acceptable to use revenues from congestion charging to improve public transport where this is a direct alternative.

This tends to focus attention on the need to obtain precise and accurate information on the costs incurred by each type of user and away from general principles. Perhaps the serious and reasonable debates which the analysts have conducted over the precise valuation of time savings or environmental damage of various types have been counter-productive, since they have provided an escape route by which both users and politicians can hide behind the uncertainty over the detail and not act, whilst ignoring the general consensus over the principle.

Implementation has also to be accompanied by more detailed analysis of the distributional effects, the way in which losers are to be compensated, or the details of accompanying measures to ensure social acceptability. Verhoef *et al.* (1997) have, for example, used a survey to analyse the reluctance of potential users in connection with an urban toll road and determined the conditions under which this could be reduced. In order to achieve increased social acceptability, we need to fill the gaps in our knowledge and two areas of research seem to be particularly important: distributional impacts and long-term effects, both in time and space.

The tendency to use revenues from charges on road users to fund expensive rail-based alternatives is a potential problem. Evidence from several countries shows that even when revenues are not being spent on roads they are being spent on road-using groups. Hence there is little effort to to redress the inherently regressive nature of transport expenditure. If the objective is simply to get people out of their cars and on to a form of public transport which they see as acceptable then this may be effective. But if the objective is to achieve a transport system which is both efficient and equitable, subsidising richer people to use trains instead of cars (and typically subsidising them more on a per capita basis) this seems perverse.

It is also necessary to reduce the extent to which the results of applied studies can be manipulated, if we are to make their results more accurate, transparent and reproducible. To do this it is necessary to define more precisely the conditions under which studies were carried out, to ensure independent audit of their results and to ensure an on-going public debate, not just of important results and conclusions, but also of the methodology in order to give it a greater moral authority. For example, in some of the Nordic countries the monetary values to be applied to the environment are decided in Parliament, giving them an apparently greater measure of legitimacy.

Ensuring the correct implementation of recommendations also implies attention be given to those responsible for their implementation. We have seen in Chapter 9 the way in which the status of different operators has an impact on the cost of services they provide. In Chapter 7 we have also seen the link between the rules on choice of investments and the structure within which they are applied: direct decision or concession, public or private, and the nature of the contract. All this requires the economist to pay careful attention not just to the economic calculus, but also to the institutional structure within which such rules are to be implemented.

2. IS A COHERENT TRANSPORT POLICY POSSIBLE?

The economic analysis which has been presented in this book can improve understanding of the transport sector, and provide appropriate and convincing applications to real world problems, but there will always remain areas of uncertainty. It is necessary to examine carefully the institutional factors which provide the context within which policy is to be implemented, recognising that these cannot easily be changed. It is also necessary to analyse differences between the points of view of different actors, to understand the conditions for social acceptability, to incorporate the recognition of conflicts of interest and, critically, to provide a means of their resolution. Norman and Vickerman (1999), for example, have identified the various conflicts posed by a major infrastructure project, the UK Channel Tunnel Rail Link, and shown how these were resolved. But this raises the real question as to whether a consistent transport policy is a possibility, both within a single jurisdiction, and more especially across different jurisdictions. This is best understood by looking at a variety of concrete problems.

2.1   Market Organization and Political Will: Freight Transport

Freight transport is an intermediate good. It affects firms, although equity issues are less important than questions of efficiency. The economist's views are thus particularly relevant.

A diagnosis of the current situation identifies excessive competition, often destructive, in most segments of the road haulage market, particularly that for non-specialised transport. It is also marked by a distortion of the conditions of competition between road and rail, resulting from an under-pricing of road usage and the lack of effectiveness of existing regulation, in particular with respect to hours of work and extra charges. This distortion of competition conditions is reinforced by the dynamic inefficiency of railways, where the monopoly position has tended to lead to a high-cost service and mediocre quality. This is found most particularly in the international transport of goods in the EU. The net result of this situation has led to a high social cost, characterised by inefficiency and excessive public expenditure, and by transfers in favour of shippers through the low prices charged by road hauliers, and in favour of the employees of state-owned enterprises, such as nationally-owned railways at the cost of employees in the road haulage sector who face pressure on both their conditions of work and wages.

Restoring efficiency requires, first of all, action to re-establish the conditions of normal competition, respecting existing regulation and adjusting those taxes which affect road transport so as to require the coverage of full costs. But this is not sufficient to ensure the functioning of markets since this is also affected by barriers to entry such as conditions of access to the market (technical competence, management and financial ability).

On the other hand, it is necessary to introduce measures to the railways to achieve dynamic efficiency so as to ensure effective competition. The reforms of European railways to separate infrastructure and operations has made it possible to improve the management of both aspects and to introduce a more equal and fair treatment of freight and passenger traffic in the allocation of track access slots. At the same time, the separate management of freight operations achieved in a number of cases, with or without privatisation, has allowed for a more effective management, recognising the logistic needs of users and allowing for competition, even if only on the fringe of the market, and the potential entry of new competitors. However, it has to be recognised that these improvements have not been universal in Europe and hence international rail traffic continues to operate at a disadvantage.

These recommendations are simple. However, the difficulties of putting them into practice are considerable. In order to overcome the possible objections it is necessary to consider a variety of accompanying measures to soften the impact, as well as a considerable political will.

2.2 The Management of Infrastructure: Standards or Discretion?

It is frequently held that there are two basic modes of conduct in public affairs: the use of standards or discretion. Discretion involves taking each situation on its merits and taking the decision best suited to the particular circumstances. This might appear to be the optimal mode of action, but it leaves the way open for inaction, risks incoherence and reduced resistance to pressure, and does not easily allow for forecasting. Standards, which involve respecting a set of pre-announced rules or norms, have the opposite characteristics.

Looking at the situation pertaining to road investment, in most cases discretion is the main decision mode. There is for most toll-free roads in most European countries a dissociation between the pricing decision (typically dependent solely on automobile ownership taxes and fuel taxes) and the investment decision. Decisions tend to depend on government, and in particular budgetary considerations, but can be heavily influenced by pressure by certain groups and the political cycle. Some construction is financed by local government where it is even more directly subject to the pressure put on local elected members of councils. In both cases there is little direct link between revenue receipts and road construction (or maintenance) expenditure.

Where concessions are used, as for example in the case of French autoroutes, the situation is rather different and is more likely to depend on the application of a norm. However, given that such norms are applied to a range of independent organisations, as with the case of national and local toll-free roads it is likely to lead to a sub-optimal situation.

For State-owned railways the management of infrastructure is most frequently seen as being governed by standards. Where there are large accumulated debts, as in the case of RFF in France, or where infrastructure investment is treated as part of the potential public sector deficit, as was the case with British Rail prior to privatisation, then finance ministries play a fundamental role in the decision process. In the emerging privatised or franchised railways then a rather more fluid situation is developing. Franchising involves the application of standards, but major investments may involve a mixture of public and private funds and decisions and here an element of discretion is likely reflecting the uniqueness of each major investment.

Airport infrastructure differs in different countries. In the fully privatised system governing the major airports in the UK, there is a large element of discretion, and although the effective regulation implies some decision by standards, the uniqueness of major investments implies a large measure of discretion (as for example in the long decision-making process over the fifth terminal at London Heathrow). In other cases, where airports are heavily subsidised, for example by local or regional governments, then, even where there is an independent management, decision-making is largely governed by norm.

This brief survey demonstrates the extent to which there are substantial differences both within and between modes within individual countries, as well as differences between countries. Although this apparently arbitrary system has enabled an enormous growth in the development of infrastructure in Europe, it has done so without achieving the degree of coordination which would be necessary for achieving optimality. Decision–making procedures, which might seem to be internally consistent and rational, and in many cases developed to a very sophisticated degree, have typically failed to achieve the correct balance between modes, and indeed in many cases within modes. Principally this is due to the lack of coordination between investment decisions and pricing decisions. One effect of this has been an excessive burden placed on public finances, which in turn led to either, or both, arbitrary cut-backs in investment and privatisation. Early experience with privatisation suggests that the problem was not in the lack of efficiency of the public sector, but in the failure of the decision-making process, which has often not changed fundamentally with the change of ownership.

A more effective approach might be through the wider use of an approach based on norms, not in the traditional sense of public sector management, but using a clear economic motive of the link between revenue and expenditure which can be applied by either public or private sector managements and which leaves a considerable degree of management freedom in how to achieve the target, investment decisions and specific pricing policies. This would have the advantage of leading to a better relationship between prices and costs, but would not require the, often misplaced, belief in the superiority of competition to achieve the target. As we have seen, Ramsey–Boiteux pricing achieves a better pricing structure for the transport sector and can deal with the presence of monopoly, externalities and increasing returns.

But how could such a norm be established in a way which could lead to effective management? We examine this under a number of headings:

- *Geographical area.* Typically this will require a compromise between as large an area as possible to ensure the most complete optimisation and the desire to minimise transaction costs, which tend to grow with size. Reference to the appropriate development of networks can be helpful here, in particular to identify the degree of substitution or complementarity present. This parallels the geographical organisation of the markets which these different networks serve: for example we could distinguish urban, regional, national and European markets.

- *Scope of application.* The same basic principles should operate as for the geographical area: the main criterion is the link between markets and the degree of substitutability/complementarity between activities. Thus one might conceive of a single decision-making body for the national market, which would embrace the main highway network, principal high-speed and long-distance rail lines, major inland waterways and airports. Such a body would be responsible for decisions on construction, maintenance, pricing, regulation and providing information to users. Individual aspects could be franchised under a clear set of norms, for example construction of new infrastructure. Information could, but need not be, a monopoly of the organisation, depending on whether information on the conditions of transport should be seen as general or not. This raises the question of whether it is optimal for everyone to have such information? It may be thought initially that such a situation would lead to an optimum: however, if an equilibrium is reached, this may not be optimal because of the difference between a social and an individual optimum. It is possible to consider a situation in which basic information is provided by the infrastructure manager and sold to operators who transform it (add value) and sell it on as a service to users. The price at which this basic information is sold could be determined by the extent to which it leads to greater competitive dynamism in final services which respond to the needs of users.

- *Constraints on decision-making bodies.* This will depend on the type of organisation and the particular problem which it has to solve. Take the case of the national level. It would be expected to determine a pricing principle, for example a general principle of Ramsey–Boiteux pricing, ensuring that marginal social costs were covered and a break-even position as achieved. In this case the decision-making body would be seen as being given a standard determining a fixed budget in such a way as to ensure that it could achieve an optimal level of investment. An independent regulator would have the responsibility of reviewing prices and judging them appropriate to meet the overall target as, for example, suggested by Henry (1997b).

It is easy to see that there is a substantial gap between such a system and that which exists in most European countries today. It is also easy to see that the means of moving to such a situation would be difficult.

2.3   Controlling Mobility

The problems posed by mobility have been raised a number of times in preceding chapters, but only a partial view has been given. Here we turn to take a more complete view and relate this to key policy issues.

The facts are well known: individual mobility has increased substantially over the past 50 years, not so much in terms of the number of journeys as the distances travelled, whilst time spent travelling has remained remarkably constant as speeds have increased. This is true of both urban travel, leading to the tendency for an enlargement of urban areas, and of inter-urban travel as people seek new destinations, whether for business or leisure travel.

This changing pattern has led to a variety of responses. For some it is a key indicator of progress, allowing individuals to benefit from a greater diversity of goods and experiences as accessibility increases and firms to benefit from growing markets. Mobility and accessibility are seen as key measures of both economic progress and personal freedom. An alternative view is that these changes are in fact a sign of dysfunction or imbalance in the economy, people are forced to travel further and further to reach the benefits of the new economy: out of town shopping centres replace the local shop, huge leisure complexes replace the local cinema or theatre, and work too becomes concentrated in the largest towns and cities. This has adverse impacts on the environment, on family and social life and on the quality of life generally.

We do not propose to make a judgement here of the relative merits of one scenario of modern life or another, but simply to evaluate the factors which influence mobility and the possibility of introducing policies which could have an effect one way or the other.

Mobility has been the subject of numerous studies such that we should already have a very clear picture of the topic, but the available information gives some very different pictures according to the location and timescale considered. Looking at the short-term we have fairly reliable information from route choice and modal choice studies. These show that, although individual behaviour is very diverse, the basic parameters which characterise choice can be estimated reasonably reliably from traffic prediction models, and hence give us a basis for intervention.

It is not so straightforward for long-term effects, which require the use of information from traffic generation and distribution models. Although such models are quite good at describing behaviour, they are less good at prediction. Thus, for example, the social physics approaches encompassed in Zahavi's Law, or the gravity model, are not easy to provide a theoretical basis for. It is easy to see the reason for this: the effects on travel behaviour, for example following the completion of a new infrastructure, take time to take full effect. However, it is clear from the early results of the London Congestion Charge introduced in 2003, that traffic has fallen more than models predicted. This is not just a switch of modes or a diversion or re-timing of car trips, but appears to have involved major changes in trip generation and hence presumably activity patterns. Not only may travel patterns change, but there may also be changes in location, in the organisation of firms and in the activity patterns of individuals, but these may be confused with changes resulting from other factors.

The control of mobility would be simple if an effective system of pricing were in place. However, for car travel, there is no obvious means of pricing individual journeys as a large number of taxes and charges impinge on the traveller, some fixed and some variable, many less transparent than necessary to make individuals aware of the real costs incurred. The London charge is a blunt instrument of a cordon charge for all vehicles crossing a certain line to enter the central area. Thus it is difficult to consider mobility in the context of a simple market transaction in which there is a clear link between costs and willingness to pay.

Moreover, any such model of travel would assume that there was an optimum spatial distribution of activities for which travel is undertaken. This is typically not the case; prices of many urban activities are distorted by subsidies to housing, taxes on various activities, etc. Even if these distortions did not exist, the presence of externalities and increasing returns, as seen in Chapter 3, would lead to non-optimality. In addition, distributional issues may be of considerable importance, some areas may be advantaged, and others disadvantaged by any changes.

The lesson of economic analysis is the need to ensure coordinated use of all the possible instruments, prices, taxes and regulation, in order to achieve optimality. It is the coordination of all the relevant interventions which is significant here: there are multiple actors with manifold and divergent interests, and numerous levels of intervention. Thus the taxation of vehicles and fuel is the responsibility of national governments, which is usually determined as part of overall budgetary policy rather than the specific needs of the transport sector or transport policy. At the other extreme, parking controls are usually the responsibility of local authorities, as is the overall spatial planning of the local area. Different levels of government face different levels of pressure from specific interest groups.

Moreover, each of the various actors is likely to find themselves in a potential free-rider situation, in which he or she has an interest in everyone else following a social rule, but not following it him- or herself.

Finally, each action may have a long-term effect which is contrary to that wished for. The most obvious example is again that of the new infrastructure, designed to reduce congestion, but which due to induced and generated traffic results in congestion which may be as bad as before. This also illustrates the consequences of a poor combination of controls in which the absence of optimal pricing results in inefficient usage.

Hence, the mixture of charges which affect traffic and parking and urban policies could be combined to optimise the traffic impact. This has been done in a limited number of places, Singapore and Zurich are two examples, but in most countries instruments are torn between the protection of industry, the requirements of public finances, and the coherence of transport policy.

Thus our relative ignorance of these phenomena, above all the long-term effects, the weakness of the various instruments available to affect choices and the difficulties of mobilising these in a coherent manner, help to explain the difficulties faced in controlling mobility, and the continuing surprise at the unexpected and undesired outcomes. Nevertheless, an analysis of emerging trends and their projection, with a little optimism, into the future provides some reasons for potential change and progress.

The first cause for optimism lies in the scope for the introduction of information technology, and in particular electronic road pricing. This will provide a uniform means through which road use could be charged, eliminating the distortions inherent in the traditional variety of measures, often managed in a contradictory way. Electronic road pricing would need to incorporate all the external effects associated with transport, and overcome all the political reluctance which has been seen so far, but it is possible to believe that this is a matter of time: some politicians are beginning to act, recognising that the current situation cannot continue, and road users are beginning to recognise that we cannot go on facing increasing congestion, out of which we try and build our way. It is necessary to concentrate efforts on explaining the current situation and the options open, above all that imposing a direct charge can reduce many users' actual costs of transport by ensuring that everyone is aware of the real costs and pays their way. There is some evidence that this can begin to overcome opposition, especially in the context of a package of accompanying measures (Button and Verhoef, 1996; Verhoef *et al.*, 1997; De Borger and Proost, 2001).

Information and communications technology can bring other changes too, both directly: better information to users, the intelligent car, demand responsive public transport, electronic pricing systems; and indirectly: changing hours of work, flexitime and telecommuting or teleworking, or the increasing use of telecommunications or the Internet for shopping, banking, and above all, arranging travel. Whilst many of these changes may appear to offer the potential to reduce mobility, they may have, at least in the short to medium term, the opposite effect. Teleworking encourages people to live further from their work because they visit it less regularly and have the freedom to indulge in more off-peak travel. Tele-purchasing may reduce the number of separate visits to shops, but may replace a single multi-leg shopping trip with a larger number of separate deliveries of ordered goods. Above all this is describing a different world of spatial relationships with different types of mobility from the one to which we have become accustomed.

A further requirement is to continue to improve our understanding of the links between transport and spatial planning. Traditional planning mechanisms have tended to fix the basic objectives of the local or regional plan, identify the locations of activities and then deduce the transport requirements. But we need to consider carefully the inverse mechanism in which decisions directly affecting transport have an impact on the spatial distribution of activities and hence on land-use planning needs.

Once again, however, it is necessary to stress the importance of coordination within an overall perspective of transport policy. Such coordination requires a smaller number of key decision-makers operating within a coherent decision-making framework. This is often anathema to those who have shaped transport policy in recent years, those who have seen the basic need as that of the market as a replacement for what had become the view of coordination and planning as old-fashioned, ineffective, inefficient socialism. This is a question of perspective rather akin to the contrast between those who see federalism (which is essentially what we are proposing here, federalism on many different levels) as an anti-democratic, centralising process gathering power into a limited number of hands, and those who see it as a pro-democratic, decentralising process, allowing the exercise of political will at the appropriate level (the subsidiarity principle), but in an ordered manner.

3. CONCLUSION

The recommendations of the economist have varied ambitions. They can define a precise objective and the conditions under which that objective can be achieved. They can also help to define the conditions under which a policy can be achieved which will fulfil those objectives. But this implies a change of attitude and of the way of defining and implementing policy and that requires a great collective will to move us forward. We have set out the principles under which this move can be made, to achieve it will require much debate and the abandonment of many entrenched positions. The role of the transport economist is to provide a consistent story and set of implementable principles, backed up by solid objective research.

References

ACTRA (Advisory Committee on Trunk Road Assessment) (1977), *Report of the Advisory Committee on Trunk Road Assessment*, chair Sir George Leitch, London: HMSO

Abraham, C. and A. Laure (1959), 'Etude des programmes d'investissement routier', *Annales des Ponts et Chaussées*, **30**, 736-760.

Amano, K. and M. Fujita (1970), 'A long run economic effect analysis of alternative transportation facility plans', *Journal of Regional Science*, **1**, 297-323.

Amici della terra, Ferrovie dello Stato (2002) *The environmental and social costs of mobility in Italy*, fourth report, Rome: Amici della terra

Anas, A. (1987), *Modelling in urban and regional economics*, New York: Harwood Academic Publishers.

Arduin, J.P (1993), 'Evaluation des grands projets ferroviaires; les modèles de prévision du trafic', in *Villes et TGV, sixièmes entretiens Jacques Cartier*, Lyon

Arduin, J.P., J. Ni and O. Picq (1994), 'Valeur du temps, log-normalité des revenus et choix modal', *Communication à WC RR 1994*, Paris.

Arnott, R., A. de Palma and R. Lindsey (1994), 'Welfare effects of congestion tolls with heterogeneous commuters', *Journal of Transport Economics and Policy*, **28**, 139-161.

Arnott, R.J. and J.E. Stiglitz (1979), 'Aggregate land rents, expenditure on public goods and optimal city size', *Quarterly Journal of Economics*, **93**, 471-500.

Aschauer, D.A. (1989), 'Is public expenditure productive?', *Journal of Monetary Economics*, **23**, 177-200.

Banister, D., J. Berechman and G. de Rus (1992), 'Competitive regimes within the European bus industry: theory and practice', *Transportation Research A*, **26**, 167-178.

Barro, R.J. (1991), 'Economic growth in a cross-section of countries', *Quarterly Journal of Economics*, **106**, 407-443.

Barro, R.J. and X. Sala-i-Martin (1995), *Economic Growth*, New York: McGraw Hill.

Bassanini, A. and Pouyet, J. (2000), 'Access pricing for interconnected vertically separated industries', in C. Nash, and E. Niskanen, *Helsinki Workshop on Infrastructure Charging for Railways*, VATT Discussion Paper 245, Helsinki: VATT

Bates, J., J. Polak, P. Jones and A. Cook (2001), 'The valuation of reliability for personal travel', *Transportation Research E*, **37**, 191-229.

Battiau, M. (1991), 'Effets des évolutions socio-économiques sur la dynamique spatiale', *L'information Géographique*, **1**, 34-57.

Baum, H. and N.C. Behnke (1997), *Der volkswirtschaftliche Nutzen des Straßenverkehrs*, Schriftenreihe des Verbandes der Automobilindustrie e.V. (VDA), 82, Frankfurt am Main: VDA.

References

Baumol, W., J. Panzar and R. Willig (1982), *Contestable Markets and the Theory of Industrial Structure*, New York: Harcourt Brace Jovanovich.

Bayliss, B and A. Millington (1995), 'Deregulation and logistic systems in a single European Market', *Journal of Transport Economics and Policy*, **29**, 305-316.

Beckmann, M.J. (1956), *Studies in the Economics of Transportation*, New Haven, CT: Yale University Press for the Cowles Commission or Research in Economics.

Ben Akiva, M. and S. Lerman (1991), *Discrete Choice Analysis*, Cambridge, MA: MIT Press.

Ben Akiva, M., J. Bowman and A. de Palma (1996), 'Activity based travel demand model systems', *Communication au 25è anniversaire du CRT*, Montreal., October 1996.

Benabou, R. (1996), 'Equity and efficiency in human capital investment: the local connection', *Review of Economic Studies*, **63**, 237-264.

Bennathan, E., J. Fraser and L. Thompson (1992), 'What determines demand for freight transport?', *WPS 998*, Washington DC: World Bank

Bensimon, E. (1993), *La Concurrence et les Couts du Transport Aérien de Marchandises*, Memoire, DEA Transport, ENPC-Paris XII, Paris: ENPC.

Berechman, J. (1983), 'Costs, economics of scale and factor demand in bus transport', *Journal of Transport Economics and Policy*, **17**, 7-24.

Bernard, A. (1983), 'La congestion peut-elle constituer un mode de régulation?', mimeo, Conseil Général des Ponts et Chaussées, Ministère de l'équipement, Paris.

Berndt, E.R. and B. Hansson (1991), 'Measuring the contribution of public infrastructure capital in Sweden', *NBER Working Paper* No 3842.

Beuthe, M. and A. Savez (1994), 'The multiproduct cost function of long distance trucking in France', *Proceedings of the 29th Annual Meeting of the Canadian Transportation Research Forum, Victoria.*

Blain, J.C. and L. Nguyen (1994), 'Modélisation de trafics de voyageurs', *Notes de synthèse OEST*, January.

Boiteux, M. (1956), 'Sur la gestion des monopoles publics astreints à l'équilibre budgétaire', *Econometrica*, **24**, 22-40.

Boiteux, M. (1994), 'Transport: pour un meilleur choix des investissements', Report of a working group chaired by M. Boiteux, Paris: *La Documentation Française*

Boiteux, M. (2000), 'Transports: choix des investissements et prise en compte des nuisances', Report of a working group chaired by M. Boiteux under the aegis of the Commissariat Général du Plan, Paris: *La Documentation Française.*

Borenstein, B. (1992), 'The evolution of US Airline competition', *Journal of Economic Perspectives*, **6**, 45-73.

Botham, R. (1983), 'The road program and regional development' in K. Button and D. Gillingwater (eds), *Transport, Location and Spatial Policy*, Aldershot: Gower.

Bradshaw, B. (1996), 'The privatization of railways in Britain', *Japan Railway and Transport Review*, Sept.

Braess, D. (1968), 'Uber ein paradoxon der verkehrsplanung' *Unternehmens-forschung*, **12**.

Brander, J. and A. Zhang (1993), 'Dynamic oligopoly behaviour in the airline industry', *International Journal of Industrial Organization*, **11**, 407-435.

Brewer, C.J. and C.R. Plott (1996) 'A binary conflict ascending price auction (BICAP) mechanism for the decentralized allocation of the right to use railroad tracks', *International Journal of Industrial Organization*, **14**, 857-886.

Briggs, R. (1982), 'Interstate highway system and development in non-metropolitan aeras', *Transportation Research Record*.

Bristow, A. and J. Nellthorp (2000), 'Transport appraisal in the European Union', *Transport Policy*, **7**, 51-60.

Bröcker, J. (1998), 'Spatial effects of trans-European networks: preliminary results from a spatial computable general equilibrium model', *Diskussionsbeiträge aus dem Institut für Wirtshaft und Verkehr der Technischen Universität Dresden*, 4/98, Dresden: TU Dresden.

Bröcker, J. (2000), 'Trans-European effects of trans-European networks' in F. Bolle and M. Carlberg (eds), *Advances in Behavioural Economics*, Heidelberg: Physica.

Bröcker, J. (2003), 'Computable general equilibrium analysis in transportation economics' in K.J. Button, and D.A. Hensher (eds) *Handbooks in Transport Volume 5*, Oxford: Pergamon Press.

Bröcker, J., A. Kancs, C. Schürmann, M. Wegener (2002), *Methodology for the Assessment of Spatial Economic Impacts of Transport Projects and Policies*, IASON Project Deliverable 2, Kiel/Dortmund: Christian-Albrechts-Universität, Kiel/Institut für Raumplanung, Universität Dortmund.

Brossier, C. (1991), 'Nouvelle étude de l'imputation des coûts d'infrastructure de Transports', Ministère des transports, Paris.

Brua, J. (1993), 'L'accessibilité des zones à faible densité', *rapport commun CGPC-CGGREF*,

Bruckner, J. and P. Spiller (1991), 'Competition and mergers in airline networks', *International Journal of Industrial Organization*, **9**, 323-342.

Bruinsma, F., P. Nijkamp and P. Rietveld (1989), 'Employment impact of infra-structure investment', in K. Peschel (ed.) *Infrastructure and the Space Economy*, Heidelberg: Springer Verlag.

Bruzelius, N., B. Flyvberg and W. Rothengatter (1998), 'Big decisions, big risks: improving accountability in mega-projects', *International Review of Administrative Sciences*, **64**, 423-440.

Bundesministerium für Verkehr (2003), *Federal Transport Infrastructure Plan 2003: Basic Features of the Macroeconomic Evaluation Methodology*, Berlin: Bundesministerium für Verkehr, Bau- und Wohnungswesen.

Bureau, D. and C. Cipriani (1986), 'Impacts macro-économiques du TGV Paris Sud-Est', mimeo, Paris: Ministère des Finances.

Burmeister, A. and K. Colletis-Wahl (1996), 'TGV et fonctions tertiaires: grande vitesse et entreprises se service à Lille et à Valenciennes', *Transports Urbains*, October–December.

Burmeister A. and G. Joignaux (eds) (1996), *Infrastructures de Transport et Territoires*, Paris: l'Harmattan.

Button, K. (1991), 'Discussion of airline deregulation and market performance: the economic basis for regulatory reform and lessons from US experience' in D. Banister and K. Button (eds) *Transport in a Free Market Economy*, London: Macmillan.

Button, K. (1996), 'Liberalising European aviation: is there an empty core problem', *Journal of Transport Economics and Policy*, 30, 275-291.

Button, K. (2001), 'Economics of transport networks' in K.J. Button and D.A. Hensher (eds) *Handbook of Transport Systems and Traffic Control*, Oxford: Pergamon.

Button, K. and Verhoef, E. (1996), *Road Pricing, Traffic Congestion and the Environment: Issues in Efficiency and Social Feasibility*, Cheltenham, UK and Brookfield, USA: Edward Elgar.

Caillaud, B., R.Guesnerie, P.Rey and J.Tirole (1988) 'Government Intervention in Production and Incentives Theory: A Review of Recent Contributions', *Rand Journal of Economics*, **19**, 1-26.

Caillaud, B. and E. Quinet (1993a), 'Analyse du caractère incitatif des contrats de transport urbain', document *CEPREMAP* No. 9307.

Caillaud, B. and E. Quinet (1993b), 'Faut-il pratiquer des tarifs dégressifs pour l'usage de l'infrastructure ferroviaire', report for SNCF, Paris: CERAS.

Caillaud, B., B. Jullien and P. Picard (1996), 'Hierarchical organisation and incentives' *European Economic Review*, **40**, 687-695.

Callan, S. and J. Thomas (1992), 'Cost differentials among household goods carriers', *Journal of Transport Economics and Policy*, **26**, 19-34.

Calthrop, E., S Proost and K. Van Dender (2000), 'Parking policies and pricing', *Urban Studies*, **37**, 63-76.

Calzada, C. and F. Jiang (1996), 'Comment mesurer la valeur du temps en transports de marchandises', *Synthèses SES*, July–August.

Cantos, P. (2000), 'A subadditivity test for the cost function of the principal European railways', *Transport Reviews*, **20**, 275-290.

Caves, D.W. (1981), 'Productivity growth, scale economies and capacity utilization in US railroads, 1955-1974', *American Economic Review*, **71**, 994-1002.

Caves, D.W. (1983), 'The structure of airline costs and prospects for the US airline industry under deregulation', Social Systems Research Institute Report No. 8313, Madison: University of Wisconsin.

Caves, D.W., L.R. Christensen and M.W. Tretheway (1984), 'Economies of diversity versus economies of scale. Why trunk and local service airlines costs differ?', *Rand Journal of Economics*, **15**, 471-489.

CERAS, CERTU, SES (1997), 'Le modèle Dépense Publique', mimeo, Paris.

CERTU (1996) 'Evaluation des transports en commun en site propre', study carried out by O. Cormier, Lyon: CERTU.

Charmeil, C. (1968), *Investissement et Croissance Economique*, Paris: Dunod.

Chiang, W., S. Judy and A. Friedlander (1984), 'Output aggregation, network effects, and the measurement of trucking technology', *Review of Economics and Statistics* **66**, 267-276.

Chin, A. and P. Smith (1997), 'Automobile ownership and government policy: the economics of Singapore's vehicle quota scheme', *Transportation Research A*, **31**, 129-140.

Christaller, W. (1933), *Central Places in Southern Germany*, (translation 1966), New York: Prentice–Hall.

Ciccone, A. (2002), 'Agglomeration effects in Europe', *European Economic Review*, **46**, 213-227.

Ciccone, A. and Hall, R.E. (1996), 'Productivity and the density of economic activity', *American Economic Review* **86**, 54-70.

Clement, L. (1996), 'Review of existing land use-transport models', Report, Lyon: CERTU.

Clement L., and D. Peyrton (1997), 'Test of a land use and transport modelling system', Mimeo, Lyon: CERTU.

Clement, L., A. Lauer, J. Maurice and J-P Taroux (1997), 'Le modèle dépense publique', Note, Paris: Ministère des Transports.

Cline, W.R. (1992), *The Economics of Global Warming*, Washington, DC: Institute for International Economics.

Cochrane, R.A. (1975), 'A possible economic basis for the gravity model', *Journal of Transport Economics and Policy*, **9**, 34-49.

Commissariat General du Plan (1981), 'Les choix d'infrastructure en période de croissance ralentie', report of a working group chaired by E. Malinvaud.

Commissariat General du Plan (1983), 'Calcul économique et résorption des déséquilibres' report of a working group chaired by E. Malinvaud.

Comissariat General du Plan (1992), *Transports 2010*, Paris: La Documentation Française.

COST 317 (1995), *The Socio-Economic Effects of the Channel Tunnel*, Brussels: European Commission.

Costa, A. (1996), 'The organization of urban public transport systems in western European metropolitan areas', *Transportation Research A*, **30**, 349-359.

Costa, J. da Silva, R.W. Ellson and R.C. Martin (1987), 'Public capital, regional output and development: some empirical evidence', *Journal of Regional Science*, **27**, 419-437

Courcelle, C., B. de Borger and D. Swysen (1998), 'Optimal pricing of transport externalities in a federal system; a theoretical analysis', paper presented to the World Conference on Transport Research, Antwerp.

Croissant, Y. (1996), 'Les performances des firmes françaises de transport urbain', *Revue d'Economie Politique*, May–June.

Crowley, J. (1997) in ECMT *Which Changes for Transport in the Next Century,* Report of the 14th Symposium on Theory and Practice in Transport Economics, Innsbruck, Paris: OECD.

Curien, N and G. Dupuy (1996), 'Réseaux de communication', *Marchés et territoires*, Paris: Presses des Ponts et Chaussées.

Curien, N. and M. Gensollen (1992), 'L'économie des télécommunications: ouverture et réglementation', *Economica-ENSPTT*, Paris:

DAEI-SES-INSEE (1996a), 'Les Transports en chiffres', pamphlet, SES, Paris.

DAEI-SES-INSEE (1996b), 'Note de conjoncture des Transports', pamphlet, SES, Paris.

Dang N'Guyen, G. (1995), *Economie Industrielle Appliquée*, Paris: Vuibert.

Danzanvilliers, P., C. Duchen and O. Morellet (1980), 'Les effets indirects des transports interurbains', SETRA, Paris.

De Borger, B. and S. Proost (eds) (2001), *Reforming Transport Pricing in the European Union*, Cheltenham, UK and Northampton, MA, USA: Edward Elgar.

De Jong, G. and M. Gommers (1992), 'Time valuation in freight transport; method and results', paper presented to the PTRC 20th Summer Annual Meeting.

de Palma, A. (1992), 'A game theoretic approach to the analysis of simple congested networks' *Transportation Economics*, **82**(2).

de Palma, A., and F. Marchal (1996), 'Métropolis: un outil de simulation du trafic urbain', *Revue Transports*, **378**, July–August, 204-215.

de Palma, A. and F. Marchal (1998), 'Présentation du projet Meteor', Université de Cergy-Pontoise.

de Palma, A. and D. Rochat (1996), 'Urban congestion and commuters' behaviour: the departure time context', *Revue d'Economie Régionale et Urbaine*, **3**, 467-488.

de Palma, A., F. Marchal and Y. Nesterov (1997), 'METROPOLIS: A Modular System for Dynamic Traffic Simulation', *Transportation Research Record*, **1607**, 178-184.

Debene, M. and O. Raymundie (1996), 'Sur le service universel: renouveau du service public ou nouvelle mystification', *Actualité juridique – Droit Administratif*, 20 March.

Deboulet, A. and V. Renard (1992) 'Les plus values induites par les infrastructures de transport', research report, Association pour le développement des études foncières, Paris.

Denan-Boemont, L. and C. Gabella (1991), 'Les effets structurants. Analyse bibliographique', Lyon: Laboratoire d'Economie des Transports.

Denoix de Saint-Marc, R. (1996), 'Rapport à Monsieur le Premier Ministre sur le Service Public', La Documentation Française, Paris.

Department for Transport (2003), 'GOMMMS Supplement: Transport appraisal and the new Green Book', London: Department for Transport.

Derycke, P.H. (1997), *Le Péage urbain*, Paris: Economica.

Dickerson, A., J. Peirson and R. Vickerman (2000), 'Road accidents and traffic flow: an econometric investigation', *Economica*, **67**, 101-121.

DIRECTION (1992), 'The final report of the Royal Commission on National Passenger Transportation', Ministry of Supply and Services, Ottawa, Canada.

Dixit, A. (1973), 'The optimal factory town', *Bell Journal of Economics and Management Science*, **4**, 637-651.

Dodgson, J.S. (1973), 'External effects in road investment', *Journal of Transport Economics and Policy*, **7**, 169-185.

Dodgson J.S. (1974), 'Motorway investment and sub-regional growth. A case study of the M62', *Regional Studies*, **8**, 75-91.

Doganis, R. and G.F. Thompson (1975), 'The economics of regional airports', *International Journal of Transport Economics*, **2**.

Douglas, G.W. and J.C. Miller (1974), *Economic Regulation of Domestic Air Transport: Theory and Policy*, Washington, DC: The Brookings Institution.

DTLR (Department of Transport, Local Government and the Regions) (2000), *Guidance on the Methodology for the Multi-Modal Studies (GOMMMS)*, London: Department for Transport.

DTLR (Department of Transport, Local Government and the Regions) (2001), *Focus on Personal Travel*, London: The Stationery Office.

Duffy-Deno, K.T. and R.W. Eberts (1991), 'Public infrastructure and regional economic development: a simultaneous equation approach', *Journal of Urban Economics*, **30**, 329-343.

Dupuit, J. A. (1844), 'De la mesure de l'utilité des travaux publics', *Annales des Ponts et Chaussées*, **8**.

Dupuy, G. (1985), *Systèmes, Réseaux, Territoires*, Paris: Presses des Pont et Chaussées.

Dupuy, G. (1995), 'The automobile system: a territorial adapter', *Flux*, 21, July-Sept.

Duranton, G. (1997), 'La nouvelle économie géographique', *Economie et Prévision*, 131.

Duranton, G. (1998), 'Labor specialization, transport costs and city size', *Journal of Regional Science*, **38**, 553-573.

Duranton, G. and D. Puga (2000), 'Diversity and specialisation in cities: why, where and when does it matter?', *Urban Studies*, **37**, 533-555.

Eads, G.C., M. Nerlove and W. Raduchel (1969), 'A long-run cost function for the local airline industry', *Review of Economics and Statistics*, **51**, 258-270.

Eberts, K. (1986), 'Estimating the contribution of urban public infrastructure to regional growth', *Working Paper 8610*, Cleveland, OH: Federal Reserve Bank of Cleveland.

ECMT (European Conference of Ministers of Transport) (1998), *Efficient Transport for Europe*, Paris: OECD.

ECMT (European Conference of Ministers of Transport) (2001), *Assessing the Benefits of Transport*, Paris: OECD.

ECMT (European Conference of Ministers of Transport) (2003), *Managing the Fundamental Drivers of Transport Demand*, Proceedings of the International Seminar December 2002, Paris: OECD.

Encaoua, D. and A Perrot (1992), *Concurrence et coopération dans le transport aérien en Europe*, Report to European Commission, Luxembourg: Office for Official Publications of the European Commission.

EURET (1996), *Transport Research Concerted Action 1.1, Report*, Brussels: European Commission, DG Transport.

European Commission (1997), *The Likely Macroeconomic and Employment Impacts of Investments in Trans-European Transport Networks*, Commission Staff Working Paper, SEC(97)10, January, Brussels: European Commission.

Fankhauser, S. (1994), 'The economic costs of climate change', *Global Environmental Change*, **4**, 301-319.

Fischer, M. (2000), 'Travel demand' in J. Polack and A. Heertje (eds) *Analytical Transport Economics: An International Perspective,* Cheltenham: Edward Elgar.

Florian, M. (1991), 'The network equilibrium model', presented at the seminar 'Optimierung in Verkehrsplanung', ETH, Zurich.

Flyvbjerg, B., N. Bruzelius and W. Rothengatter, W. (2003) *Megaprojects and Risk: An Anatomy of Ambition*, Cambridge: Cambridge University Press.

Fogel, R.M. (1964), *Railroads and American Economic Growth: Essays in Economic History*, Baltimore, MD: Johns Hopkins Press.

Ford, R. and P. Poret (1991), 'Infrastructure and private sector productivity', *OECD Economic Studies* **16**(1), 79-131.

Friedlander, A. and R. Spady (1981), *Freight Transportation Regulation*, Cambridge, MA: MIT Press.

Friedlander, A., E. Berndt, J. Shaw, E.W. Chiang, M. Showalter, and C Vellturo (1993), 'Rail costs and capital adjustments in a quasi-regulated environment', *Journal of Transport Economics and Policy*, **27**, 131-152.

Friedriech R. and P. Biekel (eds) (2002), *Environmental External Costs of Transport*, Berlin: Springer Verlag.

Fritsch, B. and R. Prud'homme (1997), 'Measuring the contribution of road infrastructure to economic development in France' in E. Quinet and R. Vickerman (eds), *The Econometrics of Major Transport Infrastructures*, London: Macmillan.

Frybourg, M. and J. Orselli (1997), Evaluation technique, économique et sociale de Sirius, report, Ministère des Transports, Paris:

Fujita, M. (1989), *Urban Economic Theory*, Cambridge: Cambridge University Press.

Fujita, M. and J.F. Thisse (1996), 'Economics of agglomeration', *Journal of the Japanese and International Economy*, **10**, 339-378.

Fujita, M. and J.F. Thisse (2002), *Economics of Agglomeration*, Cambridge: Cambridge University Press.

Fujita, M., P. Krugman and A.J. Venables (1999) *The Spatial Economy: Cities, Regions and International Trade*, Cambridge, MA: MIT Press.

Gaegler, A. and J. March (1978), 'Dynamic social and economic effects of the Connecticut Turnpike', *Transportation Research Record*.

Galland, C. and E. Quinet (1995), 'Les dépenses de sécurité et la valeur de la vie humaine dans les transports collectifs de voyageurs', Report by CERAS-ENPC for Ministère des Transports, Paris.

Gannon, F. (1996) 'La péri-urbanisation', paper presented to seminar on economic analysis, MELTT, Paris

Gathon, H.J., and P. Pestieau (1995), 'La performance des entreprises publiques: une question de propriété ou de concurrence?' CREPP 95/06, Université de Liège.

Gaudry, M. and M. Wills (1978), 'Estimating the functional form of travel demand models', *Transportation Research*, **12**, 257-289.

Gerondeau C. (1996), 'Les Transports en Europe', EDS, Paris.

Gillen, D., TH. Oum and M. Tretheway (1990), 'Airline cost structure and policy implications', *Journal of Transport Economics and Policy*, **24**, 9-34.

Girault, M. and J. C. Blain (1997), 'La demande de Transport en 2015', *Etudes du SES*, Ministère des Transports, Paris.

Girault, M. and J.M. Kail (1997), 'Perspectives de la demande de transport et des émissions de polluants à l'horizon 2015', *Actes du Congrès de l'ATEC*, Paris: Presses de l'Ecole des Ponts et Chaussées.

Girault, M., J.C. Blain and K. Meyer (1995), 'Elasticités de court et de long termes des trafics de marchandises à la croissance économique', notes de synthèse, OEST, Paris, March.

Glaeser, E. (1998), Are cities dying?, *Journal of Economic Perspectives*, **12**, 139-60.

Glaister, S. (2002a), 'UK transport policy 1997-2001', *Oxford Review of Economic Policy*, **18**, 154-186.

Glaister, S. (2002b), 'La concurrence dans les transports; l'expérience britannique, in C. Henry and E. Quinet (eds) *Concurrence et Service Public*, Paris: Harmattan.

Golob, E (1995), 'Impact of deregulation on investment and production strategies in the commercial aircraft industry', *Transportation Research Record*, **1480**.

Gomez-Ibanez, J. (1995), 'Pitfall in estimating whether transport users pay their way', paper presented at the Conference: 'Measuring the full social costs and benefits of transportation', Irvine, June 1995.

Gomez-Ibanez, J. (1997), 'Estimating whether transport users pay their way. The state of the art', in D. Greene, D. Jones and M. Delucchi (eds), *The Full Social Costs and Benefits of Transportation*, Berlin: Springer-Verlag.

Gomez-Ibanez, J. and J. Meyer (1993), 'Going private: the international experience with transport privatization', Washington, DC: Brookings Institution.

Goodwin, P. (1992), 'A review of new demand elasticities with special reference to short and long run effects of price changes', *Journal of Transport Economics and Policy*, **26**, 155-169.

Goodwin, P. (1996), 'Extra traffic induced by road construction, empirical evidence, economic effects and policy implications' in ECMT, *Infrastructure Induced Mobility*, Report of Round Table 105, Paris: OECD.

Gourvish, T. (2002), *British Rail: 1974-1996*, Oxford: Oxford University Press.

Gravel, N., M. Martinez and A. Trannoy (1996), 'Evaluation des prix hédoniques du logement dans les communes du Val-d'Oise de plus de 10 000 habitants', Rapport du centre THEMA, Université de Cergy-Pontoise.

Greene, D., D. Jones and M. Delucchi (eds) (1997), *The Full Social Costs and Benefits of Transportation*, Berlin: Springer-Verlag.

Guitard, B., and A. Plaud (1991), 'Impacts et mise en valeur des voies rapides', DDE Morbihan.

Hafner P., (1996), 'The effects of railroad reform in Germany', *Japan Railway and Transport Review*, Sept.

Hainault, M. and J. Karam (1998) 'Les modèles de choix modal. Recherche d'élasticités', Mémoire , ENPC, Paris.

Hakfoot, J. (1996), 'Public capital, private sector productivity and economic growth: a macro-economic perspective' in D. Batten and C. Karlsson (eds), *Infrastructure and the Complexity of Economic Development*, Berlin: Springer-Verlag.

Harmatuck, D.J. (1981), 'A motor carrier joint cost function', *Journal of Transport Economics and Policy*, **15**, 135-153.

Harmatuck, D.J. (1991), 'Economies of scale and scope in the motor carrier industry', *Journal of Transport Economics and Policy*, **25**, 135-151.

Harris, C.C. (1980), 'New developments and extensions of the multi-regional multi-industry forecasting model', *Journal of Regional Science*, **20**, 159-171.

Harris, R.G. (1977), 'Economics of traffic density in the rail freight industry', *Bell Journal of Economics*, **8**, 556-563.

Haudeville, B.(1994), 'Les stratégies concernant l'entrée dans un oligopole étroit: l'exemple de la construction aéronautique civile', *Revue d'Economie Industrielle*, 3rd quarter.

Hayashi, Y. and H. Morisugi (2000), 'International comparison of background, concept and methodology of transport project appraisals', *Transport Policy*, 7, 73-88.

Helm, D. and D. Thompson (1991), 'Privatized transport infrastructure and incentive to invest', *Journal of Transport Economics and Policy*, **25**, 231-246.

Henderson, J.V. (1985), *Economic Theory and the Cities*, Orlando: Academic Press.

Henderson, J.V. (1988), *Urban Development. Theory, Fact and Illusion*, Oxford: Oxford University Press.

Henderson, J.V. (2003,) 'Marshall's scale economies', *Journal of Urban Economics* **53**, 1-28.

Henry, C. (1997a), 'Cours d'économie publique', volume 2, Ecole Polytechnique, Paris.

Henry, C. (1997b), *Concurrence et Service Publique dans l'Union Européénne*, Paris: PUF.

Henry, C. and E. Quinet (1996), 'Service public, efficacité et concurrence dans le système ferroviaire français', *Transports*, July/August.

Hensher, D. (1997), 'Value of travel time savings in personal and commercial automobile travel', in D. Greene, D. Jones and M. Delucchi (eds), *The Full Social Costs and Benefits of Transportation*, Berlin: Springer-Verlag.

Hilvert, L., J.P. Orfeuil and P. Troulay (1988), 'Modèles désagrégés de choix modal', Rapport INRETS 67, Paris.

HM Treasury (2003), *The Green Book: Appraisal and Evaluation in Central Government*, London: Stationery Office.

Holliday, I.M., G. Marcou and R.W. Vickerman (1991), *The Channel Tunnel: Public Policy, Regional Development and European Integration*, London: Belhaven Press.

Hong, S. and P. Harker (1992), 'Air traffic network equilibrium : toward frequency, price and slot priority analysis', *Transportation Research A*, **26**(2).

Huang, Y. (1997), 'Identifying the link between transportation and land use density with accessibility', paper presented to 76th meeting of Transportation Research Board.

Hylen, B., (1997), 'Sweden', in ECMT, *The Separation of Operations from Infrastructure in the Provision of Railway Services*, Report of Round Table 103, Paris: OECD.

Infras-IWW (2000), *External Costs of Transport. Accident, Environmental and Congestion Costs in Western Europe*, International Union of Railways (UIC), Paris.

Inman, R.P and D.L Rubinfeld (1996), 'The political economy of federalism', in D. Mueller (ed.), *Perspectives on Public Choice*, Cambridge: Cambridge University Press.

INSEE (1986), 'Effets d'entraînement multisectoriels à court et moyen termes des investissements en infrastructures et matériel de transport', mimeo, Paris.

Isard, W. (1956), *Location and the Space-Economy*, New York: Wiley.

Ising, H., W. Babish and B. Gruppa (1995), *Traffic noise and risk of myocardial infarction*. 18th International Congress for Noise Abatement, Association internationale contre le bruit (AICB), Bologna.

Ivaldi, M. and G. McCullough (2001), 'Density and integration effects on class I US freight railroads' *Journal of Regulatory Economics*, **19**, 161-182.

Jansson, J.O. (1994), 'Accident externality charges', *Journal of Transport Economics and Policy*, **28**, 31-43.

Jansson, J.O. (2000a), 'Transport infrastructure: the investment problem', in J. Polack and A. Heertje (eds), *Analytical Transport Economics: An International Perspective,* Cheltenham, UK and Northampton, MA, USA: Edward Elgar.

Jansson, J.O. (2000b), 'Transport infrastructure: the problem of optimum use', in J. Polack and A. Heertje (eds), *Analytical Transport Economics: An International Perspective,* Cheltenham, UK and Northampton, MA, USA: Edward Elgar.

Jara-Diaz, S.R. (1986) 'On the relationships between users' benefits and the economic effects of transportation activities', *Journal of Regional Science*, **26**, 379-391.

Jara-Diaz S.R. (1990), 'Consumer's surplus and the value of travel time savings', *Transportation Research B*, **24**, 73-77.

Jara-Diaz, S.R. and C. E. Cortes (1996), 'On the calculation of scale economies from transport cost functions', *Journal of Transport Economics and Policy*, **30**, 157-170.

Jara-Diaz, S., and M. Munizaga (1992), 'The effects of network density on European Railway costs', paper presented to World Conference on Transport Research, Lyon.

Jara-Diaz, S. and C. Winston (1981), 'Multiproduct transportation cost functions: scale and scope in railway operations', in N. Blattner (ed.) *Eighth European Association for Research in Industrial Economics*, Basel: University of Basel.

Jeanrenaud, C. (1993), 'Les coûts sociaux des transports en Suisse', IRER, Neuchâtel.

Jensen-Butler, C. and B. Madsen (1996), 'Modelling the regional economic effects of the Danish Great Belt Link', *Papers in Regional Science*, **75**, 1-21.

Jiang, F. and C.Calzada (1997), 'Shipper's demand characteristics and their value of time: an analysis on the freight mode choice', memo, Ministère des transports and INRETS, Paris.

Johansson, O. and L. Schipper (1997), 'Measuring the long run fuel demand of cars', *Journal of Transport Economics and Policy*, **31**, 277-292.

Jones-Lee, M.W. (1990), 'The value of transport safety', *Oxford Review of Economic Policy*, **6**, 39-60.

Jones-Lee, M.W. and G. Loomes (1994), 'Towards a willingness to pay based value of underground safety', *Journal of Transport Economics and Policy*, **28**, 83-98.

Kail, M., J. Lambert and E. Quinet (2000), 'Evaluer les effets des transports sur l'environnement; le cas des nuisances sonores', CADAS Report, Paris.

Kanemoto, Y. and K. Mera (1985), 'General equilibrium analysis of the benefits of large transportation improvements', *Regional Science and Urban Economics*, **15**, 343-363.

Kawakami, S., Y. Hirobata, and Z. Xu (1989), 'A general comparison of stochastic and deterministic equilibrium traffic assignment models', paper presented to 5th World Conference on Transport Research, Yokohama.

Kechi, L. (1996), 'Synthèse de documents sur les élasticités tarifaires', mimeo, CETUR.

Keeler, R. (1973), 'Airport cost and congestion', *The American Economist*.

Keeler, T.E. (1972), 'Airline regulation and market performance', *Bell Journal of Economics*, **3**, 399-424.

Keeler, T.E. (1974), 'Railroad costs, returns to scale and excess capacity', *Review of Economics and Statistics*, **61**, 201-208.

Kerstens, K. (1996), 'Technical efficiency measurement and explanation of French urban transit companies', *Transportation Research A*, **30**, 431-452.

Kirby, M. (1986), 'Airline economies of scale and Australian domestic air transport policy', *Journal of Transport Economics and Policy*, **20**, 339-352.

Koenig, J.G. (1974), 'Théorie de l'accessibilité urbaine', thesis, Université de Paris VI.

Koenker, R. (1977), 'Optimal scale and the size distribution of American trucking firms', *Journal of Transport Economics and Policy*, **11**, 54-67.

Kogan, J. (1997), 'The new structure of Argentine Railways', World Railways, Kensington Publications.

Kogan J., and L. Thompson (1994), 'Reshaping Argentina's Railways', *Japan Railway and Transport Review*, June.

Kolm, S. C. (1968), 'Prix publics optimaux', *Cahiers du séminaire d'économétrie*, 9, CNRS, Paris.

Kolm, S.C. (1970a), 'L'inégalité des valeurs des vies humaines', *Cahiers du séminaire d'économétrie*, 18, CNRS, Paris.

Kolm, S.C. (1970b), *Le Service des Masses*, Paris: Dunod.

Kreps, J. and J. Scheinkman (1983), 'Quantity precommitment and Bertrand competition yield Cournot outcomes', *Bell Journal of Economics*, **14**.

Krugman, P.R. (1991), 'Increasing returns to scale and economic geography', *Journal of Political Economy*, **99**, 483-499.

Krugman, P.R. (1993a), 'On the number and location of cities', *European Economic Review* **37**, 293-298.

Krugman, P.R. (1993b), 'First nature, second nature and metropolitan location', *Journal of Regional Science*, **33**, 129-144.

Laffont, J.J. (1982), *Cours de théorie micro-économique*, Paris: Economica.

Laffont, J.J., and J. Tirole (1986), 'Un théorie normative des contrats Etat-entreprise', *Annales d'Economie et de Statistiques*, no 1.

Laffont, J.J., and J. Tirole (1993), *A Theory of Procurement and Regulation*, Cambridge, MA: MIT Press.

Laffont, J.J., and J. Tirole (1994), 'Access pricing and competition', *European Economic Review*, **38**, 1673-1710.

Lam, T.C. and K.A. Small (2001), 'The value of time and reliability: measurement from a value pricing experiment', *Transportation Research E*, **37**, 231-251.

Lau, S.H.P. and C.Y. Sin (1997), 'Public infrastructure and economic growth: time series properties and evidence', *Economic Record*, **73**, 125-135.

Le Jeannic, T. (1997), 'Trente ans de péri-urbanisation: extension et dilution des villes', *Economie et Statistique*, **307**, 21-41.

Lefevre, C. and J.M. Offner (1990), 'Les transports urbains en question', *Editions CELSE*.

Lesourne, J. (1969), *Le Calcul Economique*, Paris: Dunod.

Leurent, F. (1991), 'Traitement mathématique d'un modèle de choix d'itinéraire sur un réseau', mimeo, INRETS, Arcueil.

Leurent, F. (1997), 'Modèles de choix binaires: une comparaison sur les observations du tunnel Prado-Carénage', working paper 97-5, INRETS, Arcueil.

Levinson, D., D. Gillena, Kanafani and J.M. Mathieu (1996), 'The full cost of intercity transportation', Research Report, Institute of Transport Studies. UCB ITS RR 96-3, University of California at Berkeley.

Levy-Lambert, H. (1968), 'Tarification des services à qualité variable: application aux péages de circulation', *Econometrica*, **36**, 241-259.

Liew, C. (1985), 'Measuring the impact of a transportation system: a simplified approach', *Journal of Regional Science*, **25**, 241-259.

Link, H., L.H. Stewart, C. Doll, P. Bickel, S. Schmid, R. Friedrich, S. Suter and M. Maibach (2001), *Pilot Accounts for Switzerland and Germany*, UNITE Deliverable D5 Funded by EC 5th Framework Transport RTD.

Littman, T. (1999), *Transportation Cost Analysis: Techniques, Estimates and Implications,* Victoria, BC: Victoria Transport Policy Institute (http://www.vtpi. org/tca).

Looney, R. and P. Frederiksen (1981), 'The regional impact of infrastructure investment in Mexico', *Regional Studies*, **15**.

Lösch, A. (1940), *The Economics of Location*, translation of 1954, New Haven, CT: Yale University Press.

Lundberg A. (1996), 'Restructuring of the Swedish State Railways', *Japan Railway and Transport Review*, Sept.

McCann, P. (2001), *Urban and Regional Economics*, Oxford: Oxford University Press.

McGeehan H. (1993), 'Railway costs and productivity growth', *Journal of Transport Economics and Policy*, **27**, 19-32.

Mackie, P. (1997), 'Regulation or competition', in ECMT *Which Changes for Transport in the Next Century,* Report of the 14th Symposium on Theory and Practice in Transport Economics, Innsbruck, Paris: OECD.

McKinnon, A. (2003) 'Influencing company logistics management' in ECMT, *Managing the Fundamental Drivers of Transport Demand*, Proceedings of the International Seminar December 2002, Paris: OECD.

Madre, J.L. (1997), 'Is the growth of passenger transport inevitable?', in ECMT *Which Changes for Transport in the Next Century,* Report of the 14th Symposium on Theory and Practice in Transport Economics, Innsbruck, Paris: OECD.

Madre, J.L. and T. Lambert (1989), 'Prévisions à long terme du trafic automobile', CREDOC, Paris.

Mandel, B., M. Gaudry and W. Rothengatter (1996), 'A disaggregate Box-Cox logit mode choice model of intercity passenger travel in Germany', in E. Quinet and R. Vickerman (eds), *The Econometrics of Major Transport Infrastructures*, London: Macmillan.

Marshall, A. (1920), *Principles of Economics*, 8th edn, London: Macmillan.

Massiani, J. (1997), 'La non-linéarité de la valeur du temps' Mémoire, DEA Transport ENPC-Paris: XII.

Mauch, H. and W. Rothengatter (1996), *External Cost of Land Transport*, Report to UIC, Paris.

Mera, K. (1973), 'Regional production functions and social overhead capital: an analysis of the Japanese case', *Regional and Urban Economics*, **3**, 157-185.

Mera, K. (1975), *Income Distribution and Regional Development*, Tokyo: University of Tokyo Press.

Merlin, P. (1991), *Géographie, Economie et Planification des Transports*, Paris: PUF.

Metzler, J.M. (1995), 'France', in ECMT, *Interurban Transport Costs,* Report of Round Table 98, Paris: OECD.

Meyer, J.R. (1982), *Techniques of Transport Planning*, Washington, DC: The Brookings Institution.

Meyer, K. (1997), 'L'économétrie au service du fret ferroviaire', *Rail & Recherche*, February, Paris

Milgrom, P. and J. Roberts (1992), *Economics, Organization and Management*, New York: Prentice-Hall.

Miller, C., D. Coomer and R. Jameson (1985), 'Role and function of transit in growth management', *Transportation Research Record.*

Mills, E.S. (1993) 'The spatial pattern of office asking rents in the Chicago Metropolitan Area', in H. Ohta and J.F. Thisse (eds), *Does Economic Space Matter*, New York: St Martin's Press.

Mills, E. and G. Carlino (1989), 'Dynamics of country growth', in O. Andersson, D. Batten, B. Johansson and P. Nijkamp (eds), *Advances in Spatial Theory and Dynamics*, Amsterdam: North Holland.

Mirrlees, J. (1972), 'The optimum town', *Swedish Journal of Economics*, **74**, 114-135.

Mituzani, F. and H. Nakamura (1997), 'Privatization of the Japan National Railways: overview of performance changes' *International Journal of Transport Economics*, **24**(1).

Modelistica (1995), 'Tranus System Overview' mimeo.

Mohring H. (1976), *Transportation Economics,* Cambridge, MA: Ballinger Press.

Mohring, H. and M. Harwitz (1962), *Highway Benefits: An Analytical Framework*, Evanston, IL: Transportation Center, Northwestern University.

Monopolies and Mergers Commission (1989), *Cross Channel Car Ferries*, Cm 903, London: HMSO.

Monopolies and Mergers Commission (1994), *National Express Group PLC and Saltire Holdings Ltd: A report on the merger situation*, Cm 2468, London: HMSO.

Montagu, N. (1997), 'Progress with rail privatization in Great Britain', World Railway Update.

Morellet, O. (1997), 'Modèle Matosse. Validation du partage du trafic entre itinéraires routiers à péage et hors péage', memo 23 June, INRETS, Arcueil.

Morisugi, H. (1983), 'A basic definition of transport benefits: advocating equivalent variation', *Proceedings of the World Conference on Transport Research, Hamburg.*

Morisugi, H. and Y. Hayashiyama (1997), 'Post-evaluation of the Japanese railway network; 1875-1940', in E. Quinet and R. Vickerman (eds), *The Econometrics of Major Transport Infrastructures, London:* Macmillan.

Morrison, C. and A.E. Schwartz (1996), 'State infrastructure and productive performance', *American Economic Review*, **86**, 1095-1111.

Morrison S. and C. Winston (1987), 'Empirical implications and tests of the contestability hypothesis', *Journal of Law and Economics*, **30**, 53-66.

Mougeot, M and F. Naegelen (1994), *La Discrimination par les Prix*, Paris: Economica.

Munnell, A.H. (1992), 'Infrastructure investment and economic growth', *Journal of Economic Perspectives*, **6**, 189-198.

Nadiri, M.I. and T.P. Mamuneas (1996), 'Contribution of Highway Capital to Industry and National Productivity Growth', mimeo, NBER and Cyprus University.

Nakamura, H. and T. Ueda (1989), 'The impacts of the Shinkansen on regional development, mimeo, Tokyo.

Nash, C. (1997a), 'Does monetary valuation of environment make sense?', in G. de Rus and C. Nash (eds), *Recent Developments in Transport Economics*, Aldershot: Ashgate.

Nash, C. (1997b), 'The separation of operations from infrastructure in the provision of railway services: the British experience', in ECMT, *The Separation of Operations from Infrastructure in the Provision of Railway Services*, Report of Round Table 103, Paris: OECD.

National Audit Office (1988), *Road Planning,* London: HMSO.

National Audit Office (2003), *Maintaining England's Motorways and Trunk Roads,* London: Stationery Office.

Nellthorp, J., T. Sansom, P. Bickel, C. Doll and G. Lindberg (2001), *Valuation conventions for UNITE*, Funded by EC 5th Framework Transport RTD.

N.E.R.A. (1998) 'An examination of rail infrastructure charges', Report to European Commission, London: NERA

Nero, G. (1996), 'A structural model of intra-European union duopoly airline competition', *Journal of Transport Economics and Policy*, **30**, 137-155.

Newbery, D. (1998a), 'Road user charges in Britain', *Economic Journal*, **98** (Conference), 161-176.

Newbery, D. (1988b), 'Road damage externalities and road user charges' *Econometrica*, **56**, 295-319.

Newbery, D. (1995), 'Royal Commission Report on Transport and the Environment - Economic Effects of Recommendations', *Economic Journal*, **105**, 1258-1272.

Nicolas, J.P. (1998), 'Circulation routière et évolution des nuisances sonores' paper presented to World Conference on Transport Research, Antwerp.

Nilsson, J.E. (1991), 'Investment decisions in a public bureaucracy: a case study of Swedish road planning practices', *Journal of Transport Economics and Policy*, **25**, 163-175.

Nilson, J.E.(1992), 'Second best problems in railways infrastructure pricing and investment', *Journal of Transport Economics and Policy*, **26**, 245-259.

Nilsson, J.E. (1995), 'Allocation of track capacity', working paper 1995-1, CTS.

Nordhaus, W. (1991), 'To slow or not to slow? The economics of the greenhouse effect', *Economic Journal*, **101**, 920-937.

Norman, C. and R.W. Vickerman (1999), 'Local and regional implications of trans-European transport networks: the Channel Tunnel Rail Link', *Environment and Planning A*, **31**, 705-718.

OEST (1994), 'La déréglementation du transport routier de marchandises. Essai de bilan', working paper, Ministère de l'Equipement, Paris.

Offner J.M. (1993), 'Les effets structurants des transports: mythe politique, mystification économique', *l'Espace géographique*, **3**.

Okano, Y. (1994), 'The backdrop to privatization in Japan', *Japan Railway and Transport Review*, June.

Oosterhaven J. and T. Knaap (2003) 'Spatial economic impacts of transport infrastructure investments' in A. Pearman, P. Mackie. J. Nellthorp & L. Giorgi (eds), *Transport Projects, Programmes and Policies: Evaluation Needs and Capabilities*, Brussels: European Commission.

Orfeuil, J.P. (1997), 'Les coûts externes de la circulation routière', Report No 216, INRETS, Arcueil.

Ortuzar, J. and L. Willumsen (1994), *Modelling transport*, 2nd edn, Chichester: John Wiley.

Orus, J.P. (1997), 'Les conséquences économiques des grandes infrastructures routières' in O. Heddebaut (ed.), *Grandes Infrastructures de Transport et Territoires*, Actes INRETS 60, Arcueil: INRETS.

Oum, T.H. and M. Tretheway (1988), 'Ramsey pricing in the presence of externality costs', *Journal of Transport Economics and Policy*, **22**, 307-317.

Oum, T.H. and C. Yu (1994), 'Economic efficiency of railways and implications for public policy', *Journal of Transport Economics and Policy*, **28**, 121-138.

Oum, T. and Y. Zhang (1990), 'Airport pricing: congestion tolls, lumpy investments and cost recovery', *Journal of Public Economics*, **43**, 353-374.

Oum, T.H. and Y. Zhang (1991), 'Utilisation of quasi-fixed inputs and estimations of cost functions', *Journal of Transport Economics and Policy*, **25**, 121-134

Oum, T.H. and Y. Zhang (1997) 'A note on scale economies in transport', *Journal of Transport Economics and Policy*, **31**, 309-315.

Oum, T.H., W.C. Waters II and J.S. Yong (1992), 'Concepts of price elasticities of transport demand and recent related estimates', *Journal of Transport Economics and Policy*, **27**, 139-154.

Oum, T., A. Zhang and Y. Zhang (1996), 'A note on optimal airport pricing in a hub and spoke system', *Transportation Research B*, **30**, 11-18.

Papapanagos, H. and R.W Vickerman (1999), 'Borders, migration and labour market dynamics in a changing Europe', in M. van der Velde, M. and H van Houtum (eds), *Borders, Regions and People*, European Research in Regional Science 10, London: Pion.

Papon, F. (1996), 'Méthodes innovantes de financement des routes de France' Report, INRETS, Arcueil.

Pavaux, J. (1994), *L'Economie du Transport Aérien*, Paris: Economica.

Pearce, D. and A. Markandya (1989), *Monetary Evaluation of the Benefits of Environmental Policies*, Report to OECD, Paris.

Peeters, D., J. F. Thisse, I. Thomas (1998), 'Transportation networks and the location of human activities', *Geographical Analysis*, **30**, 355-371.

Peirson, J. and R. Vickerman (2001), 'Computation of the internal costs of transport', in B. De Borger and S. Proost (eds), *Reforming Transport Pricing in the European Union*, Cheltenham, UK and Northampton, MA, USA: Edward Elgar.

Peirson, J., I. Skinner and R. Vickerman (1994), 'The taxation of external effects and the efficient supply of transport', Discussion Paper 94-3. CERTE, Department of Economics, University of Kent, Canterbury:

Peirson, J., I. Skinner and R. Vickerman (1995), 'Estimating the External Costs of UK Passenger Transport: The First Step Towards an Efficient Transport Market', *Environment and Planning A*, **27**, 1977-1993.

Peirson, J., I. Skinner and R. Vickerman (1998,) 'The microeconomic analysis of the external costs of road accidents', *Economica*, **65**, 429-440

Pels, E., P. Nijkamp and P. Rietveld (1997), 'Substitution and complementarity in aviation : Airports vs Airlines', *Transportation Research E*, **33**, 275-286.

Perrett, K.E. and A. Stevens (1996) 'Review of the potential benefits of road transport telematics', TRL Report No. 220, Crowthorne: TRL

Perrot, A. (1993), 'Compatibility, networks and competition: a review of recent advances', *Transportation Science*, **27**, 55-61.

Perroux, F. (1955), 'Note sur la notion de pôles de croissance', *Economie Appliquée*, **7**, 307-320.

Pindyck, R.S. (1991), 'Irreversibility, uncertainty and investment', *Journal of Economic Literature*, **29**, 1110-1148.

Planco (1991), *Externe Kosten des Verkehrs: Schiene, Straße, Binnenschiffahrt*, Essen: Planco Consulting GmbH.

Plassard, F. (1990a), 'Axes autoroutiers et développement des régions', *Les Cahiers Scientifiques du Transport*, **25**.

Plassard, F. (1990b), 'France' in, ECMT, *Transport and the Spatial Distribution of Activities*, Report of Round Table 85, Paris: OECD.

Politano, A. and C. Roadifer (1989), 'Regional economic impact model for highway systems', *Transportation Research Record,* 1229.

Polydoropoulou, A., M. Ben Akiva, A. Khattak and G. Lauprete (1997), 'Modelling revealed and stated in route travel response to advance traveller information systems' *Transportation Research Record,* 1537.

Ponsolle, P. (1996), 'Le financement privé des grands projets d'infrastructure : l'expérience Eurotunnel', *Revue Transports,* Sept-Oct.

Porte, O. and A. Remy (1995), 'La déréglementation du transport interurbain par autocars en Grande-Bretagne : bilan 1950-1995', Synthèse OEST, December.

Preston, J. (1994), 'The economics of rail privatization', paper presented to a seminar at l'Ecole Polytechnique, Paris, October.

Prud'homme, R. (1996), 'Assessing the role of Infrastructure in France by Means of Regionally Estimated Production Functions' in D. Batten and C. Karlsson (eds) *Infrastructure and the Complexity of Economic development*, Berlin: Springer Verlag.

Prud'homme, R. and Chang-Woon Lee (1999), 'Size, sprawl, speed and the efficiency of cities', *Urban Studies*, **36**, 1849-1858.

Quin, C. (1994), 'Analyse des coûts de déplacement: élaboration d'une méthodologie dans le cadre d'un compte transport de voyageurs', Report for the Ministère des Transports, Paris.

Quinet, E. (1969), 'L'incertitude dans les calculs et rentabilité routiers', *Annales des Ponts et Chaussées*, **3**, 268-294.

Quinet, E. (1988), 'Transport et espace économique', *Communication à l'Académie des Sciences Morales et Politiques*.

Quinet, E. (1991), 'Organizational structure of public transport and assessment of schedules', *Transport Planning and Technology*, **16**, 145-152.

Quinet, E. (1992a), *Infrastructures de transport et croissance*, Paris: Economica.

Quinet, E. (1992b), 'Route, Air, Fer', Report for the Ministère des Transports, Paris.

Quinet E. (1993), 'Transport between monopoly and competition', in J. Polack and A. Heertje (eds), *European Transport Economics*, Oxford: Blackwell.

Quinet, E. (1994), 'Rapport Route-Air-Fer, Propositions pour l'harmonisation des tarifications d'infrastructures aériennes, ferroviaires et routières', Report for *the* Ministère des Transports, Paris.

Quinet, E. (1994), 'The social costs of transport', in OECD, *Internalizing the Social Costs of Transport*, Paris: OECD.

Quinet, E. (1997a), 'Issues in building the European high speed train network', *Journal of Infrastructure Systems*, **3**, 49-54.

Quinet, E. (1997b), 'Full social cost of transportation in Europe', in D. Greene, D. Jones and M. Delucchi (eds), *The Full Social Costs and Benefits of Transportation*, Berlin: Springer-Verlag.

Quinet, E. (1997c), Evaluation économique des projets de transports urbains. Report of a working group led by E. Quinet for the Ministère de l'Equipement and ENPC-CERAS, mimeo, Paris.

Quinet, E. (2000), 'Imperfect competition in transport markets' in J. Polack and A. Heertje (eds) *Analytical Transport Economics: An International Perspective,* Cheltenham, UK and Northampton, MA, USA: Edward Elgar.

Quinet, E. (2003), 'Short-term adjustments in rail activity: the limited role of infrastructure charges, *Transport Policy,* 10, 73-79.

Ramsey, F.P. (1927), 'A contribution to the theory of taxation', *Economic Journal,* 37, 47-61.

Ratner, J.B. (1983), 'Government capital and the production function for US private output', *Economics Letters,* 13, 213-217.

Remy, A. (1996), 'Performances économiques des principaux opérateurs ferroviaires de l'O.C.D.E.', SES Ministère de l'Equipement, Paris.

Rietveld, P. and P. Nijkamp (2000), 'Transport and regional development', in J. Polak. and A. Heertje (eds), *Analytical Transport Economics,* Cheltenham, UK and Northampton, MA, USA: Edward Elgar.

Rietveld, P. and R. Vickerman (2003) 'Transport in regional science: is the "death of distance" premature?, *Papers in Regional Science,* 82.

Rothengatter, W. (2000), 'Evaluation methodology of transport projects in Germany', *Transport Policy,* 7, 35-53.

Rousseau, J. and C. Saut (1991), 'Tests de politiques de transport', RATP Etudes-Projets, 4th quarter.

Rousseau, J. and C. Saut (1997), 'Un outil de simulation de politiques des transports: IMPACT3', *Revue Générale des Chemins de fer,* December.

Roy, R. (2000), 'Revenues from efficient pricing. Evidence from the member states ', UIC/CER/European Commission DG-TREN study.

SACTRA (Standing Advisory Committee on Trunk Road Assessment) (1986), *Urban Road Appraisal,* London: HMSO.

SACTRA (Standing Advisory Committee on Trunk Road Assessment) (1992), *Assessing the Environmental Impact of Road Schemes,* London: HMSO.

SACTRA (Standing Advisory Committee on Trunk Road Assessment) (1994), *Trunk Roads and the Generation of Traffic,* London: HMSO.

SACTRA (Standing Advisory Committee on Trunk Road Assessment) (1999), *Transport and the Economy,* London: Stationery Office.

Sansom, T., C. Nash, P. Mackie, J. Shires and P. Watkiss (2001), *Surface Transport Costs and Charges: Great Britain 1998,* Institute for Transport Studies, University of Leeds.

Sanchez, P.C. (2000), 'Vertical operations between infrastructure and the operations, the European case', in C Nash and E Niskanen (eds), *VATT Discussion Paper No. 245,* Helsinki: VATT.

Sauvant, D. (1996), 'Cours d'économie des transports', Université de Paris II.

Savy, M. and P. Veltz (1993), 'Les nouveaux espaces de l'entreprise', DATAR, Paris: Editions de l'Aube.

Schumpeter, J.A. (1942), *Capitalism, Socialism and Democracy,* New York: Harper.

Segonne, C. (1998), 'Comportement de choix d'itinéraires', thesis Université de Lyon 2.

Selvanathan, E.A. and S. Selvanathan (1994), 'The demand for transport and communication in the United Kingdom and Australia', *Transportation Research B,* 28, 1-9.

SES (1996), 'Les transports en 1995', *Rapport de la Commission des Comptes de la Nation,* La Documentation Francais, Paris.

SETRA (1993), 'Les prévisions de trafic 20 ans après', mimeo.

Sharkey, W. (1982), *The Theory of Natural Monopoly*, Cambridge: Cambridge University Press.

Simmons, D. and N. Jenkinson (1996), 'Les impacts économiques régionaux du tunnel sous la Manche' in A. Burmeister and G. Joignaux (eds), *Infrastructures de Transport et Territoire*, Paris: Harmattan.

Simon, D. (1987), 'Spanning muddy waters: the Humber bridge and regional development', *Regional Studies*, **21**, 25-36.

Skamris, M. and B. Flyvbjerg (1996), 'Accuracy of traffic forecasts and cost estimates on large transportation projects', *Transportation Research Record*, **1518**, 65-69.

Small, K. (1992), *Urban Transportation Economics*, Chur: Harwood Academic Publishers.

Small, K. and M. Rosen (1981), 'Applied welfare economics with discrete choice models', *Econometrica*, **49**, 105-130.

Small, K., C. Winston and C.A. Evans (1989), *Road Works: A New Highway Price and Investment Policy*, Washington, DC: Brookings Institution.

SNCF (1993), 'Evaluation des grands projets ferroviaires', mimeo.

Song, S. (1996), 'Some tests of alternative accessibility measures: a population density approach ', *Land Economics*, **72**, 474-482.

Spady, R. and A. Friedlander (1978), 'Hedonic cost functions for the regulated trucking industry', *Bell Journal of Economics*, **9**, 154-179.

Spiekermann, K. and M. Wegener (1997), 'The Channel Tunnel and regional development: combining qualitative and quantitative methods', in E. Quinet and R. Vickerman (eds), *Econometrics of Major Transport Infrastructures*, London: Macmillan.

Stabenau, H. (1997), 'New trends in logistics in Europe' in ECMT, Report of Round Table 104, Paris: OECD.

Starkie, D. (1994), 'The US market in airport slots', *Journal of Transport Economics and Policy*, **28**, 325-329.

Stephanides, Y. and D. Eagle (1986), 'Highway expenditures and non-metropolitan employment', *Journal of Advanced Transportation*, **20**.

Stoffaes, C. (1995), *L'Europe de l'utilité publique*, ASPE Europe Editions.

Suga, T., (1997), 'The separation of operations from infrastructure in the provision of railway services: the case of Japan', in ECMT, *The Separation of Operations from Infrastructure in the Provision of Railway Services*, Report of Round Table 103, Paris: OECD.

Szymanski, S. (1991), 'The optimal timing of infrastructure investment', *Journal of Transport Economics and Policy*, **25**, 247-258.

Szymanski, S. (1993), 'Making hay when the sun shines', working paper, Imperial College Management School.

Szymanski, S. (1996), 'Rational pricing strategies in the cross channel tunnel', in E. Quinet and R. Vickerman (eds), *The Econometrics of Major Transport Infrastructures*, London: Macmillan.

Taroux, J.P. (1995), 'Modèle IMPACT. Rapport d'actualisation', OEST, Ministère des Transports, Paris.

Taroux, J.P. and G. Buchmuller (1980), 'PRETRAP: modèle de prévision de trafic de personnes', SAE. Ministère des Transports, Paris.

Tauchen, H., F. Fravel, and G. Gilbert (1983), 'Cost structure of the intercity bus industry', *Journal of Transport Economics and Policy*, **17**, 25-47.

Thisse, J. (1988), 'La concurrence spatiale' in C. Ponsard (ed.), *Analyse Economique Spatiale*, Paris: PUF.

Thisse, J. (1993), 'Oligopoly and the polarization of space', *European Economic Review*, **37**, 299-307.

Tinch, R. (1996), 'Estimation des prix fictifs des externalités dans les transports', Rapport CEMT/CS/SOC (96)5.

Tirole, J. (1988), *The Theory of Industrial Organization*, Cambridge, MA: MIT Press.

Toen-Gout, M.W. and M.M. Jongeling (1993), 'Investeringen in infrastructuur en economische groei', *ESB* 12-5.

Tol, R. (1994), 'The damage costs of climate change: a note on tangibles and intangibles applied to DICE, *Energy Policy,* **22**, 436-438.

Tolofari, N., N. Ashford and R. Caves (1990), 'The cost of air service fragmentation', working paper, Loughborough University.

Toutain, J.C. (1967), 'Les Transports en France', *Archives de l'ISEA* September–October.

Transportation Research Board (1997), *Macroeconomic Analysis of the Linkages between Transportation Investments and Economic Performance*, NCHRP Report No. 389, Washington, DC: National Academy Press.

Treyz, G. (1980), 'Design of a multiregional policy analysis model', *Journal of Regional Science*, **20**, 191-206.

Vacher, J.F. (1997), 'L'évolution des Transports depuis 40 ans', *INSEE première*, **522** June, Paris.

Van De Voorde, E. and H. Meersmann (1997), 'Is freight transport growth inevitable?' in ECMT, *Which Changes for Transport in the Next Century,* Report of the 14th Symposium on Theory and Practice in Transport Economics, Innsbruck, Paris: OECD.

Varian, H. (1992), *Microeconomic Analysis,* 3rd edn, New York: Norton.

Venables, A.J.(1999), 'Road transport improvements and network congestion', *Journal of Transport Economics and Policy*, **33**, 319-328.

Venables, A. and M. Gasiorek (1999), *The Welfare Implications of Transport Improvements in the Presence of Market Failure Part 1*, Report to Standing Advisory Committee on Trunk Road Assessment, London: DETR.

Verhoef, E., P.Nijkamp and P. Rietveld (1997), 'The social feasibility of road pricing', *Journal of Transport Economics and Policy*, **31**, 255-276.

Vickerman, R.W. (1984), 'Urban and regional change, migration and commuting: the dynamics of workplace, residence and transport choice', *Urban Studies*, **21**, 15-29.

Vickerman, R.W. (1999), 'The transport sector, new economic geography and economic development in peripheral regions', in M. Beuthe and P. Nijkamp (eds), *New Contributions to Transportation Analysis in Europe*, Aldershot: Ashgate.

Vickerman, R.W. (2000a), 'Economic growth effects of transport infrastructure', *Jahrbuch für Regionalwissenschaft*, **20**, 99-115.

Vickerman, R.W. (2000b), 'Evaluation methodologies for transport projects in the UK', *Transport Policy*, **7**, 7-16.

Vickerman, R.W. (2002a), 'Transport and economic development', in ECMT *Transport and Economic Development*, Report of Round Table 119, Paris: OECD.

Vickerman, R.W. (2002b), 'Sustainable mobility in an age of internationalisation', in, Y. Higano, P. Nijkamp, J. Poot and K. van Wijk (eds), *The Region in the New Economy*, Aldershot: Ashgate.

Vickerman, R.W. (2003a), 'Freight traffic', in ECMT, *Managing the Fundamental Drivers of Transport Demand*, Proceedings of the International Seminar December 2002, Paris: OECD.

Vickerman, R.W (2003b), 'Public and private initiatives in transport infrastructure supply', in P. Rietveld and R. Stough (eds), *Institutions, Regulation and Sustainable Transport*, Cheltenham, UK and Northampton, MA USA: Edward Elgar.

Vickerman, R.W., K. Spiekermann and M.Wegener (1999), Accessibility and regional development in Europe, *Regional Studies*, **33**, 1-15

Vickers J. and G. Yarrow (1988), *Privatization: an Economic Analysis*, Cambridge, MA: MIT Press.

Vickrey W.S. (1963), 'Pricing urban and suburban transport', *American Economic Review*, **59**, 452-465.

Ville, J. (1970), 'Le paradoxe de la congestion', mimeo, Ministère de l'Equipement, Paris.

Viscuse, W. Kip (1993), 'The value of risks to life and health', *Journal of Economic Literature,* **31**, 1912-1946.

Vogelsang, I. and J. Finsinger (1979), 'A regulatory adjustment process for optimal pricing by multi-product monopoly firms', *Bell Journal of Economics*, **10**, 157-171.

Walker, T. (1992), 'Network economics of scale in short hand truckload operations', *Journal of Transport Economics and Policy*, **26**, 3-17.

Wang, J.S. and A. Friedlander (1981), 'Mergers, competition and monopoly in the regulated trucking industry', MIT Working Paper no. 289, Cambridge, MA: MIT.

Wardman, M. (1998), 'The value of travel time: a review of British evidence', *Journal of Transport Economics and Policy*, **32**, 285-316.

Wardman, M. (2001), 'A review of British evidence on time and service quality valuations' *Transportation Research E*, **37**, 107-128.

Wardrop, J. (1952), Some theoretical aspects of road traffic research', *Proceedings of the Institute of Civil Engineers*, **1**, 325-378.

Weber, A. (1909), *Über den Standort der Industrien*, transl. by C.J. Friedrich (1929), *Alfred Weber's Theory of the Location of Industries*, Chicago: University of Chicago Press.

Webster, F.V., P.H. Bly, and N.J. Paulley (1998), '*Urban Land use and Transport Interaction*, Aldershot: Gower.

Wegener, M. and D. Bökemann (1998), *The SASI Model: Model Structure*, SASI Deliverable 8. Berichte aus dem Institut für Raumplanung 40, Dortmund: Institut für Raumplanung, Universität Dormund.

Weinberger, M. (1992), 'Gesamtwirtschaftliche Kosten des Lärms in der Bundesrepublik Deutschland', *Zeitschrift für Lärmbekämpfung*, **39**, 91-99.

Weitzmann, M.L. (1974), 'Prices versus quantities', *Review of Economic Studies*, **41**, 477-491.

White, P (1995), 'Deregulation of local bus services in Great Britain: an introductory review', *Transport Reviews*, **15**.

Wie, B., R. Tobin, D. Bernstein and T. Friess (1995), 'A comparison of system optimum and user equilibrium dynamic traffic assignments with schedule delays', *Transportation Research C*, **3**, 389-411.

Wiel, M. (1997), 'Comportements de mobilité et évolution de l'organisation urbaine' Research Report, GERME, Brest.

Williamson, O.E. (1975), *Markets and Hierarchies: Analysis and Antitrust Implications*, New York: Free Press.

Wilson, A.G. (1998), 'Land use/transport interaction models: past and future', *Journal of Transport Economics and Policy*, **32**, 3-26.

Wilson, F., A. Stevens and T. Holyoke (1982), 'Impact of transportation on regional development', *Transportation Research Record*, 851.

Winston, C. (1985), 'Conceptual developments in the economics of transportation: an interpretative survey', *Journal of Economic Literature*, **23**, 57-94.

Winston, C. (1993), 'Economic deregulation: days of reckoning for micro-economists', *Journal of Economic Literature*, **31**, 1263-1289.

Winston B., and C. Kuranami (1997), 'Effects of rail privatization in Japan', *World Railways*, Kensington Publications.

Xu, K., R. Windle, C. Grimm and T. Corsi (1994), 'Re-evaluating returns to scale in transport', *Journal of Transport Economic and Policy*, **28**, 275-286.

Yang, H. and H. Huang (1998), 'Principle of marginal cost pricing: how does it work in a general road network?', *Transportation Research A*, **32**, 45-54.

Index

Index